Music-making in the Hertfordshire parish 1760 to 1870

Music-making in the Hertfordshire parish 1760 to 1870

Maggie Kilbey

HERTFORDSHIRE PUBLICATIONS
an imprint of
University of Hertfordshire Press

First published in Great Britain in 2020 by
University of Hertfordshire Press
College Lane
Hatfield
Hertfordshire
AL10 9AB
UK

© Maggie Kilbey 2020

The right of Maggie Kilbey to be identified as the author of this work has been asserted by her in accordance with the Copyright, Designs and Patents Act 1988.

All rights reserved. No part of this book may be reproduced or utilised in any form or by any means, electronic or mechanical, including photocopying, recording or by any information storage and retrieval system, without permission in writing from the publisher.

British Library Cataloguing in Publication Data
A catalogue record for this book is available from the British Library

ISBN 978-1-912260-26-3

Typeset in Sabon

Design by Arthouse Publishing Solutions
Printed in Great Britain by Hobbs the Printers Ltd

Contents

List of figures	vii
List of tables	ix
List of abbreviations	x
Notes relating to the text	xi
Introduction	1
1 Background	9
2 Charity schools	33
3 Psalms and hymns	68
4 Singers and bands	90
5 Organs and organists	115
6 Church barrel organs	143
7 Disputes and Tractarianism	180
8 Singing classes and choirs	203
9 Church buildings	219
Conclusion	249
Appendices	253
Bibliography	260
Index	287

Figures

1.1	Value of Hertfordshire livings in 1835	13
1.2	Johan Joseph Zoffany, *The Gore family with George, 3rd Earl Cowper* (c.1775)	14
1.3	William Henry Hunt, *Interior of Bushey Church* (1815–20)	20
2.1	Decennial totals of births and deaths in England 1710s–1850s	34
2.2	Organs in the west galleries of St Peter's, St Albans and St James's, Piccadilly	37
2.3	Edward Pugh, 'The Annual Meeting of the Charity Children in St Paul's Cathedral' (1804)	40
2.4	Samuel Hieronymus Grimm, *St Wilfred's church, Kirkby-in-Ashfield* (1786) and *A Service at Bath Abbey* (1788)	42
2.5	'The Gamut' from Matthew Wilkins, *A Second Book of Psalmody* (London, 1750)	55
3.1	J.P. Neale, *St Albans Abbey Church, the Choir looking West* (1824)	75
3.2	T.W. Luppino, *Psalms and Hymns for Ware Church* (c.1821)	76
4.1	Goulding & D'Almaine bassoon with trumpet top and Cuvillier bassoon (both 1800–50)	108
5.1	Map of North Mymms, showing the seats of subscribers towards music-making at St Mary's church	119
5.2	Reed organ at St Mary the Virgin, Clothall (2015)	122
5.3	Interior of St Laurence's, Wormley (c.1860)	123
5.4	Subscriptions to organ funds at St Andrew's, Hertford, in 1861 and 1865–7	125
5.5	J. Stadler, after Richard Livesay, *The Royal Review in Hatfield Park* (1802)	130
5.6	Memorial window to the organist Emily Ryley at Holy Cross, Sarratt (c.1919)	134
6.1	Barrel-and-finger organ at St Mary's, Stanstead St Margaret	144
6.2	T.C. Bates & Son barrel organ at St Andrew's, Letheringsett (Norfolk)	145

6.3	T.C. Bates & Son barrel organ used at St Mary's, Stocking Pelham, until 1917	146
6.4	J.C. Buckler, 'Westmill Church' (1841)	147
6.5	T.C. Bates & Son dumb organist at St Andrew's, Fersfield (Norfolk)	149
6.6	Alice Mary Oliver, 'Bovinger church' (1862)	153
6.7	George Cruikshank, 'The Self-Playing Organ' (1843)	160
6.8	Gray's improved church barrel organ (1839)	165
6.9	John Tenniel, 'Clearing the Streets' (1864)	174
9.1	St Lawrence's, Ayot St Lawrence (2013)	220
9.2	Interior of St James's, Stanstead Abbots (2014)	222
9.3	Daniel Hollingsworth, *Plans and elevations of gallery, St Michael's, St Albans* (1846)	223
9.4	Benches provided for the poor at St Mary's, Albury (1866)	226
9.5	W.W. Malet, *Proposed relocation of organ at St Lawrence's, Ardeley* (1844)	229
9.6	Elevation of gallery, St John's, Markyate (1843)	230
9.7	Dennis Tucker, *Western end of All Saints, Sandon, showing the proposed new gallery* (1841)	232
9.8	Richard Kelsey, *Reordering of galleries at St Mary's, East Barnet* (1829)	234
9.9	Music cupboard presented to the Watton-at-Stone choir by Robert Hanbury (1853)	242
9.10	G.E. Pritchett, *Detailed plans of St Luke's, Widford* (1868)	243
9.11	Gray organ relocated next to the chancel of St Faith's, Hexton (2017)	244

Tables

2.1	Examples of Hertfordshire elite with metropolitan addresses during the late eighteenth century	36
2.2	Sunday schools established in Hertfordshire during the late eighteenth century	44
2.3	Hertfordshire children's singing teachers	54
5.1	Mid- to late eighteenth-century Hertfordshire organs and organists	116
5.2	Organists' salaries in Hertfordshire parish churches	132
6.1	Barrel-organists' salaries in Hertfordshire parish churches	163
6.2	Tunes known to have been played by Hertfordshire church barrel organs, as classified in *The Parish Choir* (1846)	171
8.1	Vice-presidents of the Hertfordshire Church Choral Association (1861)	210
8.2	Members of St Andrew's, Hertford, church choir (1864)	214

Abbreviations

BARS	Bedfordshire Archives and Record Service
BL	British Library
CCS	Cambridge Camden Society
CRL	Cadbury Research Library
HALS	Hertfordshire Archives and Local Studies
HG	*The Herts Guardian, Agricultural Journal, and General Advertiser for Hertfordshire, Essex, Beds, Bucks, Cambridgeshire and Middlesex*
HMR	*The Hertford Mercury and Reformer.* This was entitled *The Reformer and Herts, Beds, Bucks, Essex, Cambridge and Middlesex Advertiser* 1834–43, *The Hertford Mercury and Reformer* 1844–68, and *The Hertford Mercury and County Press* 1868–72
ICBS	Incorporated Church Building Society
LPL	Lambeth Palace Library
ODNB	*Oxford Dictionary of National Biography* (Oxford, 2004–, online edn), accessed at <http://oxforddnb.com>
SPCK	Society for Promoting Christian Knowledge
VCH Herts	William Page (ed.), *The Victoria History of the County of Hertfordshire*, 5 vols (London, 1902–23), accessed at <http://www.british-history.ac.uk>

Notes relating to the text

Unless indicated otherwise, all places referred to in the text are located in Hertfordshire, and all census returns are for England.

The locations of Hertfordshire properties and parishes are shown in Appendices 1 and 2.

Before the introduction of decimal currency on 15 February 1971, guineas, pounds (£), shillings (s) and pence (d) were used in the UK. 1 guinea = £1 1s; £1 = 20s; 1s = 12d.

See <http://measuringworth.com> to calculate current relative values of sums given in this book.

Publication Grant

The publication of this volume has been supported by a generous subvention from the Aurelius Charitable Trust.

Introduction

This book examines the introduction, development and consequences of various attempts to improve congregational singing from the 1760s to 1860s. In England, the history of music in the established church often focuses on the repertoire of organists and choristers in cathedrals and the Chapel Royal, yet relatively few people today have had personal experience of hearing or making music in these places. By contrast, this book focuses on the social history of music-making in the parish church, where historically far more parishioners have worshipped, and in many places continue to do so. This important topic has received very little attention, but is perhaps of far more general interest to both worshippers and non-churchgoers.

Those with a particular interest in church organs, architecture, choral music or 'west gallery music' have their own special interest groups and societies, yet there is often little cross-over between them, and perhaps less still with historians who have an interest in social, economic, educational and religious issues. This book investigates these largely unexplored influences on parochial music-making and reveals that, rather than being isolated strands, in Hertfordshire all were inter-related and instrumental in an overarching drive to encourage the congregation to fulfil their duty to sing. This drive endured for several generations during the period from the 1760s to the 1860s, and the legacy of attempts to achieve this result can still be seen in many churches today.

Until recently, this period was considered to have been one of stagnation during which psalmody (psalm-singing) in most churches was either erratic or conspicuous by its absence, despite the fact that all were expected to join in. The population at large had become alienated from church music-making during the interregnum, and this was still the case a century later. A major obstacle was the fact that it was considered ungenteel to sing in church, leaving any congregational singing to the poor and artisan classes, or, in certain metropolitan parishes, to professional musicians. To make matters worse, non-participation by the gentry may have been compounded by reluctance on the part of their servants and tenants, who 'no doubt felt too inhibited to sing heartily in their presence'.[1] Furthermore, many parishioners were tempted away from their parish church to Nonconformist meetings, often attracted by their more inclusive music-making. According to the composer Andrew Gant, 'England expected little from its church music at this period. And it got it.'[2] But instead of being a lethargic era for church music-making, this book demonstrates that the period from the 1760s to the 1860s was dynamic, with many attempts made to overcome these issues and encourage congregational singing.

The accepted view is that music-making developed differently in town and rural parishes during the eighteenth and early nineteenth centuries. Town churches had organs and parishioners with the means to pay for them, and often choirs of charity children. By contrast, rural churches were left to their own devices, with music-making provided by groups of rustic singers with or without the support of bands of instrumentalists. But in Hertfordshire, the focus of this book, no clear distinction between music-making in town and country parishes has been found by the author. 'Country psalmody' was found in some town churches, and charity children in some rural parishes, where music-making, rather than being left solely in the hands of self-motivated singers, was significantly influenced by the local elite and their experience of metropolitan fashion. The effects of the presence or absence of elite influence on parish music-making is apparent throughout this book, and the inter-connectedness of the clergy and elite families is an important feature.

Music-making in Hertfordshire parish churches developed in response to the influence of bishops, their clergy and local nobility and gentry. The drive to improve congregational singing was taken up by new landowners and householders attracted to the county by its proximity to London. Support for Sunday and charity schools was allied with the desire to improve parochial psalmody, and church organs were given with this objective in mind. Over 80 per cent of organs installed in Hertfordshire parish churches between 1760 and 1850 are thought to have been barrel organs, in most cases for reasons of economy. Elite involvement with amateur military bands of music influenced the instrumentation of church bands, and organs and band instruments alike had the potential to support singing in the church. These actions formed part of a complex pattern of support for church music-making that was mirrored by those further down the social scale.

The suggestion that teaching charity school children to sing would result in a congregation of singing adults became a recurring theme throughout the entire period, yet time and time again attempts met with little success. This objective led, however, to a lack of available seating in many Hertfordshire parish churches, owing to the requirement for charity school children to attend every Sunday. Another unintended consequence was that compulsory attendance as children may have instilled a rooted disinclination to attend as adults.

During the early to mid-1800s church rate disputes driven by both dissent and objections to new styles of worship became a source of conflict, particularly in town parishes. In many cases these were centred around opposition to funding for organs and organists, with long-lasting repercussions for church music-making. The mid-nineteenth century saw the beginnings of a more settled era for parochial music-making, with the abolition of compulsory church rates and a widespread, albeit in many cases short-lived, enthusiasm for singing classes and societies. The choir-stalls found in many Hertfordshire churches today have seen little use since the transitory enthusiasm for singing classes that led to their installation in the first place.

Historiography

Historians of church music-making usually refer to Nicholas Temperley's *The Music of the English Parish Church* (1979), which was concerned with parochial church music from the middle ages to the 1970s.[3] Although published over forty years ago, this work has been summarised and updated by Temperley in more recent publications and articles.[4] Prior to this work, the only monographs devoted to music-making in the parish church were those written by Canon K.H. MacDermott: *Sussex Church Music in the Past* (1922), based on his own fieldwork, was followed by *The Old Church Gallery Minstrels* (1948), which drew on anecdotal evidence submitted by listeners following a 1935 BBC radio broadcast.[5]

During the late nineteenth century a number of clergymen – typical of the clerical antiquaries described by the historian Kate Tiller as 'jackdaw-like accumulators of both gems of information and unconsidered trifles'[6] – had begun to collect and study redundant church band instruments and tunebooks. The prolific musical instrument collector Canon Francis W. Galpin reported an encounter with a surviving church band at Winterbourne Abbas (Dorset) during the early 1890s, and this inspired others to explore the subject.[7] These included the educationalist John Spencer Curwen, following a request in the *Church Times* asking clergymen all over the country if they knew of any 'old men who forty or fifty years ago' played the clarinet, bassoon or bass viol (cello) in their parish churches.[8] He received an 'overwhelming' response, enabling him to interview and photograph some of the surviving musicians for *Strand Magazine*.[9] Another was Canon Peter H. Ditchfield, who published *The Parish Clerk* (1907), comprising 'anecdotes, recollections, facts and biographical sketches of many clerks in different parts of England' submitted by elderly correspondents recollecting 'scenes of their youth'.[10] Some, owing to the parish clerk's duty to lead the congregational singing, were related to church music-making.

Thomas Hardy's *Under The Greenwood Tree* (1872) has been, and continues to be, cited by many historians and others as the authoritative account of the activities of rural singers and bands, and their inevitable replacement by a harmonium or organ.[11] But the extent of Hardy's first-hand knowledge of church music-making during the nineteenth century should be questioned. After all, his experience was restricted to stories from Dorset handed down by his father and grandfather, both church band members. Hardy himself explained that his descriptions of 'west-gallery musicians' were intended to be a 'fairly true picture' of village customs common during the 1830s and 1840s, but these customs may not have been so widespread elsewhere in England, particularly in counties much closer to the influence of London, such as Hertfordshire.[12]

In February 1905 Canon Galpin gave a paper to the Dorset Natural History and Antiquarian Field Club on the 'Old Church Bands and Village Choirs of the Past Century', in which he said 'How graphic a picture Thomas Hardy gives us of these old Dorset choirs in his charming tale of village life *Under the Greenwood Tree*.'[13] Intriguingly, Hardy himself was present, and questioned Galpin about the manner in which church bands played. In Hertfordshire, shortly after his meeting with Hardy, Galpin lectured on 'The By-gone Music of our Parish Churches' at the 1905 English Church History Exhibition held at St Albans Town Hall, now the St Albans Museum + Gallery.[14] St Albans had been chosen to host this very well-attended exhibition owing to its national ecclesiastical and archaeological significance, but also because of the ease with which it could be reached by large numbers of visitors travelling by train via London.[15] On display were almost 700 artefacts drawn from museums, cathedrals, churches and private collections across the country, including relics dating back as far as the fourth century, needlework, communion plate, bibles, prayer books and music books. Galpin demonstrated a selection of items from his 'really wonderful collection of musical instruments used at different times in church services', and these were on display together with a handful of others sourced locally.[16]

The historiography – often informed by Hardy's writings – usually presents the development of church music-making as a clear-cut progression, with the replacement of singers and church band first by a barrel organ or harmonium and then by a 'finger' organ (in other words, not barrel-operated).[17] This book demonstrates, however, that in Hertfordshire these phases were sometimes parallel rather than sequential, with no inevitable outcome. This was probably also the case in many other counties.

Despite the fact that church barrel organs became increasingly common from *c.*1800 onwards, little research has been undertaken into the circumstances surrounding their introduction and use. During the 1950s Canon Noel Boston began to compile a list of church barrel organs, concentrating on their repertoire rather than their use.[18] Following Boston's untimely death in 1966 his research notes were used by Lyndesay Langwill to publish a work concerned with both chamber and church barrel organs.[19] According to Galpin, the barrel organ 'supplanted the Church Bands in towns and villages during the early part of the last century'.[20] This appears to have been coloured by his own reading of Hardy's works, and perhaps by their encounter in Dorset. It seems likely that Hardy and Galpin reinforced each other's theories. The suppression of singers in this manner has since been seen by many historians as part of a wider conflict between elite and popular cultural values.[21] Yet MacDermott suggested that barrel organs were used only in churches with no band.[22] Christopher Turner noted that their use was contemporaneous with the main church band period, but his research was largely focused on barrel-organ tunes and the tempo at which they could be played.[23] In this book it will be argued that in many cases the main impetus for the introduction of a barrel organ was the establishment of a charity school associated with the church, owing to the organ's intended function of supporting singing by both school children and the general congregation. Rather than supplanting church bands, in many churches they were installed where there had been no singing at all.

Although it was easy enough for antiquarians such as Galpin to acquire redundant church tunebooks, barrel organs and other instruments, MacDermott argued in 1922 that the two main sources of information concerning these were the musicians' children and grandchildren and the musicians' tunebooks, and that 'Time is relentlessly calling away the one class, while the kitchen fire is too frequently the finale of the other.'[24] Private instrument collections made by antiquarians during the late nineteenth and early twentieth centuries have for the most part now ended up in local or national museums, often with no record of who used them or where they were used. Regrettably, few Hertfordshire instruments are known to have survived locally. Those that have include a handful of woodwind instruments and barrel organs spread between museum stores in St Albans, Hertford, Bedford and Luton, in addition to the last remaining working church barrel organ in the county at Stanstead St Margaret and a pitch-pipe at Aldbury.

Despite the lack of surviving instruments and tunebooks in Hertfordshire, the availability of online resources such as The British Newspaper Archive has now opened up new fields of enquiry.[25] By linking newspaper reports and other primary sources, this book reveals a fascinating story of the changing involvement of men, women and children in church music-making that includes both episodes of enthusiastic support and, at times, discordant dispute.

The history and legacy of Hertfordshire church music-making during the period from the 1760s to the 1860s reveals, for example, how repeated attempts to use children's voices to encourage congregational singing went hand in hand with new seating arrangements in the church; how a mid-nineteenth-century singing craze influenced the widespread church restoration projects undertaken during this period; and the financial difficulties faced by those involved in church music-making during the nineteenth century, which are still faced today. It is to be hoped that the new findings presented in this book will encourage other researchers to undertake studies in their own regions, adding even more to our growing understanding of the development of music-making during this important period.

Endnotes

1. N. Temperley, 'John Wesley, Music, and the People Called Methodists', in N. Temperley and S. Banfield, *Music and the Wesleys* (Urbana, 2010), p. 5.
2. A. Gant, *O Sing unto the Lord: A History of English Church Music* (London, 2015), p. 284.
3. N. Temperley, *The Music of the English Parish Church*, Cambridge Studies in Church Music, 2 vols (Cambridge, 1979), 1.
4. For example, N. Temperley, 'Music in Church', in H.D. Johnstone and R. Fiske (eds), *The Eighteenth Century: Music in Britain*, The Blackwell History of Music in Britain, vol. 4 (Oxford, 1990), pp. 357–95; N. Temperley *et al.*, 'Psalms, metrical', *Grove Music Online*, accessed at <http://www.oxfordmusiconline.com>.
5. K.H. MacDermott, *Sussex Church Music in the Past* (Chichester, 1922); K.H. MacDermott, *The Old Church Gallery Minstrels: an Account of the Church Bands and Singers in England from about 1660 to 1860* (London, 1948), p. 67; *Radio Times* (18 January 1935), p. 64.
6. K. Tiller, *English Local History: An Introduction*, 2nd edn (Stroud, 2002), p. 15.
7. F.W. Galpin, 'The Village Band. An Interesting Survival', *Musical News*, 5 (8 July 1893), pp. 31–2 and (15 July 1893), pp. 56–8.
8. *Church Times* (1 November 1895), p. 488.
9. *Ibid.*, p. 553; J.S. Curwen, 'The Old Village Musicians', *Strand Magazine*, 33 (11 September 1897), pp. 137–9.
10. P.H. Ditchfield, *The Parish Clerk* (London, 1907), Preface.
11. T. Hardy, *Under the Greenwood Tree or the Mellstock Quire. A Rural Painting of the Dutch School* (London, 1872). For example, see MacDermott, *Minstrels*, p. 37; I. Bradley, *Abide with Me. The World of Victorian Hymns* (London, 1997), p. 5.
12. 'Preface', in Hardy, *Greenwood Tree* (London, 1896 edn), pp. v–vi.
13. F.W. Galpin, 'Notes on the Old Church Bands and Village Choirs of the Past Century', *Proceedings of the Dorset Natural History and Antiquarian Field Club*, 26 (1905), pp. xl and 172–81.
14. Anon., *English Church History Exhibition: at the Town Hall, St Albans, from 27th June to 15th July 1905* (St Albans, 1905); *Church Times* (30 June 1905), p. 842; *Musical Times* (1 August 1905), p. 526.
15. *Yorkshire Post and Leeds Intelligencer* (29 June 1905), p. 8.
16. *Herts Advertiser* (8 July 1905), p. 6.
17. Temperley, 'Music in Church', p. 387.
18. N. Boston, 'Barrel Full of Tunes', *Church Times* (9 July 1954), p. 531; 'The Barrel-Organ', *Transactions of the Ancient Monuments Society*, New Series, 7 (1959), pp. 99–124.
19. N. Boston and L.G. Langwill, *Church and chamber barrel-organs: their origin, makers, music and location: a chapter in English church music* (Edinburgh, 1967); see also L.G. Langwill and N. Boston, *Church and chamber barrel-organs: their origin, makers, music and location: a chapter in English church music*, 2nd edn (Edinburgh, 1970).
20. F.W. Galpin, *Old English Instruments of Music: their History and Character* (London, 1910), p. 174.
21. For example, V. Gammon, '"Babylonian Performances": the Rise and Suppression of Popular Church Music, 1660–1870', in E. Yeo and S. Yeo (eds), *Popular Culture and Class Conflict 1590–1914: Explorations in the History of Labour and Leisure* (Brighton, 1981), pp. 62–88; J. Obelkevich, *Religion and Rural Society: South Lindsey 1825–1875* (Oxford, 1976), p. 147; D. Adelmann, *The Contribution of Cambridge Ecclesiologists to the Revival of Anglican Choral Worship 1839–62*, Music in Nineteenth-Century Britain (Aldershot, 1997), p. 7.
22. MacDermott, *Sussex*, p. 50.
23. C. Turner, 'The Decline of the Gallery Tradition', in C. Turner (ed.), *Georgian Psalmody 1. The Gallery Tradition* (Corby Glen, 1997), p. 78; see also C. Turner, 'Miserable Machines: The Role of the Barrel Organ within Georgian Psalmody', in C. Turner (ed.) *Georgian Psalmody 2. The Interaction Between Urban and Rural Practice* (Corby Glen, 1999), pp. 65–72; C. Turner,

'Psalmody Singing and the Role of the Barrel Organ in the Anglican Church of the Nineteenth Century', in Dibble and Zon, *Nineteenth-Century British Music Studies*, Music in Nineteenth-Century Britain (Aldershot, 2002), pp. 32–45.

24   MacDermott, *Sussex*, pp. 5–6.
25   *The British Newspaper Archive*, accessed at <http://www.britishnewspaperarchive.co.uk/>.

Chapter 1
Background

This chapter explains the origins of the need for improvement in congregational singing witnessed during the mid-eighteenth century, and introduces the context for parochial music-making in Hertfordshire. The approach to singing adopted in London churches influenced the involvement of certain elites in their Hertfordshire parishes, probably more so than in counties distant from the capital.

A brief account of the administrative duties of the clergy and churchwardens is also given, together with an explanation of the bishop's involvement with his diocese. As Hertfordshire towns grew, so did the number of Nonconformist meetings, and they attracted both non-churchgoers and members of the parish church. An outline of the Nonconformist groups that presented the greatest challenge to the established church is therefore given here.

A summary of the main weekday occupations many poor children were obliged to pursue is also given in this chapter. This provides context for the often arduous requirement that children attending charity schools associated with the Church of England should attend church on Sunday, where it was hoped that their singing would lead to an improvement in congregational psalmody.

Psalmody
The poor state of congregational singing during the mid-eighteenth century had its origins in the Civil War a century earlier. In May 1644 a parliamentary ordinance ordered that 'all Organs […] in all Churches and Chapels aforesaid, shall be taken away and utterly defaced, and none other hereafter set up in their Places'.[1] Most parish churches were not immediately affected by this order because they had no organ, but of more serious consequence was the associated disbanding of choral foundations in cathedrals, the Chapel Royal and Oxford and Cambridge colleges. This is because it led to a shortage of choristers suitable to become musically trained clergymen or parish clerks. According to Shaw's *Parish Law*, the parish clerk needed to be

a competent singer because his duties included 'setting the psalms': in other words, leading congregational singing.[2] By 1709 one parish clerk found that, although there had once been enough clerks to supply 'the whole Kingdom', so few boys and youths had been taught to sing 'that the most Common tunes in use amongst us neither are, nor can be but seldom, sung in our Parish-Churches'.[3]

Before the Civil War, the words sung by congregations in the established church were taken from Sternhold and Hopkins' English metrical version of the psalms, later known as the Old Version (OV).[4] One relic of this version still familiar today is the hymn known as the 'Old 100th', with the first line 'All people that on earth do dwell' (Psalm 100, OV). After the restoration of the monarchy a new metrical translation of the psalms by Tate and Brady was finally approved in 1696, and became known as the New Version (NV).[5] Some hymns taken from the New Version are still sung today, such as 'Through all the changing scenes of life' (Psalm 34, NV).

Although tune supplements were available and sometimes included in the revised prayer book, New Version psalms were written in the same metres as the Old Version so that familiar tunes could continue to be used. The number of tunes sung was limited to those that could be learnt by ear, since musical notation was indecipherable to the untutored. Furthermore, because few in the congregation could read, the parish clerk led the singing by 'lining out' the psalm – that is, reading each line out loud before it was sung. With no instrumental support, the singing became slower and slower over time, and this became known as the 'old way of singing'.[6]

The Society for Promoting Christian Knowledge (SPCK), founded in 1698, subsequently encouraged the spread of religious societies and the teaching of simple harmonised psalm tunes to groups of young men.[7] The intention was that they would reform the old way of singing by sitting among and leading the congregation, but little had changed by the mid-eighteenth century. This book examines the ensuing attempts made to encourage the congregation to sing.

The location and population of Hertfordshire

Covering just over 630 square miles, Hertfordshire is one of England's smallest counties and, with no large towns or cathedral until the late nineteenth century, it has been described as a 'county of small towns'.[8] There is a marked contrast between the hillier west bordering the Chilterns and the flatter eastern region. Clockwise from the west, Hertfordshire is bordered by Buckinghamshire, Bedfordshire, Cambridgeshire, Essex and Middlesex (London), and its proximity to London was key in the development of parochial music-making in the county. Several major routes from London pass through it, including the Great North Road to York (now the A1), the Old North Road (Ermine Street, now the A10) and the Holyhead Road (Watling Street, now the A5) (see Appendix 1). This made it relatively easy for psalmody teachers, organists and other musicians to travel to and from London, and likewise for the elite to attend, and be influenced by, musical events in the capital. But it also facilitated the spread of Nonconformity, as explained later in this chapter.

In 1801 the population of Hertfordshire was *c.*97,000, with only eleven towns greater than 2,000, but by 1851 the number of inhabitants had reached *c.*167,000.[9] The 1851 census revealed that for the first time over half the nation lived in urban areas, yet in Hertfordshire 76 per cent still lived in rural areas.[10] By the end of the nineteenth century Hertfordshire was still an agricultural rather than an industrial county, and therefore throughout the entire period the county appealed to London elites wishing to purchase a country house with easy access to the capital, as continues to be the case today.

Landowners, patrons and clergy

The relative ease with which Hertfordshire landed estates could be reached from the capital meant that they have been considered desirable by successful Londoners ever since the sixteenth century, resulting in a steady influx of wealthy families.[11] The county was considered sufficiently distant for most new landowners to maintain their London address, with the associated advantages of metropolitan society and taste, while also becoming prominent members of the local community.[12] In a recent assessment of Dury and Andrews' 1766 *Topographical Map of Hartfordshire* it was noted that half the 169 properties with named occupiers had been purchased since 1700; 14 per cent of the purchasers were lawyers and 40 per cent city merchants, overseas traders, brewers and bankers.[13] This trend continued into the nineteenth century, with the addition of mill owners such as paper manufacturer John Dickinson, who built Abbots Hill, Abbots Langley, in 1836.[14]

As parks were the most conspicuous status symbols in eighteenth-century rural society, landowners spent fortunes on landscaping by leading figures such as 'Capability' Brown and, later, Humphry Repton. In Hertfordshire the consequence was the enlargement of parks, the closing of footpaths and the alienation of landowners from the poor.[15] By contrast, nineteenth-century improvements tended to focus more on rebuilding the main house. Both approaches often led to bankruptcy and a rapid turnover of ownership, with the capital providing a 'perpetual fountain of wealth for new building'.[16] Foremost among the London bankers who made their home in Hertfordshire was Abel Smith MP (d. 1859). In 1834 he inherited Woodhall Park, which had been purchased by his father. With close family ties to many prominent Evangelicals, Abel Smith used part of his immense wealth to improve the county's social fabric by endowing schools, building and renovating churches. By 1873, his son Abel Smith MP (d. 1898) owned in excess of 10,000 acres, and had become second only to James Gascoyne-Cecil, 4th Marquess of Salisbury, in the hierarchy of Hertfordshire land ownership.[17]

Many landowners, including Salisbury and members of the Smith family, among others, were church patrons. Church patrons had the right to choose which clergyman to appoint as the parish church's incumbent, a right known as the advowson. Although advowsons were often inherited, during this period they were sometimes purchased, and a succession of new Hertfordshire landowners became church patrons. Old and new Hertfordshire patrons alike were familiar with the London scene, and brought metropolitan fashions to their country houses and parishes. McVeigh noted the 'effect on musical dissemination' as the elite 'journeyed between London and their country seats', and Cowgill and Holman have also remarked upon the 'extraordinary amount of musical activity outside London'.[18] Yet neither considered the influence of the elite's experience of metropolitan church music-making on their rural parishes, which forms a key part of this book.

For arcane historical reasons, in most cases the incumbent of an ecclesiastical parish was known as either the rector or the vicar. Suffice to say that vicars held the living of parishes where the local landowner, often the church's patron, had become the 'lay rector' following the dissolution of the monasteries. Unlike the vicar (if there was one), the rector, whether clerical or lay, was responsible for the upkeep of the church's chancel. He, or in the case of a lay rector sometimes she, also had the right to determine who was seated there during divine service. The result was that in some churches the chancel was left empty apart from bulky monuments commemorating the patron's family, while the rest of the church was crammed with inconvenient seating. No member of the congregation could be seated in the chancel without the rector's permission, and a similar restriction applied to the location of musicians or organs until the 1860s.

The values of Hertfordshire livings were diverse. Unsurprisingly, those yielding the greatest income were in the hands of powerful patrons, and were frequently given to their relatives. Yielding an annual income of £2,318 in 1835, by far the most valuable was Hatfield, with the Marquess of Salisbury (until 1789, Earl) as patron.[19] In 1772 the 6th Earl installed as rector one of his illegitimate sons, William Cecil Grave.[20] The Bishops of London and Lincoln held several advowsons, including the second and third most valuable livings. These were Much Hadham with Little Hadham

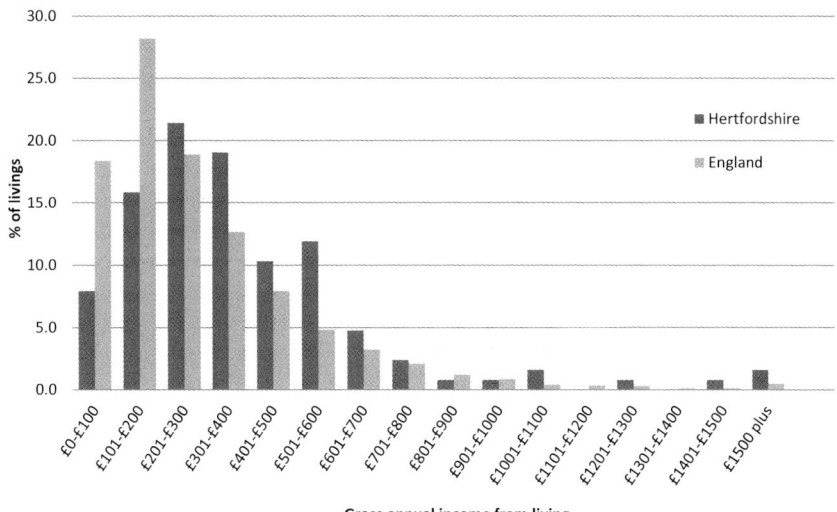

Figure 1.1. Value of Hertfordshire livings in 1835. Based on PP 1835 [67] Royal Commission to inquire into Ecclesiastical Revenues and Patronage of England and Wales Report, pp. 510–613, 634–81 and 1053–56.

(£1,654) and Wheathampstead with Harpenden (£1,404), where the sons of bishops John Randolph and George Pretyman were installed as rectors. These figures were in marked contrast to poor livings such as Kings Walden, which yielded £57, and Little Wymondley, only £20. The Ecclesiastical Revenues Commission of 1835 found that the typical gross income of an English incumbent was £275, but in Hertfordshire the mean, excluding Hatfield, was approximately £375, as summarised in Figure 1.1.[21]

Many Hertfordshire clergy were therefore part of the close-knit county hierarchy, related by birth or marriage to landowners, church patrons, MPs and other clergy. James Carpenter Gape, vicar of Redbourn and St Michael's, St Albans, from the 1770s to the 1820s, was cousin to the patron James, 3rd Viscount Grimston, who owned the Gorhambury estate. The connections of the poet William Cowper also illustrate the inter-relatedness of the elite and clergy. Son of the rector of Berkhamsted, his first cousins included William Cowper MP and Rev. Martin Madan, chaplain of the Lock Hospital in London. Furthermore, George, 3rd Earl Cowper, was a second cousin, with a seat at Cole Green Park near Hertford. The family group shown in Figure 1.2 depicts the 3rd Earl with his future wife's family, and conveys their shared taste, politeness and exquisite refinement, hinted at by the inclusion of a newly invented square piano.

MUSIC-MAKING IN THE HERTFORDSHIRE PARISH

Figure 1.2. Johan Joseph Zoffany, *The Gore family with George, 3rd Earl Cowper* (*c*.1775). Yale Center for British Art, USA, Paul Mellon Collection, B1977.14.87.

According to Holman, 'it could be argued that England was the most musical country in Europe in the second half of the eighteenth century', with the 'average Georgian gentleman' regularly participating in music-making in both London and the provinces.[22] However, during this period English chamber music was dominated by the playing of stringed and keyboard instruments, as seen in the depiction of the Gore family group. The only wind instrument regularly played by gentlemen during this period was the flute, as brass and other wind instruments were considered unsuitable for chamber music around the keyboard.[23] Attention has been drawn to the dependency of gentry music-making on professional musicians or members of the local militia band when playing pieces requiring wind instruments, and the possibility of links between military and church bands has been highlighted.[24] Until now little research has been undertaken, but evidence presented in this book suggests that certain elites may have supported and funded both ventures.

Close familial ties and shared cultural values such as those exhibited by the Cowper family suggest that many Hertfordshire clergy would have not only enjoyed listening to music but also been willing and able to participate on suitable occasions, and may therefore have taken an interest in church music-making. One such was the harpsichordist Edward Garrard Marsh, son of the Sussex gentleman composer John Marsh, who was appointed vicar of Sandon in June 1828 and of Ardeley six months later.[25]

Another clergyman–musician was Thomas Hutchinson, vicar of Sawbridgeworth. Following his death in 1856 the auction of his goods at the vicarage included:

> a very powerful rich-toned Finger ORGAN with swell, in handsome solid mahogany case, with gilt front and two rows of keys, 10ft. 8in. high and 6ft. 9in. wide, with composition and German pedals, 12 stops, &c., quite complete. A 5-Octave Patent HARMONIUM, in beautiful rosewood case, 4ft. 1in. wide, with 14 stops (perfect). A 5-Octave SERAPHINE, in mahogany case, 3ft. 6in. wide. TWO GRAND PIANOFORTES (Maelzel's Metronome). A fine collection of Cathedral Music …[26]

Yet the apparent indifference of many eighteenth- and early nineteenth-century incumbents to their cures is well rehearsed. Once instituted, it was almost impossible to remove a clergyman from his living, because it was treated as his property rather than an appointment. Examples of a variety of neglect on the part of Hertfordshire clergy during this period set the surviving evidence for music-making in context. In 1847 the Baptist minister William Upton described William John Moore, vicar of Sarratt, as 'Worldly and useless'.[27] Upton added: 'Sarratt would be in a deplorable state, but for the Dissenting Chapel. The Clergyman is non-resident and only comes on the Sabbath.' With such a lack of supervision it is perhaps unsurprising that in Sarratt parish church 'the only music provided was by the [parish] clerk, who performed on the flute until he became too asthmatical to do so any longer, when his place was taken by a lame boy who played a concertina'.[28]

Many Hertfordshire clergy were frequently absent from their parishes. These included pluralists, who held more than one living, such as the Hon. & Rev. Frederick de Vere Beauclerk, great-great-grandson of Charles I and Nell Gwynn. He was vicar of Kimpton 1797–1827, before succeeding Gape as vicar of both Redbourn and St Michaels, St Albans, in 1827, livings that he held until his death in 1850. Beauclerk was also a professional cricketer and a gambler, who claimed that his average annual winnings of £600 matched the income from his two livings.[29] He played for the All England Eleven forty-six times between 1796 and 1823, and was often absent from his parishes. Some Hertfordshire clergymen held livings in neighbouring counties or the capital, but other livings were much further afield, including those held by William Skynner, vicar of Rushden but also rector of Bradley (Derbys.) and Cuxwold

(Lincs.) in the early 1800s. Those with London livings spent the Season there, where they lived alongside the Hertfordshire elite, and so were only partially resident. These included Edmund Gibson, son of the late Bishop of London, who in London was rector of St Benet & St Peter and precentor of St Paul's Cathedral, and in Hertfordshire vicar of Bishops Stortford 1766–98.[30]

In 1790 many incumbents were found to be non-resident, including William Langford, vicar of Sandridge, who lived at Eton College, where he was a master, and Thomas Davies, vicar of Newnham, who lived at his patron's seat at Erddig, North Wales.[31] During the 1870s the historian John Edwin Cussans commented:

> Churchmen of today are surprised why in the western part of Hertfordshire there are so many Dissenters. The reason is obvious. I could name twenty parishes, where, fifty years ago, there were no resident Incumbents, although they never failed to put in an appearance for the purpose of receiving the tithes and other emoluments which they had not earned.[32]

The church had no responsibility for the provision or upkeep of the parsonage, and some clergy were unwilling or unable to maintain one, using this as a reason for their absence. In 1810 William Cross, vicar of Great Amwell, explained that 'the vicarage of Amwell is a small cottage, not fit for the residence of a clergyman and has not been inhabited by one within the memory of the oldest parishioners'.[33]

The poet William Cowper (see above), who wrote for *The Connoisseur* under the nom-de-plume 'Mr Village', had in 1756 drawn attention to the precedence given by many clergymen to parsonage rather than church repairs:

> It is no uncommon thing to see the parsonage-house well thatched, and in exceeding good repair, while the church perhaps has scarce any other roof than the ivy that grows over it. The noise of owls, bats, and magpies, make the principal part of the church-music in many of these ancient edifices.[34]

Even if the incumbent was resident in his parsonage house this usually meant that his other livings were served by a curate. It seems probable that in many instances they undertook their duties conscientiously, but this was not always so. In 1772 the Bovingdon churchwardens reported to their archdeacon that 'we have no curate resident in our Parish and when he appears for the performance of his duty is often disguis'd in liquor'.[35] Curates sometimes served several parishes on the same day, resulting in hastily said or cancelled services. During the absence of William Cowling, pluralist vicar of Albury, it was said that:

the people never knew whether there would be a service or not, and the non-resident curate would ride over from Stortford, leap his horse over the churchyard fence, and if he found only two or three people waiting, would give them a shilling to go to the public-house instead of holding a service.[36]

The rector of both Hertingfordbury and St Andrew's, Hertford, from 1755 until his death in 1804 was the Hon. & Rev. Robert Cholmondeley, often resident at the family seat, Cholmondeley Castle in Cheshire. Non-resident in both of his Hertfordshire parishes, he too had failed to appoint a suitable curate, since in May 1780 the vestry resolved to write to his son George 'to know whether his father Robert Cholmondeley Esq will appoint a proper person to act as curate to the Parish of St Andrews Hertford [...] If this is not complied with in a small space of time the Parish will apply directly to the Bishop of the Diocese of Lincoln for redress.'[37]

Neglected parishes allowed dissent to thrive. With little or poor music-making in churches such as these, it became more likely that their congregations would be attracted to Nonconformist meetings where it was good. The Hon. & Rev. Cholmondeley's neglected parishioners went on to erect a singing gallery, presumably in an attempt to improve the singing in their church in the face of local Methodism, which had flourished in the rector's absence.

Other clergyman who showed little interest in their duties included the notorious Hon. & Rev. William Robert Capel, vicar of Watford from 1799 to 1854. Appointed by his brother and patron, the 5th Earl of Essex, in 1823 he had the dubious distinction of appearing in the short-lived fortnightly *Crimes of the Clergy* produced by Nonconformist preacher and publisher William Benbow. Benbow described 'Tally-ho' Capel as a 'bon vivant, fox hunter, farmer, crop-buyer, horse-dealer and general lover', and commented that 'a more desirable situation than his, for a sporting parson is not to be found; his brother keeps a fine pack of foxhounds, who are more used to his voice in the field than his parishioners are in the church, where he speaks so low that he is scarcely audible'.[38]

Capel, too, refused to appoint a curate and, when one was appointed by the Bishop of London in 1829, 'Capel resisted stoutly, and on one occasion the rector and the curate had a race for the reading-desk in church.'[39] In 1832 the dispute was brought to the Hertfordshire Assizes, where Bishop Blomfield lost the case on a technicality. Watford parish church later became the scene of several acrimonious disputes over the funding of music-making, which could probably have been avoided if Capel had made an attempt to secure long-term funding from his wealthy parishioners.

Nevertheless, more conscientious clergy did promote music-making in their parish church, as demonstrated throughout this book. This included subscribing to books of psalmody, supporting charity schools and children's singing in church and contributing towards the purchase of organs. Indeed, during the nineteenth century many clergymen were indefatigable in their attempts to raise money for organs, sometimes paying for them themselves. But, as explained in the next section, the duties of the clergy and churchwardens were not restricted to ecclesiastical matters.

Parishes, dioceses and churches

During the period from the 1760s to the 1860s, 136 parishes lay wholly or partly in Hertfordshire, the majority having parish churches (see Appendix 2). The remaining parishes – that is, Bayford, Markyate and Totteridge – were ancient chapelries of Essendon, Flamstead and Hatfield respectively, while both Bovingdon and Flaunden were chapelries of Hemel Hempstead. In most respects the chapels in these settlements functioned as parish churches, and are therefore treated as such in this book.

Organisation

Parishes were grouped together into archdeaconries, themselves grouped into dioceses, which were under the control of a bishop. Archdeacons held regular church visitations (inspections) to identify problems in the parish and, every three years or so, the bishop toured the diocese himself, holding visitations in selected churches, attended by both the clergy and churchwardens from nearby parishes. Visitations gave churchwardens the opportunity to present any problems concerning the clergy, parishioners or church fabric. Printed articles (questions) were distributed at the visitation and, once the returns had been received, the bishop preached a Charge (sermon) to all the clergy of the diocese addressing the problems identified. Like other important sermons, this was published, and Charges now form an important primary source regarding the day-to-day running of churches and how this may have affected music-making.

Before any alterations could be made to the church's fabric it was necessary to obtain a faculty – legal permission to undertake a specific alteration – from the bishop. In theory a faculty was needed before any galleries could be built or organs installed, but few such faculties survive for Hertfordshire churches during this period. In all likelihood this is because few applications were actually submitted, but many Hertfordshire parishes changed diocese twice during the nineteenth century, perhaps leading to the loss of evidence.

Until 1845 Hertfordshire parishes were divided between two dioceses, but no discernible difference in music-making has been found between them. Parishes in the west of the county were part of the archdeaconry of Huntingdon, Lincoln diocese. Parishes in east Hertfordshire were in the diocese of London, either in the archdeaconry of Middlesex or 'peculiars',[40] while those in the south-west and other scattered parishes were in the archdeaconry of St Albans.[41] To complicate things further, in 1845 the archdeaconry of St Albans was reconstituted to include the whole of Hertfordshire and transferred to the diocese of Rochester. The new St Albans diocese did not come into being until 1877, when the Abbey Church was elevated to the status of Cathedral and Abbey Church of St Alban. In 1553 the abbey church of the recently dissolved monastery had been purchased by the town for use as the parish church of their small, newly created parish. Although civic services were held here, and indeed the mayor and corporation held the advowson until 1835, there was little or no attempt to provide fashionable music-making in this town church until the installation of an organ in 1820.

Parish finances

Since the sixteenth century parishes had had both ecclesiastical and civil duties, and were responsible for collecting rates from all householders to fund local concerns, as agreed by each parish. These rates were based on a valuation of the property the householder occupied, so the poor were usually exempt. The sums collected were used under the supervision of the churchwardens to make provision for the poor, keep order, maintain the highways and other items approved by the vestry, which was a meeting of ratepayers assembled for parochial business. In addition, a 'church rate' was levied to fund articles 'necessary for the decent performance of Divine Service' and repairs to the church, excluding the chancel, which, as explained above, was the responsibility of the rector.[42] Because church rates were collected from all householders in the parish, in addition to members of the congregation, ratepayers included non-church-goers and dissenters in varying proportions.

The spending of the church rate was scrutinised by the parish vestry. Written notices announced the date of the next vestry meeting, which was normally held in the church under the chairmanship of the incumbent. Usually all ratepayers were entitled to vote, and consequently it was common for vestry decisions to be affected by some persons whose main concern was financial. At the Easter vestry parish officers were appointed and church rates proposed by churchwardens, based on an estimate of what would be needed during the coming year. The outgoing churchwardens' accounts were scrutinised and taken into consideration by the vestry when authorising items to be budgeted for in the new rate. Churchwardens would therefore have been reluctant to make payments for unauthorised items, which on occasion related to music-making, because these could be disallowed at the

Figure 1.3. William Henry Hunt, *Interior of Bushey Church* (1815–20). This shows pews and galleries typical of an unrestored Hertfordshire church. The patron's pew, just seen on the right, is directly opposite the pulpit. National Gallery of Art, USA, 1992.96.3 Ailsa Mellon Bruce Fund.

end of the financial year, leaving them out of pocket. This was not unknown. In 1809 the churchwardens' accounts of Madron (Cornwall) included 'Pair of clarinets and reeds and music, £5 14s 0d', but this was disallowed by the vestry.[43] This left the instruments to be funded privately, perhaps by the churchwardens themselves.

Each parish decided what should be covered by the church rate and, as is all too apparent, items considered 'necessary' by one parish were not by another. In Hertfordshire, payments were often made to the parish clerk, pew-openers and vermin catchers, and on occasion for items as diverse as candles, brooms and umbrellas. Because no vocal or instrumental music of any kind was actually essential for the performance of divine service, there was no compulsion for it to be funded out of the church rate. Nevertheless, until the early nineteenth century certain vestries considered music-making a legitimate expense, whether by custom, vestry resolution or informal agreement, and therefore sanctioned small payments for music, instruments and singers from the church rate. This indicates not only that they considered music-making 'necessary' but also that the church rate-payers were able to afford these sums, and that there was little or no opposition to making a financial contribution towards parochial music-making.

Pews and seats

During the 1760s most English churches had pews. These were high-sided private seats, usually with doors, as at Bushey (Figure 1.3), and often lockable. In 1802 the churchwardens of St Stephen's, St Albans, reported to their bishop that the 'Seats are locked up by the parishioners who seldom attend divine service'.[44] Had the seats been occupied, it might have offered those wishing to improve congregational singing better material to work with, and perhaps encouraged music-making by those accommodated elsewhere in the church. These pews should not be confused with the open seating that replaced them during the nineteenth century, now also known as pews.

Appropriated pews were allocated to a particular property or family, and others could be rented, the income from which contributed to church funds. Renting a pew in fashionable London churches was a very expensive but highly sought-after privilege, and something to be emulated in wealthy Hertfordshire parishes such as All Saints, Hertford, and St Peter's, St Albans. In addition, many churches had galleries built by the patron or other prominent parishioners for their own use, as seen at Bushey. Private galleries were built in the most prestigious part of the church, usually a prominent location as near as possible to the pulpit.[45] As seen above, seating in the chancel was under the control of the rector and, because most naves were filled with exclusive pews, there was often no room in the church for the poor, charity children, singers, bands or organs. These were therefore often accommodated in galleries, but in the less prestigious parts of the building, usually the west end.

Accommodation was not usually such an issue in Nonconformist meetings and this, in addition to preaching and inclusive worship, proved to be an attraction for poor parishioners. But the Nonconformists' music-making, described in the following section, may have been even more influential in drawing away members of the established church.

Nonconformity

The focus of this book is music-making in the parish church rather than in Nonconformist meetings, but the two were often closely related. Indeed, provincial Anglican and Nonconformist church music is collectively known as psalmody, reflecting the fact that some pieces were used in both church and chapel. Inclusive music-making in Baptist and Methodist meetings in particular became an attractive draw, a challenge which the established church countered in some parishes by attempts to improve their own music-making. As a result, Nonconformist tunes were sometimes used in an effort to retain worshippers.

In 1851, for the first and last time, a national Census of Accommodation and Attendance at Worship, or 'Religious Census', was held on the same March weekend as the decennial population census. The Religious Census was organised by the civil servant Horace Mann, with the object of discovering whether religious and educational provision had kept pace with the increasing population and its changing distribution.[46] It tried to determine the number of attendees and seats at all known places of worship, and how many of these places had been established since 1800, but its imprecise questions were open to interpretation. Unfortunately the day chosen for the count, Mothering Sunday, may have given atypical results owing to certain workers returning home to visit their mothers, and widespread poor weather lowered attendance figures, but these factors probably affected all denominations.

A more significant problem for Mann was that no attempt was made to record how many people attended more than one service. In his Report tables Mann decided to convert 'attendances' into 'individuals' by approximating that half those attending in the afternoon had not been present in the morning, and a third attending in the evening had not been there earlier in the day.[47] This made the assumption that all places of worship held three services a day, yet many opened only in the afternoon or evening, so only half or a third of their attendees were recorded in Mann's calculations. Nonconformists objected to this conclusion because they tended to worship later in the day, unlike Anglicans, who tended to worship in the morning. Others may have attended church in the morning and chapel in the evening, or even three different denominations, as did Edwin Chapman when visiting St Albans in 1835, but there is no way of ascertaining this from the returns.[48] Because the returns do not record who actually attended they tell us very little about the social status of the congregations, but they do provide valuable information regarding mid-century patterns of worship in Hertfordshire, as outlined below.

Nonconformity can be divided into old dissent, including Quakers, Baptists and Independents, and new nonconformity – Methodism – as explained in the following sections.

Old dissent

The inhabitants of the southern part of the diocese of Lincoln, which included Hertfordshire, had a long history of nonconforming activity, and were described by Bishop Laud in 1637 as being 'very giddy in matters of religion'.[49] With so many small towns, which in comparison with rural parishes were very hospitable to Nonconformists, this was still the case following the restoration of the monarchy. St Albans was the first staging post north from London on the busy Holyhead Road as it passed through west Hertfordshire, and it was the centre of county activities for various Nonconformist groups during the eighteenth century. A strong and enduring Nonconformist presence was found among gentry and commoners alike, and this was also the case in Hemel Hempstead, and further east in Hertford.

In south-west Hertfordshire, Rickmansworth had become an important centre of Quakerism owing to its proximity to Jordans (Bucks.), home of the Quaker leader William Penn.[50] Although a number of prominent Quakers were also based in Hertford, it was Baptists whose presence was felt most keenly in Hertfordshire during this period.[51] A strong Baptist presence endured in north-west Hertfordshire because of the influence of John Bunyan, who had made preaching visits on a circuit that included Flamstead and Markyate.[52] Neighbouring Kensworth had been the headquarters of Hertfordshire Baptists before the Toleration Act of 1689, serving more than thirty villages and towns in Hertfordshire and Bedfordshire.[53] Many private dwellings had been registered as Baptist meeting places in this part of Hertfordshire and, according to the Religious Census, by 1851 Baptists comprised almost 45 per cent of all attendances in the west of the county.[54] The influence of Baptist hymns and the use of Baptist tunebooks in some parish churches grew towards the end of the 1700s.

Independents were strongest in the areas where there was less Baptist influence: that is, areas bordering Essex and Middlesex. In 1810 Charles Chester, rector of Barley (population *c.*600), reported that about 120 parishioners 'consisting of the principal farmers and their families' were in the habit of crossing the border into Essex to attend an Independent meeting house in Chishall.[55]

In April 1810 the 'Hertfordshire Union' of Baptist and Independent churches was instituted at St Albans with the aim of spreading the gospel throughout the county, with Sir Culling Eardley Smith as its first president.[56] In 1847 William Upton, minister of Dagnall Street Baptist church, St Albans, undertook an independent survey of Hertfordshire places of worship to assess the progress of both Baptist and Independent ministry for the Hertfordshire Union. Upton's 1847 survey and the 1851 Religious Census returns can therefore be compared with, and supplement, each other.[57]

Methodism

During the 1730s and 1740s Methodism emerged, so-called because its early followers adopted a particular method of religious study. Having come under the influence of religious revival, John Wesley, an ordained clergyman in the established church, began to preach at open-air meetings and in rooms provided by those sympathetic to his Evangelical cause. Wesley himself always claimed that Methodism formed part of the Church of England, and early Methodists attended their parish church and taught its doctrines. Referring to Methodists, in 1762 the psalmody teacher William Riley cautioned that 'people of weak minds are fond of novelty, and this frothy way of singing seems to be of a piece with the flighty method of preaching adopted by their teachers'.[58]

In 1795, four years after Wesley's death, Methodists finally split from the established church to become a Nonconformist church. Although Methodism itself split into several branches, in this book references can be assumed to refer to Wesleyan Methodists, during this period the most prominent branch in England.

Methodism appeared in Watford, Barnet, Stevenage, Hatfield and St Albans in the decades from the 1770s to the 1790s, and meetings spread to these towns' hinterlands.[59] Again, the major London routes that pass through Hertfordshire influenced the spread of Methodism (see Appendix 1). John Wesley himself first preached in Hertford in 1763 on his way north to Norwich. A Methodist chapel was established in Hertford within five years, but by 1772 meetings were discontinued.[60] He also stopped to preach at Hatfield on several occasions as he made his way up the Great North Road. Welwyn is the next town north of Hatfield along this route, where in May 1792 the diarist John Byng, later Lord Torrington, discovered that 'they are building a new, large meeting house, sad omen of the downfall of the churches! For the dissenters will soon chuse the parliament; and then look to yourselves, my Lord the Bishop, Mr Dean, ye fat prebends, and ye idle, absent rectors.'[61]

Wesley journeyed further up the Great North Road to Hinxworth, where many of the villagers flocked to hear him at the house of Elizabeth Harvey, a prominent Methodist supporter.[62] The Methodist style of worship particularly appealed to women such as Miss Harvey. By tradition, women generally sang very quietly in the parish church, but lively and inclusive Methodist meetings were often held in ordinary houses, and communal singing was successfully encouraged in these less intimidating surroundings.[63] Wesley visited Hinxworth many times, and at Miss Harvey's in December 1784 he met the Evangelical Charles Simeon, vicar of Holy Trinity, Cambridge, who became a pioneer in attempts to encourage his congregation to sing by installing a barrel organ in his church.[64]

Parishes situated on or within easy reach of the Old North Road received particular attention from Methodist preachers. In January 1762 Wesley had preached at both Barley and Barkway, where 'The preaching-place was exceeding large; yet it was well filled, and the people were wedged in as close as possible.'[65] In 1790 few Hertfordshire parishes reported Methodist meetings in the Bishop of London's visitation returns, but the 1810 returns indicated a growing concern among the clergy. Thomas Cockshutt, rector of Little Hormead and curate of Great Hormead, 'The vicar not being resident', stated that 'The Methodists are numerous, and their number seems to increase, there are no teachers resident in the parish, tho' many I believe occasionally visit it. Their meetings are held in a barn, which as I conceive cannot properly be licensed so long as it is used as a barn.'[66] Similarly, Henry Allen Lagden, vicar of Ware, reported that 'The number of Methodists has increased very much. They have a licenced meeting house in the town. Their service is performed in it on Sunday evening and supplied with teachers from Cheshunt or London.'[67]

Teachers from Cheshunt attended the training college for the ministry of the Countess of Huntingdon's Connexion, an Evangelical sect within the Methodist church, which had relocated from Wales to a building near Cheshunt parish church in 1792.[68] The vicar, John Collins, reported that 'the number of students which are educated and preach here and from hence in the neighbouring parishes vary from six to twelve'.[69] Indeed, many of the neighbouring parishes felt the effects of their preaching, and the incumbents of Broxbourne, Stanstead Abbots and Standon reported preaching by Cheshunt teachers at local meeting houses or in private rooms.[70]

Nonetheless, by the time of the 1851 Religious Census only 11 per cent of attendances at Hertfordshire places of worship were attributed to Methodist meetings, compared with the national average of 25 per cent.[71] This may have contributed to the county's relatively strong Anglican attendance of 56 per cent, compared with the national average of 48 per cent.[72]

Inclusive worship and music-making in Baptist and Methodist meetings were considered rival attractions by the established church. This led to attempts to retain worshippers by improving parochial music-making and, in some parishes, to the inclusion of works by Nonconformists in collections of psalms and hymns, and tunes pinned on church barrel organs.

Children of the poor

An explanation of the Church of England's desire to use charity children's voices to promote congregational singing, and the ways in which this was attempted, is central to this book. Although Church of England 'National Schools' were established from 1811, the establishment of 'British Schools' by the British and Foreign School Society from 1814 enabled other poor children to receive an education free from Anglican control. This society was non-denominational, but principally supported by Nonconformists, and, because Nonconformist numbers were greatest in towns, this is where the majority of British Schools were established. In Hertfordshire the main British Schools attended before 1870 were in Baldock, Berkhamsted, Bishops Stortford, Broxbourne, Bushey, Cheshunt, Chipping Barnet, Hitchin, Rickmansworth, Royston, St Albans, Ware and Watford.[73]

Many children of the poor were obliged to work for their living, attending charity schools only on a Sunday or when they could be spared from work during weekday hours. This section outlines the children's main occupations, providing context for the expectation that many of these same children would attend church every Sunday and be expected to contribute towards the improvement of congregational singing.

Employment of children

In 1851 the population of Hertfordshire was 54,350, of whom 32,576 – that is, 60 per cent – were aged under fifteen.[74] Nationally, of the 4.6 million children aged under fifteen, only half were recorded as receiving an education, either at home or school.[75] In Hertfordshire approximately 5.7 per cent of boys and 7.4 per cent of girls aged five to nine were employed.[76] The percentages for older children are unknown as this information was not recorded in Mann's summaries of census returns, but would have been significantly higher. Because children formed such a high proportion of the population, impoverished parents relied on their earnings, no matter how small.

Agriculture

In east Hertfordshire the main employment was in agriculture. Reports from the 1867 Parliamentary Commission on the Employment of Children, Young Persons and Women in Agriculture gave an indication of the extent of their workload.⁷⁷ Several Hertfordshire respondents were the very clergymen eager to promote children's attendance at the parish church on Sunday, yet few saw a real problem with the age children started work or the working hours, chiefly because of their families' reliance on their wages. This was the harsh reality of childhood for the children of the Hertfordshire poor during the early to mid-nineteenth century.

Recalling his late 1860s childhood, during his seventies Edwin Grey remembered several Harpenden boys hired by farmers at the age of nine or ten and returning home only for occasional Sunday visits.⁷⁸ In addition to supplementing the family's income, this allowed more sleeping room at home for the younger children. Hugh Rayner, a Wallington landowner, wrote 'How is the parent to maintain the children if they remain at home till 11 or 12 years of age? They must begin early, otherwise they are not fitted for agricultural labourers.'⁷⁹ Boys often worked a twelve-hour day bird-scaring or weeding. In Hemel Hempstead the charity school boys were obliged to attend church on Sundays, Thursdays and Saints' days throughout the year 'unless hindered by sickness or other good cause', but were allowed a month to help with the harvest and a fortnight at stone-picking time to help the family finances.⁸⁰

Walter Wortham, vicar of Shephall, wrote that boys generally started work at the age of ten and that boys were not employed on the land at an even younger age simply because their work would not have been productive.⁸¹ C.H. Lattimore of Wheathampstead wrote 'I think boys ought not to work on land under 9 to 10 years of age, as they are unable to earn anything by work; still they get an insight and acquaintance with the rudiments of their occupation by a moderately early contact with it.'⁸²

Straw plait
The straw plait and hat-making industries became significant in Hertfordshire following the stoppage of supplies of Italian straw hats at the onset of the Napoleonic Wars. Although the pay was initially higher than for agricultural work this was variable, and in the 1830s the Children's Employment Commission found the trade in a very depressed state.⁸³ By 1851 more than 30 per cent of the population in Hertfordshire straw-plait areas were employed in the industry. Workers were predominantly girls, women and young boys from the age of two upwards, the children either plaiting at home or in small schools, usually run by a local woman in her own home. Parents paid around 2d a week for each child to attend a plaiting school, often while they themselves worked, and usually supplied the straw that the children used so that they could sell the finished plait.⁸⁴ Children were frequently obliged to keep working until they had produced the amount of plait required by their parents.⁸⁵ In most cases little attempt

was made to teach them anything except plaiting, but when George Gaisford became the incumbent of Wigginton in 1854 he found that one hour a day was allowed for the 'three Rs' at the plaiting school, and noted that 'it was wonderful how well the children did with that one hour'.[86] The dominance and economic importance of straw plaiting was such that it was also taught in certain church charity schools.[87]

By 1851 St Albans had become the centre of the local straw plait industry and the associated silk and trimmings trades, with an influx of workers from outlying villages working in factories making 'Brazilian' and other hats. This contributed towards the near doubling of the St Albans district population from 9,834 in 1801 to 18,004 in 1851, with the town itself now the largest in Hertfordshire.[88] In addition to St Albans, until the late nineteenth century the west Hertfordshire districts of Hemel Hempstead and Berkhamsted were also centres for the straw trades.

Silk and papermaking
During the eighteenth and nineteenth centuries twelve silk mills and around twenty paper mills were located in towns and villages along Hertfordshire rivers, mostly in the south-west of the county. Many women and children worked in the silk mills, and on average 30 per cent of the workforce was aged fourteen or under throughout the nineteenth century.[89] The Woollam family owned silk mills in St Albans and Redbourn, where children comprised approximately 60 per cent of the workforce.[90] Smaller silk mills were built in Rickmansworth and Hatfield, but the most important were located on the river Ver in St Albans, the Gade in Watford and the Bulbourne in Tring.[91] As these were also straw-plait districts it is unsurprising that they saw the fastest population growth in the county between 1801 and 1851.[92] Perhaps it was only to be expected that, after working twelve hours, six days a week in the Watford silk mills, in 1833 a number of children were reported as playing truant from Sunday school 'to ramble in the fields'.[93] It became increasingly difficult to recruit local women and children because of the dominance of the straw plait industry.

Paper was made on the river Lea at Hatfield and Wheathampstead, and on the river Rib at Standon.[94] But the papermaking industry was most prominent in settlements located along the river Gade and Grand Union canal near Hemel Hempstead – the river provided the water needed to make paper, the canal the means to transport it. These settlements included Frogmore, where the Fourdrinier brothers installed a machine to produce continuous rolls of paper in 1801, and Apsley, where John Dickinson established a works in 1809 to produce high-quality paper.[95] Girls were employed in sorting and cutting up rags, and glazing paper, while boys kept the pulp-grinding engines running smoothly.⁹⁶ In 1866 'nearly 250 lads from the age of 11 upwards' were employed at Apsley mill, but it was a rule that all the younger ones were compelled to attend Sunday school.⁹⁷

This chapter has explained the background to attempts made to encourage Hertfordshire Anglican congregations to sing during the period from the 1760s to the 1860s. Chapter 2 explains the significance of the Church of England's desire to use charity children's voices to promote congregational singing, and the methods adopted to do so. During the late eighteenth century charity schools were supported by prominent members of the Hertfordshire elite and, across Hertfordshire as a whole, by 1851 five times as many children attended schools associated with the Church of England than any other charity schools. The church was therefore able to exert a significant influence on children and their parents.

Chapter 3 describes the nature of psalms and hymns sung in the parish church during this period. Singing in the growing number of Nonconformist meetings was instrumental in attracting people away from the church and led to the use of Nonconformist hymns and tunebooks in some parish churches. Chapter 4 describes the activities of church bands and singers and those who funded and supplied them, and the influence of Nonconformity on them is also considered.

In Chapter 5 it will be argued that, although fashionable among the gentry, organs were rarely found in Hertfordshire churches at the beginning of the period, but by the 1860s most churches aspired to own one. Organists were held in high esteem during the late eighteenth century, but by the mid-1800s usually held a more lowly position in society. Throughout almost the entire period it was far more common for churches to have a barrel organ. They played a very important role in music-making in the Hertfordshire parish church, and Chapter 6 is devoted to this topic.

Chapter 7 examines mid-nineteenth-century church rate disputes in several Hertfordshire towns, which became the scene of heated arguments over the funding of church music-making. These included parishes that had been neglected by their clergy, those with large numbers of dissenters, and often both. In some cases disputes were driven by objections to newly appointed clergy who introduced forms of worship unfamiliar to their parishioners.

By the mid-nineteenth century prominent Hertfordshire families were still involved in promoting congregational singing, and Chapter 8 discusses the craze for singing classes and church choirs. Chapter 9 examines the influence of changing approaches to music-making on the church fabric itself. The need to accommodate choirs and organs became a top priority in the widespread nineteenth-century restoration of church buildings, resulting in the layout still found in many Hertfordshire parish churches today.

Endnotes

1. 'House of Lords Journal Volume 6: 9 May 1644', in *Journal of the House of Lords*, 6 (1643), pp. 545–7. *British History Online* <http://www.british-history.ac.uk/lords-jrnl/vol6/pp545–547>.
2. J. Shaw, *Parish Law* (London, 1733), p. 43.
3. B. P[ayne], *The Parish-Clerk's Guide* (London, 1709 edn), p. 5.
4. T. Sternhold, J. Hopkins et al., *The Whole Book of Psalms* (London, 1562).
5. N. Tate and N. Brady, *A New Version of the Psalms of David, fitted to the Tunes used in Churches* (London, 1696).
6. Temperley, *Parish Church*, pp. 92–3.
7. S. Drage, 'A Reappraisal of Provincial Church Music', in Wyn Jones, *Music*, p. 173.
8. See, for example, T. Slater and N. Goose, *A County of Small Towns: The Development of Hertfordshire's Urban Landscape to 1800* (Hatfield, 2008).
9. PP 1852–53 [1631] Census of Great Britain, 1851. Population tables. I. Numbers of the inhabitants, in the years 1801, 1811, 1821, 1831, 1841 and 1851, vol. I, pp. 14–21 and 82.
10. F.M.L. Thompson, 'Town and City', in F.M.L. Thompson (ed.), *The Cambridge Social History of Britain*, vol. 1 (Cambridge, 1990), p. 3; PP 1852–53, p. cvi.
11. L. Stone and J.C.F. Stone, 'Country Houses and their Owners in Hertfordshire, 1540–1879', in W.O. Aydelotte, A.G. Bogue and R.W. Fogel (eds), *The Dimensions of Quantitative Research in History* (London, 1972), pp. 58–9; see also L. Stone and J.C.F. Stone, *An Open Elite? England 1540–1880* (Oxford, 1984).
12. K. Harwood, 'Some Hertfordshire Nabobs', in A. Rowe (ed.), *Hertfordshire Garden History: A Miscellany* (Hatfield, 2007), p. 71.
13. A. Macnair, A. Rowe and T. Williamson, *Dury and Andrews' Map of Hertfordshire: Society and Landscape in the Eighteenth Century* (Oxford, 2016), pp. 145–8.
14. H. Prince, *Parks in Hertfordshire since 1500* (Hatfield, 2008), p. 183.
15. *Ibid.*, pp. 57–66.
16. Stone and Stone, 'Country Houses', p. 123.
17. PP 1874 [C.1097] Return for each County in England and Wales of Name and Address of every Owner of Acre and upwards […].
18. S. McVeigh, 'Introduction', in S. Wollenberg and S. McVeigh (eds), *Concert Life in Eighteenth-Century Britain* (Aldershot, 2004), pp. 4–7; 'Preface' in R. Cowgill and P. Holman (eds), *Music in the British Provinces 1690–1914* (Aldershot, 2007), p. xxi.
19. PP 1835 [67] Royal Commission to inquire into Ecclesiastical Revenues and Patronage of England and Wales Report, pp. 510–613, 634–81 and 1053–56.
20. Hatfield W.E.A., *Hatfield and Its People: Part 7: Churches* (Hatfield, 2014), p. 13.
21. P. Virgin, *The Church in an Age of Negligence: Ecclesiastical Structure and Problems of Church Reform 1700–1840* (Cambridge, 1989), p. 90.
22. P. Holman, 'Eighteenth-Century English Music: Past, Present, Future', in Wyn Jones, *Music*, p. 3.
23. J. Brewer, *The Pleasures of the Imagination. English Culture in the Eighteenth Century* (London, 2013), p. 443.
24. M.J. Lomas, 'Militia and Volunteer Wind Bands in Southern England in the late Eighteenth and Early Nineteenth Centuries', *Journal of the Society of Army Historical Research*, 67 (1989), pp. 158–9; M.J. Lomas, 'The Wiltshire Militia Band, 1769–c.1831', *Wiltshire Archaeological and Natural History Magazine*, 85 (1992), pp. 93–100; T. Herbert and H. Barlow, *Music and the British Military in the Long Eighteenth Century* (Oxford, 2013), p. 108.
25. B. Robins (ed), *The John Marsh Journals. The Life and Times of a Gentleman Composer (1752–1828)*, Sociology of Music, no. 9, 2 vols (New York, 1998–2013) II, p. 397.
26. *HMR* (27 September 1856), p. 2.
27. J. Burg, *Religion in Hertfordshire 1847 to 1851*, Hertfordshire Record Society, vol. XI (Hertford, 1995), p. 67.

28 G. Anderson, 'The Old Church Bands', *The Antiquary*, 10 (July 1914), p. 267.
29 E. Midwinter, 'Beauclerk, Lord Frederick de Vere (1773–1850)', *ODNB*.
30 LPL, FP Porteus 24/65 (1790).
31 LPL, FP Porteus 29/4 (1790); 30/8 (1790).
32 J.E. Cussans, *History of Hertfordshire*, 3 vols (London, 1870–81), III, p. 163.
33 LPL, FP Randolph 9/107–14 (1810).
34 *Connoisseur* (19 August 1756).
35 HALS, AHH10/1 Churchwarden's presentment (1772).
36 W.B. Gerish, 'Albury Church', *Transactions of the East Herts Archaeological Society*, 2/3 (1904), p. 237.
37 HALS, DP/49/8/2–5 Vestry minutes (1779–1867).
38 W. Benbow, 'Account of the Honourable and Rev. William Capel', in *The Crimes of the Clergy, or, the Pillars of Priestcraft Shaken*, no. 2 (London, 1823), pp. 28–30.
39 C.C.F. Greville, *The Greville Memoirs*, 3 vols (London, 1885), II, p. 113.
40 Peculiar = a parish, church or chapel exempt from the jurisdiction of the diocese in which it is physically located.
41 J. Hunn, 'County, Hundred and Ecclesiastical Boundary Changes', in Short, *Historical Atlas*, pp. 12–13; S. Flood, 'Probate Divisions', in Short, *Historical Atlas*, pp. 14–15.
42 PP 1831–32 (199) Royal Commission to inquire into practice and jurisdiction of Ecclesiastical Courts in England and Wales: Reports, Appendix; 1868 c. 109 (Regnal. 31 and 32 Vict).
43 *Cornishman* (6 August 1924), p. 3.
44 HALS, ASA17/14/1 Churchwardens' presentment (1803).
45 W.M. Jacob, '"… This congregation here present …": Seating in Parish Churches during the Long Eighteenth Century', in K. Cooper and J. Gregory (eds), *Studies in Church History, 42: Elite and Popular Religion* (Woodbridge, 2006), pp. 297–8.
46 D.M. Thompson, 'The Religious Census of 1851', in R. Lawton (ed.), *The Census and Social Structure* (London, 1978), p. 241.
47 H. Mann, *Census of Great Britain, 1851: Religious Worship, England and Wales – Report and Tables* (London, 1854).
48 A.R. Ruston, 'Sermon Tasting in St Albans 1835', *Hertfordshire's Past*, 22 (Spring 1987), pp. 12–17.
49 W. Urwick, *Nonconformity in Herts. Being Lectures upon the Nonconforming Worthies of St. Albans, and Memorials of Puritanism and Nonconformity in all the Parishes of the County of Hertford* (London, 1884), p. 90.
50 'Parishes: Rickmansworth', *VCH Herts*, 2, pp. 371–86.
51 L.M. Munby, *The Common People are not Nothing. Conflict in Religion and Politics in Hertfordshire 1575–1780* (Hatfield, 1995), p. 117.
52 A. Deacon, 'John Bunyan in Hertfordshire', *Hertfordshire's Past*, 22 (Spring 1987), pp. 5–8; 'Parishes: Caddington', *VCH Herts*, 2, pp. 187–93.
53 'Parishes: Kensworth', *VCH Herts*, 2, pp. 231–4.
54 Urwick, *Nonconformity*, pp. 440–1; J. Burg, 'Religious Worship in 1851', in Short, *Historical Atlas*, pp. 140–1.
55 LPL, FP Randolph 9/301–8 (1810).
56 Urwick, *Nonconformity*, p. 232.
57 See Burg, *Religion*.
58 W. Riley, *Parochial music corrected. Containing remarks on the performance of psalmody in country churches, and on the ridiculous and profane Manner of Singing practised by the Methodists* (London, 1762), p. 8.
59 J.G. Greaves, *Wesleyan Methodism in the City of the Proto-Martyr and the St Albans Circuit* (St Albans, 1907); A. Ruston, 'Protestant Nonconformity', in Short, *Historical Atlas*, p. 134.
60 S.G. Corke, *John Wesley and the Methodists in Hertford* (n.d.).
61 C.B. Andrews (ed.), *The Torrington Diaries*, 4 vols (London, 1934–8), 3, pp. 6–7.

62 J. Wesley, *The Journal of the Rev. John Wesley in Four Volumes*, 4 vols (London, 1827), 4, pp. 226, 286 and 462.
63 Temperley, 'John Wesley', pp. 5–6.
64 M. Kilbey, 'The early use of barrel organs in the English parish church', *Journal of the British Institute of Organ Studies*, 43 (2019), pp. 67–9.
65 Wesley, *Journal*, 3, p. 75.
66 LPL, FP Randolph 10/100 (1810).
67 LPL, FP Randolph 12/94 (1810).
68 B.S. Schlenther, 'Hastings, Selina, countess of Huntingdon (1707–1791)', *ODNB*.
69 LPL, FP Randolph 9/784–91 (1810).
70 LPL, FP Randolph 9/651–8 (1810); 10/66 (1810; 12/30 (1810).
71 Burg, 'Religious Worship', pp. 140–1.
72 *Ibid.*
73 Burg, *Religion*, pp. 12–81; E. Wallace, 'Schools 1833–1902', in Short, *Historical Atlas*, pp. 148–9.
74 PP 1852–53, p. ccii.
75 *Ibid.*, p. lxxxix.
76 Wallace, 'Schools 1833–1902'.
77 PP 1868–69 [4202] [4202-I] Royal Commission on Employment of Children, Young Persons and Women in Agriculture, Second Report, Appendix.
78 E. Grey, *Cottage Life in a Hertfordshire Village* (Harpenden, 1977), pp. 57–8.
79 PP 1868–69 [4202] [4202-I].
80 PP 1833 (60) 25 Reports of the commissioners appointed in pursuance of an act of Parliament, made and passed in the 1st and 2nd years of His Present Majesty, c. 34, intituled, 'an act for appointing commissioners to continue the inquiries concerning charities in England and Wales for two years, and from thence to the end of the then next session of Parliament'.
81 PP 1868–69 [4202] [4202-I].
82 *Ibid.*
83 N. Goose, 'Straw-Plaiting and Hat-Making', in Short, *Historical Atlas*, pp. 90–1.
84 L. Gróf, *Children of straw: the story of straw plait, a vanished craft and industry* (Buckingham, 2002); E. Wallace, *Children of the Labouring Poor: The working lives of children in nineteenth-century Hertfordshire* (Hatfield, 2010), pp. 56–9.
85 *Ibid.*
86 HALS, DP/124/29/1 George Gaisford, Some notes concerning Wigginton (1901).
87 H.J. Burgess, *Enterprise in Education. The Story of the work of the Established Church in the education of the people prior to 1870* (London, 1958), p. 40.
88 PP 1852–53 [1631].
89 S. Jennings, 'The Silk Industry', in Short, *Historical Atlas*, pp. 96–7.
90 *Ibid.*
91 Wallace, *Children*, p. 71.
92 N. Goose, 'Population, 1801–1901', in Short, *Historical Atlas*, pp. 56–7.
93 Wallace, *Children*, p. 6.
94 M. Stanyon, 'Papermaking', in Short, *Historical Atlas*, pp. 80–1.
95 'Parishes: Hemel Hempstead', *VCH Herts*, 2, pp. 215–30; J. Evans, *The Endless Web* (London, 1954).
96 Wallace, *Children*, pp. 94–5.
97 *Ibid.*, p. 104.

Chapter 2
Charity schools

Children's singing has been heard in the Anglican parish church right from its beginnings, when many late sixteenth-century grammar school children were taught metrical psalms in order to lead the singing during divine service.[1] This was encouraged by the church in order to familiarise congregations with the tunes associated with the Old Version of the psalms. The same approach was taken a century later in an attempt to reintroduce these tunes and improve parochial singing after the interregnum, and repeated attempts to use children's voices to improve congregational psalmody were made until the 1860s.

In addition to supporting the training of singing youths, the SPCK encouraged the founding of numerous charity schools to educate poor children in preparation for a lifetime of obedience and work. By 1715 almost 5,000 charity children in and near London had been taught reading, writing, the catechism and psalmody.[2] In Hertfordshire there were at least twenty-four such schools, while in Great Britain as a whole some 1,193 had been founded, teaching more than 24,000 poor children of both sexes.[3] SPCK charity school rules demanded that masters and mistresses 'bring the children to Church twice every Lord's Day and Holy Day […] and to join in the publick service'.[4] Among the books recommended by the SPCK in 1713 for use in their schools were 'a Common-Prayer Book with singing Psalms', 'Some Book of Psalmody' and *Hymns for the Charity Schools*.[5] As with their plan for singing youths to be dispersed among the congregation, it was not the SPCK's intention that children should form a separate choir, leaving the congregation to listen in silence, but rather that they would lead the singing.

According to the historian W.M. Jacob, the establishment of charity schools in the early eighteenth century reflected a modest increase in the national birth rate: 'There were more children around, and a more obvious need to educate them' (Figure 2.1).[6] Following a sharp increase in the death rate during the 1720s the emphasis shifted from the establishment of charity schools to the establishment of hospitals for the sick poor, in order

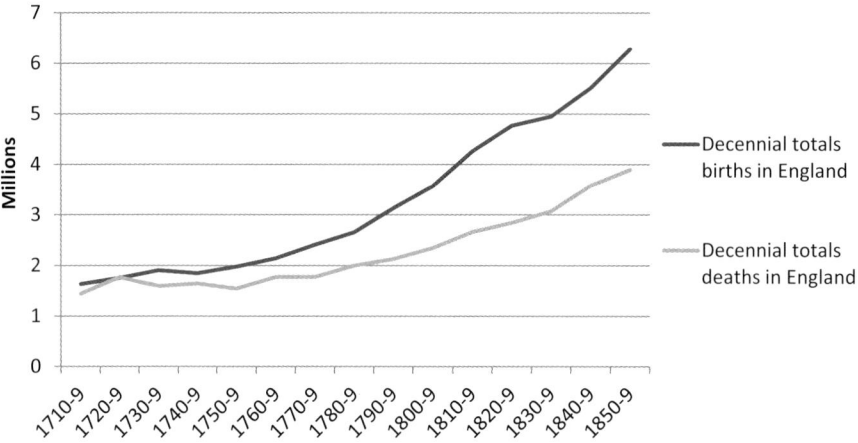

Figure 2.1. Decennial totals of births and deaths in England 1710s–1850s. Based on E.A. Wrigley and R.S. Schofield, *The Population History of England 1541–1871: A Reconstruction*, Cambridge Studies in Population, Economy and Society in Past Time (Cambridge, 1981), p. 494.

to maintain a workforce.[7] As outlined in the following section, music heard in the chapels of metropolitan hospitals for the poor exerted an influence on music-making in certain Hertfordshire parishes. The late eighteenth century saw more rapid population growth, with children forming an increasing proportion of the population. A drive to educate children was therefore seen in both the early and the late eighteenth century, and this was most apparent in the capital.

Metropolitan influence

During the 1730s, with a declining population and the threat of war, there had been a real concern that the country would have neither a firm war footing nor a sufficient workforce.[8] In London this influenced the establishment of the Foundling Hospital 'for the Maintenance and Education of Exposed and Deserted Young Children' in 1739 – the year in which Britain declared war on Spain.[9] Other London hospitals concerned with promoting a healthy workforce followed in quick succession, including the Lock Hospital, the Asylum for Female Orphans and the Magdalen Hospital. Like charity schools, hospitals relied on income from bequests, subscriptions and charity sermons but, in an innovation, these four establishments all had chapels in which choirs of singers attracted support. Chapels such as these were outside episcopal jurisdiction and their chaplains were therefore able to introduce hymns without opposition, despite the fact that some questioned the legality of using them in parochial worship, a topic discussed further in Chapter 3.[10] Many of the governors and directors of the Foundling Hospital, which maintained a mixed children's choir, owned estates or country houses in Hertfordshire (Table 2.1), and the girls' choir at the Magdalen Hospital also attracted support from those living in Hertfordshire. In October 1803 William Jones, vicar of Broxbourne, recorded in his journal:

> The last Sunday evening I spent in Town I went to the Magdalen Chapel and was very much affected with the whole service, particularly the singing [...] What a heavenly charity! Blessed for ever be the men who instituted it! Blessed be all those who now patronize and support it.[11]

The popularity of the children's singing led to a demand for the music they sang, and collections of hymns used in the Foundling and Magdalen Hospital chapels were published from the 1760s onwards.[12] This enabled Hertfordshire landowners who had heard these hymns during the Season to encourage their use in their own parishes, and in 1784 'Magadalen Hymn Books' were used by the singers in Essendon church.[13]

London and Westminster were highly desirable residential areas for the elite, especially for MPs wishing to live within easy reach of parliament. Parcels of land began to be sold off for development; St James's Square was built in the 1660s, followed in the early 1700s by Hanover and Grosvenor Squares.[14] Many properties were occupied only during the Season, which coincided with the parliamentary session. Newly built places of worship, including St James's, Piccadilly, St George's, Hanover Square, and the Grosvenor Chapel, accommodated the influx of worshippers, many of whom lived in Hertfordshire country houses for the rest of the year (see Table 2.1). As elsewhere in the capital, these three churches installed organs in the centre of their west galleries shortly after completion. With wealthy, albeit seasonal, congregations, pew rents were high, and their occupants willing and able to pay for an organ by subscription. These congregations also funded large charity schools, whose pupils were then seated on either side on the organ and sang with its support. The deep, narrow design of English church organs has its origins in the fact that space had to be left on either side of the gallery for charity children.[15] Metropolitan churches such as these were both popular and at the forefront in the 'improvement' of town psalmody. Yet the consequence of funding both organ and charity school children was that, instead of singing themselves, fashionable congregations paid to have God's praises sung on their behalf.[16] This was not the original object of teaching charity children to sing.

Table 2.1
Examples of Hertfordshire elite with metropolitan addresses during the late eighteenth century (see Appendix 1 for location of their Hertfordshire seats).

Name	Hertfordshire address	Metropolitan address
Thomas Brand MP, Lord Dacre	The Hoo, Kimpton	St James's Square
William Capel, 3rd Earl of Essex*	Cassiobury Park, Watford	Grosvenor Square
James Cecil, Marquess of Salisbury*	Hatfield House	Arlington Street
James, 3rd Viscount Grimston, MP for St Albans	Gorhambury, St Albans	Grosvenor Square
Francis Osborne MP, 5th Duke of Leeds*	North Mymms Park	St James's Square and Grosvenor Square
Lionel Lyde, Bart., tobacco merchant	Ayot St Lawrence	Bedford Square
Thomas Plumer Byde, MP for Hertfordshire*	Ware Park	Palace Yard
John Radcliffe, MP for St Albans	Hitchin Priory	Grosvenor Square
Georgiana, Countess Spencer	Holywell House, St Albans	Grosvenor Street
George Townshend, Earl of Leicester*	Balls Park, Hertford	Grosvenor Square
Philip Yorke, 3rd Earl of Hardwicke	Tyttenhanger, St Albans	St James's Square

* Governor or director of the Foundling Hospital.
Sources: Anon., *A list of the governors and guardians, of the Hospital for the Maintenance and Education of Exposed and Deserted Young Children* (London, 1740–99); *The History of Parliament*, accessed at <http://www.historyofparliamentonline.org/>; F.H.W. Sheppard (ed.), *Survey of London*, accessed at <http://www.british-history.ac.uk/search/series/survey-london>.

Gentry familiar with this arrangement during the Season would have aspired to similar in their country parishes, and this approach may have been adopted as early as 1678 in Hertfordshire. Christ's Hospital, or the Bluecoat school, had rural branches in Hertford and Ware where girls were taught, as were young boys before being sent to the school's main site in London.[17] In 1678 the 'Mayor, steward, chiefe burgesses and comonalty of the Burrough of Hertford, minister and churchwardens' purchased an organ for All Saints, making it possible for the children to sing with an organ, as in London.[18] Although the organ was originally located above the mayoral seat, in 1684 it was relocated to a gallery built at the west end 'for the use of the Blew Coat Boys', ideally placed to support their singing.[19]

Figure 2.2. Organs in west galleries. Left: Ralph Dallam organ in St Peter's, St Albans. W.C. Morgan, 'St Peter's Church, St Albans', *Transactions 1897 & 1898*, St Albans Architectural and Archaeological Society, New Series, 1 part II (St Albans, 1899), p. 153. Reproduced by permission of the St Albans Architectural and Archaeological Society. Right: St James's, Piccadilly. Royal Commission on Historical Monuments (England), *An Inventory of the Historical Monuments in London, 2: West London* (London, 1925), Plate 157.

In 1723 a prestigious organ was installed in the wealthy parish of St Peter's, St Albans, when Dr Christopher Packe, of whom little is known, acquired an organ built by Ralph Dallam from St Martin-in-the-Fields, following its replacement by a superior instrument.[20] A west gallery was built by subscription to house the St Peter's organ, implying – despite the lack of a record of the subscribers' names – popular support for the introduction of the organ and its use to support charity children's singing. As seen in Figure 2.2, the arrangement of organ and gallery at St Peter's bore a marked similarity to that found in metropolitan churches. As the Dallam organ had originally been built for St George's Chapel, Windsor, its acquisition and installation in the church would have been seen as a great honour. It remained the only St Albans organ until 1820, when the Abbey Church was itself able to secure a second-hand metropolitan organ.

In response to the installation of organs and trained choirs of charity children, in 1724 Edmund Gibson, Bishop of London, cautioned London schoolmasters and mistresses against providing poor children with a 'polite' education in case they got ideas above their station:

> if the Boys should be taught fine writing, and the girls fine working, and both of them fine singing [...] the masters and mistresses would hardly refrain from teaching the children to *value* themselves upon these attainments; all this, I own, would have a natural tendency to set them above the meaner and more laborious stations and offices of life. And therefore all these things should be carefully kept out of our charity-schools [...].[21]

Gibson was trying to avoid the teaching of an obscure or exclusive repertoire by restricting children's singing to the common psalm tunes, thus preventing psalmody from becoming the preserve of the elite, whether adult or child. He continued:

> many wise and considerate men have condemn'd the custom in some charity-schools, of teaching the children to sing anthems, and such psalm-tunes as are uncommon and out of the way; and have wish'd that they were absolutely restrain'd to the learning five or six of the tunes most usually sung in churches; and that not only some few of the children but all of them in general might be equally bound to learn and sing them to the best of their capacities, in order to be able to join with the congregation, wherever their lot shall fall, in that useful and edifying part of Divine Service.[22]

In a Charge to his London clergy, Gibson reinforced the objectives of the SPCK and expressed a wish that 'the People of every Parish, and especially the Youth, were trained up and accustomed to an orderly way of singing some of the Psalm-Tunes, which are most plain and easy, and of most common use'.[23] Gibson encouraged his clergy in the attempt to bring:

> your *whole* Congregation, Men and Women, Old and Young, or at least as many as you can, to sing five or six of the plainest and best known Tunes, in a decent, regular, and uniform Manner, so as to be able to bear their Part in them at the Publick Service of the Church.[24]

He cautioned against complicated tunes such as those introduced by itinerant singing teachers, because 'the greatest part of the Congregation being unaccustom'd to them, are silenc'd, and do not join in this exercise at all'. In an attempt to achieve his aims a course of singing-psalms was circulated with his Charge, listing three or four verses of specific psalms to be sung each Sunday, and by 1733 the common tunes are said to have been taught in all charity schools.[25]

Significantly, Gibson claimed that being able to sing would also 'incline' children to acquire the habit of attending church, an argument also put forward by Rev. Samuel Wesley, father of the Methodist John Wesley, when he advocated the use of children to lead the singing. Clearly influenced by London churches, in *c*.1726 Samuel Wesley advised the curate of his Epworth (Lincs.) parish to improve congregational psalmody by teaching singing on weekday evenings: 'you will find it will have a very good effect on your congregation, especially if you could get the scholars to sing, as they do in London.'[26] As will be seen, Gibson's advice had a lasting influence on subsequent attempts to reform music-making in the parish church.

Anniversary Meetings
Children in many charity schools in London and the provinces were provided with specific clothing. In addition to the pre-existing Bluecoat school, in 1760 a Greencoat school was founded in Hertford, where the boys were taught 'reading, writing and arithmetic, and singing of psalms'.[27] Elsewhere 'Redcoat', 'Greycoat' or 'Browncoat' uniforms were adopted. Just as the installation of an organ and associated festivities drew attention to the munificence of school patrons, contemporary evidence suggests that a display of 'clothed' objects of charity could have the same desirable consequence. Statues of uniformed charity children were proudly displayed outside certain schools in London, Hertford, Ware, Dunstable (Beds.) and elsewhere for the same reason.

Uniformed children from all the London and Westminster charity schools processed through the streets to a joint annual Anniversary Meeting, and by combining forces were able to produce a much larger volume of sound and attract a very eminent preacher. The benevolence of each parish to its poor was there for all to see, both in the procession and prominently on display during the service. This spectacle helped to maintain funding, as few parishes would have wanted to send poorly turned-out children to the Anniversary Meeting, especially when they could be identified so easily and compared with those of neighbouring parishes. From 1782 onwards the Anniversary Meetings were held at St Paul's Cathedral, where groups of children filled specially erected tall galleries centred around the organ (Figure 2.3).[28] Elite 'Patrons of the Anniversary of the Charity Schools' were guaranteed seats at this very popular event, a highlight of the Season.[29]

Beilby Porteus, Bishop of Chester, preached at the first Meeting held at St Paul's in 1782, which was attended by almost 5,000 charity children. Deeply impressed, he described the spectacle as 'impossible for any man of the least sensibility to contemplate without emotions of tenderness and delight'.[30] Likewise, in 1787 William Vincent, Dean of Westminster, commented that

Figure 2.3. Edward Pugh, 'The Annual Meeting of the Charity Children in St Paul's Cathedral', in Richard Phillips, *Modern London: Being the History and Present State of the British Metropolis* (London, 1804). Children from many different metropolitan charity schools were accommodated in very tall raked galleries on either side of the organ, seen here in the central arch.

'Reflections upon the probable advantages accruing to so many human creatures rescued from total ignorance, steal upon the mind […] one of the most heart-moving spectacles ever exhibited in this or any other country.'[31] When the Evangelical educationalist Sarah Trimmer attended the 1788 Meeting she estimated that some 10,000 children were present. Overcoming initial reservations that the display of so many children could be regarded as ostentatious, she too was in favour of the meeting, as it attracted funding from both new and existing subscribers.[32] The contrast between the children's youthful voices and those of professional singers heard in London music rooms, opera houses and even many churches must have been striking to the congregation, and Joseph Haydn was overwhelmed by their singing while visiting London in the 1790s.[33]

It seems very likely that the success and popularity of the Anniversary Meetings encouraged the elite to promote similar schemes when they returned home to Hertfordshire and other counties. By the end of the eighteenth century charity schools were found throughout the country, particularly in market towns. Figure 2.4 shows a large number of 'clothed' charity children entering St Wilfrid's church in Kirkby-in-Ashfield (Notts.), a small market town with a population of around 1,000 in 1801.[34] Executed in 1786, this work is one of a series commissioned from Grimm by Sir Richard Kaye, who had become rector in 1765. Kaye improved not only the church and rectory but also the psalmody, recording in his notebook: 'Men & boys taught to sing plain Psalm tunes congregationaly instead of anthems in singing seats.'[35] Two years later Grimm was attracted to the same subject matter in Bath (Somers.), depicting the Abbey nave filled with charity children. With no galleries to seat the children, most of the adults were confined to the aisles and the back of the nave.

The practice of parading children to church persisted well into the nineteenth century, probably owing a great deal to the popularity of the Anniversary Meetings. They continued at St Paul's until 1870, when it was deemed unacceptable to close the building for a week to erect and dismantle the temporary galleries.[36] The Anniversary Meetings are usually discussed by scholars simply in terms of being a grand spectacle, overlooking the fact that their impact on parochial music-making was of enduring significance.

In addition to Anniversary Meetings, charity children also sang at state occasions, including a service held in April 1789 to give thanks for the apparent recovery of George III from a bout of madness that later became permanent. Yet the prospect of establishing ubiquitous massed choirs of children was viewed with alarm in some quarters. An anonymous critic cautioned against the increasing dominance of charity children's singing in churches:

Figure 2.4. Above: Samuel Hieronymus Grimm, *St Wilfred's church, Kirkby-in-Ashfield* (1786), showing charity school children processing to church © The British Library Board, Add. 15544, f. 10. Below: Samuel Hieronymus Grimm, *A Service at Bath Abbey* (1788), showing the entire nave filled with charity children © The British Library Board, Add. 15546, no. 101.

the effects of simplicity and power of unisons were never better applied and illustrated, than at St Paul's on the King's recovery: but, because the united voices of six thousand children [...] had all the impressive energy so well described by the Bishop of London, are oratorios, anthems, services, and psalmody in different parts to be laid aside, and no music to be heard in our churches but in a similar unisonous mass of infant voices?[37]

This suggests again that, rather than leading the singing, children were singing on behalf of the congregation, which was not the original intention of those who praised the Anniversary Meetings.

Sunday schools

The founding of the Sunday School Society in 1785 was a direct result of the Anniversary Meetings. Its founders, impressed by the contrast between the 'present comfortable situation' of the charity children and the 'vicious ignorance' in which they must otherwise have been left, intended it to be 'for the support and encouragement of Sunday-Schools in the different counties of England'.[38] Schools of various denominations were promoted, and the twenty-four-strong Sunday School Society committee comprised equal numbers of members of the Church of England and dissenters.[39] Unlike other charity schools, there were no paid teachers, and therefore no requirement for an endowment to maintain the school. Sundays were free from business, enabling middle-class Evangelicals to become voluntary teachers, and a further financial advantage was that children would not be kept from paid employment during the remainder of the week.[40]

With James, Marquess of Salisbury, as the Society's first president, early Sunday schools were founded in a number of Hertfordshire towns and villages. In St Albans, Viscount Grimston chaired a meeting in 1785 'to consider the expediency of establishing Sunday schools in the town'.[41] The meeting resolved that 'the establishment of such schools, supported by voluntary contributions, in the several parishes of this town, distinct and independent from each other' would be 'highly proper', and might 'serve to promote an early habit, among the lower class of inhabitants, of attending church', give them 'additional opportunities of learning the duties of religion' and tend to the suppression of 'idleness, ignorance, and immorality'.[42]

Addressing the lack of congregational singing, in 1787 William Vincent suggested that, if Sunday school children were taught to sing, 'here may be opened the means of rendering the whole body of the lower people capable of feeling and joining in this service'.[43] Similarly, in 1791 the Doncaster organist and composer Edward Miller argued that

Table 2.2
Sunday schools established in Hertfordshire during the late eighteenth century, ordered by size of parish.

Sunday school established by	Parish	Diocese	Population (1801)	Finger organ?
1786	Watford	London	3530	Yes
1794	Hertford	Lincoln	3360	Yes
1785	St Albans	London	3177*	Yes
1789	Cheshunt	London	3173	Yes
1790	Ware	London	2950	Yes
1788	Hemel Hempstead	Lincoln	2722	No
1794	Hatfield	Lincoln	2442	No
1790	Bishops Stortford	London	2305	Yes
1788	Braughing	London	972	No
1786	Kings Langley	Lincoln	970	No
1788	Buntingford	London	799	No
1800	Hertingfordbury	Lincoln	625	No
1790	Barley	London	494	No
1792	Tewin	Lincoln	494	No
1788	Pirton	Lincoln	481	No
1790	Thundridge	London	437	No
1788	Ickleford	Lincoln	337	No
1789	Hinxworth	Lincoln	228	No

*This figure includes the parishes of St Peter, St Michael, St Stephen and the Abbey. St Peter's was the only St Albans church which had an organ at this date.
Sources: Sunday School Society, *Sunday-Schools* (1788), p. 55; LPL, FP Porteus 24/20–65 (1790), 25/5 (1790), 30/64 (1790), 30/92 (1790) & 30/95 (1790); HALS, DP/23/3/1 Vicar's notes (1714–88), DP/29/8/48–52, DP/64/25/9–10 Sunday School minutes & accounts (1786–1827); *Universal British Directory*, 3, pp. 360 and 371; *Digest of the Reports made to the Commissioners of Enquiry into Charities* (London, 1841), p. 42; PP 1852–53 [1631] Population Tables, 1851, Part I. Numbers of the Inhabitants in 1801, 1811, 1821, 1831, 1841, & 1851, Vol. I, pp. 38–61; Grimston, *Manuscripts*, p. 132; Carrington and Johnson, 'Memorandoms.', p. 25; J.S. Hurt, *Bringing Literacy to Rural England. The Hertfordshire Example* (Chichester, 1972), p. 3.

The establishment of *Sunday schools* offers a finer prospect for the improvement of parochial music, than was ever before presented to us. The number of scholars in various parts of the kingdom, are supposed to amount to 300,000. The parish ministers are always trustees for these and all other charity schools and it is needless to mention how much they must have it in their power to be of essential service towards the improvement of congregational psalmody.[44]

Sunday schools were established in all six Hertfordshire towns with church organs during the late eighteenth century, as summarised in Table 2.2 and Appendix 3; consequently, children in these towns could be selected to sing in imitation of metropolitan fashion. Thus, following the founding of the Watford Sunday school by Thomas Villiers, Earl of Clarendon, in 1786, the children from both this and other charity schools sang with the organ.[45] Again, the intention was that their singing would encourage, rather than act as a substitute for, congregational singing.

Evangelical influence
The late eighteenth century was characterised by a general sense of social dislocation prompted by industrialisation, anxiety about revolution and disillusionment with the church. One result of this was the emergence of Evangelicalism, both in the Church of England and among Nonconformists, which led to a cult of duty, self-discipline and 'seriousness'. Sunday schools were particularly promoted by those sympathetic to the Evangelical cause, including the writer and philanthropist Hannah More and her circle, many of whom saw psalmody as an important part of both worship and education. Several high-profile members of the Hertfordshire nobility sympathetic to the Evangelical revival supported church leaders in their drive to establish Sunday schools. Foremost among these in north Hertfordshire was Philip Yorke (1757–1834), who supplemented the parishioners' subscription towards the Sunday school in Braughing.[46] MP for Cambridge from 1780 until elevated to the peerage as 3rd Earl of Hardwicke in May 1790, he was described as a 'godly noble'.[47]

The most significant promoter of Sunday schools in south Hertfordshire was Georgiana, Countess Spencer (1737–1814). The Spencers were the most influential St Albans family throughout the eighteenth century, and heavily involved in political and social activities. The countess was a talented musician, and as a girl had harpsichord lessons from the Hertfordshire organist Thomas Green.[48] With a Grosvenor Street address, she was familiar with the metropolitan musical scene. On the death of the earl in 1783 the countess took the family's Holywell House, St Albans, as her dower house.[49] She was a renowned philanthropist and during the 1780s, hoping to establish a school in St Albans, visited the Reading charity school in Berkshire. During her visit she 'personally furnished herself with the knowledge she wished to obtain of this Foundation, and expressed her great approbation'.[50] At Reading, the children attended church on certain weekdays and twice every Sunday, 'when they likewise bear no inconsiderable part in the Psalmody of the Church, from the gallery, in which they are placed during Divine Service', so, in this church too, the charity children were prominently displayed. In 1788 she spent six weeks in Norfolk with her brother Charles Poyntz, rector of North Creake, where she established a Sunday school. According to the local landowner Thomas Herod, the countess, 'a most amiable character', 'constantly attended the school herself from eight o'clock in the morning till night, to teach them to read and sing psalms'.[51] Although strongly opposed by many local farmers, the school continued to flourish after her departure.[52] In 1824 Herod directed that after his death, on the decease of his main beneficiary, 'every thing should be sold, except the organ, which he desired might be given to the school, as a means to teach the poor children to sing psalms'.[53] In St Albans the countess not only funded the clothing and education of girls at an industrial school but also started the Bluecoat school and taught Sunday school children both in the Abbey Church and at her own home.[54] It seems very likely that they would have been taught psalmody, as at North Creake, and took their part in leading the Abbey Church congregation. Her actions suggest not only an interest in teaching children psalmody but also that she considered this a necessary requirement when establishing a school.

Countess Spencer's involvement typifies the growing national vogue among well-to-do ladies and gentlemen for setting up Sunday schools. This cause was encouraged in Sarah Trimmer's *The Oeconomy of Charity* (1801), in which she urged ladies to take a personal interest in Sunday schooling. While praising all who made a financial contribution, Trimmer advised such ladies to teach charity school girls 'to sing psalms in a proper manner, when they have no master, or by joining with them at Church when they are taught psalmody'.[55] She continued, 'Not that I would by any means recommend [...] teaching *Charity Children* to sing in a superior stile, so as prevent the congregation from joining with them, for this would entirely defeat the purpose of their being taught.'[56] This significant statement indicates that many members of the elite encouraged singing by charity school children not so that they would sing on their behalf, but in an attempt to improve congregational psalmody. Since the countess had consulted Trimmer, it is highly likely that her methods informed the teaching and objectives in St Albans.[57] Again suggesting this was a charitable cause particularly favoured by ladies, in 1788 Trimmer had noted that at the St Paul's Anniversary Meeting 'there appeared at least six ladies to one gentleman'.[58] Robert Raikes, Sunday school pioneer, neatly observed 'At Windsor Ladies of Fashion pass their Sundays in teaching the poorest children.'[59]

In 1773 John Ivery of Northaw explained in the preamble to his *Hertfordshire Melody* that 'The psalm-tunes […] are set in three and four parts, so as to be sung either in the choir or in the school.'[60] But publications such as this may have troubled Trimmer, who was concerned that if children were taught to sing 'in a superior stile' it might result in them singing with 'sets of *anthem singers*, who, it is to be feared, have but little thought of devotion'.[61] Here, Trimmer was referring to church singers, who were considered to overestimate their own importance by singing anthems instead of restricting their contribution to the singing of psalms.

Episcopal influence
In 1787 Beilby Porteus, who had preached at the first St Paul's Anniversary Meeting as Bishop of Chester, became Bishop of London. His first visitation articles of 1790 asked: 'Have you any public or other school […] in your parish?' The returns for the forty-nine Hertfordshire parishes in his diocese gave an indication of the task before him – only five had Sunday schools, and twenty-seven had no school whatsoever.[62] To many Hertfordshire clergy this seemed to be of no personal concern. At Little Hormead the return was completed by the curate, who reported that the pluralist rector Dr Drake 'resides personally at his living of Hadleigh in Suffolk'.[63] Seemingly untroubled, he added 'There is no school in the parish and the parents of children cannot read so that the children of the few poor families are not able to say their catechism.' Similarly, at Stocking Pelham the rector Nicholson Calvert reported 'No catechizing in the church, out of the few residing in the parish but two can read'.[64]

Porteus used the material given in the visitation returns to inform a 1790 Charge to his clergy that addressed the need for an improvement in parochial psalmody. Although he reiterated much of Bishop Gibson's 1724 Charge, there was one major difference. Whereas Gibson had urged that all children should participate, Porteus now suggested that only those with the best voices should do so. This was not in the spirit of elitism, but rather to give the congregation a greater incentive to sing – in some London churches there was now perhaps an excess of children's singing, coupled with insensitive organ-playing. Indeed, William Vincent had cautioned that much of the Anniversary Meetings' success could be attributed to the unusual circumstance of the children having been rehearsed. Conversely, in their own metropolitan churches he would find 'fifty or an hundred trebles, strained to their highest pitch, united to the roar of the full organ'.[65] Vincent's direction that children should be taught to sing 'in their natural tone' rather than 'strained to their highest pitch' gives the first indication that, even if they felt inclined to do so, in some cases it might have been difficult for adults to join children singing at an uncomfortably high pitch outside their natural range.

Perhaps influenced by Vincent, Porteus suggested that in London

> it would be extremely useful to select a few of the charity-children, who have the best voices, and the best ear for music, from the rest, and have them taught to sing well and in their natural tone. And directions should be given to the organist not to drown and overpower the singers by the unremitted loudness and violent intonations of the full organ [...] This would render the psalm-singing so pleasing and melodious that the greater part of the congregation would soon be tempted and [...] enabled to join in it.[66]

This was the approach adopted at All Saints, Hertford, and in 1809 the diarist John Carrington attended a service where 'some of the Blew Boys about 20 of them sung a psalme'.[67] 'Unremitted loudness' from the organ would not have been a widespread problem in Hertfordshire, where only six town and two country parishes had organs during the 1780s–1790s. By contrast, Porteus observed, 'In country parishes, where there are in general neither charity-children nor organs, it may be more difficult perhaps to restore the psalmody to its primitive state, and banish the corruptions of it introduced by the select village choir.'[68]

Although a High Churchman, Porteus was a warm supporter of many Evangelical initiatives and encouraged the founding of Sunday schools. He particularly encouraged their establishment in rural parishes, again believing that children's voices would encourage congregational psalmody. Porteus, like Gibson, placed an emphasis on plain tunes, but rather than trying to do away with singers *per se* he suggested persuading them to use 'proper portions of the Psalms from the new version, which should be adapted to some of the plainest, simplest and easiest of our most ancient and popular melodies'. In country parishes 'This will be greatly aided by training up some of the most promising children of the parish in the constant practice of plain psalmody, till by degrees a large part of the congregation have been thus instructed from their youth, and a select band will no longer be necessary.'[69] Porteus further argued that this had

> been already done in several parishes with great success, especially in those where Sunday-Schools have been established; [...] By these means a considerable choir of well taught young people may in a few years be formed in every church, who will serve as guides and instructors to the rest of the congregation [...][70]

Porteus was not alone in seeing the potential benefits to be derived from using children to improve the psalmody in rural parish churches. Shortly after touring Hertfordshire in 1788 the diarist John Byng claimed, presumably from experience, that were he 'Squire of a country Village' he would offer 'Premiums and Encouragements' to found 'a little Chorus of Children; than which nothing is more Elevating and Grateful and Sublime, hearing Innocence exert their little Voices in praise of their Creator'.[71] Like Porteus, Byng alluded to the potential of using youthful singing to attract larger parochial congregations: 'Nothing should be more encouraged, as drawing both Young and Old to Church, than Church Melody.'[72]

Leading by example, Porteus began to install clergymen sympathetic to his cause in those Hertfordshire livings of which he held the patronage. One such was Rickmansworth, where he installed his nephew Edward Hodgson as rector in 1805. Despite being one of the largest towns in Hertfordshire, Rickmansworth had no organ at this date and, prior to the introduction of a barrel organ in 1826, 'the school children vocalized Tate and Brady to the accompaniment of the frolicsome fiddle, the melancholy flute, and the rumbling bass-viol'.[73]

About half of Hertfordshire parishes came under the jurisdiction of the Bishop of Lincoln, where George Pretyman was bishop 1787–1820. As summarised in Table 2.2, early Hertfordshire Sunday schools were equally distributed between the dioceses of London and Lincoln, indicating that Bishop Pretyman also looked favourably upon the establishment of Sunday schools. When Pretyman held his first visitation at Baldock in 1788, Sir Adam Gordon, rector of Hinxworth, preached a sermon supporting them.[74] By 1789 Gordon had himself established a Sunday school, urging parents to support the endeavour. Moreover, in 1791 he took the call to improve psalmody one step further and made his own selection of psalms suitable for parish use, set to tunes edited by Samuel Arnold.[75] It seems most probable that this was also prompted by the strong Methodist presence in Hinxworth and the rival attraction presented by their music-making. In 1794 William Dechair Tattersall attributed the poor state of congregational psalmody to a want of encouragement by both gentry and clergy, while praising Gordon for his 'assiduous endeavours to serve the Church'.[76]

Bishop Gibson's 1724 directions for singing psalms were still considered essential reading in 1807 when John Randolph, then Bishop of Bangor, included them in a select collection of tracts entitled *The Clergyman's Instructor*.[77] By highlighting Gibson's directions he clearly attached importance to promoting psalmody and in his own 1808 Charge addressed the problem of the rival attractions of Methodist meetings:

> I would also suggest whether an attention to the Psalmody of the Church would not be a likely means of keeping your congregations regular in their attendance, and earnest in their worship. Our adversaries, as is well known, and they are much

to be commended in this particular, render their meetings attractive by a careful attention to this custom, and by the skilful practice of it.[78]

Gibson's argument against teaching complex psalmody to the children of the poor continued to be used, particularly with regard to girls. But in an account of her Brentford Sunday schools, in 1787 Sarah Trimmer mounted a spirited defence of both girls' education and their participation in psalmody:

> Those children who have voices are exceedingly fond of singing psalms, and others have great pleasure in hearing them. Some people object to girls being indulged in this particular, from an idea that it will give their thoughts an improper turn: but surely this is an illiberal as well as mistaken notion; for why should we suppose that directing the application of their talent to its noblest use will lead to the perversion of it? And why in this age, when a taste for sacred music prevails among the higher ranks of people, should we wish to debar the lower ones from the recreation which psalmody gives to their minds; unless it could be proved that it actually takes them off from any religious or moral duty? Our great Creator has not confined the relish for music to any rank of his creatures; and I do not think that any can claim an exclusive privilege to the moderate enjoyment of its delights.[79]

But controversies surrounding Sunday schools jeopardised their potential to improve church music-making. Despite the limited education that they provided, any education of the poor remained a contentious issue, particularly during the Napoleonic Wars, when Pitt's government considered introducing legislation against Sunday schools.[80] This was partly because of concerns that the educated poor would be able to read subversive political tracts such as Thomas Paine's *Rights of Man*, leading to revolution in England, as in France. In 1803 Porteus delivered a Charge to his clergy during a period when hostilities were thought to be over. In this Charge, largely overlooked by scholars, Porteus said that he was encouraged to have received from various parts of his diocese 'most favourable accounts of the effects produced by the Sunday schools lately established there. […] In some places […] churches, which before were almost deserted, are now crowded with hearers and with communicants.'[81] He then directly addressed the 'problem' of educating the poor, setting out a forceful case against those who equated the education of the poor with training up a rebellious populace. Porteus argued that any sort of education was better than none, and contended that there had been no revolution in England because so many children had received an education of some sort. This resulted in a significant proportion of the populace being able to read the counter-revolutionary discourses, sermons and tracts distributed just as widely as the feared subversive literature.[82] This successful defence of Sunday schools enabled them to continue to form the basis of attempts to use charity children's voices to improve congregational singing.

Polite children

So far, only the involvement of charity children in church music-making has been considered, for the simple reason that more fortunate children followed the example set by their families, and remained silent. William Riley, who described himself as 'Principal Teacher of Psalmody to the Charity-Schools in London, Westminster, and Parts adjacent' and therefore may have taught in Hertfordshire, published in 1762 a book of psalmody entitled *Parochial Music Corrected. Containing remarks on the performance of psalmody in country churches, and on the ridiculous and profane Manner of Singing practised by the Methodists; Reflections on the bad Performance of Psalmody in London, Westminster, &c. [...] the Utility of Teaching Charity-Children Psalmody and Hymns [...]*. Advertisements were often placed in newspapers inviting individuals or groups to subscribe to works such as this, which would be published once enough subscriptions had been received to make it economical to do so. The lengthy sub-title gave the subscriber an indication of its content without seeing the book in advance. The subscribers not only received the publication but, by being listed in the book itself, would have their names associated with the other subscribers, usually including clergymen, gentry and sometimes nobility. In this case the 389 subscribers included several prominent London organists and organ-builders, in addition to William Hatfield, who was rector of Lilley and vicar of Caddington, parishes in which musical instruments were used to support singing.[83] Despite praising his subscribers for their support of charity children, Riley berated them for the misdirected education of their children and noted, in reference to Bishop Gibson, that 'It is plain that his Lordship thought it as necessary for these poor Children to be taught to sing the Praises of their bountiful creator, as those who are blest with a higher Birth, Education and Fortune.'[84]

Like Gibson, Riley argued that, if children were to be taught singing, this would lead to an improvement in congregational psalmody. Poor children should be taught to sing psalmody, but he argued that, in addition, 'polite' children in receipt of a musical education should put their talents to good use. Children of 'superior condition' were very often taught the harpsichord, but Riley found that they were 'seldom, if ever, permitted either to play or sing a psalm-tune, because that cannot so well shew the abilities of their children, as in playing or singing a song. Thus a contempt for psalmody is commonly very early contracted.'[85] He added that many 'superior' children shared the somewhat cavalier attitude of the Page in Otway's *Tragedy of the Orphan*, who opined 'Boys that go to school sing psalms, but pages, that are better bred, sing lampoons.'[86] Riley claimed that 'their parents[,] giving themselves no manner of concern about it, [think] it a matter of little or no importance, or a qualification too mean and unpolite for children of superior condition'.[87]

Concerning the silence of young ladies in church, Riley much regretted that they 'should be so bashful and ashamed of doing their duty to God; when asked to sing at home, it would be looked upon as a breach of good manners to refuse'. Many contemporary writers found Riley's a compelling argument, including John Arnold, organist of Great Warley (Essex). In the preface to his own *Church Music Reformed* (1765) he said 'How excellent would the sweet Female Trebles likewise render the Performance, if young Ladies, who learn to sing, and play on the Harpsichord, Spinnet, &c. could be persuaded to join?'[88] But other 'polite' children received no musical education at all, leading Riley to suggest that

> between those who are not taught, and those who think it mean to employ their talents this way, this exercise is almost totally neglected; and were it not for charity-children being taught psalmody, the performance would be very indecent indeed, especially in churches which have no organs, and unskilful clerks.[89]

Riley's plea appears to have had little response, and in 1827 the Congregationalist minister and composer David Everard Ford wrote:

> There are many Christian parents who devote large sums of money to the musical education of their children, and expect them, in return, to gratify their visitors, by playing and singing for hours together; yet who would think themselves insulted, if any one were to hint, that such talents and attainments might be serviceable in public worship [...] Perhaps the excuse may be, that some of the persons with whom, in that case, they would be expected now and then to associate, are a few degrees beneath themselves in the scale of society [...].[90]

These comments reveal one of the unforeseen results of associating church music-making with charitable objectives. In 1791 the organist Edward Miller commented on the lack of participation among the greater part of the congregation, who during psalm-singing would be 'Irreverently *sitting* – talking to each other – taking snuff – winding up their watches, or adjusting their apparel'.[91] Among the gentry he attributed this to feelings of superiority, since they were acquainted with metropolitan music-making: 'Perhaps the excellent musicians we hear at the opera, have in some measure contributed to render the present performance of *Parochial Psalmody* so intolerable to our ears.' But he also suggested that it could be attributed to '*pride*, and the fear of appearing vulgar'.[92] According to Temperley, 'the gentry would not so far demean themselves as to sing in church', but were prepared 'with Christian charity to endow a school for poor children who, in return, would be trained to provide a more elegant song of praise'.[93] It could also be suggested that, rather than it being merely considered 'unpolite' to sing in church, certain elite families in Hertfordshire and elsewhere felt that they would be tainted by association with the objects of their charity if they did so.

Children's singing teachers

Although charity children were sometimes taught to sing by school patrons, as discussed above, in churches with an organ it was usually the organist who taught children to sing. Shaw described the organist as 'a master of musick, so does he often teach some of the younger parishioners musick', and in Hertfordshire most of the identifiable children's singing teachers were organists.[94] It is therefore unsurprising to find payments for charity school children's singing lessons following the acquisition of an organ. Although Table 2.3 gives some indication of the range of teachers' occupations, it does not include clergy family members and others who taught *gratis*.

In 1774 the churchwardens of St Peter's, St Albans, purchased six copies of 'Wilkins's Psalm Books', which included 'easy instructions for young beginers' (Figure 2.5).[95] The daunting chart of the Gamut, or scales, in Wilkins' *Psalmody* illustrates why teaching children to sing with the aid of a barrel organ later came to be seen as an easier option in so many churches. Presumably these books were purchased on the recommendation of Anna Sophia Sherman, who was appointed organist at around this date, almost certainly with the obligation of teaching the charity children to sing. The appointment of a woman organist during this period was not as unusual as it might at first appear, and this issue is discussed further in Chapter 5.

Edward Miller's *Psalms* attracted a number of Hertfordshire subscribers, including Mr Yardley, churchwarden of Bishops Stortford, where a Sunday school had already been established. Miller emphasised the important role of organists such as himself: 'It is chiefly from *his* exertions, that a reformation in the performance is to be hoped for. Let him not shrink from the trouble of attending once a week, for a few months, to instruct the *charity* or Sunday school children.'[96] This suggestion was adopted at Bishops Stortford, where between 1793 and 1799 Yardley authorised payments to the organist 'for teaching the Children of the Sunday School to sing Psalms' (see Table 2.3). In 1787 William Vincent advised that one method of obtaining better instruction for children would be 'for them to come to church half an hour before the service commences; during which time they might practise or rehearse with the organ'.[97] Miller's own church in Doncaster introduced a routine whereby

Table 2.3. Hertfordshire children's singing teachers. Ordered by date of earliest known payment.

Parish	Date	Teacher	Details
Rickmansworth	1761–1802	Richard and William Halsey, breeches makers; H. Tomlinson, barber	Regular payments for 'teaching the Charity boys to sing' and 'teaching the children psalmody'
Cheshunt	1788–1814	Thomas Leach, organist	1788: 'to teach the children in the Free School Psalmody' 1814: 'additional duty of teaching the Charity school boys Psalmody for half an hour before church service every Sunday morning'
Bishops Stortford	1793	Robert Perry, organist	'teaching the Children of the Sunday School to sing Psalms'
Ware	1794	Henry Tillcock, labourer	'teaching the children to sing'
St Peter's, St Albans	1815–18	Thomas Fowler and Mr Castell, organists	'playing the organ and teaching boys to sing'
Abbey Church, St Albans	1818	John Higdon, clarionet player	'instructing the Blue Coat boys to sing at the Abbey Church'
East Barnet	1824–29	Elizabeth Neave, schoolmistress	'teaching the children to sing' & 'turning the organ'
Little Gaddesden	1824	John Osmond, ?clarinettist	'teaching boys & girls the art of singing'
St Andrew's, Hertford	1825	Henry Bridgeman, organist	'teaching the children of this parish to sing'
Bishops Stortford	1827	James Hyde	'teaching children singing'
Kings Langley	1827	Unknown	'Proposed that some of the Girls should be instructed in singing in the Church'
Totteridge	1827	George Miller, organist	Appointed on condition he 'give instructions to the children in singing'
Chipping Barnet	1829	William Easton	'to conduct the singing in church … and to give necessary instructions to the children'
Abbey Church, St Albans	1831	Edwin Theodore Nicholls, organist	Appointed on condition 'he is to teach twelve of the boys belonging to the Blue Coat School at least one day in each week to sing'
Watford	1833	Edward Hackman, organist	Charity children 'taught to sing by the organist'
Braughing	1835	Barrel organist	Instructed girls of the National School in psalmody
Essendon	1835	John Bamford, smith and parish clerk	Duties included 'Teaching Singing children'
Hitchin	1838	Godwin, organist	Duties included 'teaching singers [including] 11 girls, 6 boys & 6 men'
Cheshunt	1840	Sarah Wood, organist	Reappointed 'on condition of her teaching the charity children psalmody agreeably to her first appointment'
London Colney	1860s	Markland Barnard, vicar, and his wife	Taught singing and chanting to the schoolchildren

Sources: HALS, DP/15/8/3, DP/16/5/2, DP/21/5/5–11, DP/29/8/48–54, DP/37/5/4, DP/46B/12/5, DP/49/8/2–5, DP/53/7/4, DP/64/25/9–10, DP/85/25/1, DP/90/5/1, DP/90/7, DP/90/8/1–3, DP/93/5/3–5, DP/116/5/1, DP/117/5/1; Little Gaddesden, Churchwardens' bills & vouchers; PP 1833 (60) 25; PP 1835 (216) 29; 1841 Census HO107/441/f.11/p.16, HO107/444/f.26/p.3; Hertfordshire Family History Society, Militia Ballot Lists: Rickmansworth & Ware; *HG* (February 1866), p. 5.

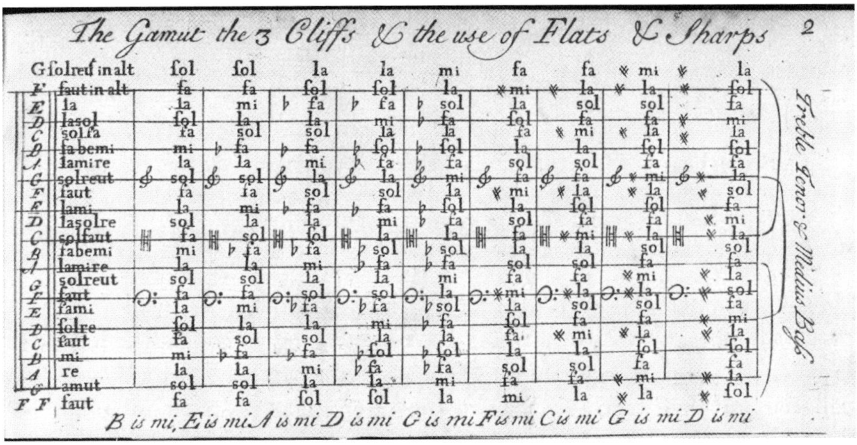

Figure 2.5. 'The Gamut', from Matthew Wilkins, *A Second Book of Psalmody* (London, 1750) © The Bodleian Library, University of Oxford, Mus. 32 e.61.

the Sunday school masters and school mistresses, along with their pupils, would attend church for half an hour before morning and evening service, 'to be instructed in properly singing the psalms to be used in this church'.[98] This practice was also adopted in Hertfordshire, and in 1814 Thomas Leach, organist of Cheshunt, was required to teach the charity school boys psalmody 'for half an hour before church service every Sunday morning'.[99]

In some churches a select group of children formed a choir to lead the congregation. At Cheshunt, the Abbey Church and St Peter's, St Albans, boys were selected in preference to girls, presumably because these particular town parishes aspired to follow the ancient choral tradition of cathedrals and collegiate places of worship. But in 1787 Trimmer argued that charity boys and girls alike should be encouraged to sing psalms.[100] This was already the case in Watford, where in 1766 'both Boys and Girls' from local charity schools sang with the organ, and at Little Gaddesden boys and girls were taught 'the art of singing' in 1824.[101] Yet in 1827 David Everard Ford suggested that psalmody could be improved by teaching a selection of Sunday school boys aged between seven and fourteen, practising two evenings a week.[102] He argued that by these means 'a most excellent quire may be raised with little trouble' and, in similarly optimistic vein, since the elder boys would instruct the younger, he suggested 'the master will have little more to do than to enforce subordination and punctuality'. He explained that trebles were needed to lead congregational singing because they could be heard more distinctly than low voices, and added 'To expect any man to organize a quire, without a good selection of treble voices, would be as unreasonable as was the requisition of the Egyptian taskmasters.' Nevertheless, in 1840 'T.V.' suggested that girls showed a greater aptitude for sight-reading music:

> there can be no excuse for continuing the execrable psalmody usual in village churches, where there is a charity school and a good singing-master within a moderate distance. It is astonishing how soon a selected class of children, particularly girls, acquire the habit of singing at sight, under good instruction.[103]

How the congregation was expected to learn from the children is a question barely addressed by historians, but the evidence indicates that the half-hour instruction sessions held before divine service were not aimed solely at children and their teachers. Vincent suggested that 'it is not impossible that rehearsals of this kind should attract several of the parishioners', and Miller agreed: 'The congregation will soon learn to join them, and the result will amply repay him for all his labour.'[104]

In charity and Sunday schools in rural parishes, and in those with no wealthy patron or landowners, it was very difficult to find funding for an organ or organist, and singing instruction in these parishes was initially undertaken by the parish clerk. In 1715 it was found that some country parishes appointed parish clerks 'on condition they would teach a certain number of children'.[105] This was the case at Furneux Pelham, where as early as the 1720s the duties of the parish clerk Mr Beard included schooling in addition to psalmody and 'setting ye psalms at church'.[106] During the nineteenth century the roles of parish clerk and teacher were still often combined, as, for example, by John Parker of Abbots Langley and Henry Broderick of Watford.[107] In other cases children were taught to sing by adult singers or members of the church band, and this is discussed in Chapter 4. Perhaps more commonly, the teaching of psalmody was undertaken by the school master or mistress. According to Vincent, 'the school-master is usually the instructor in music, [...] always attendant on them at church, and the regulator of their behaviour there'.[108] The importance of this duty was emphasised by Miller in 1791, who suggested that the clergy should choose as Sunday school masters 'one or two persons who know enough of music to teach, *by the ear*, the children of their schools, the tunes that are to be used in the church'.[109] As explained in the following section, teachers employed by the National Society were often required to teach psalmody.

National Schools

At the beginning of the nineteenth century a group of High Churchmen again saw an opportunity to increase church attendance by educating the young. In this way, they hoped to instil a lifelong habit of attending church.

In October 1811 they were instrumental in founding the National Society for Promoting the Education of the Poor in the Principles of the Established Church (National Society), potentially bringing a charity school education within the reach of children in parishes with no existing school. National Schools quickly began to be founded in Hertfordshire, in line with the Society's aim of establishing one in every parish in the country.

In addition to newly created National Schools, numerous, but by no means all, existing charity and Sunday schools associated with the established church joined the Society because they shared many of its objectives. These included the hope expressed by clergy and laity alike that children's singing would encourage congregational singing and maintain, or even increase, the number attending church. In 1847 Rev. Richard Gee advertised for a National School mistress at Abbots Langley, saying 'She must be a good needlewoman, thoroughly competent to teach a Village School on the National System, and able to lead the children in singing', while a schoolmaster was wanted near Tring 'with ability to lead in congregational singing, to take charge of a small village day and Sunday school'.[110] In 1854 advertisements for National School teachers at Essendon stated 'either master or mistress must be able to teach Psalmody'.[111] Similarly, the Aston National School master sought a new appointment, explaining that he had 'some knowledge of music', and would be 'happy to assist the choir'.[112]

The incorporation of a charity day or Sunday school into the National Society, or the founding of an entirely new National School, was often associated with the installation of a church organ, in practice usually a barrel organ, a theme developed in Chapters 5 and 6. As Vice-President of the National Society, evidence of the Earl of Hardwicke's interest in promoting church music-making in this manner comes from Aspenden and Westmill, two parishes of which he was the patron.[113] In 1818 Henry Pepys was presented by Hardwicke to the living of Aspenden, which he left in 1827 to become rector of Westmill. In order to support the children's singing, barrel organs were purchased by subscription during Pepys' incumbency at both Aspenden in 1821 and Westmill in 1829.[114]

But it was only children whose parents could afford the National School's fee, usually a penny a week, who were able to attend at all. As outlined in Chapter 1, in Hertfordshire many poor children were employed in agriculture, the straw-plait industry, silk and paper mills and other occupations. The 'Rules for the Guidance of the Parents' issued when Baldock National Schools opened in June 1834 were therefore typical in stipulating that all boys and girls aged four and over were expected to attend, except those 'whose necessary employment prevents their coming in the week-days'.[115] Low attendance figures at National Schools in some parts of Hertfordshire were attributed to the large proportion of young children employed in the straw trade, and this almost certainly contributed to the decision to teach straw plaiting in some National Schools.[116]

Unlike 'clothed' charity schools, there was no uniform and, because of financial constraints felt by both the parents and the teachers themselves, some National Schools were open only on Sundays. Yet those who only attended on Sundays *and* those who attended during the week were expected to attend church on Sundays.[117] By doing so, they would have had the potential to play their part in the drive to improve congregational singing. When a proposal was put forward for the establishment of the Elstree National School in 1814, Rule 3 stipulated:

> All the children to assemble every Sunday morning at the School-house, by half past nine o'clock; and in the afternoon by two, for the purpose of attending divine worship; and if any of them shall, without sufficient cause to be allowed by the mistress, fail to do so, it is to be a ground of expulsion from the school.[118]

And in 1839 Barkway National School rigorously enforced National Society rules, stipulating that 'The master and mistress [...] shall always attend church with the children, whether in holiday time or otherwise, whenever it is open for Divine Service. The children shall proceed to church from school in order together, and return after church to school in like manner.'[119]

Typical hours for 'Daily Schools' during the 1830s were 9 a.m.–12 noon and 2–5 p.m. from Ladyday to Michaelmas, with afternoon lessons finishing an hour earlier during the winter.[120] Although there was no school on Saturday afternoons at certain times of year, the children's week was almost entirely timetabled.

In 1851 a one-off Census of Education was held on the same weekend as the Population and Religious Censuses, again organised by the civil servant Horace Mann. Unlike the Population Census, it was not compulsory for the Census of Education returns to be completed. Furthermore, many schools gave only the total number of pupils, but in these cases Mann split the figures equally between boys and girls to give an approximation of their actual numbers. Because so few returns survive it is impossible to use this census alone to identify the Hertfordshire schools that sent them. Nevertheless, Mann's Report indicates that, in Hertfordshire, although 2,163 children attended British schools, 11,171 attended charity schools connected with the Church of England.[121] In many villages a school associated with the Church of England or National School was the only school. The clergy were therefore able to have a direct influence on children and, through them, their parents. These schools were attended by children of those who attended the church, but also by those of non-churchgoers and dissenters alike. In such circumstances certain clergymen took a more liberal attitude to church attendance, only demanding it of children whose parents belonged to the established church.[122]

Because it was obligatory for the church to provide some sort of seating for National School children this contributed to a shortage of accommodation in many churches, the consequences of which are examined in Chapter 9. There was, however, no requirement, and often no room, for their parents to attend at all. George Gaisford became the incumbent of Wigginton in 1854, and later recalled:

> The church – it was like many other rural churches in those days – untidy, mean, dilapidated – a gallery at the west end into which the schoolchildren were with difficulty squeezed, the usual 3-decker arrangement of pulpit &c in short everything as bad as could be. But worse still was the congregation, a few very aged women & the schoolchildren.[123]

Despite accommodation problems in some parishes, others found that children's singing was successful in attracting both their parents and people who would otherwise have stayed away, perhaps to attend dissenting meetings. The Lincolnshire vicar George Davys promoted this aim in his 1820 *Village Conversations* between 'William' and 'Thomas':

> William: [...] I hope if Sunday-schools, and day-schools, go on and prosper, our congregations will, in time, be all able to read, and so all join in the service [...]
> Thomas: And they tell me, that, in many of these schools, the children learn to sing too; so that, in time, we may expect the whole congregation to join in singing the praises of God, instead of leaving this part of the service to only a few of the people, as is too much the way now-a-days. When a psalm is given out, the clerk says, 'Let us sing to the praise and glory of God'. This shows that we should all join if we can; it is not, 'Let us listen, whilst others sing', it is 'Let us sing'.[124]

In 1840 'E.T.' wrote to the *Educational Magazine* about the continuing poor state of congregational psalmody, arguing:

> In any place where there is a daily boys' or girls' school [...] and singing established as a regular part of school tuition, the clergyman and his people will be secure of a succession of tolerable vocalists. Though the children pass off from the school, some remain in the village; and these, whether in the gallery or in the body of the Church, are useful both by their better singing and better taste.[125]

However, in 1821 Samuel Wilks, editor of the *Christian Observer*, had cautioned that 'Much might be done in most parishes, and *is* done in many, by teaching the charity children to *sing* – not *vociferate* – and taking care that no tunes are sung but what a plain congregation can easily join in.'[126] To vociferate is 'to cry out loudly', 'bawl' or 'shout' – again suggesting that the congregation may have found difficulties in singing with poorly taught children's choirs. But such difficulties were symptomatic of far wider problems associated with the compulsory church attendance of charity children, as explained in the following section.

A qualified success

In the preface to his Census of Education report, Mann noted that the number of dissenters was far higher than should have been expected had National School children continued to attend church as adults:

> At first sight it appears inevitable that in course of time the mass of the population, educated of necessity in Church of England schools, must gradually return to that community; but, in opposition to this natural anticipation, is the curious fact, that – while for many years past at least four fifths of all the children who have passed through public schools must have been instructed in the schools of the Church of England – concurrently with this, a very considerable augmentation has (according to the tables of Religious Worship) been proceeding in the number of Dissenters; so that now they number very nearly half of the total population.[127]

Mann suggested that this could be attributed either to some laxity on the part of the established church or to the superior persuasiveness of the dissenting influence. The teaching of Nonconformist hymns to National School children may also have been a contributory factor. But a further, more uncomfortable, conclusion that Mann did not consider presents itself: namely, that by compelling children to sing psalms and attend church in the few hours each week when they were not required to work, the established church had actually managed to dissuade children from attending as adults.

By 1856 letters to the National Society began to acknowledge that compelling unwilling children to attend church was not conducive to willing voluntary attendance as adults, and 'G.W.O.' described as mischievous 'the fashion of marching our school-children to church on a Sunday'.[128] Because children who attended National Schools were required to meet at the schoolroom to 'proceed to church' in a body, the parents were deprived of both the pleasure and pride of escorting their children to church and sitting with them. According to G.W.O., 'They may often be seen after the services of the day, with evident sentiments of parental pride, […] but not having been allowed to accompany [their children] to the house of God, have themselves refrained from going thither.'[129] Furthermore, the sheer number of children needing to be accommodated in the church meant that in many cases there was no room for their parents. G.W.O. continued:

> In many instances, it may be feared, [the parents] seek at a Dissenting conventicle a substitute for the enjoyment of taking their own children to a place of worship, which our pernicious though well-intended school-regulations have refused them in connection with that church in which their fathers assembled to adore their fathers' God in the beauty of holiness. Thus are we unwisely alienating our respectable poor from our church, and contributing to swell the ranks of Dissent.[130]

During the 1860s Harpenden children attended the Sunday school attached to St Nicholas's, where classes were held for two hours until it was time to process to the church for the 11 a.m. service, just as charity children had processed during the eighteenth century. The more daring boys seized this opportunity to run away across Harpenden common rather than be trapped in church for another hour and a half.[131] The Berkhamsted businessman Henry Nash reminisced about the 'dismal' atmosphere of St Mary's when he had attended Sunday school during this period:

> The children were sent as a duty by their parents without much regard as to the kind of instruction they received; they were expected to assemble at nine o'clock in the morning, when they were kept standing on the cold stones for two hours, then required to remain for the service, which kept them nearly two hours more through a dreary service that had no meaning to them. The prayers were long and monotonous; the singing, accompanied by a barrel organ, was of such a dismal character, that it would not be tolerated in a ragged school today. It is not surprising, therefore, that those who had to pass through this ordeal should have forsaken the church altogether.[132]

Perhaps as a result of his experience at Sunday school, in adulthood Nash was willing to have his goods seized rather than pay the church rate.[133] Strict discipline did little to ameliorate the situation. At Westmill the barrel-organist was 'a stern disciplinarian and kept order among his choir of Sunday scholars with a stick'.[134] The master of the Royston Sunday school wielded a ten-foot wand over the heads of his scholars during divine service and, if any misbehaved, 'down came the wand, whack' upon the back of the seat.[135]

The efforts of the National Society to encourage congregational singing seem to have had limited success, with adults remaining silent while the children sang. In January 1852 Novello advertised his *169 Psalm and Hymn*

Tunes thus: 'At the request of many friends and others connected with churches where the singing is confined to Treble voices, or to the children, the whole of the 169 Psalm and Hymn tunes have been adapted for one, two or three treble voices.'[136] 'G.W.O.' commented:

> It is frequently to be observed, that where school-children are placed together at church, and required [...] to form a choir, the adult members of such congregations are generally disposed to praise their Almighty Creator by deputy, and to accept the services of our scholars as such. Disperse these children amongst the people; enjoin them [...] to take their part in singing; they will then afford an example worthy of imitation, and one that can scarcely fail to promote congregational worship.[137]

Consciously or unconsciously, 'G.W.O.' was repeating a complaint made time after time since the late eighteenth century.

By the early 1860s the 'novelty' of teaching children to lead congregational singing appears to have worn thin. From December 1860 onwards the newly published *Oxford Parochial Magazine* ran a three-part guide to 'Things to be Said or Sung' in church. In the first part, the anonymous contributor commented:

> Of all long-suffering generations that ever existed there have been none certainly so patient as those which have listened for these many years past to the execrable stuff foisted upon them as devotional music in their Churches. Turn into a town Church, for instance, and what does one hear? Fifty charity children squalling their little windpipes to pieces in uninstructed efforts to sing a psalm tune or hymn tune which no effort in the world could make singable by the congregation at large.[138]

The *status quo* in Hertfordshire during the 1860s was pithily appraised by an anonymous Watford resident when a local lecture on church music prompted them to write to the *Watford Observer*. They commented that, although 'more than common attention' was now being given to the subject of church music, 'While our congregations are satisfied to listen to a few poor children singing because they are compelled, poor things, no improvement can possibly take place.'[139] The contributor argued that congregations were unable to join in because the range or arrangements of the tunes made them unsingable, saying:

> The majority of the congregation do not sing because it is impossible to do so. The arrangements very often seem to be made as if it were intended that they should not sing. Even the few who are disposed to join in the singing cannot do so. The tunes are selected which require a great compass of voice. Even the sopranos among the

ladies, and tenors among the men, cannot reach the upper notes without drawing the attention of the congregation upon them, and so they remain silent. In the case of the contralto and bass voices, they find it simply impossible, and they give it up as hopeless.[140]

He or she clearly sympathised with the children who were compelled to attend church on the one day a week they were not obliged to work:

In this way silence is the rule in our churches, and the singing is left to a few poor children, frequently those who are engaged in work all the week, and whose only attendance at church is on Sundays, when they are mercilessly criticised by the listening congregation, whose educated ears are offended by the attempts to do what they would rather let quite alone.[141]

Teaching psalmody to charity school children was seen to be of great importance throughout the period from the 1760s to the 1860s, with the repeated expectation that their singing would encourage the congregation and attract worshippers. Unfortunately this outcome was rarely achieved and, as seen in this Watford example, the congregation studiously refused to sing.

The psalmody that children and adult members of the congregation were expected to sing is the subject of the next chapter.

Endnotes

1. Temperley, *Parish Church*, p. 63.
2. Anon., *Methods used for erecting Charity Schools, with the Rules and Orders by which they are governed* (London, 1715), pp. 16 and 20.
3. Ibid.; Anon., *An Account of Charity Schools in Great Britain and Ireland [...]* (London, 1713).
4. Anon., *Methods used for erecting Charity Schools*, p. 8.
5. Anon., *Account of Charity Schools*, pp. 76–7.
6. W.M. Jacob, *Lay People and Religion in the Early Eighteenth Century* (Cambridge, 1996), p. 179.
7. Ibid.; D.T. Andrew, *Philanthropy and Police. London Charity in the Eighteenth Century* (Princeton, 1989), p. 54.
8. Jacob, *Lay People*, p. 179.
9. Anon., *An Account of the Hospital for the Maintenance and Education of Exposed and Deserted Young Children* (London, 1749), p. 4.
10. See Chapter 3, pp. 68 and 79.
11. HALS, DE/Hd/F3 Journal of William Jones (1802–5).
12. N. Temperley, 'The Hymn Books of the Foundling and Magdalen Hospital Chapels', in D. Hunter (ed.), *Music Publishing and Collecting: Essays in Honor of Donald W. Krummel* (Urbana, 1994), p. 9.
13. H.R.W. Hall, 'Essendon Church', *Transactions of the East Herts Archaeological Society*, 3/III (1907), p. 255.
14. T. Longstaffe-Gowan, *The London Square* (London, 2012), pp. 30 and 43.
15. P. Williams, 'English Organ Music and the English Organ under the First Four Georges', PhD thesis (Cambridge Univ., 1962), p. 116.
16. Temperley, *Parish Church*, p. 116.
17. 'Parishes: Hertford (All Saints' & St John's)', *VCH Herts*, 3, pp. 490–501; F.M. Page, *Christ's Hospital Hertford* (London, 1953).
18. Lincolnshire Archives, DIOC/FAC/1/26 Faculty (1678).
19. J.F.B. Sharpe, 'Christ's Hospital at Ware and Hertford', *Transactions of the East Herts Archaeological Society*, 3/III (Hertford, 1908), p. 305; G. Sheldrick, *Three Centuries of Music at All Saints Church Hertford* (Hertford, 1987), p. 39.
20. W.C. Morgan, 'St Peter's Church, St Albans', *Transactions 1897 & 1898*, St Albans Architectural and Archaeological Society, New Series, 1 part II (St Albans, 1899), pp. 135–73.
21. E. Gibson, *Directions given by Edmund Lord Bishop of London to the Masters and Mistresses of the Charity-schools* (London, 1724), pp. 5–6.
22. Ibid.
23. E. Gibson, *Directions given to the Clergy of the Diocese of London, in the year 1724* (London, 1727), pp. 9–12.
24. Ibid.
25. A. Bedford, *The Excellency of Divine Music* (London, 1733), p. 31, cited by Temperley, *Parish Church*, p. 104.
26. T. Jackson, *The Life of the Rev. Charles Wesley*, 2 vols (London, 1841), 2, p. 509.
27. Cussans, *History*, II, pp. 96–7.
28. D. Keene, R.A. Burns and A. Saint (eds), *St Paul's: the Cathedral Church of London, 604–2004* (London, 2004), pp. 348–50.
29. Anon., *List of the Patrons of the Anniversary of the Charity-Schools* (London, 1790).
30. B. Porteus, 'Sermon XII', in *Sermons on Several Subjects*, vol. II (London, 1794), p. 267.
31. W. Vincent, *Considerations on parochial music* (London, 1787), p. 9.
32. S. Trimmer, *Family Magazine*, 1 (June 1788), p. 427.
33. I. Spink, 'Haydn at St Paul's: 1791 or 1792?', *Early Music*, 33/2 (May 2005), pp. 273–80.
34. B. Dolman, '"Everything Curious": Samuel Hieronymus Grimm and Sir Richard Kaye', *Electronic British Library Journal* (2003), pp. 4–6, accessed at <http://www.bl.uk/eblj/2003articles/article2.html>.

35 *Ibid.*
36 B. Rainbow, 'Singing for Their Supper', *Musical Times* (April 1984), p. 229.
37 *Monthly Review* (1796), pp. 402–3.
38 Sunday School Society, *Plan of a Society established in London, AD 1785, for the support and encouragement of Sunday-Schools in the different counties of England* (London, 1793), pp. 1–14.
39 *Ibid.*; W.R. Ward, *Religion and Society in England 1790–1850* (London, 1972), p. 13.
40 Burgess, *Enterprise*, p. 12.
41 J.W. Grimston (3rd Earl of Verulam), *Report on the Manuscripts of the Earl of Verulam, preserved at Gorhambury*, Historic Manuscripts Commission, no. 64 (London, 1906), p. 132.
42 *Ibid.*
43 Vincent, *Considerations*, pp. 28–9.
44 E. Miller, *Thoughts on the Present Performance of Psalmody in the Established Church of England* (London, 1791), p. 9.
45 HALS, DP/64/25/9–10 Sunday School minutes & accounts (1786–1801).
46 HALS, DP/23/3/1 Vicar's notes & memoranda (1680–1912).
47 B. Hilton, *A mad, bad, and dangerous people? England 1783–1846* (Oxford, 2008), p. 178.
48 G. Sheldrick (ed.), *The Accounts of Thomas Green, Music teacher and tuner of musical instruments 1742–1790*, Hertfordshire Record Society, vol. VIII (Hertford, 1992), p. 135.
49 S. Shaw, *History of Verulam and St Albans*, (St Albans, 1815), p. 221.
50 C. Sturges, *Mr West's Annual Charity Sermon* (Reading, 1795), pp. 10–14.
51 Sunday School Society, *Sunday-Schools* (1793), pp. 78–80.
52 *Ibid.*
53 PP 1835 (216) 29, Commissions of Inquiry into Charities in England and Wales: Twenty-ninth Report, p. 502.
54 *Universal British Directory*, Appendix, p. 178; W. Urwick, *Bible Truths & Church Errors* (London, 1888), p. 211; Shaw, *History*, pp. 203–4 and 212.
55 Trimmer, *The Oeconomy of Charity, or, An address to ladies concerning Sunday-schools*, 2 vols (London, 1801), 1, pp. 107–8.
56 *Ibid.*
57 B.B. Schnorrenberg, 'Trimmer, Sarah (1741–1810)', *ODNB*.
58 Trimmer, *Family Magazine*, p. 427.
59 J. Nichols, *Literary Anecdotes of the Eighteenth Century*, 9 vols (London, 1815), IX, p. 543.
60 J. Ivery, *The Hertfordshire Melody; or, Psalm-Singers Recreation* (London, 1773), Preface.
61 Trimmer, *Oeconomy* (1801), p. 108.
62 LPL, FP Porteus visitation returns (1790).
63 LPL, FP Porteus 27/40 (1790).
64 LPL, FP Porteus 29/34 (1790).
65 Vincent, *Considerations*, p. 8.
66 B. Porteus, *A charge delivered to the clergy of the diocese of London at the primary visitation of that diocese in 1790* (London, 1790), pp. 17–19.
67 HALS DE/X3/12 Diaries of John Carrington, senior, vol. XII (April–December 1809).
68 Porteus, *A charge* (1790), pp. 17–19.
69 *Ibid.*
70 *Ibid.*
71 C.B. Andrews (ed.), *The Torrington Diaries: A Selection from the Tours of the Hon John Byng* (London, 1954), p. 160.
72 *Ibid.*
73 Cussans, *History*, III, pp. 149–50.
74 A. Gordon, *Sermons on several subjects and occasions*, 2 vols (London, 1790), 1, p. 304.
75 S. Arnold, *The Psalms of David […] The words selected by the Revd. Sir Adam Gordon Bart.* (London, 1791).
76 W.D. Tattersall, *A version of the Psalms […]* (London, 1797), p. iii.
77 J. Randolph (ed.), *The Clergyman's Instructor* (Oxford, 1807).

78 J. Randolph, *A charge delivered to the clergy of the diocese of Bangor* (Bangor, 1808), pp. 23–7.
79 Trimmer, *The Oeconomy of Charity, or, An address to ladies concerning Sunday-schools* (London, 1787), pp. 151–2.
80 B. Rodgers, *Cloak of Charity. Studies in Eighteenth-Century Philanthropy* (London, 1949), p. 109; Ward, *Religion*, p. 40.
81 Porteus, *A charge delivered to the clergy of the diocese of London, in the year 1803* (London, 1804), pp. 21–9.
82 *Ibid.*
83 See Appendix 4.
84 Riley, *Parochial music*, pp. 24–5.
85 *Ibid.*
86 T. Otway, *The Orphan, or, the Unhappy Marriage* (London, 1680), n.p.
87 Riley, *Parochial music*, pp. 24–5.
88 J. Arnold, *Church Music Reformed* (London, 1765), p. 5.
89 Riley, *Parochial music*, pp. 24–5.
90 D.E. Ford, *Observations on psalmody, by a composer* (London, 1827), pp. 114–15.
91 Miller, *Thoughts*, pp. 4–6.
92 *Ibid.*
93 Temperley, *Parish Church*, p. 101.
94 Shaw, *Parish Law*, p. 45.
95 HALS, DP/93/5/3–5 Churchwardens' accounts (1760–1870); M. Wilkins, *An Introduction to Psalmody. Containing some easy instructions for young beginers […]* (London, 1750)
96 E. Miller, *The Psalms of David for the use of Parish Churches the words selected from the version of Tate & Brady by the Revd. George Hay Drummond* (London, 1790), pp. v–vi.
97 Vincent, *Considerations*, p. 24.
98 Miller, *Psalms*, pp. x–xi.
99 HALS, DP/29/8/48–54 Churchwardens' accounts & vestry minutes (1750–1857).
100 Trimmer, *Oeconomy* (1787), pp. 151–2.
101 HALS, DP/117/8/1–3 Vestry minutes (1766–1862); Little Gaddesden, Churchwardens' bills & vouchers (1824).
102 Ford, *Observations*, p. 63; J. Brown, rev. I. Sellers, 'Ford, David Everard (1797–1875)', *ODNB*.
103 *Educational Magazine* (November 1840), pp. 312–13.
104 Vincent, *Considerations*, p. 24; Miller, *Psalms*, pp. v–vi.
105 Anon., *Charity Schools*, p. 5.
106 HALS, DP/78/3/3 Vicars' account book (1725–47).
107 1841 Census HO107/438/f.23/p.15; 1851 Census HO107/1714/f.260/p.11; *Kelly's Post Office Directory of Hertfordshire* (1851), pp. 207–8.
108 Vincent, *Considerations*, p. 22.
109 Miller, *Thoughts*, p. 9.
110 *Ecclesiastical Gazette* (September 1847), p. 71.
111 National Society, *Monthly Paper* (April 1854), pp. 64 and 142.
112 *Ibid.*
113 National Society, *First Annual Report* (London, 1812), p. 13.
114 HALS, DP/8/1/3 Register of baptisms, includes list of subscribers to new organ (1821); DP/120/1/4 Register of baptisms (1829); DP/120/8/1 Vestry minutes (1829).
115 HALS, DP/12/29/5 Miscellaneous papers (1814–34).
116 Burgess, *Enterprise*, p. 40.
117 National Society, *First Annual Report* (1812), pp. 27–8; Burgess, *Enterprise*, p. 157.
118 HALS, DP/3/25/12 Establishment of Elstree National School (1814).
119 HALS, DP/13/25/14 National School minute book (1839–54).
120 *Ibid.*; HALS, DP/12/29/5.
121 H. Mann, *Census of Great Britain, 1851. Education in Great Britain, the official report of H. Mann* (London, 1854).

122 Burgess, *Enterprise*, p. 157.
123 HALS, DP/124/29/1.
124 G. Davys, *Village Conversations on the Liturgy of the Church of England* (London, 1820), pp. 61–7. Davys became Bishop of Peterborough in 1839.
125 *Educational Magazine* (May 1840), pp. 309–14.
126 S.C. Wilks, *Correlative Claims and Duties; or, an Essay on The Necessity of a Church Establishment in a Christian Country [...]* (London, 1821), pp. 434–5.
127 Mann, *Education in Great Britain*, p. 50.
128 National Society, *Monthly Paper* (October 1856), pp. 275–7.
129 *Ibid*.
130 *Ibid*.
131 Grey, *Cottage Life*, p. 142.
132 H. Nash, *Reminiscences of Berkhamsted* (Berkhamsted, 1890), p. 56. Not to be confused with Henry Nash of Frogmore paper mill.
133 *HMR* (30 July 1887), p. 4.
134 G. Ewing, *Westmill. The Story of a Hertfordshire Parish* (Tunbridge Wells, 1928), p. 95.
135 A. Kingston, *Fragments of Two Centuries, Glimpses of Country Life when George III was King* (Royston, 1893), p. 118. A similar wand can be seen in Figure 6.6.
136 *Musical Times* (1 January 1852), p. 323.
137 National Society, *Monthly Paper* (October 1856), p. 277.
138 *Oxford Parochial Magazine* (December 1860), pp. 31–3; (February 1861), pp. 113–17.
139 *Watford Observer* (27 February 1864), p. 1.
140 *Ibid*.
141 *Ibid*.

Chapter 3
Psalms and hymns

Ever since the first years of Elizabeth I's reign the singing of 'hymns', in practice often metrical psalms, has been permitted before and after morning and evening prayer in parish churches.[1] In addition to the Old and then the New Versions, in 1700 a Supplement to the New Version was published that included six new hymns. These were the Christmas hymn 'While shepherds watched their flocks by night', two Easter hymns and three for communion.[2] Until the early 1800s the Old and then the New Version with its Supplement were commonly held to be the only authorised verses, but many eighteenth-century parochial collections also included a few hymns, especially 'Morning Hymn' (Awake my soul and with the sun) and 'Evening Hymn' (Glory to Thee my God this night). Both these hymns were written by Bishop Thomas Ken, who was born in Little Berkhamsted in 1637. In this chapter it will be seen that parochial psalmody in Hertfordshire was not restricted to settings of the approved versions and this handful of hymns that fell into a 'grey area'.

Generally, it is only since the publication of nineteenth-century hymn books that words have become associated with specific tunes; before this, metrical psalms and hymns could be sung to any tune of the same metre. Tate and Brady, authors of the New Version, recommended that those in common metre could be sung to 'the most usual' or common psalm tunes, namely 'York', 'Windsor', 'St David's', 'Litchfield', 'Canterbury', 'Martyrs', 'St Mary's alias Hackney', 'St Anne', and those in long metre, if of praise or cheerfulness, to the 'Old 125th' or 'Old 100th'. Psalms written in other metres could be sung to the 'Old 25th', 'Old 113th', 'Old 148th' or 'Old 104th [Hanover]'. These titles refer to the tunes most often used for the psalms with these numbers. All these tunes were commonly found on church barrel organs, a topic discussed in Chapter 6.

But, before examining psalmody in the established church, it is important to consider the influence of Nonconformist singing on parochial music-making.

Nonconformist singing

As Hertfordshire Methodist, Baptist and Independent meetings grew during the late eighteenth and early nineteenth centuries, clergymen faced the twin challenges of worshippers being enticed away by uplifting and inclusive Nonconformist singing and raised expectations for music-making in the established church itself. In 1829 a *London Literary Gazette* music review referred to the poor state of congregational singing in town parishes:

> it is well known that the great success of some classes of dissenters in making converts from the established church is mainly to be attributed to the attraction of sacred music, which, in many meeting-houses has been rendered more impressive and affecting than in our parish churches, where this elevating part of public worship has been consigned either to ill-taught charity children, or else to one or two hired and careless singers concealed in the organ-gallery [...][3]

It was Methodists who gave the most concern to church leaders during this period, partly because of the considerable appeal of the tunes they sang. Some were 'parody' hymn tunes – that is, taken from popular or 'art' sources and given new words. Setting words to popular tunes helped the congregation to remember them, which was greatly advantageous when so many could not read. Methodist hymnody presented an attractive alternative to disenchanted members of the church accustomed to having psalms 'lined out' by the parish clerk.[4]

John Wesley's collection of hymn tunes 'for use of the People called Methodists' included 'Directions for Singing'. These emphasised not only that all should sing but, more importantly, that all should be able to understand what they were singing: 'Have an eye to God in every word you sing.'[5] The implication is that neither was common. In 1787 William Vincent had warned of the attractive nature of 'the psalmody of the Methodists', suggesting that, for every person drawn to them from the established church by preaching, 'ten have been induced by music'.[6] Edward Miller echoed this in 1791, observing 'It is well known that more people are drawn to the tabernacles of *Methodists* by their attractive harmony, than by the doctrine of their preachers.'[7]

In Hertfordshire, evidence of Methodist singing comes from three towns located on the main routes out of London. Although the first Methodist chapel in Hertford was short-lived, in 1775 a 'large and serious congregation' of Methodists was reestablished in Castle Street.[8] This may have been the impetus behind the building of a singing gallery in nearby St Andrew's in 1779.[9] With the absent and indifferent Hon. & Rev. Cholmondeley as rector, the congregation seem to have taken matters into their own hands in an attempt to raise the standard of music-making in their church in order to retain worshippers, and possibly even attract new ones.

In St Albans, Wesleyan Methodists first met in a licensed outhouse almost adjacent to the Abbey Church in 1793, and one of their members was John Leifchild, 'a preacher of no mean pulpit power, a constant singer of psalms, hymns and spiritual songs'.[10] In 1801 their nineteen members relocated to a building in St Peter's Street and in 1810 John Nicholson, rector of the Abbey Church, reported numerous Methodists in the parish, 'who are certainly upon the increase'.[11] By 1824 their numbers had swollen to fifty-two, necessitating a move to an even larger meeting place in Dagnall Street.[12]

Further north at Baldock an anonymous verse, written at around the time John Simpson became rector in 1815, alluded to his attempts to reform church music-making. The rector attempted to do this by imposing his own choice of psalm rather than allowing the singers to choose for themselves. He also objected to them playing a 'symphony' (short interlude) between verses, and complained that their psalmody lasted too long. The fourth stanza also referred to William Stockese, the parish clerk:

> Our church Clerk too so wondrous wise
> He thus pretends to criticize
> Good author's work of modern date
> Which shows the weakness of his pate
> Says he, those words are not quite right
> His tune too airy, brisk & light
> That symphony does not agree
> With the strict rule of Psalmody[13]

The references to 'work of modern date' and the words being 'not quite right' suggest that the singers may have been singing hymns that had not been specifically authorised, rather than restricting themselves to the approved wording of the Old and New Versions. Moreover, the verse recorded the singers' intent to decamp to the Methodist chapel, or perhaps to carry on singing there, as the verse continued

> So now to chapel we'll away
> And hear no more he's got to say
> And there the singers we will aid
> In those good hymns John Wesley made [...]

before concluding defiantly 'If we in church sing any more/We'll sing the same we sung before'.

Although Methodists were at the forefront of promoting hymn-singing in the later eighteenth century, by the turn of the century Independent and Baptist congregations also sang enthusiastically.[14] The Independent Isaac Watts was the foremost hymn-writer of the early eighteenth century, publishing his *Divine Songs* for the use of children in 1715 and following it in 1719 with a metrical version of the psalms considered more singable than the New Version.[15] As a result of Watts' verses, by the early 1800s hymnody was at the heart of nineteenth-century Nonconformity.[16] Despite the fact that Watts' hymn-writing has been described as 'unmistakably that of a non-Anglican', the use of hymns in the established church, particularly those by Watts, became increasingly accepted during the eighteenth century.[17] In 1820 Kings Langley Sunday school purchased 'Watts' Hymns',[18] indicating that Nonconformist hymns were considered suitable for use by children in the established church. It is unclear whether they were intended for use in the Sunday school alone or also used in divine service. An idea of how they may have been used can be gained from North Creake, where Countess Spencer had established a Sunday school.[19] In 1792 Thomas Herod, the school patron, reported:

> I bought a quantity of Dr Watts songs, and let every scholar have one [...] We have about 60 that will say the whole of Dr Watts songs by rote, some of which I have fixed to some easy psalm tunes, and learnt them to sing them, they frequently assemble by themselves, and are amused with those.[20]

This suggests that certain words and tunes taught to children were different from those sung by adults, perhaps laying up trouble if the children became too attached to them. Indeed, hymns may have gained in popularity because the congregation had been taught them as children, rather than metrical psalms alone.[21] As seen from the continuing repeated calls for the improvement of psalmody, Porteus's hope that children taught to sing would continue to sing as adult members of the congregation did not meet with the anticipated success. Perhaps some became Nonconformists when an appetite for hymns instilled in childhood was not satisfied in the established church.

There is no evidence that Nonconformist hymns were used in Hertfordshire parish churches until the early years of the nineteenth century, when certain church bands may have played in both their parish church and one or more local Nonconformist chapels. In St Albans, Dagnall Street Baptist chapel purchased 'Rippons Collection of Hymns' in 1790, perhaps for use in both the chapel and their Sunday school, established at around this date.[22] This may have contributed to a subsequent decision taken in 1818 by the Abbey Church vestry to authorise John Higdon's purchase of

'Rippons Selection with 2 Supplements' and 'Walkers Companion with 3 additional Supplements'.[23]

Rippon's *Selection* was a landmark Baptist hymnal compiled and part-written by the minister John Rippon and later used as the basis for the *Baptist Hymn Book*. The two supplements purchased by the Abbey Church were a *Selection of Psalm and Hymn Tunes* (1791), also known as the *Tune Book*, and an arrangement of the *Psalms, Hymns, and Spiritual Songs of Isaac Watts* (1801).[24] The *Tune Book* was produced with the assistance of Thomas Walker, and was the largest hymnal produced in England up to this date.[25] Rippon included verses from 'different Denominations of Ministers, and Christians on Earth, in the same noble Work' with the objective that 'Churchmen and Dissenters, Watts and Tate, Wesley and Toplady, England and America' would be able to 'sing Side by Side'.[26] When Rippon's *Selection* and Watts' works were bound together 'they comprised the complete dissenters' hymn-book'.[27] The Abbey was not the only St Albans parish church to use this hymn book; in September 1819 the churchwardens of St Michael's paid Job Nash, bookseller and stationer of Holywell Hill, for 'Binding Rippons Selection of Tunes'.[28] Furthermore, Walker's *Companion* was used at Aldbury in 1810, and in 1827 Bishops Stortford also purchased 'Rippon's and Walker's tune books'.[29]

In June 1820 the Baldock churchwardens authorised the purchase of two single volumes of 'Sacred Music', presumably for the use of the singers.[30] The purchase of 'Fawcet's Set of Music' in September 1831 suggests that the two earlier volumes of 'Sacred Music' were also by John Fawcett, since his *New Set of Sacred Music* was first published in around 1811, followed by further sets at regular intervals until the publication of the seventh in 1830.[31] This choice was perhaps influenced by a wish to placate the singers, and perhaps to enable the music to be played at both church and chapel, again suggesting that the boundaries between church and chapel music-making were much more permeable than previously thought. Although Fawcett had a Wesleyan Methodist background, during his twenties he was choirmaster of St George's, Kendal (Westmorland), and intended his work to appeal to Anglicans and Nonconformists alike.[32] Like Rippon, the tunes in his first *Set* were intended to be 'sung by different Denominations of Christians', and included settings of works by John Wesley, Isaac Watts, John Rippon and others.[33]

In *c.*1820 the St Albans composer W.J. White published his *Sacred Herald*, almost certainly to further the work of the Hertfordshire Union of Baptists and Independents. By way of introduction he explained: 'The express design of this Work is to promote Congregation singing and assist in Private Devotion.'[34] White also composed *Sacred Melodies*, which ran through several editions, finishing with an eighth in *c*.1830. The third edition, 'adapted to the Psalms and Hymns in the New Version, Dr Watts, Dr Rippon's, Dr Collyer's, Mr Wesley's, Countess of Huntingdon's and Dr Doddridge's Hymn Books', was reviewed in the *New Evangelical Magazine* in 1823. Describing his melodies as 'simple, chaste, and elegant', the reviewer portrayed them as 'affording the finest specimen of the present improved state of Church Music, that is before the public', striking a happy medium between the 'doleful ditties' of the 1770s and the 'light, airy, theatrical jiggings' introduced in the early 1800s, echoing sentiments attributed to the Baldock parish clerk.[35] In 1820 Abbots Langley parish church employed William James White, a singing teacher, and in all likelihood the composer W.J. White of St Albans. This suggests that Nonconformist musicians were welcomed by certain parish churches in their drive to improve music-making, again providing evidence that boundaries between church and chapel were more flexible than previously thought.

A further example of Baptist music-making comes from Boxmoor, in the parish of Hemel Hempstead. One of those applying for certification of Boxmoor Baptist chapel as a place of worship in 1825 was Henry Nash, manager of the Frogmore paper mill, who was married to the sister of William Carey, founder of the Baptist Missionary Society. A book of tunes used in this chapel was compiled in 1830 by one of the mill workers and carries the inscription 'This book belongs to Stephen Cox who made the paper ruled the lines and pricked out the tunes.'[36] He included pieces by local Nonconformist and Anglican composers, including W.J. White and the Watford parish church organist William Bird, indicating either that the same tunes were used in both the established church and chapels or that Cox played or sang in both.

Anglican singing

The importance of Bishop Porteus's 1790 Charge concerning psalmody was such that it was summarised or quoted in the prefaces to subsequent abridged collections of psalms with simple tunes. One such was Edward Miller's *Psalms of David*. Miller wrote the preface in March 1790, but, following the publication of Porteus's Charge shortly afterwards, extended it to explain how effective his work had already been in improving the psalmody in his own church; advertisements for Miller's *Psalms* appeared in many newspapers.[37] In 1793 Peter Hellendaal inscribed a collection of psalm tunes 'to the Worthy Patrons of the Charity & Sunday schools of Great Britain'.[38] Hellendaal's *Collection* attracted subscriptions not only from the clergy and elite, such as the Earl of Hardwicke, but also from Hertfordshire 'Societies of Singers', including those of Hitchin and Royston. This may have been because they were attracted by the simple arrangements, or perhaps because they had been advised to sing a less complicated repertoire alongside children, as envisaged by Porteus.

In neighbouring Bedfordshire, John Gresham was master of Chew's charity school in Dunstable, and his son William was organist of the parish church. In 1797 they attracted a number of Hertfordshire subscribers to their *Psalmody Improved*, which was 'intended to promote general singing in Public Worship'.[39] The Greshams suggested that by using their *Psalmody* 'the unskilled in music, as well as Sunday School and other children, may, with a little practice and attention, be able to sing in Public Worship'.[40] Further copies were purchased for use at Harpenden and Caddington and as late as 1856 it was claimed that Gresham's compositions were 'yet the favourite music of several neighbouring choirs'.[41] In addition to supplying music, the Greshams also supported music-making in several Hertfordshire church bands by repairing musical instruments, as is discussed further in the following chapter.

New books of psalms and hymns were introduced in some Hertfordshire churches during the 1810s and 1820s following the appointment of a new organist or the installation of an organ. In 1811 William Bird published *A Set of Psalm and Hymn Tunes*, and it seems probable that this work was written to mark his appointment as organist of Watford parish church. With a number of other published compositions, Bird must have had some talent, as the composer and organist Samuel Wesley, nephew of John Wesley, travelled to Watford in November 1829 to prepare a concert with him.[42]

When Miss Sherman died in 1815 Thomas Fowler succeeded her as organist and charity boys' singing teacher at St Peter's, St Albans. In 1817 he took the opportunity to order new 'Hymn books for the Gallery'.[43] Rather than simply purchasing new books, however, these were copies of *An Enlarged Selection of Psalms and Hymns*, which he had compiled himself and had printed in St Albans.[44] His action met with disapproval from both vicar and vestry and led to his subsequent decisions being subjected to strict scrutiny. Although many of the metrical psalms included in his *Selection* were from the authorised Old and New Versions, others were by Watts or the poet James Merrick. Furthermore, the collection included seventy-four hymns, whose authors included Rippon, Fawcett and other Nonconformists. The vestry agreed

> that no alteration take place for the future without the consent of the minister and vestry. Ordered that Mr Fowler the organist do produce a list of sacred music to be played on the organ at the next vestry, that a selection may be made from such list by that vestry and that he provide them according to such order.[45]

Figure 3.1. J.P. Neale, *St Albans Abbey Church, the Choir looking West* (1824). The recently installed Father Smith organ can be seen in a gallery beyond the pulpit.

Figure 3.2. T.W. Luppino, *Psalms and Hymns for Ware Church* (*c.*1821).

Later that year Fowler lost his job – because of 'atrocious and hardened conduct' in his private life, rather than his controversial selection of psalms and hymns – but in 1818 he was listed as a subscriber to Jacob's *National Psalmody*, perhaps having subscribed while still organist at St Peter's.[46] Although an organist himself, Jacob's intention was that his work should be used whether or not the church had an organ, explaining that the dynamics should be left to the 'good sense of the Clerk, Organist, or Leader of the Singers', according to the sentiment expressed in the psalm.[47] Hertfordshire subscribers included Hitchin parish, which had acquired an organ in 1803, but it was also purchased for use at Totteridge, the Abbey Church and St Stephen's, St Albans, none of which had organs at the time.[48] Jacob's *Psalmody* was therefore used in at least three of the four St Albans parishes. This may have been the beginnings of a show of strength in the face of the many local Nonconformist chapels. These purchases were almost certainly influenced, too, by the heavy promotion of Jacob's *Psalmody*, and possibly by the fact that one of the new tunes commissioned from Vincent Novello for the book was entitled 'St Alban's'.

Perhaps a reformed character, Fowler was appointed organist of the Abbey Church when a Father Smith organ was obtained second-hand from St Dunstan-in-the-East, London, in 1820 (Figure 3.1).[49] The installation of the organ provided the impetus for Fowler to compile another collection, *A Selection of Psalms and Hymns adapted for the use of the Abbey Church in St Albans*.[50] The Abbey Church purchased six copies from the printer William Langley, who took in part exchange 'several old books as waste paper',[51] but members of the congregation were expected to purchase their own, of which more below.

Following his appointment Fowler purchased Joseph Kemp's *New System of Musical Education* and the first and second volumes of *The Seraph*.[52] The purchase of John Whitaker's *Seraph* is of particular significance for a church such as the Abbey where charity children sang. Recommending his collection, Whitaker criticised other psalm tune compositions as 'sameness personified, applied indiscriminately to the language of the Psalmist, whether *joyful* or *melancholy*'.[53] He claimed this mismatch between words and sentiment often resulted in meaningless renditions: 'Thus I have frequently heard in parish churches some scores of charity children, who, in singing a *penitential psalm*, or *invoking the mercy of the Deity*, have been so vehement, that their *vocal efforts* have rather resembled *a shout* or *a scream*.'[54] Whitaker's description suggests that 'strained' and 'squalling' children's voices continued to be a problem in some churches, and would have done little to encourage congregational participation.

It could be argued that displays such as those described by Whitaker gave the impression that, unlike Methodists, neither the children nor their teachers attached any importance to singing with understanding. But, just as significantly, according to Whitaker the congregation found the whole exercise of singing psalms something to be endured, so that '[...] the congregation being thus nearly deafened by such a sacrifice of sense to sound, becomes as indifferent to this essential and delightful part of divine worship, as they would be to the noise of passing carriages in the streets'.[55] Instead, Whitaker took a leaf out of the Methodists' book by also including adaptations of operatic and chamber music familiar to the gentry and those able to afford the price of a ticket to a public concert. Although not the first to adopt this method, Whitaker's preface must have struck a chord with many potential purchasers. Thomas William Luppino, organist of Ware church, also tried to address this problem, stating in his *Psalms and Hymns* that 'In selecting the Melodies, care has been taken to adapt the stile to the words'[56] and explaining, 'The present publication of Sacred music, is chiefly intended as an Inducement to the Congregation to join more generally, in that delightful part of divine worship, the singing Praises to Almighty God.'[57] Luppino was able to attract over 130 Hertfordshire subscribers from thirty-one parishes for his *Psalms and Hymns*, compiled in 1821 and featuring the new organ on the title page (Figure 3.2). New editions such as these thus had the potential to introduce the congregation to a new repertoire and encourage them to sing.

In 1821 Charles Bridgeman, organist of All Saints, Hertford, also produced a *Collection of Psalms and Hymns* for use in his church, stating 'the choral praises of a devout congregation may justly be esteemed the most delightful part of divine worship' before criticising the congregation of his church for not singing: 'This very impressive act of the Christian worship is, indeed, left wholly unperformed by many persons, who sit in cold indifference, and silent unconcern, resigning to an appointed few the mere ceremony of singing.'[58]

Edward Bickersteth was rector of Watton-at-Stone when his *Christian Psalmody* was published in 1833. He too saw psalm-singing as an obligation and a means of improvement rather than a pleasure:

> The duty of singing praises and hymns to God is very clearly expressed in the Scriptures. [...] The privilege of singing is as great as the duty is clear. [...] It furnishes constant subjects of devout meditation. The heart is prepared for and supported under trials, and many a vital and precious truth is received and expressed in a hymn, which the unhealthy moral atmosphere of the world would otherwise quench and suppress.[59]

Further emphasising the devotional nature of psalm-singing, Bickersteth urged the whole congregation to participate, with 'those unable to sing remaining silent, yet joining in heart and affection'.

It seems probable that the sudden appearance of several Hertfordshire collections of psalms and hymns from 1820 onwards was not merely a response to a new appointment or the introduction of a new organ. During the eighteenth century some English parishes had begun to have their own books of psalms and hymns printed, which, in addition to New Version psalms, sometimes included other metrical psalms and devotional hymns. Yet certain High Churchmen continued to believe that only the Old and New Versions were permitted. It was not until 1820 that a widely publicised case heard in the ecclesiastical Consistory Court in the diocese of York ruled that both metrical psalms and other hymns were authorised for use, and these collections may have been part of the response.[60] According to Temperley, the ruling led to 'an unedifying stampede to commission hymns and tunes from well-known authors and composers, and to get selections adopted by fashionable churches and recommended by bishops'.[61] Some of the collections most widely adopted in Hertfordshire are considered below.

The Mitre Hymn Book
William John Hall's *Psalms and Hymns*, better known as 'The Mitre Hymn Book' (1836), was one product of the publishing frenzy that formed part of this renewed drive to improve congregational singing.[62] Hall was rector of Sandon and, at the time of publication, editor and proprietor of the *Christian Remembrancer*. A High Churchman, in the preface to his collection he did not comment on the obligation to sing psalms, but stated that usually only four verses of each were included 'in compliance with the custom which has obtained in most of our churches'.[63] Used at Bishops Stortford, St Andrew's, Hertford, and other Hertfordshire churches, the *Mitre* was so-called because it was approved by Charles Blomfield, Bishop of London, and had a deep impression of a mitre on the cover to emphasise this.

The Union Tune Book
The interdenominational Sunday School Union's first book of tunes, *The Union Tune Book* was published in 1837.[64] It included arrangements of many traditional psalm tunes, suggesting that they were considered suitable for both children and adults. No claim was made for the originality of the selection; indeed, it was the 'extremely low' price and simplicity of the arrangements that appealed to the *Educational Magazine*, which also commented that 'Very little oral instruction will be necessary to the rules laid down, as their perspicuity and simplicity are such as children may understand them; an advantage rarely found in works of this character.'[65]

Unsurprisingly, the *Union Tune Book*'s simple tunes and arrangements did not find favour with all. The following year Vincent Novello published the third volume of his *Psalmist*, with which the *Eclectic Review* unfavourably compared the *Union Tune Book*.[66] Describing the *Union Tune Book* as an attempt 'to prolong the reign of vulgarity and common-place over our sacred music', it praised the *Psalmist* for being 'the very opposite'.[67] However, the *Union Tune Book* went on to become very successful. A much revised second edition published in 1842 under the editorship of the Nonconformist composer Thomas Clark of Canterbury included thirty-six of his own tunes.[68] It ran to at least thirteen more editions, and was still in print in 1879.

In most cases, surviving barrel organs with barrels pinned after the publication of the Sunday school *Union Tune Book* in 1837 used its arrangements of psalm tunes, providing further evidence that church barrel organs were used to support children's singing.

William Mercer

William Mercer's *The Church Psalter and Hymn Book* was published in 1855.[69] Mercer's innovation was to issue an edition 'with the unharmonised tunes as well as the words, so that all could have the tunes before them' – one of the first times this had been done since the last musical edition of the Old Version in 1688.[70] More significantly, he also advocated associating a specific tune with each particular hymn:

> The advantages of this arrangement are obvious and manifold. The Clergy are spared the weekly trouble of selecting the tunes: the choice of music inappropriate to the words is avoided: a due variety of chants and tunes is secured: the people know the music they will have to sing, and by practising it at home can become thoroughly familiarized with it; and above all, the melody becomes associated and intertwined in the people's minds with the Psalm or Hymn.[71]

Mercer suggested that tunes appointed for the following Sunday could be taught in National Schools, and in the second edition addressed clergymen's doubts over 'whether the music can be of any use to the poorer members of their flocks'. He argued that

> the poor are as partial to the music as to the Hymns; and even assuming [...] that many of the present generation of adult poor can benefit but little by it, yet their children will. By being familiarized from their infancy in the Church and in the school, to the sight of a given number of notes, they will gradually acquire the use of them, and so be enabled to take a more intelligent part in the choral praises of the congregation.[72]

Like Bickersteth, Mercer emphasised the fact that congregational psalmody was a duty, saying 'The Church of England does not content herself with simply recognizing it, but she requires it of her members.'[73] But, as demonstrated throughout this book, despite the fact that children were taught to sing, there is little indication that they continued to do so as adult members of the congregation, a pattern repeated every generation from the mid-eighteenth to the mid-nineteenth century.

The tunes in Mercer's collection had been harmonised by John Goss, organist of St Paul's Cathedral, and it saw massive sales, going through fifteen editions in 1857–8, during which time Mercer added a large number of additional hymns and Goss revised some of the harmonies.[74] Because it included many traditional metrical psalms but placed them among other hymns, it 'caught both high and low in its net'.[75] Sales were boosted by widespread advertising and the growing insistence of the clergy on providing copies of hymnals for all the congregation, but this was by no means universal. Often, it was still the case that members of the congregation were expected to supply their own copies. In 1866 Pain & Brook's, printers, stationers and bookbinders of Hitchin, advertised 'Hymn Books – The different arrangements for use in the Churches and Chapels in Hitchin and neighbourhood'.[76] Similarly, in 1835 the St Albans printer and stationer Richard Gibbs had advertised in the *Hertford Mercury and Reformer*: 'A large assortment of Bibles, Testaments, Prayer and Hymn Books, in Plain and Elegant Binding'.[77]

The *Hertford Mercury and Reformer* had been founded in 1834 by the printer, stationer and bookseller Stephen Austin. Elected to Hertford Town Council in 1848, he was Honorary Secretary of the Hertfordshire Liberal Association, and edited the paper until his death in 1892.[78] The newspaper was published in Fore Street, near All Saints' church, where Austin was a member of the choir.[79] In February 1852 a rival Hertford newspaper entitled the *Herts Guardian, Agricultural Journal and General Advertiser* was launched to support the Conservative cause at the approaching election. The paper was published in the parish of St Andrew's, and its proprietor and editor was William Pollard, whose move to Hertfordshire had been brought about by Sir Edward Bulwer-Lytton, MP for Hertfordshire.[80] Pollard was described as 'ever ready to plead the cause of the workers', and consequently had a large working-class following 'amongst whom he was held in high respect'.[81]

Predictably, the editors of the Liberal *Hertford Mercury and Reformer* and Tory *Herts Guardian* disagreed with each other on many subjects and, as will be seen later in this section, this included the choice of hymn-books. Until the 1830s a tax of fourpence a copy meant that newspapers were unaffordable to many members of the general public, but following a tax reduction to a penny in 1836 local papers such as these had large circulation figures.

Temperley argued that the use of Mercer's collection at St Paul's Cathedral boosted the book's popularity because of 'the widespread acceptance of the cathedral as the model for parochial worship'.[82] This is borne out by the justification of this choice of hymnal made by John Marchant, choir director of St Andrew's, Hertford. According to the *Herts Guardian*, based in the same parish, he said:

> The fact too, that 'Mercer's Hymn Book' was a favourite with the late Prince-Consort, who had a soul for music as well as for everything else that was good; that it is in regular use in her Majesty's Private Chapels as well as in St Paul's Cathedral; and that the harmonies have been twice carefully revised by that good musician John Goss, is sufficient justification one would think, for its adoption at St Andrew's, Hertford.[83]

But William Pollard, the editor, was not convinced, and commented 'even if it *were* authenticated that the book was a favourite with Prince Albert, that would have no weight with us. The Prince was brought up in the Lutheran religion – and that assimilates more to the Independents than to the Church of England.'[84] In response to Pollard's comments, in 1864 a correspondent identified only as 'Delta' criticised the psalmody in All Saints' and commented that on moving to Hertford three years earlier he or she found it

> greatly inferior to any other town or even village I have visited. I believe this disgraceful state of things springs mainly from want of judgement as to what is *sound church music*. Until within the last two years [...] even such sublime tunes as St Ann's and London New were played in triple time, and 'grace' crochets and quavers introduced seemingly *ad libitum*.[85]

Hymns Ancient and Modern

It has been stated that the final catalyst for significant change in music-making during the nineteenth century was the 1861 publication of *Hymns Ancient and Modern*, with its collection of approved hymns and standardised hymn tunes rather than metrical psalms.[86] 'Delta' praised *Hymns Ancient and Modern*, 'which is of great merit, the words especially; the tunes, too, are at any rate, in such easy time, that the congregation can join in them, which was impossible under the system in vogue two or three years back'.[87] Yet he or she criticised the editors for including some of the old favourite psalm tunes, singling out 'the worn-out jig called Helmsley' and saying 'I am still more sorry that such fanciful tunes should ever have been popular in the Church.'[88]

By 1868 some 4.5 million copies had been sold, which the historian Vic Gammon argued represented 'national and standard triumphing over the local and various'.[89] Yet many churches refused to use it owing to its Tractarian origins. One manifestation of this was its inclusion of reverential Tractarian tunes such as William Henry Monk's 'Eventide', paired with the words 'Abide with me', and John Bacchus Dyke's 'Nicea', paired with 'Holy, Holy, Holy'.[90] Evidence for the use of several other hymnals in Hertfordshire during this period indicates that its success was neither immediate nor universal. In 1869 Richard Gibbs published a list of hymn books used at the different places of worship in St Albans. Although *Hymns Ancient and Modern* was used at the Abbey and St Michael's churches, *Bickersteth's Hymns* was used at St Peter's.[91]

Other hymnals
In July 1864 'E.K.S.' asked readers of the *Musical Standard* to consider the respective merits of a new edition of the SPCK's *Psalms and Hymns for Public Worship*, Mercer's *Psalter*, Chope's *Congregational Tune Book* and *Hymns Ancient and Modern*, with particular reference to 'freedom from modern rubbish', good harmony, cheapness and good sub-editing.[92] 'E.K.S.'s own opinion inclined towards the SPCK collection, which, according to Temperley, held the middle ground between Evangelical and High-Church hymnals.[93] The SPCK hymnal was adopted in a number of Hertfordshire parish churches, including Bengeo and Sandridge.[94]

Thomas Baker Morrell and William Walsham How's *Psalms and Hymns* was used in the newly restored church at Tring.[95] In their preface, Morrell and How criticised the SPCK's *Psalms and Hymns* for classifying hymns according to the church calendar, restricting their use.[96] Moreover, they were not in favour of allocating a specific tune to each hymn, arguing that this was 'of little use in country choirs possessing only a limited number of tunes' – perhaps suggesting that they expected them to be sung with the support of a barrel organ.

Evidently disagreements over the choice of tunes and hymnals were not confined to Hertfordshire. The following month, the *Musical Standard* published an anonymous article identifying the congregation as the real obstacle to introducing 'improvements' in church music-making and suggesting that the clergy should

> delegate the task of regulating the music unreservedly to a competent organist, holding him responsible, not for pleasing the congregation, but for being able to show at any time that his choice of music is artistically defensible. As for the congregation, they soon get accustomed to be treated with the contempt they

deserve. If an improvement be introduced, like a flock of sheep when scared by some unaccustomed object, they will stand off stupidly staring for a while; after a time, they will come back, and find that there was nothing to be afraid of. The very tune or chant which originally set them scampering will very likely come to be a favourite, and the next scare be the result of some attempt to go back to its once-cherished predecessor.[97]

The article was reprinted verbatim in the *Hertford Mercury and Reformer* in what may be presumed to be a veiled attack on William Pollard, editor of the *Herts Guardian*, and his criticism of Mercer's *Psalter*.[98] Yet Pollard's campaign against Mercer's *Psalter* continued into 1865, insinuating its way into seemingly unrelated news items such as this:

Three or four recent trials deserve more space than we can afford for comment. One is a heartless case of breach of promise of marriage, where either the defendant or his mother sent the young lady a lot of trashy hymns, which, as was truly stated were but a poor consolation to the deserted plaintiff; and they were not even good of their kind, but poor, sad stuff, like much of what we meet in Mercer's collection.[99]

Pollard's opinions received national coverage in the *Musical Standard*, which took a continuing interest in his campaign for an improvement in church music-making.[100]

Supply of music

No matter which tunes were sung in the church, it was first necessary to obtain the music. Although several tunes would have been known already, itinerant singing teachers taught additional tunes in some parishes. In certain cases tunes were introduced by musically literate clergy or parishioners who had subscribed to printed books of psalmody. Some groups of singers were fortunate enough to subscribe to several copies, but it was usual to share or borrow just one and compile individual tunebooks with music copied, or 'pricked', from a variety of sources. In 1816 J. Noble of Boston (Lincs.) advertised 'Blank Music-books and Ruled paper, on a plan particularly convenient for psalmody'.[101] In 1761 the Rickmansworth churchwardens purchased eight blank psalm books for a guinea, plus 6d for carriage from London, with an additional 10s 6d 'For pricking eight psalm books' – in other words, for copying music into the blank books.[102] This practice was by no means unique to Hertfordshire; for example, at Oakham (Rutland) a payment was made in 1783 for 'pricken tunes'.[103] Blank tune or psalm-books were also purchased between 1773 and 1840 at Aldbury, Caddington and Pirton, and at Baldock ruled music paper was purchased in 1819.[104] In Hertfordshire it seems almost certain that James Whitaker, papermaker and manager of the Standon papermill, supplied his own paper for his blank tunebooks, as was the case in other papermaking parishes, including Hemel Hempstead.[105]

Local collections such as Gresham's *Psalmody Improved* and Ivery's *Hertfordshire Melody* tended to attract local subscribers, but as the eighteenth century progressed advertising became more widespread and many composers attracted purchasers from further afield. Orders could also be sent or collected from London. Some Hertfordshire parishes patronised the Thompson family of musical instrument makers, dealers and publishers of St Paul's Churchyard: Aldbury purchased the Dorset composer Joseph Stephenson's *Church Harmony* from them in 1773 and Caddington purchased a Hautboy (oboe) and two copies of the Kentish composer Abraham Adams' *Psalmist's New Companion* in 1787.[106] Tunes by these composers were also used at Essendon and Standon.[107] But the increasing commercial opportunities available in market towns during this period gave access to a wide range of merchandise, making churches independent of itinerant singing teachers, salesmen or purchases commissioned from London.

The fact that members of the congregation were usually expected to provide their own books suggests a further hindrance to congregational singing. J. Warren, 'Hair dresser, perfumer, bookseller and stationer', supplied music books to Baldock parish church.[108] In St Albans, the St Peter's churchwardens purchased 'Psalm Books' and 'Music Paper' from the local 'Musician, Dealer and Chapman' George Sherman in 1806, while the bookseller and stationer Job Nash sold music books and paper to the other three parish churches.[109] When St Mary's, Hitchin, adopted *Hymns Ancient and Modern* in 1864 the stationers Pain and Brook's offered a choice of no fewer than nineteen different editions, ranging from a 'Glazed cloth' binding for 4d a copy to 'Best Morocco, gilt edges' for 12s.[110] Market-town booksellers and stationers such as these also supplied rural churches further afield, and in 1827 the Kensworth churchwardens paid Job Nash 7s 'for binding two Psalm Books'.[111]

When a new church barrel organ was acquired it was probably common to order new psalm-books, and during the 1820s 'psalm books' were purchased for use with both the Aspenden and Westmill barrel organs.[112] At Chipping Barnet 250 'Books for Psalms' were purchased for use with their newly purchased barrel organ in 1824, perhaps for use by the charity school children, who already numbered 230 by 1818.[113] Barrel organs could play only the tunes set on their barrels, but the new books suggested which of these tunes would be appropriate for the chosen psalm. The organ-builders Flight & Son advertised 'Books of the most appropriate Psalms [...] as set on their organs'.[114] Books such as these had the potential to make the church's music-making an inclusive activity, but in churches where the congregation had to purchase their own copies this did little to encourage the participation of the poor.

In addition to supplying music, some booksellers and stationers also acted as agents for sales of musical instruments. These are discussed in the following chapter, as is the involvement of Hertfordshire singers and church bands, who in certain churches led congregational singing with varying degrees of success.

Endnotes

1. Temperley *et al.*, 'Psalms, metrical'.
2. Temperley, *Parish Church*, p. 123.
3. *London Literary Gazette* (31 October 1829), p. 716.
4. M.R. Watts, *The Dissenters*, vol. II. *The Expansion of Evangelical Nonconformity* (Oxford, 1995), p. 182.
5. 'Directions for Singing', in J. Wesley, *Select Hymns: with Tunes annext: Designed chiefly for the use of the People called Methodists*, 4th edn (Bristol, 1773).
6. Vincent, *Considerations*, pp. 13–14.
7. Miller, *Thoughts*, p. 11.
8. Corke, *John Wesley*, n.p.
9. HALS, DP/49/8/2–5.
10. Greaves, *Methodism*, pp. 22–3 and 45.
11. LPL, FP Randolph 9/17–26 (1810).
12. Greaves, *Methodism*, pp. 48 and 55; Urwick, *Nonconformity*, p. 220.
13. HALS, DP/12/29/5.
14. I. Bradley, 'Nonconformist Hymnody', in R. Pope (ed.), *T & T Clark Companion to Nonconformity* (London, 2013), pp. 238–9.
15. I. Watts, *Divine Songs Attempted in Easy Language, for the Use of Children* (London, 1715); I. Watts, *The Psalms of David Imitated in the Language of the New Testament* (London, 1719).
16. Bradley, 'Nonconformist Hymnody', p. 237.
17. J.R. Watson, 'The Hymns of Isaac Watts and the Tradition of Dissent', in Rivers and Wykes, *Dissenting Praise*, p. 33.
18. HALS, DP/64/25/9–10.
19. See Chapter 2, p. 46.
20. Sunday School Society, *Sunday-Schools* (1793), pp. 80–1.
21. T.K. McCart, *The Matter and Manner of Praise. The Controversial Evolution of Hymnody in the Church of England 1760–1820*, Drew Studies in Liturgy Series, 5 (Lanham, 1998), p. 58.
22. D. Turner, *With Cheerful Zeal: A History of Dagnall Street Baptist Church St Albans* (St Albans, 1999), p. 17.
23. HALS, DP/90/7 Bills & vouchers (1814–48).
24. K.R. Manley, 'John Rippon and Baptist Hymnody', in Rivers and Wykes, *Dissenting Praise*, p. 95.
25. *Ibid.*, pp. 117–18; see also N. Temperley, 'The Music of Dissent', in Rivers and Wykes, *Dissenting Praise*, pp. 197–228.
26. J. Rippon, *A Selection of Hymns from the Best Authors, Intended to be An Appendix to Dr. Watts's Psalms and Hymns* (London, 1787), Preface.
27. Manley, 'John Rippon', pp. 117–18.
28. St Albans, St Michael's, Churchwardens' papers 2 (1819).
29. T. Walker, *Walker's Companion to Dr Rippon's tune book* (London, 1811); HALS, DP/2/5/2 Churchwardens' accounts (1764–1813); DP/21/5/10–11 Churchwardens' bills & vouchers (1760–1841).
30. HALS, DP/12/5/2 Churchwardens' bills & vouchers (1821); DP/12/5/3 Churchwardens' accounts (1826–68).
31. *Ibid.*
32. S. Drage, 'John Fawcett of Bolton: the Changing Face of Psalmody', in Dibble and Zon, *Nineteenth-Century British Music Studies*, pp. 60–1.
33. J. Fawcett, *A New Set of Sacred Music* (London, *c.*1811).
34. W.J. White of St Albans, *The Sacred Herald [...]* (London, *c.*1820).
35. *New Evangelical Magazine* (October 1823), p. 341.

36 Private collection, Boxmoor (Herts.).
37 For example, *Stamford Mercury* (28 January 1791), p. 1.
38 P. Hellendaal, *A Collection of Psalms for the use of Parish Churches* (Cambridge, 1794).
39 J. Gresham, *Psalmody Improved [...]* (London, 1797).
40 *Northampton Mercury* (1 April 1797), p. 4.
41 HALS, DP/122A/5/1–2 Churchwardens' accounts (1800–18); BARS, P35/5/2 Vouchers (1787–1840); C. Lamborn, *The Dunstaplelogia* (Dunstable, 1859), p. 129.
42 P. Olleson, *Samuel Wesley: the Man and his Music* (Woodbridge, 2003), p. 207.
43 HALS, DP/93/5/3–5.
44 T. Fowler, *An Enlarged Selection of Psalms and Hymns, for the use of the parish church of St Peter, St Alban's: and adapted to the congregations of the Established Church in general* (St Albans, 1817).
45 HALS, DP/93/5/3–5.
46 HALS, DP/93/29/8 Extracts from the records of the church of St Peters (*c.*1890); B. Jacob, *National psalmody, a collection of tunes, set to a course of psalms selected from the new version by J.T. Barrett* (London, 1818).
47 *Ibid.*, Preface.
48 *Ibid.*, List of Subscribers; HALS, DP/94/5/1 Churchwardens' accounts (1805–24); DP/46B/8/12 Churchwardens' accounts (1821–3).
49 HALS, DP/90/7; *Christian Remembrancer* (January 1821), p. 60.
50 T. Fowler, *A Selection of Psalms and Hymns, adapted for the use of the Abbey Church, St Albans* (St Albans, 1820).
51 HALS, DP/90/5/1 Churchwardens' accounts (1811–49).
52 HALS, DP/90/7; J. Kemp, *The New System of Musical Education* (London, 1819); J. Whitaker, *The Seraph, a Collection of Sacred Music [...]* (London, 1818).
53 Whitaker, *Seraph*, p. 2.
54 *Ibid.*
55 *Ibid.*
56 T.W. Luppino, *Psalms and Hymns for Ware Church* (Hertford, 1821), pp. 1–2.
57 *Ibid.*
58 C. Bridgeman, *A Collection of Psalms and Hymns for the use of the Congregation of All Saints, Hertford* (Hertford, 1821), Preface.
59 E. Bickersteth, *Christian Psalmody: A Collection of Above 700 Psalms, Hymns, and Spiritual Songs; Selected and Arranged for Public, Social, Family and Private worship* (London and Hertford, 1833), pp. iv–v.
60 Temperley *et al.*, 'Psalms, metrical'.
61 N. Temperley, 'The Modern English Hymn', *Grove Music Online*, accessed at <http://www.oxfordmusiconline.com>
62 W.J. Hall (ed.), *Psalms and Hymns adapted to the Service of the Church of England, approved by Bishop Blomfield* (London, 1836), aka 'The Mitre Hymn Book'.
63 *Ibid.*, p. v.
64 J. Peck, *The Union Tune Book, being a collection of psalm and hymn tunes, adapted for use in Sunday schools and congregations. Arranged by John Peck. To which is prefixed a short introduction to singing* (London, 1837).
65 *Educational Magazine* (June 1838), p. 241.
66 V. Novello, *The Psalmist: a Collection of Psalm and Hymn Tunes, suited to all the varieties of Metrical Psalmody; consisting principally of Tunes already in general use for Congregational Worship [...]* (London, 1838).
67 *Eclectic Review*, 4 (October 1838), p. 479.
68 T. Clark, *The Union Tune Book, a selection of Psalm and Hymn tunes, suitable for use in Congregations and Sunday Schools. Arranged by Thomas Clark of Canterbury*, 2nd edn (London, 1842).
69 W. Mercer, *The Church Psalter and Hymn Book* (London, 1855).
70 Temperley, 'Modern English Hymn'.

71 Mercer, *Church Psalter* (1855), Preface.
72 Mercer, *Church Psalter*, 2nd edn (London, 1857), p. xi.
73 Mercer, *Church Psalter* (1855), Preface.
74 The 4th to 19th editions; J. Blezzard, 'Goss, Sir John (1800–1880)', *ODNB*.
75 Temperley, *Parish Church*, pp. 297–8; Temperley, 'Modern English Hymn'.
76 *Hertfordshire Express and General Advertiser* (8 December 1866), p. 1.
77 *HMR* (1 December 1835), p. 1.
78 *HMR* (28 May 1892), p. 5.
79 Sheldrick, *Three Centuries*, p. 21.
80 F. Boase, *Modern English Biography*, VI (London, 1965), p. 411.
81 *HMR* (11 July 1896), p. 5.
82 Temperley, *Parish Church*, p. 298.
83 *HG* (25 June 1864), p. 8.
84 *HG* (30 July 1864), p. 5.
85 *HG* (13 August 1864), p. 8.
86 *Hymns ancient and modern for use in the services of the Church* (London, 1861).
87 *HG* (13 August 1864), p. 8.
88 *Ibid*.
89 Gammon, '"Babylonian Performances"', p. 82.
90 I. Bradley, 'The Theology of the Victorian Hymn Tune', in M. Clarke (ed.), *Music and Theology in Nineteenth-Century Britain*, Music in Nineteenth-Century Britain (Abingdon, 2016), p. 13.
91 *Herts Advertiser* (4 December 1869), p. 4.
92 *Musical Standard* (16 July 1864), p. 22.
93 Temperley, 'Modern English Hymn'.
94 *HG* (23 July 1864), p. 4; HALS, DP/96/29/1 Accounts of various parish clubs (1831–72).
95 *HG* (13 January 1863), p. 2.
96 T.B. Morrell and W.W. How, *Psalms and Hymns* (London, 1858).
97 *Musical Standard* (27 August 1864), pp. 61–2.
98 *HMR* (29 October 1864), p. 4.
99 *HG* (18 February 1865), p. 4.
100 *Musical Standard* (6 May 1865), p. 357.
101 *Stamford Mercury* (1 March 1816), p. 3.
102 HALS, DP/85/25/1 Charity School accounts (1761).
103 H. Davidson, *Choirs, Bands and Organs. A History of Church Music in Northamptonshire and Rutland* (Oxford, 2003), p. 184.
104 HALS, DP/2/29/9 Churchwardens' bills (1772–4); DP/12/5/2; DP/80/4/1–2 Churchwardens' accounts (1791–1861); BARS, P35/5/1 Churchwardens' accounts (1779–1838).
105 HALS, DE/X228/Z5–6 ms volumes of metrical psalm tunes and church anthems, titled on spine 'James Whitaker 1829'.
106 HALS, DP/2/29/9; BARS, P35/5/2; J. Stephenson, *Church Harmony Sacred to Devotion. Being a choice Set of New Anthems & Psalm Tunes on various Subjects*, 3rd edn (London, 1760)
107 HALS, DE/X228/Z5–6; Hall, 'Essendon Church', p. 255.
108 HALS, DP/12/5/2.
109 HALS, DP/90/7; DP/93/5/3–5; DP/94/5/1; *London Gazette* (24 March 1798), p. 258; *Universal British Directory*, Appendix, p. 181; St Albans, St Michael's, Churchwardens' papers 2 (1811–20).
110 *Hertfordshire Express and General Advertiser* (19 November 1864), p. 2.
111 BARS, P34/5/1–3 Churchwardens' accounts (1805–60).
112 HALS, DP/8/1/3; DP/120/1/4.
113 HALS, DP/15/5/2 Churchwardens' accounts (1762–1840); PP 1819 (224), Select Committee on Education of Poor (1818). Digest of Parochial Returns (3 vols), I, p. 352.
114 *Ecclesiastical Gazette* (12 September 1843), p. 64.

Chapter 4
Singers and bands

This chapter explains the activities of 'singers' and instrumentalists in Hertfordshire parish churches: in other words, those singing or playing in exclusive groups distinct from the congregation. Today, such groups are usually referred to as west gallery quires (choirs), but this term was not used before the twentieth century. The use of instruments in church is considered here, as is the relationship between church bands and military bands of music formed during the period of the French Revolution and Napoleonic Wars. Evidence that music-making by singers and church bands hindered the continuing drive to encourage congregational singing is also examined in this chapter. In some churches choirs of charity children were introduced to replace singers in order to address this issue, and in others children and adult singers sang together. Neither approach had long-lasting success in encouraging congregational singing.

Although relatively little evidence of singers or church bands survives for late eighteenth- to early nineteenth-century Hertfordshire, such as there is indicates their presence in at least fifty-one of its 136 parish churches, or around 38 per cent (see Appendix 4). It is somewhat frustrating that Owen Davys, rector of Wheathampstead, gave no specific examples when he lectured his antiquarian society on 'The Choral Arrangements of Churches' in 1870, merely saying:

> I need not detain the meeting with anecdotes relating to village choirs as they were a few years ago (of which I could easily arrange an absurd series) for I doubt not that many persons present have some time in their lives gone through the infliction of a service so conducted, and I would rather spend the short time during which I desire to detain this meeting in looking at a happier present, and forward to a brighter future, than backward upon a past from which we have little to learn but what to avoid.[1]

Singers

Until the early nineteenth century, certain vestries considered music-making 'necessary for the decent performance of Divine Service' and therefore an activity that could be legitimately funded from the church rate and recorded in the churchwardens' accounts. But the scarcity of payments to singers in Hertfordshire ecclesiastical parish records indicates that they were not generally funded by parishioners. Occasional payments out of the church rate usually took the form of food and drink, and in January 1792 the Elstree churchwardens sanctioned a payment of one guinea 'for a Dinner for ye Psalm Singers'.[2] The churchwardens of St Stephen's, St Albans, were more liberal in December 1818 and paid 'Bills for Psalm singers feast £6 0s 9d'.[3] Isolated payments such as these may give the impression that these groups were either short-lived or visiting from a neighbouring parish, but it is clear that isolated December or January payments were made for singers' Christmas dinners or feasts. In January 1813 the Berkhamsted Psalm singers' dinner cost £1 11s, including reimbursements for a leg of pork, puddings, vegetables, bread, butter and cheese, and the vestry subsequently resolved 'That an annual Dinner be given to the Singers, two Guineas allowed'.[4] Similarly, the 1826–35 Aldenham churchwardens' accounts record payments for 'Refreshment for Singers at Christmas', including beer and vegetables.[5] Singers' feasts were also common elsewhere in the country, and in many Northamptonshire and Rutland parishes were a well-established tradition.[6] In other Hertfordshire parishes singers received more regular payments. In September 1825 the Kings Langley singers were paid £2 10s, accrued over '20 months at 2s 6d per month', while in Bishops Stortford beer money of between 3s and 6s was paid weekly 1829–30, presumably depending on the number who sang.[7] These indicate both that the singers sang regularly and that the parishioners were willing to support their music-making by contributing towards it out of the church rate.

By the early nineteenth century groups of singers and church bands had become widespread throughout the country, and settled into the very patterns of behaviour that had caused concern to Bishop Porteus and others during the late eighteenth century. The first, and most important, concern was the exclusion of the congregation. In some churches the singers and band were grouped together in a singing pew in the body of the church, as at Aldbury, Essendon and elsewhere, but 'singing galleries' were erected in many churches. These may have upset the congregation's hierarchy, because entry was by merit rather than status.[8] By implication, the lower orders were literally getting ideas above their station, which may have been resented by rich and poor alike. The congregation often found themselves physically separated from singers, whose singing became a performance, with the silent congregation turning or standing to 'face the music'.

Lengthy discussions about the need to reform church music appeared in the *New Monthly Magazine*, a Tory publication founded in 1814. A letter from 'P.X.' observed that 'country choirs', usually located in galleries, were 'evidently occupied in singing only to the praise and glory of themselves', and excluded the congregation.[9] Thomas Adolphus Trollope often visited his uncle Adolphus Meetkerke, patron of Rushden, and described the music-making in this parish, which appears to have been of the character described by 'P.X.', as in c.1820 'the singers were so well pleased with the exercise that they were apt to prolong it, as my uncle thought, somewhat unduly. And on such occasions he would cut the performance short with a rasping "that's enough!" which effectually brought it to an abrupt conclusion.'[10]

Another concern was the arrangement of the tunes. Collections of complex psalm tunes often repeated words for emphasis, and from the mid-eighteenth century included 'fuguing tunes', with imitative entries rather than the same words sung at the same time, and this confused the understanding of the psalm. Parts of words or phrases were also repeated for emphasis, or to fit the tune, which caused further confusion.[11] In 1779 John Wesley criticised such tunes, saying 'it is glaringly, undeniably contrary to common sense [...] allowing, nay appointing different words, to be sung by different persons at the same time! [...] Pray which of those sentences am I to attend to?'[12] In 1827 the composer David Everard Ford alluded to the use of tunes unsuited to the chosen psalm, referring to the last verse of Psalm 95, 'The Lord in vengeance drest', being sung to 'a lively tune called Falcon Street, which, to make the matter worse, requires the last verse to be concluded with a series of hallelujahs', a trait also deplored by John Wesley.[13]

The manner of performance by the church band was also a matter of debate. In 1795 William Mason, poet, garden designer, artist, musician, precentor of York Minster and rector of Aston (Yorks.), described from bitter experience 'The tintamarre which this kind of squeaking and scraping and grumbling produces'.[14] In 1819 'T.G.' also remarked upon what he or she considered to be the deplorable state of music in country churches:

> our beautiful service is disfigured and disgraced to gratify the vanity of every drivelling performer on the clarionet, flute, fiddle, or violoncello. The resemblance of all this complicated discordancy of sound, to what we usually call music, is faint indeed. I have occasionally witnessed similar performances, in which the effect produced was more like the noises of the congregation in Noah's ark, than the singing in a protestant church.[15]

Furthermore, disrespectful behaviour could be an issue in some parishes. 'P.X.' complained that even a clergyman with little or no musical knowledge should attempt some sort of control over the music-making in his church: 'such an interference would, in the outset, tend to the entire exclusion of all fiddles, oboes, flutes, clarionets &c. &c.' and 'the exhibition of such indecencies as oftentimes occur from the conduct of these parochial musicians'.[16] An example of such behaviour was seen at St Peter & St Paul, Tring, one Sunday morning in June 1827 when the singing gallery was left unoccupied following a disagreement between the rector and singers. A London newspaper reported that 'the clerk in vain announced the Psalm, with "Let us sing to the Praise, etc." – no-one answered the invitation, and the silence remained unbroken for the space of at least ten minutes'.[17] The rector sent the parish clerk to explain that it was not his intention to preach a sermon 'until the congregation had sung a psalm', but no-one took the lead because they were either unwilling or unable to sing in the absence of the singers, and so the service ended abruptly with 'no singing and no preaching'.

Disrespectful behaviour could also extend to the use of church instruments in other places of worship, or for secular purposes. The Aldenham parish clerk recalled that during the 1820s church band members insisted on taking instruments, some church property, to the public house 'to assist in revels'.[18] Furthermore, in 1820 the Abbots Langley churchwardens reported to the archdeacon that 'William James White lately employed to instruct the Choir in singing has taken away and converted to his own use a bass viol belonging to the church, which he has received notice to restore but refuses so to do.'[19] Such activity was not restricted to Hertfordshire, and in 1845 the Great Houghton (Northants.) vestry resolved 'that no musical instrument belonging to the Parish be used for any other purpose but the services of the Church'.[20]

Rather than banning the use of church-owned instruments in village festivities, it is possible that Abbots Langley and other churches were trying to prevent their use in dissenting meetings. Singers sometimes travelled several miles from their own parish to sing not only in other churches but also in Nonconformist chapels. Motives may have included the enjoyment derived from an afternoon out, payment, or friendly rivalry occasioned by augmenting or deputising for other singers.[21] Poor weather and dark evenings mitigated against such travelling during winter, but the practice of visiting other parishes appears to have been widespread during the summer months of the late 1700s and early 1800s. In 1779 the churchwardens of Caddington paid 7s 6d for 'Beear gave to ye Lutton [Luton] Psalm Singers', while the Rickmansworth singers received £1 at Kings Langley in September 1814 and 10s at Aldenham in May 1822.[22] It seems highly probable that payments made to 'Mr Godman for his Attendance with the Psalm singers' at Elstree in 1816–17 were made to singers from the neighbouring parish of St Stephen's, St Albans, some seven miles up Watling Street, where Mr Godman was both singer and parish clerk.[23] Additional motives appear to have been both vanity and the promise of a good dinner. However, when

John Kent, plumber, glazier, and parish clerk of the Abbey Church, died in 1798 *The Gentleman's Magazine* recounted that when 'country choristers' came from a neighbouring parish 'with instruments termed by him a box of whistles' the congregation could not join in, possibly because the tunes were unfamiliar or because the performance was difficult to follow.[24] A further problem was 'the generally miserable condition of the instruments on which they perform',[25] unsurprising given the tendency of wooden instruments to warp or split.

Some of the problems associated with church band members may be partially attributable to their gradual decline in status as the nineteenth century progressed. With more than twenty employees, the social standing of Standon papermaker and choir-member James Whitaker was assured.[26] Yet by the 1890s antiquarian clergymen and commentators made reference to church singers from the 'peasant' class.[27] Gammon argued that they were usually artisan tradesmen, and this is likely to be nearer the truth for the majority of the church band period.[28] Thomas Webster's famous painting of the singers and band at Bow Brickhill (Beds.), just to the north of Hertfordshire, is shown on the cover of this book. In 1942 Canon Boston was in correspondence with the clarinettist's great-grandson, who was able to name several of the members, and, using additional information from the 1851 census, it is possible to identify their occupations.[29] The conductor William Osborn was a bricklayer, the clarinettist John Wootton a wheelwright and baker, and the cellist Thomas Baskerville the village blacksmith.[30] The children at the front of the gallery included some of the straw-plaiting daughters of the conductor and clarinettist, and two of the rector's and clarinettist's sons. Although the names of few Hertfordshire singers and band members survive, in other counties more records exist, and the availability of online census records suggests that their occupations could be a fruitful area of research.

Children and adult singers

In certain churches charity school children shared a gallery with adult singers, as at Bow Brickhill. There can be little doubt that in some cases this was due to space restrictions, partly fuelled by the obligation for charity children to attend church. But the evidence suggests that in other instances this enabled them to sing with adults or with the support of instrumentalists. This may have been the case at Kings Langley, where payments to singers and instrumentalists continued from 1793 to 1853, a period when Sunday school children attended church.[31] During the 1780s Sarah Trimmer had expressed concern about children and 'anthem singers' singing together, and in 1814 'P.X.' complained:

Almost every person who is in the habit of frequenting country churches must be acquainted with the anthem 'Young men and maidens, old men and children'. This is usually commenced by boys or girls screaming in alt 'young men and maidens', and followed by the bass voices singing 'old men and children'; and it is usually considered by ignorant people as peculiarly expressive and appropriate.[32]

This complicated repertoire clearly did little to encourage congregational participation, even if they enjoyed listening to the performance.

In churches with no organist, patron or musical schoolteacher the parish clerk was often obliged to teach children to sing, but in some churches children were taught by adult singers or band members. Following the incorporation of the Abbey Bluecoat school into the National Society, in 1814–20 John Higdon was paid for both 'playing the Clarionet at the church on Sundays' and 'Instructing the Blue Coat Charity Boys to sing'.[33] A similar arrangement was found at Irthlingborough (Northants.), where the singers were paid 'for teaching the Children at the Sunday-school to sing' in 1819–20.[34]

The evidence also suggests that members of a defunct church band were sometimes drafted in to support children's singing. The Furneux Pelham churchwardens' accounts include payments to the labourer George Bayford for 'bass viol' strings and repairs in the decade 1842–52, by which time he was 68 years old.[35] No references are made to singers, and yet there were National and Sunday schools in 1847, suggesting that the children may have sung in church accompanied only by the elderly cellist.[36] Similarly, at Rickmansworth children's singing was supported by the remains of a church band prior to the introduction of a barrel organ.[37] At Little Gaddesden, John Osmond was paid 'for teaching boys & girls the art of singing' in 1824.[38] According to the village schoolmaster, the choir during this period was accompanied only by an old man who played the clarionet, perhaps Mr Osmond.[39] The novelist Anthony Trollope described a fictional, but possibly not unusual, church of the era. With a nave full of appropriated pews, the children sat in the west gallery of Allington church with the aged remnants of the old church band: 'As regards its interior, it was dusty; it was blocked up with high-backed ugly pews; the gallery in which the children sat at the end of the church, and in which two ancient musicians blew their bassoons, was all awry, and looked as though it would fall [...].'[40]

In many churches, rather than singing with adult singers, children were used to replace them on a temporary or permanent basis. After the incorporation of Elstree's charity schools with the National Society in 1818 no further payments were made to visiting singers and by 1826 the church had acquired a barrel organ, suggesting a reform of former practices.[41] Furthermore, although many churches had their own singers their attendance was not guaranteed, and some found the solution to this problem by using children's voices. In other cases children's voices were used as a means of introducing sweeping reform by replacing the singers completely, and this was not always a smooth transition. In 1819 the *Christian Observer* reported a case tried in the Court of Arches:

> in which an action was brought by the minister against the churchwarden; and the charge in the citation was, 'for obstructing and prohibiting, by his own pretended power and authority, and for declaring openly his intention still further to obstruct and prohibit, the singing and chanting of the charity-children of the parish'. Here the churchwarden supposed that he had a right to direct when the children should sing, and when they should not. The minister had directed the organ to play in certain parts of the service, and the children to chant at the same time: the churchwarden directed the contrary; and the organist obliged him in preference to the minster.[42]

Although the court decided in the minister's favour, other cases followed. In 1822 the *Christian Remembrancer* reported a significant case concerning Chardstock (Dorset), which throws light on an unhappy compromise that may have also been reached elsewhere. The previous November, several Chardstock ringers had been gaoled following a 'tumultuous' disagreement concerning the abandonment of the Pains and Penalties Bill.[43] This bill had been introduced to parliament in 1820 at the request of King George IV, with the object of dissolving his marriage to Caroline of Brunswick and depriving her of the title of Queen, but her popularity was such that the bill was withdrawn. Although the ringers were forbidden to ring in celebration, on three successive nights they forced the belfry door and rang defiantly. The significance is that some of the ringers were also singers, and the other choir members refused to sing in their absence. The curate, Thomas Babb, therefore told the Sunday school children to sing instead, and they sang in church until 'the singers, namely Benjamin Dening, and eight others, including three of the ringers (being the next Sunday after their liberation from prison) began to sing at the same time as the children, on which the latter desisted'.[44] The following Sunday the singers deliberately drowned out the curate's prayers for the king, provoking the curate to write a note banning them from singing the following Sunday. But the singers clearly felt entitled to sing, and defiantly claimed that 'they were the first singers and would sing'. Yet, instead of singing: 'after the children had sung a verse, James Smith rose from his seat, went down from the gallery in a very noisy manner, several boys following him, most of whom again returned, but he walked out of Church and remained in the churchyard till the service was over.'

The disrespectful behaviour of the singers continued to escalate. The following Saturday the curate forbade the singers to sing or play any musical instrument in church without his written consent, and on Sunday the children were allowed to sing 'without interruption'. But it was a very different story in the afternoon. Seven of the singers and 'some strangers', perhaps singers from a neighbouring parish offering their support, sat in the gallery until it was time for the children to sing, whereupon all except James Dening 'rose up hastily, and noisily lifting up the seats on which they sat, went down from the gallery and walked out of the Church'. The sole remaining singer 'was observed making signals whilst the children were singing to persons to leave the Church', and almost a third of the congregation followed the singers out. The main legal opinion sought was:

> Whether the right of controlling the choir and directing or preventing their singing altogether is not vested by law in the officiating minister, and whether in the present case the choir having ceased to sing and a new choir being formed by the minister the old choir had any right to resume and interrupt the service?[45]

The judge's opinion was that the minister had responsibility to direct 'what tunes shall be used, and at what times they shall be sung', and

> he may prevent the use of all instruments, except, perhaps, in the case of an organ erected by faculty, but I do not think that the minister can lawfully prohibit any parishioner from joining in the singing: if any parishioner so joining behave indecorously, he may be punished in the ecclesiastical court.[46]

This real-life Dorset case certainly presents a more acrimonious situation than the more familiar and much-cited fictional replacement of the Mellstock 'quire' by the National School mistress and her choir of Sunday scholars painted by Hardy in *Under the Greenwood Tree*. If the militant behaviour of the Chardstock singers was not unusual, then it is easier to understand why their music-making was considered to be in need of such urgent reform.

Church band instruments

This section describes the incidence and supply of band instruments used to support singers in the parish church. A summary of church band instrumentation for Hertfordshire is given in Appendix 4. A brief list of instruments used in churches across the country was given in Langwill and Boston's *Church and Chamber Barrel-Organs*, and evidence of church bands in specific counties has been gathered by Canon MacDermott in Sussex, Harry Woodhouse in Cornwall, Canon Davidson in Northamptonshire and

Rutland and Stephen Weston, again in Northamptonshire.[47] In his survey *Lincolnshire Church Organs* Robert Pacey also noted the use of instruments in certain parishes.[48]

References to the existence of bands have been found in approximately a quarter to two-fifths of parishes in Hertfordshire, Sussex, Cornwall, Northamptonshire and Rutland, but it is probable that they were far more widespread than this.[49] Anecdotal evidence supplied to MacDermott indicated that the flute 'nearly always figured in the old church bands'.[50] Yet little evidence of their use survives, probably because flutes have neither reeds nor strings, the purchase of which provide the main surviving evidence for clarinets, oboes, bassoons, violins and cellos in churchwardens' accounts. For example, in 1793 the parish of Kings Langley paid for 'Bassoon & hoboy repairs & reeds'.[51] But, although a cello and 'claronetts' were purchased and violin repairs sanctioned at Aldenham during the 1820s, there is no mention of the oboe known to have been used in this church.[52]

The quality of record-keeping varied from church to church, and churchwardens' accounts were often drawn up on odd sheets of paper rather than being entered into a book, or written on spare pages in books of vestry minutes, overseers' accounts and so forth. Not all of them survive. Although All Saints, Hertford, was destroyed by fire in 1891 many of its records were salvaged. During the 1870s the Hatfield vestry sought an estimate for 'making a fire proof room in the south porch [...] for the safe custody of the books and papers belonging to the parish', but, alas, not before the curate had already burnt most of them.[53] The brevity of many churchwardens' accounts is also a factor in the scarcity of evidence for music-making. Although the churchwardens of St Stephen's, St Albans, recorded a payment of five guineas in 1805 'To Mr Rumbald for his Bassoon', other churchwardens might have merely recorded the name of the recipient, with no details regarding the nature of the expense.[54] This is amply demonstrated in the few parishes where bills and vouchers survive. When the local carpenter or blacksmith undertook instrument repairs they may have been grouped, unitemised, with other work, but in Barkway a detailed carpenter's bill from June 1832 included 6d for 'Repairing the Bass Voil'.[55] Similarly, in St Albans the Abbey Church accounts for December 1817 record: 'Paid John Higdon ¼ salary as Musician, 2 guineas', but the voucher to which it relates reveals 'for Playing clarinett in the Abby Church, 2 guineas'.[56] John Higdon and other family members, including Pantamus, Thomas and Alexander, are known to have played 'orchestral instruments' in the Abbey Church during the early nineteenth century,[57] so it seems probable that Higdon received this and similar payments on behalf of all the instrumentalists.

Nostalgic novels such as Hardy's *Under the Greenwood Tree* have fuelled a romanticised picture of parochial music-making, with strings as 'soul-lifters' and serpents providing a 'good old note'.[58] Although church bands may have been common in Dorset, this may not have been the case in Hertfordshire, and there remains the possibility that no evidence of singing has been found in many parishes because there was none.

Where there was no instrumental support, a tunable pitch-pipe was sometimes used to give the first note of the psalm tune. In Hertfordshire these are known to have been used during the early nineteenth century at Aldbury, Great Gaddesden and Pirton, but their use is likely to have been far more widespread, owing to their affordability.[59]

Once instruments were in use there followed the issue of upkeep and repair. Hardy described how in Dorset a pedlar specialising in 'fiddle-strings, rosin, and music-paper' travelled from parish to parish 'coming to each village about every six months'.[60] In addition to acting as agents selling music and musical instruments, many provincial booksellers and stationers, such as Andrews of Royston, also sold consumables. In 1816 J. Noble of Boston (Lincs.) advertised 'Country Choirs of Singers supplied with Musical Instruments, *warranted*; also Reeds, Strings, and every other article, of the best description, on the most reasonable terms – A variety of new Church music lately received […]'.[61]

New evidence from a cluster of parishes in north-west Hertfordshire illustrates the role played by certain composers, charity school teachers and organists in supporting church bands. In addition to supplying books of psalmody, John Gresham also supplied reeds and undertook instrument repairs, charging the Caddington churchwardens 5s for 'rectifying and cleaning a clarinet'.[62] When Gresham died in 1812, local church bands appear to have turned to his organist son William for instrument supplies and repairs. In 1814 the Toddington (Beds.) churchwardens' accounts itemised 'Mr Gresham for a new clarionett £3 8s 6d' and 'for mending the clarionett and reeds 13s 6d'.[63] John Gresham's son-in-law and successor as master of the Dunstable charity school was John Puddephatt, whose son Alfred William Gresham Puddephatt was appointed organist of Dunstable in 1824.[64] The Puddephatts continued the Gresham family's supply and repair of musical instruments. Whereas in January 1812 the Aldbury churchwardens paid 'Mr Gresham for singing Books and Reeds', in 1813 'James Puddefoot' was paid for repairing instruments, 'claronette' and bassoon reeds.[65] Similarly, in 1810–11, in addition to '1 Psalmody improved bound', Gresham supplied Caddington church with hautboy, clarinet and bassoon reeds, but in 1822 a payment was made to 'Mr Puddephatt for 4 Music Books'.[66]

Supply and funding of instruments

If the purchase of instruments was not met by the church rate, who paid for them? Correspondence concerning music-making in Woburn, in neighbouring Bedfordshire, provides rare evidence of church musicians purchasing their own instruments. In 1816 the church band member William Harland wrote to Robert Salmon, churchwarden and the Duke of Bedford's steward, stating that the band had, by permission of both duke and incumbent, acquired flutes to supplement the church 'clarionet' and 'base viol' during afternoon service 'at an expence not very inconsiderable to persons in our circumstances'.[67] However, the flutes were considered discordant, and Harland wrote 'It has also been represented to us that you would permit Hautboys to be used instead of the flutes but as we cannot be assured but that they may in a short time be rejected as well as the flutes we have declined putting ourselves to the expence of purchasing them.'[68] He stated that the band would retire from the gallery immediately 'with feelings of pleasure mingled with regret'. Pleasure because 'we are conscious of having done every thing in our power to secure the approbation of the Community and to increase the attendance of the Public at Church (as we are well aware that many prefer the Wind Instruments &c to the Organ)',[69] but regret because 'we have not found in the parish of Woburn (tho' inhabited by so respectable a body of Gentlemen) one person to step forward to give us the least Encouragement in promoting this (the expression of which we have been honored with) our laudable undertaking'.[70] This indicates that certain elites were reluctant to make any financial contribution to church music-making, as had been noted by Crompton in 1778:

> Singers are at a considerable expence for books, and oftentimes for instruction too, and in country places frequently travel miles in an evening after the labour of the day is over, to meet together for improvement [...] it certainly is very unreasonable and very uncharitable to expect, that persons who labour for a livelihood, should not only spend so much of their time, as they of necessity must, but be at a great expence too to serve a large number of persons, who can well afford to give them a small gratuity, at least to reimburse part of the reasonable expence that necessarily attends the keeping up the decent performing this part of divine worship in their several parish churches [...].[71]

In addition to purchase by church band members, the evidence suggests a complex funding picture. In some parishes instruments were given by a local landowner, patron or clergyman. In 1742 Tristram Land, newly appointed vicar of Brent and Furneux Pelham, paid £6 9s 'To Mr Searle for instruments', and in 1746 subscribed a guinea 'Towards a singing pew'.[72] In other cases instruments were purchased by subscription. At Offley in

1818 the churchwardens authorised a payment of 5s 'towards paying for a new Clarenet to the Church'.[73] Although such a method indicates popular support, those who subscribed to instruments may have felt entitled to an opinion about their use. In 1818 subscribers towards the cello at Aston-le-Walls (Northants.) attached a list of conditions to its use and controlled the choice of instrumentalist.[74] Similarly, in 1807 the Somerset parson William Holland reflected upon the temporary absence of his church's church band: 'As we of our own Parish subscribed for the Instruments I observed that they should not forsake us in the time of our own Service, for we did not buy the Instruments for the Amusement of other Churches.'[75]

Some instruments were acquired by part exchange. In 1823 the Bushey churchwardens recorded 'To Cash for the difference between a new Violincello for the Church band & the allowance for the old one taken in Exchange £2 10s'.[76] Instruments could also be purchased in instalments, on approval or by hire-purchase.[77] In 1790 Longman & Broderip of London advertised that their instruments 'if not approved may be exchanged'.[78] This suggests that some church bands may have tried out instruments before purchase, and Hertfordshire evidence now establishes that this was indeed the case. William Andrews was a 'Stationer and Watchmaker, Dealer and Chapman' in Royston.[79] When the Barkway churchwardens purchased a second-hand clarinet from him in April 1817 Andrews employed effective sales pressure by sending his son to collect the instrument with a note that there was another interested party should the clarinet be unwanted: 'Sir, I should not have sent my son over to-day, but we have a young man waiting for the clarinett, provided it does not suit you.'[80] Provincial shops acted as outlets for London musical instrument makers and dealers such as Goulding & Co., whose 1800 catalogue claimed the contents 'may be had of every music shop in town and country, and of most of the principal booksellers in England, Scotland, and Ireland'.[81]

In some cases musicians made the instruments themselves. No evidence of amateur-built instruments survives from Hertfordshire, however, and it seems likely that, owing to its proximity to London, it was far more common for them to be acquired from professional instrument makers. Lastly, there is the possibility that some church band instruments came from military bands, as discussed in the following section.

Military influence
Mid-eighteenth-century military action on the continent led to fears of civil unrest in England, and later of invasion by Napoleonic forces. The start of this period saw militia revived by Act of Parliament in 1757, to be raised by ballot from men aged between eighteen and fifty.[82] Although supervised by

the War Office, the militia were organised by each county's Lord Lieutenant, and a strict hierarchy determined the appointment of local landowners as officers, actively involved in both recruiting and commanding. Each company received government funding via its commanding officer, and it was his responsibility to arrange the purchase of items such as clothing and weapons and the payment of wages and allowances.[83]

Militia Acts provided for two drummers per company until 1786, when the number was reduced to one, yet many colonels considered a military band, often referred to as a 'band of music', to be desirable. This could be financed by judicious spending of the government funding, as it was accepted that officers could use any 'profit' as they thought fit.[84] Militia Acts of 1786 and 1794 formalised this arrangement, decreeing that 'Officers may keep extra Drummers as Musicians if they defray the Expence'.[85] Commanding officers may have taken advantage of this ruling to create their own private bands relatively cheaply.[86] The 1786 Militia Act was quickly satirised in *The Times*:

> Advice to the Lord Lieutenants of Counties. It is absolutely necessary to the dignity of yourself and your corps, that you should have a band of music. You will contrive to raise it by conscription among your Captains; but when it is raised you will consider it entirely as your own, and not let them have a tune without your express leave. The raising and instruction of the musicians will occasion a considerable expence, and though not to yourself only, yet it is proper you should have the whole advantage of it [...].[87]

Despite this overt criticism, adverts appeared almost immediately from makers and dealers such as Longman & Broderip offering to supply 'a great variety of military musical instruments'.[88] By 1790 they boasted 'instruments sent out, conveyed, and tuned in town and country on the shortest notice, and if purchased and paid for within eight months, the hire will be abated. [...] Regiments supplied with complete sets, or any parts of such [...]'.[89]

Although drummers were used for signalling and maintaining a steady marching pace on parade, it is unlikely that the elite invested in militia bands solely for this purpose. Bands would have helped to create an air of ceremony, in addition to serving as signs of patriotism and prosperity, and may therefore have been a source of competition between different units.[90] Furthermore, the commanding officer, who would usually also have been patron of at least one parish church, could take pride in having a renowned band, particularly if loaned to another landowner.

Rivalries became evident when militia from across the nation convened in military camps established near the east and south coasts to enable quick deployment to the continent or to repel French invaders. One of the most important camps was in Coxheath (Kent), where the Hertfordshire and other militia were stationed in 1778, including 'his Grace the Duke of Grafton, at the head of his battalion of Suffolk militia, with their band of music' and the Derbyshire militia led by the Duke and Duchess of Devonshire, 'with a good band of music'.[91]

The following year the Hertfordshire militia were stationed at another important camp, Great Warley (Essex), less than twenty miles east of the Hertfordshire border and home of the composer John Arnold.[92] In June 1778 the *Ipswich Journal* reported 'Warley Common begins now to have a very fine appearance, and vast crowds of people are continually repairing thither to see the camp.'[93] Visits to these camps fuelled the fashion for all things military, and Countess Spencer's daughter the Duchess of Devonshire organised a short-lived women's auxiliary corps, complete with fashionable uniform.[94]

Over winter invasion was considered less likely, and troops were quartered in towns and villages. When Warley camp broke in 1779 many of the militia overwintered in Hertfordshire – the West Suffolk at Hitchin, Stevenage and Baldock, and the West Kent at Royston.[95] The following year the Earl of Hardwicke's Cambridgeshire militia were quartered at Royston and Baldock.[96] In 1794 the Derbyshires, under the command of the Duke and Duchess of Devonshire, overwintered at Hertford, Ware and surrounding villages.[97] These regiments all had renowned bands and, as explained below, their effect on local music-making was surely significant, as they were in residence for a considerable period.

The Volunteer movement
Under imminent threat of invasion, in March 1794 the Secretary of State for War sent a circular to all Lords Lieutenant proposing local defence forces to augment the militia. Again, officers were permitted to supplement government funding to create bands of music. In 1798 an Oxford dealer announced to 'Gentlemen who have taken arms in defence of their country, that he furnishes musical bands with the following instruments', listing French horns, clarionets, flutes, bassoons, serpents and other instruments.[98] The London musician and dealer William Napier took advantage of the situation by sending an unsolicited circular to the commanding officers of Volunteer associations, including Lieutenant Colonel William Wilshere of Hitchin, which read 'Having been honoured with the Appointment of Music Seller and Musician to His Majesty for the last Thirty Years, I take the Liberty of soliciting the Honour of being employed by your Regiment to furnish Military Instruments and Music.'[99] Although more than £56 was spent on musical instruments for the Hitchin Volunteer band in 1803–4, the

name of the supplier is unknown.[100] Wilshere was not the only Hertfordshire commanding officer to seize this opportunity to form a band of music. In June 1805 the diarist John Carrington visited Ware with 'Mr Allington Gent & his Band of Musick', the significance of which is that Allington had just been appointed Captain of the Ware Volunteers.[101] As seen, militia bands had overwintered at both Hitchin and Ware, perhaps influencing Wilshere and Allington's desire to establish Volunteer bands.

Few clergymen were willing or accepted to serve in the Volunteers except as chaplains.[102] The appointment of Thomas Shield, vicar of Royston, as Captain in July 1798 was clearly a notable exception perhaps encouraged by his parish's anti-Revolutionary patron, Thomas Brand Hollis.[103] It was left to Captains to timetable the drill days, but Sundays became common following legislation stipulating that Volunteers would be paid 'provided they had been drilled on the SUNDAY preceding the day for which they claimed pay'.[104] At Royston the vicar would 'ascend the pulpit wearing his surplice over his uniform, and having finished his sermon would descend from the pulpit, slip off his surplice, and march to the Heath at the head of his company of Volunteers for drill on a Sunday afternoon'.[105]

It has been suggested that church band instrumentalists may have been encouraged to join militia and Volunteer bands owing to their knowledge of music.[106] It is possible that this was the case in Royston. When Thomas Shield left church for the drill ground he was accompanied by the parish clerk John Warren, both 'bass viol' player and leader of the church band.[107] In Norfolk, George Walpole, 3rd Earl of Orford, was Lord Lieutenant and colonel of the county militia. Among the subscribers to John Crompton's 1778 *Psalm Singer's Assistant* were three from East Dereham, namely John Taylor, 'Musician, Master of Lord Orford's Band of Music', James Philoe 'of the Band, in Lord Orford's Company of the Norfolk Militia' and John Wilson 'of Lord Orford's Music Band'.[108] It seems highly likely that they were members of the East Dereham church band before being recruited as members of Orford's band.

On occasion the influence of military band members was also seen in church bands. In July 1771 the gentleman composer John Marsh found that the church singers in Romsey (Hampshire):

> had engaged a Mr Roe, a soldier (who had formerly belong'd to a cathedral) to attend & instruct them, in which he was of some service, tho' he had no great depth of theoretical knowledge & was very illiterate. He however taught them a few very pleasing anthems, Psalms etc. [...][109]

In addition to their official function, militia and Volunteer bands contributed extensively to provincial music-making in a number of ways.

The first of these was by enhancing social life, and Viscount Grimston hired the 'militia music' to play at Gorhambury in 1789.[110] In 1787 the *New Lady's Magazine* reported that Salisbury had made great alterations to Hatfield Park and gardens, including enlarging the canal, which

> has induced the Earl and his Countess, with their visitors, to divert themselves a few evenings during the summer with regattas, in elegant barges for that purpose, that have accommodations for the band of music belonging to the Hertfordshire militia, of which his Lordship is colonel.[111]

Military bands' second contribution was towards music-making by the nobility and gentry themselves, both privately and at subscription concerts. During this period they depended on military instrumentalists because, despite the growing popularity of orchestral music, brass and reed instruments such as oboes, clarinets and bassoons were not usually considered suitable for members of the elite to learn. Lastly, it seems likely that the increasing use of wind instruments in church during this period was another result of this military influence, as discussed below.

Military and church bands
John Arnold's *Complete Psalmodist* 'for the use of country choirs' ran through seven editions between 1740 and 1779. Although scholars have commented on his prefaces, none appear to have remarked that the last two provide useful accounts of the development of church music-making in the Great Warley area, and almost certainly in neighbouring Hertfordshire. In 1761 Arnold observed:

> The Bassoon being now in great Request in many Country Churches, I presume therefore, it will not be improper for me here to acquaint my Reader, that it makes an exceeding good Addition to the Harmony of a Choir of Singers, where there is no Organ, as most of the Bass Notes may be played on it [...].[112]

Arnold seems to have noticed the growing use of the bassoon in church bands, an instrument that until recently would have been unfamiliar to many. This supports the growing evidence that bass instruments were the earliest to be used in church bands, where they supported bass voices or provided a bass line where there was none.

Yet, in his final preface of 1779, Arnold observed 'of late years several kinds of musical treble instruments have been introduced into many country churches, to accompany the voices, as violins, hautboys, clarinets, vauxhumanes, &c'.[113] The militia had taken up residence at Warley Camp near

Arnold's parish church a few months after the publication of the 1761 edition, and following their stay in 1779 Arnold wrote about the marked increase in the use of clarinets and other instruments in church bands. So by the end of the eighteenth century treble instruments were used to support the higher voices, perhaps influenced by the availability of military band instruments.

Evidence of the fashionable military influence on both costume and church music-making comes from Ayot St Lawrence. Following the consecration of Lionel Lyde's rebuilt parish church in 1779 *The Gentleman's Magazine* reported:

> the neighbouring nobility and gentry, with their ladies, attended, together with many hundred persons of all denominations from different parts of the county. The procession was preceded by a band of music; upwards of twenty men and women, dressed in neat uniforms at the expense of Sir Lionel, followed the music, and after them the bishop, clergy, and the rest of the company in regular procession.[114]

The use of a band of music on such a prestigious occasion, rather than the immediate installion of an organ in the church, suggests that this was something to aspire to.

The inter-related nature of the instruments used in church and military bands is also revealed in contemporary advertisements and bills. In July 1809 the Barkway churchwardens paid for bassoon and clarinet reeds and a redbox from the London instrument maker Thomas Key, who described himself as 'military musical instrument maker to their Majesties Prince Regent, Dukes of York, Kent, Cumberland, and army in general'.[115] Before the singers' stand-off with the rector, discussed in the previous chapter, Tring churchwardens had sanctioned a payment to Goulding & Co. in December 1824 'for a Clarinet & carriage of it £2 13 6'.[116] Goulding's 1800 catalogue listed instruments manufactured on their premises at 76 James Street, Covent Garden, 'Where Gentlemen of the Army may be supplied with regular sets of instruments for a Military Band, upon the shortest notice'.[117] Similarly, an oboe by George Astor & Co., who advertised complete sets of military band instruments, was used in Aldenham church.[118] By the 1820s advertisements appeared to suggest that instruments were suitable for both military and church bands, as in an advertisement from Stamford (Lincs.): 'Country Choirs, and Military and other Bands, supplied with complete Sets of Instruments, in tune with each other, on the most reasonable terms'.[119]

If the local landowner felt the need for instruments in both the military and the church band, would it not have made sense to have them serve both purposes? The Hatfield church band was discontinued in 1848, but in 1866 James Grimston, 2nd Earl of Verulam, recalled its 'gallery full of fiddlers and some few old musicians from the militia'.[120] A permanent militia camp had been established in Hatfield Park, only a few yards from the parish church of the Marquess of Salisbury, Lord Lieutenant and colonel of the Hertfordshire militia, who encouraged the use of militia instruments in the church.

A close connection between military and church bands, and possible overlap between them, was also evident in Welwyn parish church. In May 1807 the diarist Carrington had spent an evening at Tewin 'with Mr Otway, Schoolmaster at Wellwin, who Brought over with him the Wellwin Band of Music, 4 Clarernetts, 2 Buzzoons, 1 french horne, Tumbrean & Simbolds &c &c [...] Mr Otway plaid the flute as Master'.[121] The Welwyn vestry resolved in April 1812 'that the middle of the Charity Boys gallery be lowered and that Mr Otway be allowed a little piece of it',[122] suggesting that as well as being schoolmaster he was the church band leader. Instead of being restricted to instruments more typically associated with church bands, the Welwyn 'band of music' – a term usually applied to military bands – included a brass instrument, tambourine and cymbels. It seems possible that Otway may have directed both the church band and local band of music. Perhaps Otway had joined the Welwyn band of music as a means of gaining access to instruments, as had the Kendal choirmaster John Fawcett, who joined his local Volunteers and 'acquired a knowledge of a few instruments, with the view to get into the band'.[123] When militia and Volunteer companies were disbanded their instruments became redundant, and the parish church may have been the obvious home for some of them. One of the Welwyn 'buzzoons' was by William Milhouse of London, who described himself as a 'Military Instrument Maker', and is stamped R.E.I.V., suggesting that it was acquired second-hand from the Royal East India Volunteers band.[124]

A further example of the inter-relatedness of church and military bands comes from Oakham (Rutland) where an 1806 inventory of church goods included, in addition to an organ and violoncello, two bassoons, two hautboys, two 'clarrinets' and one French horn.[125] Significantly, among the churchwardens' bills and vouchers was an invoice from Köhler & Percival, 'Martial Musical Instrument Makers' for a bassoon with a trumpet top.[126] Between 1786 and 1793 Köhler advertised his 'Bassoon tops &c in silver, brass and copper, manufactured in the best manner [...] having been master of the band of his majesties Royal Lancashire Volunteers &c'.[127] The implication of these unusual tops may be explained by correspondence between John Pearce and Nathaniel Winchcombe, bandmaster and captain respectively of the Frampton-on-Severn Volunteers in Gloucestershire.[128] Pearce advised Winchcombe to 'order ... the Bassoons [to] have Trumpet Bell tops and common tops to use occasionally which will render them fit for concerts or Church Music when wanted – the Trumpet tops to correspond with the Horns &c.'[129] With flared metal trumpet tops the bassoons would

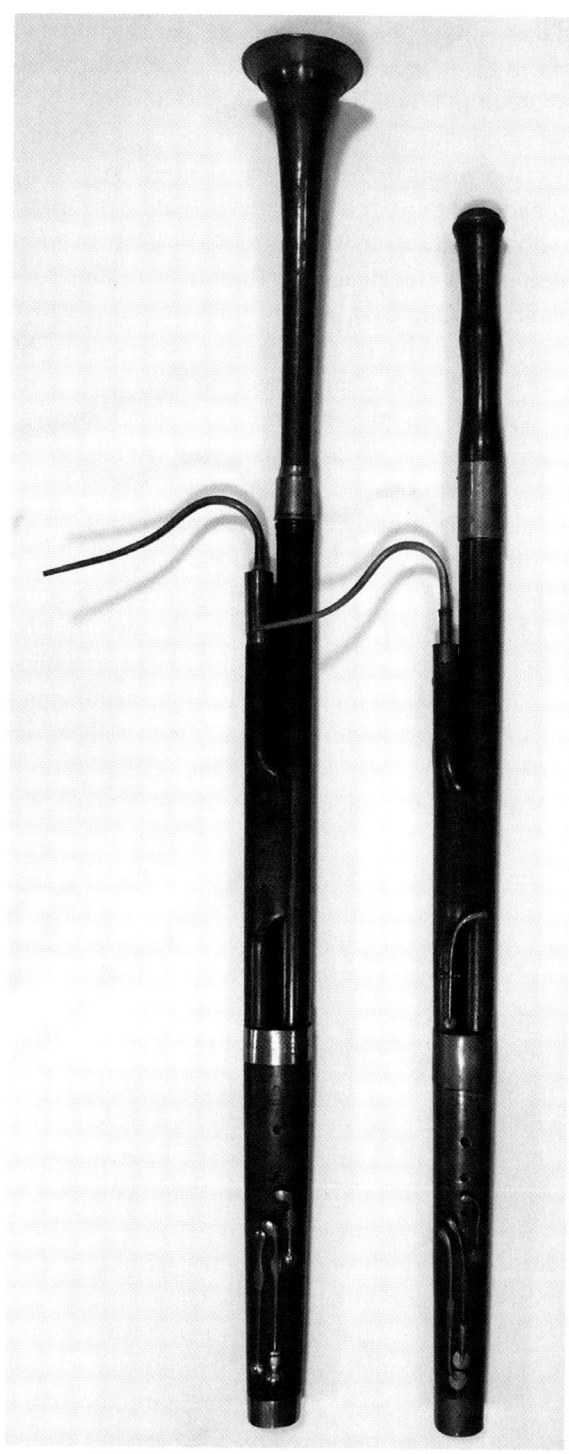

Figure 4.1. Left: Goulding & D'Almaine bassoon with trumpet top; right: Cuvillier bassoon (both 1800–50). Bate Collection, University of Oxford, 310 & 309.

better match military instruments such as horns and trumpets in terms of both appearance and loudness, while a standard wooden bell would give a softer appearance and volume that would blend better with church band instruments (Figure 4.1).

In some cases the church's existing instruments appear to have been pressed into military use. Elsewhere in the Lincoln diocese, the Rippingale (Lincs.) churchwardens' accounts of 1790 include payments 'for repairing the bassoon some years standing 6s 6d' and 'To Mr Rouse trumpet top and repairs bassoon 17s'.[130] This suggests that the trumpet top was purchased to adapt the church's existing bassoon for occasional use in the Volunteer band. Other churches known to have used bassoons with trumpet tops include Ridlington (Rutland), Oundle (Northants.) and Balsham (Cambs.).[131]

A bassoon had been used in Woburn parish church since 1778, but in 1801 the churchwardens paid a guinea 'for a trumpet top to the bassoon', presumably so that it could be used in the local Volunteer band.[132] It is surely significant that the Duke of Bedford purchased a barrel organ for the church shortly afterwards, for reasons that will become apparent.[133] The installation date is unknown, but it may have marked the 6th Duke's accession in 1802, and certainly pre-dates the purchase of a new barrel made in 1813.[134] As seen above, although band instruments had been purchased for use during afternoon service in the church they were later banned.[135] In 1816 Robert Salmon, churchwarden and the Duke of Bedford's steward, explained to band members 'With respect to my having insisted on your introducing clarinets or hautboys I must beg to correct that misrepresentation. […] your instruments were considered discordant and disapproved of by His Grace.' He continued:

> I thought if you used wind instruments at all in an afternoon that perhaps a Clarinet with the Base Viol would be sufficient and Less objectionable altho' His Graces opinion is that the Instruments are altogether improper. Thus you must understand that my insisting on the use of any instrument is altogether as incorrect as it would be contrary to the Duke's request […] I have not heard any of the Inhabitants express their preference of Instruments to the Organ.[136]

So, despite the duke's opinion that the use of wind instruments was 'altogether improper', references to using instruments 'in an afternoon' suggest that during this period it may have been the practice for the Woburn barrel organ and children's voices to lead the congregation during morning service, but instrumentalists during afternoon service. Perhaps, as in other churches, humbler classes attended Woburn church in the afternoon, but superior music-making – including the use of a barrel organ while still a fashionable novelty – was expected by the elite who attended in the morning.

When church reform began to take hold in the 1830s, rather than doing away with all instruments at a stroke, John Antes Latrobe, a Bristol curate, advised clergymen newly inducted into country livings to replace wind with stringed instruments: 'The bassoon must be dispensed with at all hazard, and if a violoncello can be introduced into its place an important object is effected.'[137] This attitude may have had its origins in a desire to disassociate church music-making from military bands of music, and may have influenced the Duke of Bedford's decision to give a barrel organ to his church. Once again, the music trade saw a marketing opportunity, and in the early 1800s the London dealer John Watlen seized it: 'It is now found of the greatest utility to have a Barrel Organ in every Church and Chapel, it not only keeps the Singers together, but saves the great and continual expence of an Organist, and also precludes the necessity of introducing military wind Instruments into the Church.'[138]

Before embarking upon a detailed explanation of church barrel organs and their use in Chapter 6, the next chapter discusses the difficulties involved in obtaining, maintaining and finding organists to play 'finger organs': that is, those without barrels.

Endnotes

1. O.W. Davys, 'The Choral Arrangements of Churches', *Reports and Papers of the Architectural and Archaeological Societies of the Counties of Lincoln and Northampton*, 10 (1870), p. 262.
2. HALS, DP/36/5/1 Churchwardens' accounts (1791–1826).
3. HALS, DP/94/5/1.
4. HALS, DP/19/5/4 Churchwardens' bills (1812–14).
5. HALS, DP/3/5/1–2 Churchwardens' accounts (1760–1870).
6. S.J. Weston, 'The Instrumentation and Music of the Church Choir-Band in Eastern England, with Particular Reference to Northamptonshire, during the Late Eighteenth and Early Nineteenth Centuries', PhD thesis (Leicester Univ., 1995), pp. 30–1; Davidson, *Choirs*.
7. HALS, DP/64/5/6 Churchwardens' bills & vouchers (1825–59); DP/21/5/10–11.
8. Gammon, '"Babylonian Performances"', p. 70.
9. *New Monthly Magazine* (1 July 1814), pp. 540–2.
10. T.A. Trollope, *What I Remember*, 3 vols (London, 1887), I, p. 63.
11. MacDermott, *Minstrels*, pp. 63–5.
12. J. Wesley, 'Thoughts on the Power of Music', *The Works of the Rev. John Wesley*, 16 vols (London, 1812), XV, p. 362.
13. Ford, *Observations*, p. 52.
14. W. Mason, 'On Parochial Psalmody' (1795), in *Essays on English Church Music*, 4 vols (London, 1811), III, p. 388.
15. *London Literary Gazette* (2 January 1819), pp. 9–10.
16. P.X., 'Church Music', pp. 540–2.
17. *London Courier & Evening Gazette* (23 June 1827), p. 4.
18. HALS, DP/3/29/17 Correspondence (1902–25).
19. HALS, ASA17/17/1/2 Churchwardens' presentment (1820). Probably W.J. White of St Albans.
20. Davidson, *Choirs*, p. 101.
21. MacDermott, *Sussex*, p. 12.
22. BARS, P35/5/1; HALS, DP/64/5/1–2 Churchwardens' accounts (1793–1853); DP/3/5/3 Receipted bills (1822).
23. HALS, DP/36/5/1; 1841 Census HO107/439/f.11/p.16.
24. *Gentleman's Magazine* (October 1798), pp. 905–7.
25. P.X., 'Church Music', pp. 540–2.
26. 1851 Census HO107/1705/f.558/p.21.
27. Galpin, 'Village Band', p. 58; MacDermott, *Minstrels*, p. 10.
28. Gammon, '"Babylonian Performances"', p. 65.
29. N. Boston, 'Music of the Eighteenth Century Village Church', *Archaeological Journal*, 99 (1942), p. 62.
30. 1851 Census HO107/1723/f.122/p.31; HO107/1723/f.110/p.5; HO107/1723/f.109/p.4.
31. HALS, DP/64/5/1–2.
32. P.X., 'Church Music', pp. 540–2.
33. HALS, DP/90/5/1; DP/90/7; 1851 Census HO107/1706/f.647/p.13.
34. Weston, *Instrumentation*, p. 310; Davidson, *Choirs*, p. 109.
35. HALS, DP/78/5/1 Churchwardens' accounts (1842–52); 1851 Census HO107/1706/f.647/p.13.
36. Burg, *Religion*, p. 55.
37. Cussans, *History*, III, p. 150.
38. Little Gaddesden, Churchwardens' bills & vouchers (1824).
39. V. Bell, *Little Gaddesden. The Story of an English Parish* (London, 1949), p. 145.
40. A. Trollope, *The Small House at Allington*, 2 vols, 2nd edn (London, 1864), 1, p. 12.
41. National Society, *Seventh Annual Report* (London, 1818); Langwill and Boston, *Barrel-organs*, p. 79.

42 *Christian Observer* (December 1819), p. 810.
43 *Christian Remembrancer* (June 1822), pp. 375–6.
44 *Ibid.*
45 *Ibid.*
46 *Ibid.*
47 Langwill and Boston, *Barrel-organs*, pp. 119–25; MacDermott, *Sussex*; H. Woodhouse, *Face the Music: Church and Chapel Bands in Cornwall* (St Austell, 1997); Davidson, *Choirs*; Weston, 'Instrumentation'.
48 R. Pacey, *Lincolnshire Church Organs [...]* (Burgh-le-Marsh, 2002).
49 M.J. Kilbey, 'Music-making in the English parish church from the 1760s to 1860s, with particular reference to Hertfordshire', DPhil thesis (Oxford Univ., 2017), p. 145.
50 MacDermott, *Minstrels*, p. 22.
51 HALS, DP/64/5/1–2.
52 HALS, DP/3/5/1–2; Anon., *English Church History Exhibition*, p. 187.
53 HALS, CP44/8/2 Vestry minutes (1843–87).
54 HALS, DP/94/5/1.
55 HALS, DP/13/8/21–30 Bills & vouchers (1803–33).
56 HALS, DP/90/5/1; DP/90/7.
57 G.C. Straker, *A History of the Organs at the Cathedral of St Alban* (London, 1929); P. Hurford, *The Organs of St Albans Abbey* (St Albans, 1969), pp. 6–7.
58 Hardy, *Greenwood Tree* (1896 edn), p. 25.
59 HALS, DP/2/5/2; DP/39/5/2 Churchwardens' accounts (1817–62); DP/80/4/1–2.
60 Hardy, *Greenwood Tree* (1896 edn.), pp. v–vi.
61 *Stamford Mercury* (1 March 1816), p. 3.
62 BARS, P35/5/2.
63 F.C. Hamlyn, 'In Quires and Places where they Sing ... The Gallery Musicians of Bedfordshire', *The Bedfordshire Magazine*, III/19 (Winter 1951/52), pp. 99–103.
64 *Windsor and Eton Express* (11 September 1824), p. 4; H. Garrod, 'Chew's House', *Dunstable & District Local History Newsletter*, 23 (February 2005), pp. 154–7.
65 HALS, DP/2/5/2.
66 BARS, P35/5/1–2.
67 BARS, R4/608/35/20–1 Harland and Salmon correspondence (1816).
68 *Ibid.*
69 *Ibid.* The significance of Harland's reference to the organ is explored below; see p. 109–10.
70 BARS, R4/608/35/20–1.
71 J. Crompton, *The psalm singer's assistant, or, a key to psalmody [...]* (London, 1778), pp. vii–x.
72 HALS, DP/78/3/3.
73 HALS, DP/76/5/1 Churchwardens' accounts (1810–70).
74 Weston, *Instrumentation*, p. 146.
75 J. Ayres (ed.), *Paupers and Pigkillers: The Diary of William Holland, a Somerset Parson 1799–1818* (Gloucester, 1984), p. 151.
76 HALS, DP/26/5/1–2 Churchwardens' accounts (1785–1831).
77 In 1806 the bassoon at Holcot (Northants.) was purchased in this manner. Weston, *Instrumentation*, p. 163.
78 *The Times* (2 November 1790), p. 2.
79 *London Gazette* (13 March 1829), p. 486.
80 HALS, DP/13/5/2–3 Churchwardens' accounts (1817–44); DP/13/8/21–30.
81 Goulding, Phipps and d'Almaine, *Catalogue of instrumental and vocal music* (London, 1800), p. 3.
82 30 Geo. II c.25 Militia Act (1757).
83 J.R. Western, *The English Militia in the Eighteenth Century. The Story of a Political Issue 1660–1802* (London, 1965), p. 130.
84 *Ibid.*, p. 370.

85 34 Geo. III c.81 Militia Act (1794).
86 Lomas, 'Militia', p. 163.
87 *The Times* (9 May 1786), p. 1.
88 *Ibid.* (25 May 1786), p. 1.
89 *Ibid.* (2 November 1790), p. 2.
90 Lomas, 'Militia', p. 162; Lomas, 'Wiltshire', p. 95.
91 *Ipswich Journal* (13 June 1778), p. 2; *Stamford Mercury* (25 June 1778), p. 3.
92 *London Magazine, Or, Gentleman's Monthly Intelligencer* (July 1779), p. 332; see Chapter 2, p. 52.
93 *Ipswich Journal* (13 June 1778), p. 2.
94 M. McCormack, '"Turning Out for Twenty-Days Amusement": The Militia in Georgian Satirical Prints', in E. Charters, E. Rosenhaft and H. Smith (eds), *Civilians and War in Europe, 1618–1815* (Liverpool, 2014), p. 176.
95 Kingston, *Fragments*, p. 94.
96 *Ibid.*
97 J. Breihan and C. Caplan, 'Jane Austen and the Militia', *Journal of the Jane Austen Society of North America*, 14 (1992), pp. 16–26.
98 *Northampton Mercury* (12 May 1798), p. 3.
99 HALS, Acc 13/Box 3/1–5 Hitchin Volunteer infantry (1800–04).
100 *Ibid.*
101 J. Carrington and W.B. Johnson (ed.), *'Memorandoms for …', The Diary between 1798 and 1810 of John Carrington* (Chichester, 1973), p. 116.
102 A. Gee, *The British Volunteer Movement, 1794–1814* (Oxford, 2003), p. 83.
103 *London Gazette* (3 July 1798), p. 616; C. Bonwick, 'Hollis, Thomas Brand (*c.*1719–1804)', *ODNB*.
104 *Christian Observer* (April 1806), p. 257.
105 Kingston, *Fragments*, pp. 67–9.
106 Lomas, 'Militia', p. 158.
107 Kingston, *Fragments*, pp. 67–9.
108 Crompton, *The psalm singer's assistant*, n.p.
109 Robins, *Marsh*, I, p. 90.
110 Grimston, *Manuscripts*, pp. 218–21.
111 *New Lady's Magazine, or, Polite and entertaining companion for the fair sex* (December 1787), p. 683.
112 J. Arnold, *The Compleat Psalmodist*, 5th edn (1761), p. iv.
113 Arnold, *Compleat Psalmodist*, 7th edn (1779), p. iv. Vox humana = tenor oboe.
114 *Gentleman's Magazine* (28 July 1779). See Chapter 9, p. 220–1.
115 HALS, DP/13/8/21–30.
116 HALS, DP/111/8/20 Vestry minutes (1824–33).
117 Goulding *et al.*, *Catalogue*, p. 3.
118 Anon., *English Church History Exhibition*, p. 187.
119 *Stamford Mercury* (30 November 1821), p. 1.
120 *Herts Advertiser* (3 March 1866), p. 2.
121 Carrington and Johnson, *'Memorandoms'*, p. 144. Clarernetts = clarinets, Buzzoons = bassoons, Tumbrean = tambourine, Simbolds = cymbals.
122 HALS, DP/119/8/5 Vestry minutes (1812).
123 Drage, 'John Fawcett', p. 60.
124 Now in St Albans Museum, 88.3187.
125 Davidson, *Choirs*, p. 184.
126 *Ibid.*
127 L. Whitehead and A. Myers, 'The Köhler Family of Brasswind Instrument Makers', *Historic Brass Society Journal*, 16 (2004), pp. 90–1.
128 D. Lasocki, 'New Light on Eighteenth-Century English Woodwind Makers from Newspaper Advertisements', *Galpin Society Journal*, LXIII (May 2010), p. 117.

129 Gloucestershire Archives, D149/X21/15 Frampton Volunteers, cited by Lasocki, 'New Light', p. 117; the instruments are now in the Gloucester Regimental Museum.
130 P. Shaw, 'Local History', *The Greenwood Quire*, accessed at <http://www.greenwoodquire.co.uk/GreenwoodWestGalleryQuire/Local_History.html> (accessed 19 September 2014).
131 *Stamford Mercury* (9 June 1809), p. 2; Langwill and Boston, *Barrel-organs*, p. 119; Davidson, *Choirs*, pp. 13 and 186.
132 BARS, P118/5/4 Churchwardens' accounts (1778–1813).
133 J.D. Parry, *History and description of Woburn and its abbey* (London, 1831), p. 146.
134 BARS, P118/5/4.
135 See p. 100.
136 BARS, R4/608/35/20–1.
137 J.A. Latrobe, *The Music of the Church Considered in its Various Branches* (London, 1831), p. 91.
138 Royal College of Music, F.F. Hill collection, label pasted inside a church barrel-organ supplied by John Watlen. Watlen commenced business at the address given in 1807.

Chapter 5
Organs and organists

During the late 1700s to early 1800s few Hertfordshire churches had 'finger' organs: that is, those played by organists rather than barrels. Most parishes that wanted to install an organ faced considerable financial challenges, sometimes resulting in the installation of an instrument soon considered to be inadequate. As a consequence of a growing desire for more powerful instruments as the century progressed, many replacement finger organs had been installed in Hertfordshire churches by the late 1800s, as summarised in Appendix 3.

Overall, the status of church organists declined over the course of the period. In the late 1700s male church organists were often described as gentlemen, and in addition to church duties they usually played an important role in promoting local music-making and concert-going. But by the mid-1800s in many parishes playing the organ was considered an incidental duty of elementary school teachers. Women organists were found in Hertfordshire throughout the period, where they made a considerable, but under-recorded, contribution to church music-making.

Organs

During the mid-eighteenth century Handel's music had dominated English music-making, and the English organ concerto 'essentially Handel's own personal creation' had become 'a staple ingredient in the musical diet of the nation'.[1] This coincided with an elite-led consumer boom in luxury goods that saw the commercialisation and advertising of fashionable products reach fever pitch.[2] The vogue for acquiring a chamber organ had therefore become firmly established among the elite. When the effects of Edward Smith of St Albans were auctioned in 1779 they included 'a large fine-toned Organ, a Harpsichord and a Guittar',[3] all considered *à la mode* in polite society. The fashionable nature of the appetite for chamber organs in Hertfordshire is further illustrated by a 1792 sale notice offering 'a chamber organ, and a great variety of curious and valuable effects, the property of A MAN of FASHION, gone abroad; brought from his seat in Hertfordshire'.[4]

Table 5.1
Mid- to late eighteenth-century Hertfordshire organs and organists.

Parish (date organ first installed)	Population (1801)	Organist	Notes
Ayot St Lawrence (c.1780)	115	1782: Jonas Blewitt	Blind organist & composer, also organist of St Katharine Coleman, Fenchurch Street
Bishops Stortford (1729)	2305	1729–61: William Popely 1762–82: Charles Perry 1782–1808: Robert Perry	Popely: member of Royal Society of Musicians 1739. Perrys: Charles & Robert = father and son. Robert: Gentleman, served in Bishops Stortford Volunteers
Cheshunt (1711)	3173	1738: Thomas Green 1761: Mr Ward 1780–7: John Baptiste Levesque 1787–1825: Thomas Leach	Green: instrument tuner Levesque: gentleman (previously organist of St Andrew's, Enfield) Leach: gentleman, singer, harpsichord player. Served in Cheshunt Volunteers
*Chipping Barnet (1731)	1258	Unknown	Organ removed 1749
All Saints, Hertford (1678)	872	1744–91: Thomas Green 1791: Anna Maria Bridgeman 1791–1872: Charles Bridgeman	Bridgemans: brother & sister of John, Thomas & Richard (musicians & dancing masters) and Henry (later organist of St Andrew's, Hertford). Charles & John served in Hertford Volunteers
*North Mymms (c.1784)	838	c.1784–c.1800: Matthew Cooke	Also organist of St George's, Bloomsbury. Organ removed c.1801
St Peter's, St Albans (1723)	840	c.1776–1815: Anna Sophia Sherman	Almost certainly sister of John Christopher Sherman (musician & dancing master) & George Ferdinand Sherman (musician, dealer & chapman)
Ware (1683)	2950	To 1812: Unknown 1812–43: Thomas William Luppino	Luppino: proprietor of 'Fore Street Concert Room' (Hertford), sometimes known as 'Mr Luppino's Theatre'. Brother 'professor of music'; daughter 'teacher of music'. Other family members dancers, puppet-masters and harlequins
Watford (1766)	3530	c.1766–c.1810: Felix Smith	Violinist, dancing master

* indicates that these organs were only present for a short period.
Sources: Lincolnshire Archives, DIOC/FAC 1/26; HALS, DP/21/5/10–11, DP/29/8/48–52, DP/69/5/1, DP/93/5/3–5, DP/117/8/1–3; Hertfordshire Family History Society, Militia Ballot Lists: Ayot St Lawrence, Bishops Stortford 1798, Brickendon, Cheshunt 1792, Watford; *Public Advertiser* (8 August 1766); Doane, *Directory*, pp. 8, 14, 39 and 61; C.W. Pearce, *Notes on English Organs of the Period 1800–1810* (London, 1912), p. 97; 1851 Census HO107/1711/f.285/p.12 and HO107/447/f.6/p.5; Boeringer, *Organa Britannica*, 2, p. 30; D. Burchell, 'Blewitt, Jonas (1757–1805)', *ODNB*; Forbes, *Artist*, pp. 64, 87–8 and 124; Royal Society of Musicians of Great Britain, *RSM Membership 1738–1749*, accessed 8 April 2014, at <http://www.royalsocietyofmusicians.co.uk/members-1749.html>; Sheldrick, *Three Centuries*, pp. 72–6; Williams, *Leffler Manuscript*, p. 129.

An increasing number of metropolitan churches also installed organs during the eighteenth century. In 1761 John Arnold found that this vogue for church organs was beginning to spread to 'many of our Market-Towns throughout this Nation'.[5] As was the case with 'clothed' charity children, this was partially driven by the desire for display. According to Temperley, 'the richness of the gilded organ case and pipes, like that of the rest of the church' showed both the generosity and wealth of the donors, and the organ's visual impact was as important as its musical quality in terms of drawing attention to the wealth and beneficence of those who had provided it.[6] Giving a church organ reflected the donor's social ascendancy, since this action indicated both fashion-consciousness and exclusivity. Moreover, the festivities associated with the opening of the organ drew favourable attention to the taste of the donor or subscribers.

In May 1766 the Watford vestry voted unanimously that an organ 'for which several of the inhabitants & others have subscribed' should be erected in a gallery at the west end of the church.[7] The principal subscriber appears to have been the church's patron, William Capel, 4th Earl of Essex, of Cassiobury. Indeed, when the Thomas Parker organ was opened in August 1766 the *Public Advertiser* reported that the earl was the sole contributor.[8] The opening recital was merely the prelude to a lavish musical entertainment held the following day, with a midday concert of vocal and instrumental music at the White Hart Inn given by 'a select Band from London', followed by an evening Ball. The earl's reputation as an arbiter of musical taste must have been secured when the newspapers were able to report 'The Indian Chiefs were present, and sung several of their warlike Songs'.[9] The Indian Chiefs had recently arrived in London in order to settle the limits of their hunting grounds, 'which they complain are encroached upon by the settlers from New York'.[10] But this was a rare event. Although it was by no means unusual to find a chamber organ in fashionable late eighteenth-century Hertfordshire households, the same could not be said of its parish churches, as summarised in Table 5.1. By 1800 only eight Hertfordshire parish churches had organs, all in market towns or parishes with a strong gentry presence. Perhaps parishioners and clergy in other towns were happy with the existing state of affairs, or were called upon to contribute towards more pressing causes. The result was that few churches had the funding to install an organ, pay for its upkeep and pay an organist.

With so few church organs outside London, some metropolitan organists tried to secure employment by offering to provide one themselves, in return for a good salary and some sort of job security. It seems likely that in certain cases this would have been made possible with financial assistance from the local elite, keen to improve local music-making. Despite the large initial outlay, providing a church organ where there was none gave the organist a head start over rivals. This is because a market town with no organ was less likely to already have an established music teacher, and it gave the organist access to the local demand for private lessons.[11] Many organists taught a number of musical instruments in addition to the organ and, among the household goods auctioned on the death of William Popely, organist of Bishops Stortford parish church, were 'two fine-toned harpsichords, three Spinnets, a Base Viol, a bassoon, two Violins, and several German and common Flutes'.[12]

Although not specifically naming Hertfordshire, a *Morning Post* advertisement of 1776 targeted counties adjacent to the capital:

> AN ORGANIST being desirous of residing in the country, within forty and not less than ten miles from London, will undertake, at his own expence, to furnish any parish church in or near a market town within the above circle, with a compleat Organ, upon his being appointed the Organist to and receiving from such parish a proper salary.[13]

One such was Matthew Cooke, who, during the late eighteenth century, was organist of North Mymms and St George's, Bloomsbury, both under the patronage of Francis Osborne, 5th Duke of Leeds. The congregation of St George's included many elites resident during the Season, and the church was designed with equally prestigious galleries for the landowners, Francis Russell (5th Duke of Bedford) and the Duke of Montagu. On condition that he was appointed organist, in 1788 Cooke offered to supply St George's with an organ valued at the enormous sum of 'not less than four hundred and fifty pounds'.[14] This indicates that he expected a considerable return on this investment in terms of salary, which was entirely dependent on the parishioners' subscriptions and feasible only in a wealthy parish such as this.

North Mymms is situated in the south of the county, within easy reach of London, and during the late eighteenth century had a very high concentration of wealthy parishioners, even by Hertfordshire standards. The church itself was situated within the Duke of Leeds' park. The extent of the duke's interest and involvement in fashionable music-making may be judged from the fact that he was a director of the prestigious 'Concerts of Antient Music', held in the capital.[15] Between 1786 and 1801 the North Mymms churchwardens recorded payments in excess of £396 'defraying the expences of the church and organ &c'.[16] Part of this sum was raised by a church rate, but an additional £53 was subscribed by five local landowners whose seats are shown in Figure 5.1. With the exception of Michie, all were members of parliament.[17] It is unclear exactly how much of this sum was spent on the

Figure 5.1. Map of North Mymms, showing the seats of subscribers towards music-making at St Mary's church. Based on C. Smith, *A New Map of the County of Hertford*, 2nd edn (London, 1808).

organ itself, which may have been supplied by Cooke, as in Bloomsbury. In 1790 Cooke composed a set of psalm tunes for use at North Mymms, which he dedicated to the Duke of Leeds, suggesting that the duke had made a significant contribution to the music-making in his parish church, where he wished to hear and display metropolitan-style music of a high standard.[18]

Opposition

Even if an organ was offered to a church, in certain circumstances parishioners opposed its installation. On occasion this may have been because of resistance to change, perhaps led by existing singers. Groups of singers may have been both well established and well received in certain Hertfordshire towns, in all likelihood more so than in rural parishes, because the pool of talent from which to draw musicians was larger. Some scholars interpret the introduction of an organ as an inevitable source of conflict, on the assumption that all churches had groups of singers (which was not the case), and that they would resent being replaced. Although some may have gone on to sing among the congregation, others may not have continued to attend the church at all.[19] However, in certain churches that did have groups of singers, their willingness to attend and deputise for the organist in times of emergency suggests little in the way of conflict. At Bishops Stortford the singers were paid 5s in October 1829 'for attending while the organist was ill'; likewise in 1827 the organ at Ware was out of order and £1 10 6d was paid to 'Singers while repair[ing] organ'.[20] In St Albans sporadic payments to organists at St Peter's are interspersed with payments to singers following the departure of Thomas Fowler, including in 1822 a payment to a member of the Higdon family, suggesting their continuing involvement in music-making.[21]

In most instances opposition to the installation of an organ was due to financial considerations. The more lucrative incomes available in nearby London may have made it challenging to attract organists to Hertfordshire and, furthermore, patrons and churchwardens may have been unwilling to make any provision for the running costs associated with an organ and organist. This was not an issue at All Saints', Hertford, where funding was in place to cover the organist's salary.[22] Similarly, in 1810 Raymond Rogers, vicar of Bishops Stortford, stated that his church had 'considerable benefactions', one of which was used for paying the organist and beautifying the church, '£150 of this money being paid in the last year towards a compleat repair of the organ'.[23] Yet in Watford provision was made for neither the upkeep of the organ nor the organist's salary, and by October 1785 an ever-increasing sum was owed to the organist Felix Smith, a situation that became all too common in Hertfordshire.[24] The Watford vestry agreed that the churchwardens should make up the deficiency, and that in future Smith should not be paid out of the church rental income, implying this had hitherto been the usual practice. Funding issues such as these became influential in the introduction of cheaper alternatives, including reed organs.

Reed organs

New developments in keyboard instrument manufacture led to the availability of relatively economical instruments during the mid-nineteenth century. Various free-reed organs were invented, including the Seraphine, the harmonium and the American Organ. These were much smaller and cheaper to manufacture than pipe organs, and, unlike pipe organs, firms often sold them on 'hire-purchase' agreements. Many churches were therefore able to consider using them.

Like pipe organs, harmoniums were used first in a domestic setting but later in churches. In Hertfordshire, the earliest recorded instances of church use come from Kings Langley and Kensworth during the mid-1850s.[25] While on long vacation from Oxford in 1859 Arthur Stanton, later known as 'Father Stanton', joined his family at Aldbury and introduced a harmonium to assist the singing at St Mary's.[26]

Since harmoniums are relatively easy to move, particularly the smaller models, they could not only be used in the church on a short-term basis but also be moved from site to site as required, and were sometimes used outdoors to accompany singing. This gave the church the opportunity to take its music-making to the people, rather than waiting for them to come to church. At Lilley the church band was replaced during the late 1860s by a young man paid £1 per annum to play a harmonium that was moved to the church every Sunday.[27] In 1859 a harmonium was used at Sandon temperance harvest cricket match to support singing led by the schoolmistress and children, while at Hitchin one was used in 1863 both in St Mary's National School for a Christmas treat and outdoors at the consecration of the new burial ground.[28] Yet at Little Gaddesden a suggestion that the school's harmonium could be used in church on Sundays to support chanting was considered inappropriate by the High-Church rector Rev. Jenks, and the west gallery barrel organ therefore continued in use until his death in 1870.[29] At Caddington the west gallery was considered a suitable location for the harmonium, presumably because the singers had previously been located there, but harmoniums were usually positioned at ground level. The Caddington instrument was first played by the schoolmaster, then the blacksmith and lastly the vicar's wife.[30]

There is little evidence of Seraphine use in Hertfordshire churches, and this small reed organ was too quiet to make a significant contribution to music-making. In *c.*1840 the enterprising John Godman, parish clerk and leader of the singers, made a Seraphine for use at St Stephen's, St Albans.[31] However, when one was used at the consecration of a new chapel-of-ease at Wareside the *Hertford Mercury and Reformer* reported 'The musical portion of the service was under the superintendence of Mr Luppino, who acquitted himself in a very creditable manner, notwithstanding the obvious defects of the instrument (a Seraphine).'[32]

It is sometimes stated that when reformers replaced singers and church bands with organs and organists there was often an 'intermediate stage' when a barrel organ, harmonium or Seraphine was used to support congregational singing.[33] Yet rural Hertfordshire parishes such as Caldecote, Clothall and others with dispersed settlements and small congregations appear never to have had pipe organs since the restoration of the monarchy, and still have reed organs today (Figure 5.2).[34]

Figure 5.2. Reed organ at St Mary the Virgin, Clothall (2015).

Finger organs

Instead of quiet reed organs or expensive finger organs (that is, organs with one or more manuals but no barrels), many parishes installed some sort of barrel organ, the subject of the next chapter. But from the mid-1800s others followed the advice of John Baron, rector of Upton Scudamore in Wiltshire. According to Baron, barrel organs, 'when cheap, are mere street-nuisances in church; and when costly, they are also failures, because they delegate too much of the service of praise to machinery, and are destructive of individual devotion and expression'.[35] As an economical alternative, Baron commissioned a local organ-builder to build a small finger organ for his church, and in 1858 published *Scudamore organs, or, Practical hints respecting organs for village churches and small chancels*.[36] The London organ-builder Henry Willis began to manufacture Scudamore organs, and from 1860 onwards Willis organs replaced barrel organs at Bayford, Ickleford and Wormley.[37] A drawing of St Laurence's, Wormley, made shortly after the installation of the Willis Scudamore organ, shows it located on the south side of the nave (Figure 5.3).

Until around the mid-nineteenth century organs were expected to support singing unobtrusively. In 1860 a service was held in Bengeo parish church to celebrate the building of a spire, a gallery to seat fifty children and the installation of a new organ, which was 'never permitted to drown the voices of the singers'.[38] However, a mid-nineteenth century craze for singing societies and choirs meant that organs were now expected to support a more ambitious choral repertoire. According to Nicholas Thistlethwaite, 'Organs had to become more flexible tonally and (an inevitable consequence) physically larger at just the moment when their accommodation was proving a major difficulty.'[39] In many churches it was considered necessary to replace unobtrusive organs with more powerful instruments. This often coincided with major changes in church layout, and the implications for the positioning of church organs are discussed in Chapter 9.

The acquisition of a new organ continued to provide the opportunity for a grand opening ceremony. The opening of the new Hill organ in the Abbey Church, St Albans, in August 1861 attracted an estimated congregation of 2,000 to 3,000, with many more turned away at the door owing to lack

Figure 5.3. Anon., Interior of St Laurence's, Wormley, showing the newly installed Willis organ (*c*.1860). HALS, DP/126/8/2 reproduced with permission from Hertfordshire Archives & Local Studies.

of space.[40] In addition to celebrating the opening of the organ, events such as this also allowed the church to assert its position when faced with the rival attractions of Nonconformity, raise additional funds and emphasise the donors' or subscribers' good taste and philanthropic motives. In addition, it gave local politicians an opportunity to win or retain support by showcasing their concern for local causes. When a new organ was installed at Aspenden in May 1856, the Tory *Herts Guardian* reported that 'Several of the nobility and nearly all who have any property and interest in the parish have subscribed liberally – nor must it be forgotten that our three county members assisted us with their handsome donations.'[41]

Four organs
During the mid to late nineteenth century, certain wealthy Hertfordshire parishes seemed to be almost constantly fundraising in their quest for a suitable, if not perfect, organ to support singing in the church. Much Hadham was notable for the constant reappraisal of its organs, upgrading from a variety of barrel organs to finger organs, and by 1859 had acquired its fourth organ within the space of around fifteen years.[42] This was almost certainly attributable to Thomas Randolph, their well-connected rector.[43]

Another church notable for the installation of four organs was St Andrew's, Hertford, an example which illustrates some of the ramifications associated with mid-nineteenth-century developments in the church. By October 1855 St Andrew's was evidently facing difficulties with both accommodation and its 'asthmatic' organ.[44] It was a further six years before the church was able to acquire a replacement 'of much sweetness, though of no great power', which was placed in the gallery.[45] With no private patron, funds were raised by subscription, with relatively large donations from relatively few donors.[46] But in April 1865 the newly formed choir declared that the organ was not powerful enough for the building.[47] The ladies of the choir started a subscription for another replacement organ, with the incentive that 'the power and character of the instrument will depend upon the amount raised in a given time'.[48] With ongoing accommodation and restoration issues there arose a question of priorities, and opinion was divided as to whether money should be raised at all for a new organ. 'A Parishioner' wrote to the *Herts Guardian*:

> [I] am disposed to think that the church itself has a prior claim; for if an organ be obtained to suit the present building, it is not likely to suit a new or enlarged church; and knowing the difficulty of resisting the entreaties of ladies, I really think they could and would, by their gentle persuasion, work as successfully for a church as for an organ. Some, I know would double their subscriptions promised a year or two back to the church, rather than subscribe to an organ separately.[49]

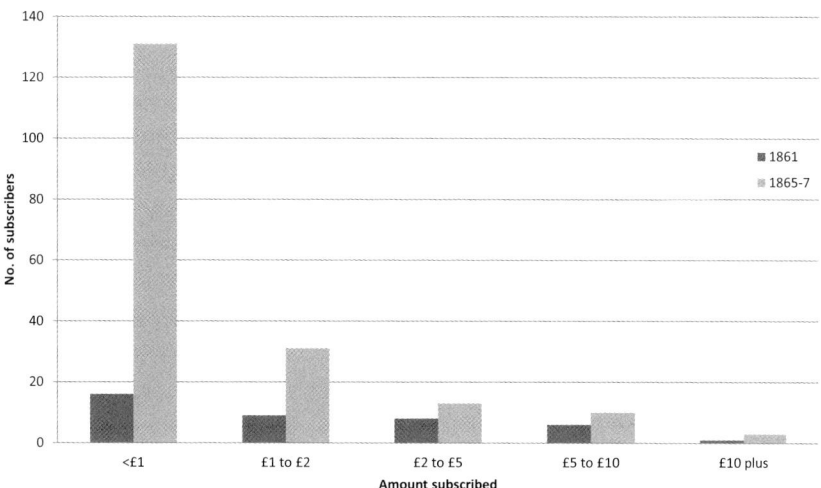

Figure 5.4. Subscriptions to organ funds at St Andrew's, Hertford, in 1861 and 1865–7. Based on *HG* (1861–67).

Those outside the parish were perhaps even more forthright. 'A Non-Parishioner' wrote to the *Hertford Mercury and Reformer* stating that the young ladies of the choir 'whose fascinations it is difficult to withstand' were soliciting subscriptions, and hoped that this time an organ would be selected 'suitable to the requirements of a larger church' and of 'the present excellent choir', a tactful remark made in deference to the editor Stephen Austin, whose daughter was a choir member.[50] However, the 'Non-Parishioner' then argued that partially or completely rebuilding the church should take priority, and that there was no shortage of locals able to supply the means to do so. Forty people had subscribed to a new organ in 1861, and now, only four years later, 213 towards another. The amounts subscribed were generally far smaller, suggesting that far more of the poorer parishioners supported the scheme (Figure 5.4). Although this appears to demonstrate how successful the new choir's fundraising had been, opponents later suggested that a significant proportion of the monies were subscribed on the misapprehension they were supporting the new church building.

By 1867 enough money had been promised, and John Marchant, St Andrew's choir director, announced his intention of purchasing a new organ immediately: 'The new instrument will be built of sufficient power for present purposes, and large enough in all necessary parts to admit of the addition of such stops as may be found requisite for a larger building.'[51] Following the death of Bishop Wigram in 1866, the *Herts Guardian* revealed the added incentive that 'It is rumoured that the new Bishop of Rochester

[Thomas Legh Claughton] will probably preach when the organ is opened.'[52] But a telling vestry minute reveals that not everything went according to plan, as Marchant explained:

> in consequence of the contracted space in the Organ Gallery it had been found impracticable to place the new organ there, but that there was a position at the end of the South Aisle in every way adapted for the instrument, and that the Organ Builder had inspected the site and reported that it was the best that could be obtained in the church.[53]

This reveals an astonishing lack of foresight. Rather than making a deliberate decision to relocate the organ from the gallery to the body of the church, the committee had simply ordered too large an organ, on the assumption it would be suitable for an as-yet-undesigned new church. Not only this, but its presence would exacerbate the church's lack of accommodation. Marchant was obliged to explain that 'the parishioners who occupied seats at the end of the South Aisle had consented to give up their sittings on condition that others were provided for them in some other part of the church'.[54] The vestry apparently had little option but to give the committee permission to place the organ 'at the end of the South Aisle or in the Gallery'.

The new Holdich organ was inaugurated in August 1867.[55] The following month William Pollard wrote to the *Musical Standard* complaining about the new organ's inappropriate registration, with its 'screaming treble pipes'.[56] He also commented on its casework and location:

> The appearance of the new one, blocking up light from one window and hiding another, was an object of wonder and surprise, and the dismantling of seven pews to make room for it, without leave from the Bishop, was a matter of regret to all who knew how deficient the church is of proper accommodation.[57]

So, to compound other errors, no faculty had been obtained for the installation. Summarising his litany of complaints, Pollard highlighted the inherent conflict of interests: 'This is the fourth organ within about six years at our Parish Church. It is very seldom indeed that a subscription can be obtained in any parish as readily as this has been, and it is very lamentable that the best has not been made of the money.'[58]

Organists

Although few Hertfordshire churches had an organ during the late eighteenth century, many elite households had chamber organs.[59] As with so many other trends, this was influenced by court fashion. Shortly after George III's accession to the throne, the *St James's Chronicle* reported 'A curious Organ is put up in one of the Apartments at St James's, upon which we are told, his Majesty performs generally about an Hour every Evening.'[60] Metropolitan organists were quick to seek additional income by offering tuition to both ladies and gentlemen, and an advertisement of 1763 offered home tuition, again suggesting that chamber organs were by no means uncommon:

> JOHN SCOTT, ORGANIST [...] continues teaching the ORGAN and HARPSICHORD, not only the Practical but Theoretical part; the want of which knowledge makes so many Ladies and Gentlemen often give it up [...] Attendance for Gentlemen are Mondays and Thursdays; and for Ladies, Tuesdays and Fridays. Likewise Ladies and Gentlemen taught at their own Houses.[61]

On a visit to Gorhambury in 1819 a guest noted that Charlotte, Countess Grimston, 'played on the organ' after dinner.[62] Certain households employed a private organist and music master to teach household members, provide music and lead psalm-singing during family prayers. Where none could be found by personal recommendation it was not unusual to advertise, as seen in a 1790 notice: 'WANTED. ORGANIST. In a gentleman's family. A person capable of conducting Psalmody in a private chapel; likewise qualified for giving instructions on the harpsichord or piano forte [...].'[63]

Church organists' association with religion may have enhanced their status, respectability and eligibility for private patronage as teachers and, in Hertfordshire, several church organists were described as 'gentlemen' during the 1780s and 1790s (see Table 5.1).[64] Nevertheless, many organists derived their income from playing in both sacred and secular venues. Rohr stated that 'London cathedrals and the royal chapels were exceptional in that they tended to hire organists and composers who had achieved prominence in the more cosmopolitan and secular London musical world.'[65] This may have had more to do with the proximity of church and theatre organs in the capital than with issues of status. It was only to be expected that organists should wish to supplement their church income in this manner, given that it was usually insufficient to live on, as is the case in most churches today. But, until the early nineteenth century, similar dual engagements were also found in Hertfordshire, where, as in London, certain church organists had strong links with the worlds of theatre and dance, which probably provided their main income.

The Hertfordshire organist with the most prominent theatrical connections was Thomas William Luppino of Hertford.[66] Luppino's grandfather had been a renowned London theatrical scene painter, employed in fitting up Westminster Abbey for the first two Handel commemorations in 1784 and 1785 before retiring to live with his grandson in Hertford.[67] By 1832 Luppino had established his 'Fore Street Concert Room', known as 'Mr Luppino's Theatre', with scenery painted by his grandfather.[68]

Organists with dual church–theatre engagements sometimes allowed secular tunes to influence their performance in church. This could result in complicated arrangements of psalm tunes, with the result that the congregation could not sing with the organ. The blind organist and prolific theatrical composer Jonas Blewitt was engaged by Lionel Lyde to play at Ayot St Lawrence (see Table 5.1). According to Blewitt:

> The giving out of a psalm tune should be played as plain as possible in order that the congregation may become acquainted with the tune they are about to sing [...] nor would I advise more than one Interlude for each Psalm, as otherwise the congregation, by a too divided attention, may forget the melody.[69]

Publishing books of psalmody was another source of income for some organists, and in 1795 Blewitt published *A Complete Treatise on the Organ*. In this work, Blewitt gave several examples of his 'plain' arrangements of psalm tunes. For Psalm 100 he gave a seven-bar prelude and a twenty-one bar 'giving out', with little clue as to the tune that followed. The tune itself lasted a mere twenty bars, followed by a nine-bar interlude (symphony) to be played between verses. If this is 'plain', it gives some idea of just how complicated other arrangements may have been.

The inter-related nature of church and theatrical performances is also indicated by the public performances given on new church organs in builders' manufactories before organs were dismantled and re-erected in their intended homes. When a new instrument was ordered for Cheshunt parish church in 1791 the organ-builders Longman & Broderip announced a public performance, Jonas Blewitt 'having very obligingly offered his assistance on the occasion'.[70]

Organist–Volunteers
During the Napoleonic Wars local church organists were actively enlisted by Volunteer associations, not only to instruct bandsmen but also for added prestige. This may have given Thomas Leach, organist of Cheshunt parish church and member of the Cheshunt Volunteers, the opportunity to obtain income from sales of his composition *The Hertfordshire Yeomanry Cavalry* (1796).[71] Songs such as this would have attracted purchases from gentry households throughout the county and perhaps further afield, providing a welcome addition to his salary as a church organist. The Bishops Stortford and Hertford Volunteers also boasted church organists among their members

(see Table 5.1); indeed, there were only two other Hertfordshire parish church organists at this time, including Felix Smith of Watford, who was already aged sixty and therefore ineligible to serve.

In October 1778 George III reviewed the militia at Warley Camp in Essex. This, and similarly prestigious reviews, inspired festivities held in June 1800, when all the Hertfordshire militia, yeomanry and Volunteers were reviewed by George III in Hatfield Park – nearly 1,600 men in total, including the Royston Volunteers, commanded by Rev. Shield, and the Hitchin Volunteers, commanded by Lieutenant Colonel William Wilshere.[72] This was an enormously important social occasion, enthusiastically reported in *The Gentleman's Magazine* and commemorated in a painting by Richard Livesay (Figure 5.5).[73] The oversized royal standard prominently displayed on Hatfield House highlighted the loyalty of James Cecil, Marquess of Salisbury – Lord Lieutenant and colonel of the Hertfordshire militia – and perhaps challenged other counties to match Hertfordshire's military resources. The painting was proudly displayed in Hatfield House, but in addition prints were sold to members of military associations and those keen to associate themselves with them.

Artists were not alone in profiting from such occasions. In 1800 Charles Bridgeman, organist of All Saints, Hertford, and member of the Hertford Volunteers, composed marches for all ten Hertfordshire Volunteer associations, those with bands being scored for clarinet, bassoon, trumpet and horn, in addition to fife and drum.[74] These marches are thought to have been played at the Hatfield Review, and Bridgeman solicited further purchases from the various captains.[75] Furthermore, in 1800 Robert Bacon wrote an *Ode on the Royal Review* set to music by Bridgeman, which complemented Livesay's work, including the verse:

And see the sons of Hertford join
All emulous in martial line
Lo! Salisbury, warm'd with patriot Fire
Th'illustrous Guardian of the Shire[76]

Similar works by church organists across the country attracted purchases from officers, including a *Slow March* and *Quick Step* by William Gresham, inscribed to the Bedfordshire Volunteers.[77] As keyboard reductions were also available, works such as these provided a patriotic souvenir to be performed at home.[78]

Clearly it was advantageous for the Volunteers to have a composer in their association, but what were the church organists' motives for joining? One may have been patriotism.[79] But for many the motives may have

Figure 5.5. Above: J. Stadler, after Richard Livesay, *The Royal Review in Hatfield Park* (1802); below: detail of George III acknowledging one of the corps, complete with fife and drum. HALS, DZ/119/6/342TT Grangerised copy of Robert Clutterbuck, *History of Hertfordshire*, 6 (1800–2) reproduced with permission from Hertfordshire Archives & Local Studies.

been more prosaic, as by volunteering men might avoid either compulsory military service or the alternative of paying for a substitute. Although militia regiments could be absent for long periods, Volunteers usually remained at or near home, and only expected to be mobilised in the event of invasion or insurrection.[80] Because church organists were in short supply during this period, much trouble and expense would have been spent finding a replacement. Consequently, remaining at home was in the interests of both the organist himself and those who wanted an organist to lead choirs of charity children in the church.

At the turn of the century, other than Felix Smith of Watford the only Hertfordshire church organist who did not serve in the Volunteers was Anna Sophia Sherman, a woman and therefore ineligible.

Women organists

Doane's 1794 *Musical Directory*, largely centred on London, named 140 organists, of whom only eight were women, but, like other directories of the time, it would probably have included only the information volunteered by those listed, and made no claim to be comprehensive.[81] Only four of the late eighteenth-century organists known to have played in Hertfordshire churches were included, all of whom were men. Although Anna Sophia Sherman, organist of St Peter's, St Albans, was not listed, this cannot be regarded as a deliberate gender-related slight as Robert Perry of Bishops Stortford and the renowned Charles Bridgeman were also left out (see Table 5.1).

In Hertfordshire the first named church organist, male or female, was Mary Battell (d. 1699), organist of All Saints, Hertford.[82] Although no evidence is known for any other women church organists in England earlier than 1753, it has been suggested that the lack of press attention given to such appointments in north-east England during the eighteenth century indicates that they were not remarkable: 'women organists were possibly more frequent than is immediately apparent from surviving evidence.'[83] Shuker has suggested that women organists were accepted on the same terms as men: 'probably one of the uncelebrated triumphs of the Georgian Anglican parish church'.[84]

Sherman was organist of St Peter's, St Albans, in 1776, and received regular payments until her death aged 69 in January 1815.[85] She and many other women church organists were the daughters of organists or otherwise connected with musical families.[86] A one-off final payment to the musician and dealer George Sherman of St Peter's Street suggests that he and John Sherman were her brothers.[87] At Cheshunt, Sarah Wood was elected organist of the parish church at successive Easter vestries during the 1840s 'on condition of her teaching the children psalmody'.[88] It might be anticipated that she was appointed because she could be paid a lower salary than a man,

Table 5.2
Organists' salaries in Hertfordshire parish churches, ordered by date.

Parish	Date	Annual salary
Cheshunt	1711–1857	£10–50
Bishops Stortford	1729–1839	£20–30
All Saints, Hertford	1748–91	c.£23
Watford	1772–1845	£20–50
North Mymms	c.1786–90	c.£42
St Peter's, St Albans	1790–1835	£15–20
Abbey Church, St Albans	1820–31	8 guineas–£30
Totteridge	1823–34	c.£15
St Andrew's, Hertford	1827–55	£15
Ware	1829–52	£35
Hitchin	1838–60	£40–20
Berkhamsted	1850	£25
Northchurch	1850–69	£21
Tring	1857	£10
Broxbourne	1860	£25

Sources: HALS, DE/Hx/F48 (1748–91), DP/19/5/2 (1850), DP/21/5/5 (1804–39), DP/21/5/10 (1729–99), DP/24/5/14 (1860), DP/29/8/49–53 (1711–1857), DP/46B/8/12 (1823–34), DP/49/8/3 (1827–55), DP/53/5/8 (1838–60), DP/53/7/4 (1829–56), DP/69/5/1 (1786–90), DP/74/5/24 (1850–69), DP/90/5/1 (1811–49), DP/90/8/2 (1828–31), DP/93/5/4–5 (1787–1835), DP/111/5/1 (1857), DP/116/5/1 (1829–59), DP/117/5/1 (1823–45), DP/117/8/2–3 (1772–1845).

but she received £30 annually throughout the period of her employment, towards the higher end of the range of salaries paid to Hertfordshire organists during this period (see Table 5.2), suggesting that she was elected on merit alone.

Like Wood, many women organists were spinsters. Although some resigned on marriage, in London there are many instances of them continuing.[89] Although Wood was replaced in 1843, she was reappointed in 1850, by which time she was married with three children, indicating no insuperable prejudice against the employment of married women.[90] Hertfordshire sources therefore support the growing evidence that it was neither unusual nor unacceptable for town churches to have a professional woman organist during the late eighteenth and early nineteenth centuries.

Nevertheless, discrimination against the appointment of women organists elsewhere became widespread, first becoming apparent during the 1830s, when Christchurch, Spitalfields, advertised for an organist stating 'N.B. No female or blind person may apply.'⁹¹ Discriminatory advertisements continued throughout the mid-1800s, and in 1865 the vicar of Great Amwell advertised 'WANTED a YOUNG PERSON (Male) capable of Playing the HARMONIUM in a VILLAGE'.⁹² It has been suggested that discrimination against women was due to 'societal conventions' that limited their public music-making.⁹³ In 1857 a male organist writing under the sobriquet 'Pedal' argued:

> their very dress is against them, since it impedes their pedalling […] if a lady to overcome this difficulty raises her dress a foot or so, I think every one will grant that it is by no means becoming […] More than this, the various positions in which a lady when pedalling is obliged to place herself […] is extremely indelicate, if not indecent.⁹⁴

He continued 'No female but a Bloomer should be an organist', referring to the craze for women cyclists to wear bloomers, perhaps out of a sense of decorum, but more importantly so that they did not catch their skirts in the moving parts of the bicycle. 'Pedal' may have had a valid point about dresses impeding the use of organ pedals when one considers the fashion for crinolines in the late 1850s and early 1860s. But another correspondent countered that, instead, women's dress showed the superiority of their pedalling technique, as

> numerous male players require to see the pedals before they can use them […] ladies are debarred from this aid to precision, as their crinoline distends their ample dresses, until the pedals are totally concealed. And yet they do use them most correctly, as I can testify, having heard several very excellent lady performers within the last two or three weeks.⁹⁵

It seems very likely that, consciously or subconsciously, most objections to women organists had their origins in financial considerations. This is because women organists often demanded only a small salary, or sometimes none at all,⁹⁶ which led to some churches preferring to appoint women and contributed to declining rates of pay for male organists. Furthermore, by paying an otherwise unprovided-for woman a small salary as organist she would be less of a drain on the parish charities or the poor rate. In 1821 Whitaker drew attention to this practice in his *Seraph*. Criticising the singing of charity children in certain churches, he attached part of the blame to the charitable motive behind the appointment of the organist: 'to heighten the effect, they have been accompanied on a fine and powerful organ by a miserable performer, who has been selected more as an object of charity than as a person of talent'.⁹⁷

Figure 5.6. Memorial window to the organist Emily Ryley at Holy Cross, Sarratt (*c.*1919).

When campaigning against the debarment of women in 1854 *The Lady's Companion* argued that this was 'one of the few appointments open to women of education', which was sought often 'to maintain respectably the slenderly remunerated visiting governess; or the humble annuitant, whose means without such assistance would be inadequate to her support'.[98] The Lady Organists' Association was founded in 1858, hoping to 'do much to silence the paltry rivalry and clamour which is now obviously rife at most organist elections'.[99]

Playing the organ was also considered a suitable occupation for trained blind persons and, again, some may have been employed for charitable reasons. When in 1858 a finger organ replaced the barrel organ in Broxbourne parish church, the first organist was Joseph George Barkwith of Woolwich, who had trained as an organist after an accident left him blind.[100] At Bengeo, 20-year-old Lydia Hawkes was the first organist when the organ was installed in the newly rebuilt church in May 1860, and the *Herts Guardian* reported 'The organist is blind, but she plays very nicely.'[101]

With payments rarely involved, the incidence of women organists is under-recorded, and so census returns, personal testimony and contemporary accounts form the core of the evidence for their involvement. In 1831 Ellen Olive wrote that she took organ lessons prior to her marriage to the rector of Ayot St Lawrence 'so as to be able to perform in his church', because 'If she did not play the organ, nobody else would.'[102]

Generally, church stained-glass windows of organists from the nineteenth century onwards depict St Cecilia, the patron saint of musicians. However, a memorial window in Sarratt parish church depicts Mrs Ryley, who had married the vicar in 1864 and became the church organist when an organ was installed shortly afterwards (Figure 5.6). According to the 1911 census she had eleven children, of whom ten survived.[103] Since barrel-and-finger organs were advertised for use when no organist was available, they may have come into their own when women organists faced similar child-rearing duties or were unable or unwilling to play regularly.

A newly introduced harmonium was often played by a woman, and in Albury parish church the men's choir, formed in 1856 to replace the singers, was accompanied by Mrs Bayliff.[104] Few harmonium players were paid, an enduring consequence of the rise in voluntary organists. At Little Munden, Elizabeth Surtees, daughter of Henry Edward Surtees, MP for Hertfordshire, gave a harmonium to the church and taught the newly formed choir. But when she married in 1864 and left the parish, her sisters were left to do 'the best they could to supply her place'.[105]

At All Saints, Radwell, the situation was perhaps worse still. In 1837 'a very neat and sweet-toned' barrel organ had been presented by Miss Horsefall of Radwell House.[106] The instrument played '33 very nice tunes, some suited to all sorts of hymns, whether of a sorrowful or a joyous nature'.[107] When a new family took up residence at Radwell House they considered a harmonium more appropriate and, with the rector's permission, placed one in the chancel, where it was played by a young lady. But the family moved away and took the harmonium with them, with the result that the young lady no longer took any part in the church's music-making. This left the barrel organ to be operated by a gardener who had never played it before. Turning the barrel erratically he 'left the congregation quite behind', which 'excited the risibilities of the young ladies, the volatile properties of whose minds exploded in a suppressed laugh'.[108] 'An Observer' commented 'If people will forego their office, and have novices to officiate and ladies to do as they please with the singing, what must they expect but that the service of God will be ridiculed.'[109]

Temperley stated that sometimes the vicar's wife or daughter was the organist in country parishes because 'a professional player was unlikely to reside within easy distance of the church'.[110] A more compelling argument is that the vicar's female relatives were able, and often willing, to work for little or nothing. In 1857 *The Church of England Quarterly Review* stated that 'the wives and sisters of the clergy form an excellent staff of organists, where there are no funds to secure professional help'.[111] In 1847 the *Parish Choir* observed 'It must often happen in country places, that were it not for the zeal of some good churchwoman, there would be no organ played; but where there is a large organ and a salary can be given, it is surely best on every account, to have a man as organist and choir-master.'[112]

Nevertheless, in some churches prejudice against women organists may have been attributable to the unwillingness of male choir members to take directions from a female.[113] Certainly, when a new organ was installed at St Michael's, St Albans, in 1867, the *Hertford Mercury and Reformer* reported 'Miss Hughes is the organist, and Mr B. Agutter, of St Augustine's, Hereford-square [South Kensington], is choirmaster'.[114] This suggests that the appointment of a male choirmaster may have been considered preferable to leaving Miss Hughes in charge, even if he had to travel a considerable distance to undertake his duties.

Schoolmaster–organists
The establishment of a charity school was often associated with the installation of a church organ of some sort, because of the expectation that the children would attend church and their singing lead to an improvement in congregational participation. In 1847 the *Parish Choir* commented on the growing phenomenon of 'the union of the offices of organist

and schoolmaster'.[115] This was seen as an economical catch-all method of replacing singers, church bands, organists and barrel organs alike. Subscriptions were initiated at Hatfield in 1851 for both the National School and a finger organ for the church, indicating that the two were still firmly linked in attempts to improve music-making in the church.[116] Ninety-one subscribed to the school, thirty-four to the organ and a further twenty-eight to both.

National School trustees often expected their teachers to teach psalmody and, of the 256 advertisements for elementary school teachers in the National Society's *Monthly Paper* for 1853, almost a third required Sunday work as organist, choirmaster, Sunday school master, parish clerk and occasionally sexton.[117] By 1855 this had risen to half.[118] Schoolmasters and schoolmistresses were expected to sit with their pupils in church, and a plan of the Barkway gallery includes a seat captioned 'Schoolmaster's and mistress's – right of office'.[119] When an organ was also located in the gallery, as in many Hertfordshire churches, the seat would have been conveniently placed for the schoolteacher to play the finger organ or operate the barrel organ. But in 1857 'Pedal' argued that women were 'not able even to properly control a pack of national schoolboys, much less a choir of men'.[120] Moreover, a typical advertisement from 1854 sought a 'Trained and Certificated' schoolmistress, stating that 'It is most probable that one would be preferred whose Husband or Brother could manage the Boys or act as Organist.'[121] This suggests that certain parishes either did not expect women to be able to play or would prefer them not to. It also implies that women found it difficult to control boys. But during the 1820s Elizabeth Neave was so successful at turning the barrel organ and teaching the charity children to sing at East Barnet that she was paid to do the same in neighbouring Chipping Barnet.[122]

Oversupply of organists
By the mid-nineteenth century there was an oversupply of organists. One reason was the recent invention of the small upright 'cottage piano', which was affordable even by tradesmen and resulted in a 'multiplication of piano players'.[123] A second reason was the National Society's success in promoting organ-playing among its teachers, and a third was an increasing obsession with gaining music diplomas, particularly among men, who were more likely to be able to study for them.[124] Although during the 1830s schoolteachers' duties may have included operating a barrel organ, by the 1850s the sheer number of trained organists meant that non-organists were at a distinct disadvantage when applying for a teaching position. In a paper given to the Ecclesiological Society in 1850, the choirmaster Thomas Helmore commented:

it is a certain fact, that whereas ten years ago, nobody, in the engagement of a schoolmaster, ever thought of inquiring about his musical capacity, men defective in this point, but otherwise of unexceptionable character and attainments, find it next to impossible to obtain employment.[125]

The ability and willingness of college-trained teachers to play a finger organ exacerbated the pressure on organists' salaries. By the 1860s the oversupply was clearly seen in Hertfordshire and, when the post of organist at St Mary's, Hemel Hempstead, was advertised in October 1863, fifty candidates applied and six auditioned, coming from such geographically diverse places as London, Kent, Chipping Norton, Sheffield and Liverpool.[126] In 1864 Dickens alluded to such a situation in a fictitious account of Grumbleton, where the vicar was swamped with applications after advertising for 'a trained and certified schoolmistress, for a mixed rural school, to teach singing and play the organ'.[127] Again, this throws into sharp focus the fact that money, rather than impropriety or incompetence, was probably the root of much of the antipathy felt towards women organists; in 1857 the editor of *The Musical World* attributed the prejudice against women to the oversupply of organists.[128] If ladies were declared ineligible, not only would there be enough places for men, but they would also receive more reasonable remuneration.

Since women were willing to work for a lower salary, the wages offered to both men and women dwindled, and in many more churches organists' posts became voluntary. In 1862 Victoria Snelling took the vicar of North Mymms to court, unsuccessfully claiming £6 5s for a quarter's salary as organist.[129] The defendant said that on the illness of the regular organist Miss Snelling had kindly offered to deputise gratuitously: 'It was very friendly of Miss Snelling to offer to help them in an emergency, but it was quite impossible to engage her as organist.'[130]

For many churches it proved very difficult to find the funding for an organ and, even where this had been possible, it was then just as difficult to find the money to pay an organist. One obvious solution was to use a barrel organ but, as will be seen in the next chapter, the motives for installing a church barrel organ were originally aspirational rather than economical.

Endnotes

1. R. McGuinness and H.D. Johnstone, 'Concert Life in England I', in: H.D. Johnstone and R. Fiske (eds), *The Eighteenth Century: Music in Britain*, The Blackwell History of Music in Britain, vol. 4 (Oxford, 1990), p. 65.
2. N. McKendrick, J. Brewer and J.H. Plumb, *The Birth of a Consumer Society. The Commercialization of Eighteenth-century England* (London, 1982), pp. 9-11.
3. *St James's Chronicle* (14 August 1779).
4. *World and Fashionable Advertiser* (18 October 1792).
5. Arnold, *Compleat Psalmodist*, 5th edn (1761), p. iii.
6. Temperley, *Parish Church*, p. 101; N. Thistlethwaite, *The Making of the Victorian Organ* (Cambridge, 1990), p. 67.
7. HALS, DP/117/8/1–3.
8. *Public Advertiser* (8 and 21 August 1766).
9. *Gentleman's Magazine* (2 August 1766).
10. *Ibid.*
11. D. Shuker, 'More than "Distinguished Ornaments"? Women Organists in Late-Georgian England', *Organists' Review*, XCVI (February 2010), p. 10.
12. *General Evening Post* (26 November 1761).
13. *Morning Post* (7 August 1776).
14. Camden Local Studies and Archives Centre, P/GB/M/1/1 Vestry minutes (1788).
15. Anon., *Concerts of Antient Music* (London, 1791), p. v.
16. HALS, DP/69/5/1 Accounts (1762–1860).
17. *The History of Parliament*, accessed at <http://www.historyofparliamentonline.org/>.
18. M. Cooke, *Twelve Psalm Tunes (in Four Parts) Composed for the Use of the Church at North Mims […]* (London, ?1790); see also I. Cutts (ed.), *Twelve psalm tunes composed for the use of the church at North Mymms* (Peterborough, 2016).
19. Gammon, '"Babylonian Performances"', pp. 72–3; Obelkevich, *Religion*, p. 147.
20. HALS, DP/21/5/5 Churchwardens' accounts (1827–29); DP/116/5/1–2 Churchwardens' accounts (1794–1868).
21. HALS, DP/93/5/3–5. See Chapter 4, p. 98.
22. Sheldrick, *Three Centuries*, p. 10.
23. LPL, FP Randolph 12/49 (1810).
24. HALS, DP/117/8/1–3.
25. HALS, DP/64/5/6; BARS, P34/5/1–3.
26. HALS, DE/X840/7/1 Sir James Craufurd, 'Aldbury Church, Hertfordshire' (1961).
27. M. Feakes, 'St Peter's Church, Lilley', *Transactions of the East Herts Archaeological Society*, 4/II (1910), pp. 188–9.
28. *HMR* (31 January 1863), p. 3; (25 July 1863), p. 3.
29. H. Senar, *Little Gaddesden and Ashridge* (Chichester, 1983), p. 165.
30. H.M. Prescott, *Notes on Caddington Church* (Luton, 1937), p. 34.
31. HALS, DP/94/8/1 Vestry minutes (1841); DP/94/29/4 Frederick Henshaw, ms history of St Stephens (1935).
32. *HMR* (4 September 1841), p. 2.
33. For example by Obelkevich, *Religion*, p. 147.
34. St Mary Magdalene's, Caldecote, is now a redundant church in the care of Friends of Friendless Churches.
35. J. Baron, *Scudamore organs, or, Practical hints respecting organs for village churches and small chancels, on improved principles* (London, 1858).
36. M. Kilbey, 'A "St Cecilia Organ" for Wormley', *Organists' Review* (September 2018), pp. 54–5.
37. HALS, DP/126/5/1 Churchwardens' accounts (1861); DP/126/8/2 Vestry minutes (1852–61); British Institute of Organ Studies, *National Pipe Organ Register*, accessed at <http://www.npor.org.uk> D00108 and D07146.

38 *HMR* (19 May 1860), p. 2; (2 June 1860), p. 3.
39 Thistlethwaite, *Victorian Organ*, p. 311.
40 *HMR* (10 August 1861), p. 3.
41 Namely the Tory MPs Henry Meux, Edward Bulwer-Lytton and Abel Smith (d. 1898); *HG* (27 May 1856), p. 3.
42 *HMR* (26 November 1859), p. 3.
43 Son of the Bishop of London. See Chapter 1, pp. 12–13.
44 *HG* (27 October 1855), p. 4.
45 *HMR* (13 April 1861), p. 2; (11 May 1861), p. 2.
46 *HMR* (29 April 1865), p. 5; (20 May 1865), p. 3; (9 September 1865), p. 2; (9 February 1867), p. 2.
47 *HMR* (15 April 1865), p. 4.
48 *HG* (29 April 1865), p. 5.
49 *Ibid.*, p. 2.
50 *HMR* (13 May 1865), p. 2.
51 *HMR* (9 February 1867), p. 2.
52 *HG* (20 July 1867), p. 4. Claughton became the first Bishop of St Albans in 1877.
53 HALS, DP/49/8/2–5.
54 *Ibid.*
55 *HG* (10 August 1867), p. 4.
56 *Musical Standard* (14 September 1867), p. 162.
57 *Ibid.*
58 *Ibid.*
59 See above, p. 115.
60 *St James's Chronicle* (20 August 1761).
61 *Gazetteer and London Daily Advertiser* (14 September 1763).
62 N. King, *The Grimstons of Gorhambury* (Chichester, 1983), p. 103.
63 *World and Fashionable Advertiser* (10 February 1790).
64 D. Rohr, *The Careers of British Musicians 1750–1810* (Cambridge, 2001), p. 93.
65 *Ibid.*, p. 90.
66 See above, p. 116.
67 *Court Magazine and Monthly Critic* (1 June 1845); D. Forbes, *The Artist and the Organist* (Ware, 2005), p. 9.
68 Forbes, *Artist*, pp. 87–8.
69 J. Blewitt, *A Complete Treatise on the Organ* (London, 1795), p. 43.
70 *World and Fashionable Advertiser* (12 October 1791).
71 T. Leach, *The Hertfordshire Yeomanry Cavalry, A new song composed by Mr Leach organist of Cheshunt, Herts* (London, 1796).
72 Anon., *A narrative of the preparations made at Hatfield* (London, 1818), p. 13; J.D. Sainsbury, *The Hertfordshire Yeomanry – An Illustrated History 1794–1920* (Welwyn, 1994), p. 29; see Chapter 4, p. 104–5.
73 *Gentleman's Magazine* (12 June 1800).
74 C. Bridgeman, *Marches composed for the Use of the Hertfordshire Volunteers* (London, 1800).
75 HALS, DE/Hx/F9 Draft of letter sent by Charles Bridgeman (1800).
76 R. Bacon, *Ode on the Royal Review of the Hertfordshire Volunteers in Hatfield Park June 13th 1800* (London, 1800).
77 *Northampton Mercury* (12 May 1804), p. 1.
78 See also Herbert and Barlow, *Music and the British Military*, p. 123.
79 R.J.S. Stevens and M. Argent (eds), *Recollections of R.J.S. Stevens, an Organist in Georgian London* (London, 1992), pp. 130–1.
80 Gee, *Volunteer Movement*, p. 3.
81 J. Doane, *A musical directory for the year 1794* (London, 1794).
82 Sheldrick, *Three Centuries*, pp. 9–10; D. Baldwin, 'Battell, Ralph (1649–1713)', *ODNB*.
83 D. Dawe, *Organists of the City of London 1666–1850. A Record of one Thousand*

Organists with an Annotated Index (Purley, 1983), p. 3; R. Southey, *Music-making in North-east England during the Eighteenth Century* (Aldershot, 2006), p. 112.
84 D. Shuker, 'The Pitfalls of Received Wisdom: Women Organists in Anglian Churches and Chapels in Great Britain from 1750 to 1850', *Organ Yearbook*, XXXIX (2010), p. 111.
85 HALS, DP/93/1/28 Register of burials (1815); DP/93/5/3–5; P. Williams (ed.), *The Leffler Manuscript*: facsimile edition (Reigate, 2010), p. 129.
86 Dawe, *Organists*, p. 4; Shuker, '"Distinguished ornaments"?', p. 8.
87 HALS, LSGB/2 Gaol Book (1798); W. Le Hardy, *Notes & Extracts from The Sessions Records*, Hertfordshire County Records, vol. IV (Hertford, 1923), pp. 132–3.
88 HALS, DP/29/8/48–54.
89 Dawe, *Organists*, p. 4.
90 1851 Census HO107/1500/f.509/p.14.
91 *Morning Post* (4 April 1837), p. 1.
92 *HG* (3 June 1865), p. 1.
93 R. Leppert, *Music and Image. Domesticity, Ideology and Socio-cultural Formation in Eighteenth-century England* (Cambridge, 1988), p. 40.
94 *Musical World* (12 September 1857), pp. 585–8, cited by J. Barger, *Elizabeth Stirling and the Musical Life of Female Organists in Nineteenth-Century England*, Music in Nineteenth-Century Britain (Aldershot, 2007), p. 41.
95 *Musical Standard* (1 May 1863), pp. 274–5.
96 Barger, *Elizabeth Stirling*, p. 46.
97 Whitaker, *Seraph*, p. 2.
98 *Lady's Companion* (August 1854), p. 100.
99 *Musical World* (1858), p. 647, cited by Barger, *Elizabeth Stirling*, pp. 44–5.
100 HALS, DP/24/6/4 Papers relating to repairs & restoration of church (1858–9); 1871 Census RG10/1349/f.29/p.16.
101 *HG* (29 May 1860), p. 5.
102 C. Oman, *Ayot Rectory. A Family Memoir* (London, 1965), pp. 125 and 144.
103 1911 Census RG14/7731/9.
104 HALS, DP/1/29/2 ms history of the parish of Albury (1939).
105 *HMR* (10 September 1864), p. 3.
106 *HMR* (31 October 1837), p. 3.
107 *Hertfordshire Express and General Advertiser* (30 September 1865), p. 3; (11 November 1865), p. 3.
108 Ibid.
109 Ibid.
110 Temperley, *Parish Church*, p. 234.
111 *Church of England Quarterly Review* (April 1857), p. 465.
112 *Parish Choir* (September 1847), p. 88.
113 Barger, *Elizabeth Stirling*, p. 65.
114 *HMR* (30 March 1867), p. 3.
115 *Parish Choir* (July 1847), pp. 154–5.
116 HALS, RDC/7/69/35 List of subscribers (1851).
117 J.T. Smith, '"The Parson's Fag": the Schoolteacher as the Servant of the Church in the second half of the Nineteenth Century', *Journal of Educational Administration and History*, 34/1 (2002), p. 7.
118 Ibid., p. 9.
119 HALS, DP/13/25/6 Rough sketch plan of the old pews in Barkway Church (*c*.1863).
120 *Musical World* (12 September 1857), pp. 585–6.
121 National Society, *Monthly Paper* (June 1854), p. 210.
122 HALS, DP/16/5/1–2; DP/15/5/2.
123 J.S. Curwen, *Studies in Church Music* (London, 1880), cited by Temperley, *Parish Church*, p. 238.
124 W. Hillsman, 'Women in Victorian Church Music: Their Social, Liturgical and Performing

Roles in Anglicanism', in W.J. Sheils and D. Wood (eds), *Studies in Church History, 27: Women in the Church* (Oxford, 1990), p. 449.
125 *Ecclesiologist* (August 1850), p. 104.
126 *HMR* (31 October 1863), p. 3.
127 C. Dickens, *All the Year Round* (26 March 1864), pp. 154–6.
128 *Musical World* (18 September 1857); Barger, *Elizabeth Stirling*, p. 41.
129 *HMR* (5 April 1862), p. 4.
130 *Ibid.*

Chapter 6
Church barrel organs

Most of the musical instruments used in parish churches during the eighteenth and nineteenth centuries are familiar; however, reference to the widespread use of church barrel organs is often met with astonishment by those unfamiliar with music-making of the period. By the mid-nineteenth century barrel organs had become almost ubiquitous in churches, particularly in rural parishes, largely because they were much cheaper to purchase than finger organs and because there was no need to pay an organist. In 1879 the musician John Spencer Curwen wrote that, some thirty years earlier, 'there would have been found in the Church of England, all the country over, a considerable majority of barrel-organs over those played by the hands and feet'.[1]

In Hertfordshire only one working barrel organ survives in the church where it was originally used – namely St Mary's, Stanstead St Margaret (Figure 6.1) – but evidence survives for their use in sixty-six of the 136 historic Hertfordshire parishes: that is, 49 per cent, as shown in Appendix 3. This compares with other studies that found barrel organs in 3 per cent of parishes in Cornwall, 6 per cent in Lincolnshire, 12 per cent in Rutland, 13 per cent in Sussex and 21 per cent in Northamptonshire.[2] Although this might suggest that Hertfordshire had an unusually high percentage, a more likely explanation is that the other studies tended to concentrate on either church band instruments or organs, without necessarily specifying whether they were finger or barrel organs. Furthermore, because some parishes replaced their original barrel organ with another, of the seventy-eight organs known to have been used in Hertfordshire churches between 1760 and 1850, sixty-two – in other words, 82 per cent of the total number – are thought to have been barrel organs.[3]

The orthodoxy is that disputes between singers and clergy often led to the installation of a barrel organ, and that it was an unwelcome innovation. Yet Drage has suggested that the decline of the church band owed much to industrialisation and the accompanying migration from country to town,

MUSIC-MAKING IN THE HERTFORDSHIRE PARISH

Figure 6.1. Front (above) and back (below) of barrel-and-finger organ in west gallery of St Mary's, Stanstead St Margaret. Photos: M. Glover.

rather than to the introduction of a barrel organ; moreover, Smith found that in Oldham and Saddleworth the introduction of an organ did not necessarily lead to the removal of the band.[4] Indeed, anecdotal circumstances surrounding the introduction of the Aldenham barrel organ provide the only known example of such an occurrence in Hertfordshire, where the vicar Caleb Lomax is said to have objected when the church band took their instruments to the public house 'to assist in revels' during the 1820s. The band resigned in a body, upon which Lomax drove up to London and returned in triumph bearing a 'grinding organ'.[5]

Disputes between singers and the clergy have been recorded in Sussex, Somerset, Norfolk and Wiltshire.[6] Yet the evidence suggests that in many cases the main impetus for the introduction of a church barrel organ was the establishment of a charity school, so that children's singing could be used to encourage the congregation to sing, and this included many churches where there had been no singing at all.

Figure 6.2. Crank handle, locking bolt and toothed bar of T.C. Bates & Son barrel organ at St Andrew's, Letheringsett (Norfolk).

Figure 6.3. T.C. Bates & Son barrel organ used at St Mary's, Stocking Pelham, until 1917. Hertford Museum, HETFM.3399.

CHURCH BARREL ORGANS

Figure 6.4. J.C. Buckler, 'Westmill church' (1841), showing the H. Bryceson organ in the west gallery. HALS, DE/Bg John Chessell Buckler, *Views of Hertfordshire* (4 vols, 1830–41), 2, p. 179 reproduced with permission from Hertfordshire Archives & Local Studies.

Types of barrel organ

Barrel organs have metal and/or wooden pipes, and are operated by a cylindrical wooden barrel, each instrument commonly having a selection of between one and six barrels. Each barrel is pinned around its circumference with flat metal staple-like bridges of varying lengths. The organ is blown by bellows, and when the barrel is turned by a crank handle (Figure 6.2, foreground), the bridges open valves in the windchest to sound the notes, the length of each bridge determining the length of the note. Most barrels for use in church were pinned with between six and twelve metrical psalm tunes, which could be changed by shifting the barrel horizontally and locking in place with a bolt located in a toothed bar. The same tune could be repeated as many times as required until the barrel was released and moved.

Two main types of barrel organ were used in churches, but the non-specific term 'barrel organ' can be applied to either of them. The first type was a barrel-and-finger organ. This instrument was the most versatile, being an ordinary 'finger organ' with a manual (keyboard), but with barrels for use when no organist was available. An existing chamber organ could be converted to a barrel-and-finger organ by the addition of a barrel mechanism, as at Stanstead St Margaret (see Figure 6.1). The second type was a barrel organ with no manuals, also known as a hand, cylinder, box, winch, psalmodic or, disparagingly, grinding organ. These were more common as they were usually smaller, lacked the full chromatic range and were therefore cheaper (Figure 6.3).

In some instruments the crank-handle operated the barrel and pumped the bellows, but in others these were separate operations, sometimes requiring the help of an additional person. Barrel organs were usually placed towards the front of a west gallery and operated from the rear, as per an advertisement of 1841: 'For SALE, an excellent BARREL ORGAN for a church [...] plays behind as usual'.[7] Figure 6.4 shows the Bryceson barrel organ located near the front of the west gallery of St Mary's, Westmill. Rarely, church barrel organs were driven by clockwork, and these were known as machine, self-acting or self-playing organs.

A barrel attachment or 'dumb organist' was occasionally purchased with a new finger organ for use in the absence of the organist. As early as 1783 the organist John Arnold offered to supply 'curious machines that will play by barrel on the keys of any organ, a set of voluntaries, psalm tunes, &c. very proper for a nobleman's chapel, or a country church, where there is an organ, and an organist not easily to be acquired'.[8] The barrel attachment was positioned above the manual with the 'trackers' (wooden fingers) placed over the keys. Although the dumb organist seldom extended for the whole compass of the manual, the section covered was, unlike the barrel organ, fully chromatic, so harmonies pinned on the barrel could be closer to those found in printed music (Figure 6.5).

CHURCH BARREL ORGANS

Figure 6.5. T.C. Bates & Son dumb organist at St Andrew's, Fersfield (Norfolk). Above: not in use; below: tipped forwards into playing position. Photos: M. Glover.

Origins

The idea of a barrel-operated mechanical organ was first suggested by the Greek inventor and mathematician Ctesibius in around 135 BC, and such an instrument had been built by the ninth century AD.[9] The building of organs, mechanical organs and clocks were parallel developments, eventually resulting in technical masterpieces such as the clockwork organ built by Thomas Dallam in 1599 as a present from Elizabeth I to Mohammed III, Sultan of Turkey.[10] During the early eighteenth century a renewed interest in barrel-operated mechanical organs developed when a fascination with automata and clocks became integrated with the fashionable taste for organ music. Certain members of the elite sought the means to display an impressive domestic instrument capable of performing many more notes than would be possible if played by a single organist. One such was Sarah, dowager Duchess of Marlborough, who in 1737 set her heart on buying a chamber organ fitted with a barrel to play music, at this date still an exotic and highly sought-after piece of machinery. She wrote:

> I am now in pursuit of getting the finest piece of music that ever was heard; it is a thing that will play eight tunes. Handel and all the great musicians say that it is beyond any thing they can do; and this may be performed by the most ignorant person; and when you are weary of those eight tunes, you may have them changed for any other that you like. This I think much better than going to an Italian opera, or an assembly. This performance has been lately put into a lottery, and all the Royal Family chose to have a great many tickets, rather than to buy it, the price being I think £1000, infinitely a less sum than some Bishopricks have been sold for. And a gentleman won it who I am in hopes will sell it, and if he will, I will buy it, for I cannot live to have another made, and I will carry it into the country with me.[11]

Unfortunately, it is not known whether she was successful in her purchase. One of the wealthiest women in the country, the duchess had spent a high-profile life in court and political circles, but had strong links with Hertfordshire. She spent lengthy periods at Holywell House, St Albans, which had been her childhood home, and it is possible that this was the 'country' property to which she referred.

In addition to playing extracts from fashionable oratorios, domestic barrel organs could be used to accompany dancing or dining and to support psalm-singing at family prayers. Such organs would be supplied with both sacred and secular tunes, usually pinned on separate barrels. The largest eighteenth-century example in the country was the barrel-and-finger organ commissioned in *c.*1767 by John Stuart, 3rd Earl of Bute, after his resignation from George III's government.[12] Having purchased Luton Hoo in neighbouring Bedfordshire in 1762, he engaged Robert Adam to redesign the mansion. Christopher Pinchbeck (d. 1783), celebrated mechanic and clockmaker to George III, is thought to have advised on the construction of the organ, which had an astonishing fifty-eight barrels, including thirty-six devoted to arrangements of Handel oratorios.[13]

Although most of the barrels were removed for use with a second organ at Bute's Hampshire residence during the 1780s, this instrument may have influenced the acquisition of organs by gentry in adjacent Hertfordshire. In 1784 an auction of the effects of Frederick Young, son of the rector of Welwyn, included 'every requisite Convenience for a genteel Family [including] a fine-toned Organ with four barrels'.[14] Similarly, in May 1774 John Radcliffe MP, who had close family ties to the county aristocracy, purchased a Charles Green chamber organ fitted with two barrels.[15] This was used at his residence at Hitchin Priory, which had been a Carmelite house until its dissolution in 1539. Radcliffe's London address was Grosvenor Square, yet it seems possible that his purchase was influenced not only by encountering similar organs in the capital but also by the organ at Luton Hoo, eight miles distant as the crow flies.[16] His subsequent hiring of 'a Band of Horns & Clarionets and Bassoon' from London indicates that the barrel organ was intended as a substitute rather than a permanent replacement for live musicians.[17] Radcliffe clearly considered the band and barrel organ alike to be both suitable and fashionable for polite music-making. Yet, as the vogue for mechanical music grew, some began to see the potential for supplanting rather than deputising for live musicians, and this had long-lasting repercussions for church music-making.

The use of barrel organs in church to circumvent the lack of an organ or organist was first suggested in 1722 by the engraver and antiquary George Vertue after learning of a musical clock made by Christopher Pinchbeck (d. 1732), the equally talented father of Bute's barrel organ builder.[18] In 1731, only nine years after Vertue's suggestion, the inventor Justinian Morse of Chipping Barnet designed a mechanical organ on which

> any person unskilled in musick may be instantly instructed to play psalm tunes, voluntaries, anthems, or any other musick, though never so difficult […] Designed for the use of churches or chapels in such parishes as cannot afford, or are unwilling to be at the expence of the constant attendance of an organist, or for gentlemen's houses.[19]

In 1732 Morse installed an organ in his parish church. It is possible that this instrument was fitted with his patented mechanism, but the organ was removed in 1749.[20] No barrel organs are known to have been used in parish churches until the 1760s, when John Arnold reported seeing advertisements for organs fitted with barrels set with voluntaries and 'most of our ancient Psalm-Tunes'.[21] Arguing that barrel organs 'are very commodious for Churches in remote Country Places, where an Organist is not easily to be had or maintained', Arnold explained they 'may also be played by a Person (unskilled in Music) who is only to turn a Winch round which causes the barrels to play the tunes they are set to'.[22] He recommended the use of barrel-and-finger organs in church because 'a person might play on them at pleasure, notwithstanding the barrels'.[23] This suggested use of church barrel organs pre-dated the use of treble instruments that he observed in 1779, as described in Chapter 4. This sequence of events is the reverse of the accepted progression whereby barrel organs were introduced to replace singers and church bands, suggesting the need for a significant amendment to the orthodoxy. Arnold himself went on to supply London-built organs, and in 1783 advertised

> Small organs, of a new construction, that will stand in a parish clerk's pew, and play by barrel a regular set of psalm tunes, and some voluntaries if required, from £10 to £20 &c. of great utility in country churches (where there are no choir of singers) to lead the congregation, in a regular performance of psalmody.[24]

This clearly indicates that barrel organs were considered appropriate for use in churches both with no organist and with no singers.

In 1824 an anonymous supporter of the 'National System of Education' wrote to the High-Church *Christian Remembrancer* outlining the advantages of introducing plain psalmody 'into every National School'.[25] Although the short-term benefits would be 'the gradual removal out of every Church of much discordant music' and the eradication of 'the irreverent behaviour of the singers' in the gallery, the long-term benefits were of prime importance. He or she argued that, 'as these children grow up, and descend into the congregation', they would carry the knowledge of singing with them, and congregational psalmody would be restored little by little, an argument used repeatedly since Gibson's 1724 Charge, but to little effect. Possibly indicating that the correspondent was a barrel-organ builder, the suggestion was then made that 'If some musical instrument be required to conduct the children, I would recommend the introduction of hand-organs, which may be purchased at all sizes and prices, and are now carried to very great perfection.'[26]

In 1829 Rev. Henry Soames also recommended the use of a barrel organ, again arguing that, 'as it plays only certain fixed tunes, the congregation, from often hearing, is likely to correctly acquire them'.[27] At the time, Soames was rector of Shelley and Little Laver and stipendiary curate of

Figure 6.6. Alice Mary Oliver, 'Bovinger church' (1862). *St Germain's, Bobbingworth* [church guide] (n.d.). The gentry are seated in appropriated pews with their backs firmly turned towards both the clergyman and the gallery, while the Capel Cure family, local landowners, are shown into their pew facing the pulpit. The detail below shows three figures standing at the front of the west gallery, and behind them a barrel-organ, a large group of school children and a schoolmaster holding a wand.

Bobbingworth, all in Essex. Soames particularly recommended the London organ-builders Flight & Robson, a very successful and popular firm. Figure 6.6 shows a drawing of Bobbingworth church by Alice Mary Oliver, the rector's daughter.[28] It is very likely that the barrel organ shown in her sketch was a Flight & Robson instrument introduced while Henry Soames was curate, as a girls' school and Sunday school had been established here in 1822 under the patronage of the Capel Cure family.[29]

Perhaps the most significant explanation for Flight & Robson's success was their completion in 1817 of an enormous instrument called the Apollonicon, at a cost of approximately £10,000.[30] Obtaining the Prince Regent's patronage for this project had a significant impact, as they could now style themselves 'organ builders to His Majesty'.[31] This vast barrel-and-finger organ was housed on the builders' premises at 101 St Martins Lane, London, where regular recitals were hugely influential, and 'practically all the organ recitals given in England' from 1817 until the mid-1830s were played on it.[32] The novelty wore off mid-century, and it was broken up for parts in 1881, but the name Apollonicon was used to attract new orders for organs and eventually came to be used as a general term to describe large barrel-and-finger organs.[33]

Reservations

Some clergymen had initial reservations about the propriety of introducing barrel organs. In 1797 *The Gentleman's Magazine* published a recommendation by 'B.S.' on this subject, which would have been a pressing concern for clergymen and patrons among its readers who wished to improve congregational singing. The editor argued that the use of barrel (or 'box') organs could hardly be worse than the *status quo*:

> B.S. recommends the introduction of *Box-Organs*, as helps to Singing, in our Village-Churches. He has mentioned it to several of the Clergy, who approved of it. The only doubt entertained was, that it might diminish the solemnity of the service. – We think this cannot be done more effectually than by the 'pipe, fiddle, and flute' of those *bands* of musicians placed in some distant village churches.[34]

But in 1791 Horace Walpole had described the unpleasantness of going to church 'to hear the dullest of all things, a sermon, and croaking and squalling of psalms to a hand-organ by journeymen brewers and charity children. As I am to go soon to church for ever, I do not think it my duty to *try on* my death before hand.'[35] 'Squalling' suggests the screaming high-pitched voices of children, and 'croaking' the inability of male adults to sing with them. Despite objections such as this, repeated attempts were made in successive generations to use church barrel organs to encourage congregational singing, so that similar complaints were still being made a century later. According to Charlton Lane, first curate and then rector of Little Gaddesden in the late 1800s, the church had a barrel organ that played 'Curious old tunes of the florid order embellished with twists and turns, soaring so high that the ordinary village voice was unable to reach the highest pitch and at this point the sound resembled the croaking of frogs, throaty and shrill'.[36]

In 1834 the editor of the Evangelical *Christian Observer* counselled a concerned clergyman seeking help after reading the SPCK's advice that 'Nothing is so objectionable as a barrel organ'.[37] Although agreeing that 'the name barrel organ sounds ill from vile associations', the editor offered the reassurance: 'what is the Apollonicon itself but a barrel organ?' He concluded that the clergyman had 'better avail himself of this secondary aid than allow the praises of God to remain unsung'. This supports the growing evidence that barrel organs were in many cases introduced to support music-making where there had been little or none, rather than solely to suppress unruly singers.

Evangelicals and High Churchmen alike wished to encourage congregational psalmody. The evidence suggests that both gave serious consideration to using barrel organs to do so, as, in addition to being heavily advertised in the Evangelical *Christian Observer*, they were also promoted in High-Church periodicals. In a letter to the High-Church *British Magazine*, in 1835 'R' advised that 'barrel organs are cheaper than finger-organs, and do very well for a country church', with the additional advantage of removing the need to find or pay an organist.[38] He also noted that finger organs could be fitted with a barrel, commenting that 'this is a good plan, in case of the illness or absence of the usual organist'. From August 1839 onwards the *Ecclesiastical Gazette*, a High-Church monthly publication sent post-free to every bishop, dean, chapter, college and church in England and Wales, carried advertisements from the organ-builder John Gray. Further advertisements specifically targeting those who wished to purchase barrel organs for church use quickly followed, including those placed by four more London firms: Bates, Flight & Son, Holdich and Eagles. In many churches the main impetus for the installation of a barrel organ was the establishment of a charity school, and some builders' advertisements highlighted the usefulness of their organs in teaching children to sing.[39] They also stressed their economical nature, sometimes selling them unfinished so that the church could employ a local carpenter to build the casework.[40]

Hertfordshire church barrel organs

In wealthy town parishes the installation of an organ reflected the prosperity of its inhabitants.[41] In 1794 the market town of Hitchin was 'reckoned the second in the county for number of streets, houses, and inhabitants'.[42] By 1805 the installation of an organ may have been seen as long overdue among the local gentry. Perhaps this is why Emilius Delmé Radcliffe offered the Hitchin Priory barrel-and-finger organ 'for the use of the church'.[43] Although he may simply have wished to dispose of it, this was also the year he was appointed High Sheriff of Hertfordshire, suggesting that, in addition to wishing to support church music-making, he may have wanted to make a grand gesture.[44] Yet, rather than accepting the organ 'as seen', the vestry resolved to 'send for a proper person from London to inspect the organ and to give an opinion whether it will be proper for the church'.[45] The organ-builder John King's estimate of £159 to alter and relocate the organ was accepted, and the money raised by subscription among the parishioners. No mention was made of removing the organ's barrel mechanism, so presumably it was left *in situ*. This is unlikely to have been considered a drawback by the incumbent, Joshua Ruddock. Trinity College, Cambridge, was patron of the living and, as a Trinity graduate, it is likely that Ruddock would have been familiar with the teachings of Rev. Charles Simeon, an early promoter of the use of barrel organs to support congregational singing.[46]

Hitchin's status was reflected by the installation of the organ, and it would have been enhanced by the consequent improvement in its music-making. The intention may have been for the organ to support the Society of Singers that had subscribed to Hellendaal's *Collection*, but it is more probable that it was in fact intended to support the singing of the Sunday school children. The date of the school's establishment is unknown, but by 1816 this large school taught 100 boys and 160 girls.[47]

By 1805 both Broxbourne and neighbouring Hoddesdon had barrel organs. These churches were under the patronage of Bishop Porteus, who installed the Evangelical William Jones as incumbent of both, serving the former in the morning and the latter in the afternoon.[48] Jones was a friend of the Methodist Thomas Charles, who was prominent in establishing Sunday schools in Wales, and visitation returns of 1810 recorded the presence of Sunday schools at both churches.[49] It is highly probable that they were established in around 1805, and the barrel organs introduced to support singing by the Sunday scholars, in accordance with Porteus's guidance. At Broxbourne, and probably Hoddesdon too, the organ was purchased by subscription. In theory this relieved the clergyman or patron of the sole burden of paying for the organ and enabled parishioners to show their support for the new venture, but Jones was not impressed by the demeanour of Admiral William Peere Williams-Freeman and his wife 'Mrs W.', a prominent local couple, recording in his journal in January 1804:

I rather apprehend, from her (Mrs. W.'s) letter on Sunday that she wishes to withdraw her promised subscription of 5 guineas towards the organ: if that is the case, I shall not be able to do otherwise than think very meanly of her Ladyship. When I showed Mr. Longman's proposal,[50] she rather haughtily asked who Captain Marsh was, who had rather liberally offered five guineas and expressed a sort of insolent surprise at seeing the same sum attached to my name. On my mentioning that I trusted the prompt liberality of my parishioners would render my subscription ultimately unnecessary, she was so good as to say she 'hoped I would, by no means, think of returning my subscription into my pocket &c'. If I could at all afford it, I would, with pleasure, subscribe still more; and verily I believe I should do infinitely more lasting and essential good by it to the souls of my people, than by relieving their bodily wants with the same sum.'[51]

This raises the question of whether it would have been deceitful for Rev. Jones to remove his name from the subscription list if enough wealthy parishioners had been found; unfortunately the subscription list does not survive, so the outcome is not known. Nevertheless, during the mid-nineteenth century clergymen and their families often made significant contributions towards the purchase of their church organs. Despite the Admiral being a grandson of Robert Clavering, Bishop of Peterborough, he rarely attended his parish church and, unlike Jones, had little interest in encouraging congregational singing. Jones continued:

To Mrs. W. and others who attend church irregularly, it is a matter of indifference whether there be any singing or not, and there are too many who think the whole service, the shorter, the more agreeable, but surely the 'reasonable' wishes of their Minister and of the majority of the congregation ought to be respected. I thought her remarks extremely rude and unfeeling.

In 1826 the London organ-builder R.W. Keith repaired the Broxbourne organ, removing 'bruises' (dents) from the pipes and 'setting up Pins & Regulating barrells', which suggests that it was in regular use.[52]

Bishop Randolph had installed his son Thomas as rector of Much Hadham and during his incumbency a schoolroom was built in 1818, followed by the building of a church gallery for the children and the installation of a barrel organ.[53] The use of the organ appears to have been successful – at least in principle – as it was replaced by a second in 1844.[54] The Wheathampstead west gallery barrel organ is also likely to have been installed when the school was first incorporated into the National Society in 1815. The following year the school governors reported that 'The parents of the children have attended Church more regularly'.[55] The Bishop of Lincoln was patron of

Wheathampstead, and George Thomas Pretyman, his son, was rector during this period. Much Hadham and Wheathampstead were among the most valuable livings in Hertfordshire, and their rectors well-placed to pay for both organs and organists, yet both chose to install barrel organs, providing further evidence that their use was both desirable and acceptable during this period, and in accordance with the guidance of bishops and their archdeacons.

Typical of the growing trend, in Kimpton, Thomas Brand MP of The Hoo built and supported a new charity school 'to accommodate 60 boys and 60 girls'.[56] As both church patron and MP for Hertfordshire it seems almost certain that Brand also gave Kimpton church its barrel organ. St Michael's, St Albans, also acquired a barrel organ during this period, perhaps given by a member of the Grimston family, as at Pebmarsh (Essex), another church of which they held the advowson.[57] At Pebmarsh the organ was placed in the west gallery and operated by the schoolmaster, and this is likely to have been the case at St Michael's too.

During the 1820s the retired guards officer Joseph Andrew De Lautour 'almost entirely rebuilt' St Faith's, Hexton.[58] As part of the refit, in 1826 he spent £217 19s 8d on a new organ by John Gray, including a sum for adjusting the barrels.[59] This was installed in a new west gallery flanked by tiered seating.[60] His wife was both patron of St Faith's and sole patron of the Hexton charity school, which was not 'in union' with the National Society.[61] Nevertheless, there can be little doubt that one of the main motives for installing the organ was to support the singing of the charity children seated on either side of it. Madame Lautour paid for the upkeep of both her own 'Apollonicon' and the less grand church organ.[62] Similarly, Robert Bevan of Trent Park near Barnet paid for the running costs of both domestic and church instruments.[63]

Hertfordshire evidence suggests that an organ purchased for a church was almost inevitably far less expensive than the donor's own house organ.[64] Rev. Richard Gee alluded to this fact in 1861, arguing that if a church was going to have an organ at all it should be a good one:

> The gentleman's house is not thought to be furnished unless it has a good and costly instrument, and in purchasing an organ for the worship of God, it would not be an extravagant suggestion that its cost should bear some proportion to the total cost of the instruments belonging to the worshippers.[65]

This intriguing statement suggests that in 1861 chamber organs were still found in the gentry households with which Gee was familiar, much as they had been a century earlier, and provides further evidence that donors typically gave their church an organ that cost less than their own.

Wealthy non-aristocrats also gave barrel organs to their parish churches. Although this may have signalled a desire to support their parish school and church, it also reflected an aspiration to emulate their social superiors and establish their place in the social hierarchy. In East Barnet the country house Oak Hill was purchased in 1810 by Simon Haughton Clarke of Kingston, Jamaica, one of the richest commoners in England after making a fortune through the slave trade.[66] A sweeping carriageway led down from Oak Hill to the parish church, where in 1815 David William Garrow became rector. In 1824 Haughton Clarke presented a Flight & Robson barrel organ, which was installed in the west gallery, and children of the National School were seated on either side during services.[67] Garrow was also rector of neighbouring Chipping Barnet, where in the same year another Flight & Robson barrel organ was introduced.[68] Although ostensibly purchased by subscription, the majority of the funds for this latter organ came from Keane FitzGerald, head of the only 'family of note' in Chipping Barnet, who later bequeathed considerable sums to numerous charitable causes.[69] Unfortunately it is impossible to tell which organ came first – were Haughton Clarke and FitzGerald responding to a direct appeal for funding from Garrow or simply trying to out-do one another?

This circumstance was embroidered upon by the 'silver-fork' novelist Mrs Gore in 'Hush!', her short story about Wheatam, 'a pleasant village in the county of Herts – a village of smock-frocks, straw-plaiting and pleasant faces', surely inspired by Wheathampstead.[70] Silver-fork novels offered an insight into aristocratic life and often ridiculed social climbers. Mrs Gore's cautionary tale did so by relating the purchase of 'Wheatam Priory' by Gamaliel Cribbs, a newly arrived 'city man'. Wishing to establish himself in the locality and keep up with 'Ashridge' and 'Brocket' (Hertfordshire estates owned by the late Earl of Bridgewater and the prime minister, Lord Melbourne), Cribbs' desire to present a barrel organ to the church rode roughshod over the wishes of the vestry. He persuaded the vestry that accepting the organ would save the organist's salary of forty to fifty pounds a year, not to mention the cost of a finger organ, and that, in this age of the Apollonicon, 'cylinder organs' satisfied the needs of nine out of ten parishes such as Wheatam. His winning card was that the money saved could be spent on the poor, presumably an argument well-versed in real life, and a machine-organ was duly installed. On the second Sunday the children sang four verses of the 'Morning Hymn' to the approbation of all present, but the organ then continued through eight more verses, followed by twelve verses of the 'Evening Hymn', after the overzealous sexton broke off the stop-bolt handle. With no possibility of silencing the organ, 'the tittering of the charity school was as though a thousand swallows' nests were rearing their young in

Figure 6.7. George Cruikshank, 'The Self-Playing Organ', from Mrs Gore, 'Hush!', a story about Wheatam church 'in the county of Herts'. Note the disgruntled Mr Cribbs, donor of the organ, in his well-placed appropriated pew immediately in front of the pulpit, members of the congregation in the gallery trying to stifle their laughter, the smock-wearing peasant with nowhere to sit hiding his amusement behind his straw hat, and, in the pulpit, the parson attempting to distance himself from proceedings. *Bentley's Miscellany*, XIV (July 1843) p. 72.

the roof', and the organ was removed to the churchyard where it could still be heard (Figure 6.7). *The Times* described Mrs Gore as 'the wittiest woman of her age', and it seems possible that her fiction may have been the origin of many anecdotes concerning unruly barrel organs.[71]

In the absence of support from local landowners, the clergy were often major contributors to organ subscriptions, their families sometimes paying for the entire instrument. It has been suggested that this may have demonstrated the clergy's desperation to improve parochial music,[72] but they also gave organs to mark important developments. In 1842 Abel Smith (d.1859) enlarged the parish church of Bramfield at his sole expense, paying for works that included erecting a tower and steeple, repairs and repewing. But a vote of thanks was given to the vicar's wife, Mrs Lewis Deedes, 'for her kind and very handsome present of a beautiful organ', almost certainly a barrel organ.[73]

In some parishes the clergy paid for both the organ and the National School, again indicating their inter-relatedness. Frederick Dudley Ryder, nephew of the Evangelical bishop Henry Dudley Ryder, supported Ickleford and Pirton National Schools during the 1840s, and was probably responsible for the installation of the barrel organs in both churches.[74] St Ippolyts and Great Wymondley shared a Trinity-educated vicar, with services held alternately morning and afternoon.[75] Thomas Henry Steel was appointed vicar in 1837 and, during his incumbency, the St Ippolyts vicarage was demolished in order to provide a site next to the church for the National School.[76] The barrel organs installed in both churches at around this time are likely to have been purchased by Steel himself.

Clergy in more straitened circumstances, or wishing to engage popular support, sought other means to raise the necessary funds. Preaching a special sermon was a long-established method, and continued to make a useful contribution. In 1842 a collection towards the new organ following a sermon at Weston parish church was particularly successful, totalling more than £30.[77] In towns, fundraising concerts of both sacred and secular music proved popular mid-century, partly because using the church itself as the venue was a novelty. In March 1840 the *Hertford Mercury and Reformer* anticipated 'a decided treat to the lovers of music' at the forthcoming concert in aid of the new organ at All Saints, Hertford, and at Codicote 'Mr Brode and twenty-two of his pupils' gave a selection of sacred and secular pieces at their organ fundraising concert in 1864.[78]

Secular fundraising events became increasingly fashionable, and had the advantage of attracting the attention of non-churchgoers. Having already fallen out with the local landowner over parish finances, in August 1840 William Wyndham Malet, vicar of Ardeley, sought alternative funding by holding a 'Fancy Fair' at the new George Hotel Assembly Rooms in Buntingford to raise money for a barrel organ.[79] By holding the event in the nearest market town, a small parish such as this, with a mainly labouring population, was able to attract funds from its wealthier neighbours, who were 'both numerous and fashionable'.[80] Similarly, in July 1864 a bazaar 'for the sale of fancy articles and toys' at The Elms, Baldock, raised funds 'for enlarging and improving the organ now in use in the parish church'.[81] The grounds of a private dwelling such as this provided a more genteel setting and attracted a better class of potential customer, and the *Herts Guardian* reported that 'the grounds and gardens at the Elms were of themselves worth a visit'.[82]

As with finger organs, even if the church acquired a barrel organ it was rare for provision to have been made for either its upkeep or its 'organist'. However, in the parish of Higham Gobion (Beds.), adjacent to the Hertfordshire parishes of Hexton and Pirton, the enterprising rector John Wardale had the foresight to purchase eight £12 10s 0d shares in the Great Northern Railway in 1849, with the specific purpose of applying the dividends 'to the maintenance of the Sunday School, the turning and maintenance of the Barrel organ, and instruction in singing'.[83] Charitable bequests made specifically to support the organist were unusual during the mid-1800s, but in 1858 Samuel Dunn conveyed land in Hoddesdon to the minister and churchwardens of Broxbourne church 'to apply the rents of the said land towards the salary of the organist of the said District Church'.[84] He may have been influenced by a long-standing family association with music-making in the church. In 1779 Samuel's father had been apprenticed to the carpenter George Cheffins, subsequently marrying his daughter, and between 1818 and 1835 the Cheffins family were paid on numerous occasions for work relating to the organs at both Broxbourne and Hoddesdon.[85]

Barrel-organists

It is reasonable to conclude that small payments made variously for 'the Organist', 'playing the Organ', 'turning the Organ', 'attending the Organ', 'grinding the Organ' and 'care of the organ' all refer to operating a barrel organ rather than exercising any trained musicianship. Prior to the onset of church rate disputes, in Hertfordshire – with the exception of wealthy Aldenham – an annual organist's salary of less than eight guineas indicates that he or she was a barrel-organist. This conclusion is supported by the stated occupations of these 'organists' in census returns (see Table 6.1). Likewise, the humble nature of the Wormley organist's task was emphasised in May 1852 when the vestry stipulated that 'The Salary of the person employed for cleaning the church & churchyard & performing the other

Table 6.1
Barrel-organists' salaries in Hertfordshire parish churches, ordered by date.

Parish	Date	Annual salary	Name	Occupation
Broxbourne	1805–57	c.£2–4	George Faint	Bricklayer
Berkhamsted	1820–45	3–4 guineas	George Margrave	Shoemaker
North Mymms	1821–53	£5	James Hutson	Beer-shop keeper
Hoddesdon	1823–51	4–6 guineas	George Faint	Bricklayer
East Barnet	1824–29	£5	Elizabeth Neave	Schoolmistress
Chipping Barnet	1826–50	£5	Charles Thompson	Labourer
Great Amwell	1826–38	£4	Unnamed	
Hunsdon	1827–79	£1	George Griffin	Gardener
Much Hadham	1827–46	2 guineas	Thomas Hobson	Schoolmaster
Chipping Barnet	1829	£5	Elizabeth Neave	Schoolmistress
Westmill	1830–52	£3	James Meredith	Millwright
Tring	1833–35	£1	Robert Cosier	Canvas weaver
Aldenham	1836–55	£10	William Boff	Sawyer
Northchurch	1836–47	£3	William Norris	Shoemaker
East Barnet	1839–60	3–4 guineas	Edward Pratchett	Blacksmith
St Michael's, St Albans	1839–58	£3	John Monk	Shoemaker & parish clerk
Ickleford	1849–59	£2	James Day	Carpenter
Great Gaddesden	1850–62	c.£5–6	George Young	Wheelwright
Essendon	1852–73	c.1 guinea	John Bamford; John Kersey	Blacksmith & parish clerk; gardener
Great Hormead	1855–59	£1	George Drage	Shoemaker
St Ippolyts	1856–61	10s	William Harris	Shoemaker
Willian	1857–60	£2	William Ellis	Blacksmith
Offley	1861–66	10s	John Church	Schoolmaster

Sources: HALS, DP/3/5/1–2, DP/4/5/1–8, DP/15/5/2, DP/15/12/5, DP/16/5/2, DP/19/5/1–2, DP/24/5/2–14, DP/24A/5/1–3, DP/37/5/4, DP/39/5/2, DP/44/5/1, DP/55/5/1, DP/57/5/2, DP/58/5/1, DP/59/5/2, DP/69/5/1, DP/74/8/1–3, DP/76/5/1, DP/120/5/1, DP/125/5/1; St Michael's, St Albans, Churchwardens' papers (1831–50); 1841 Census HO107/438/f.7/p.8, HO107/438/f.34/p.24, HO107/440/f.5/p.5, HO107/440/f.17/p.4, HO107/443/f.16/p.1, HO107/443/f.30/p.26, HO107/447/f.4/p.1; 1851 Census HO107/444/f.26/p.3, HO107/1701/f.274/p.10, HO107/1705/f.89/p.26, HO107/1705/f.205/p.12, HO107/1707/f.13/p.18, HO107/1709/f.135/p.4, HO107/1710/f.283/p.25, HO107/1712/f.5/p.3, HO107/1712/f.75/p.16, HO107/1715/f.453/p.18; 1861 Census RG9/821/f.24/p.14, RG9/820/f.28/p.5.

duties connected with his office was fixed at eight Pounds a year including all expense for tools, soap &c and his remuneration as organist.'[86]

During the 1830s the Willian barrel organ was a highly regarded novelty, and the unpaid organist was Sophia, wife of the vicar William Wollaston Pym.[87] But by the 1850s the status of barrel organs had fallen so far that the village blacksmith undertook this duty, and was paid for his trouble.[88] It seems likely that in many other churches the first barrel-organist was unpaid. In such cases the barrel organ was introduced earlier than indicated by the first known payments to an 'organist'.

Despite the widespread adoption of church barrel organs in Hertfordshire, they had many limitations, and by mid-century the demand for new instruments had fallen dramatically.

Improved barrel organs

In 1831 some of the first signs of what became a more widespread rebellion against the use of barrel organs had come from the Bristol curate John Antes Latrobe in his diatribe against faults in church music.[89] Having criticised church bands, he now concerned himself with the inflexibility of barrel organs: 'the barrel, once set, being unendowed with reason [...] must proceed doggedly in its inwrought regularity. And no alternative remains for the congregation, but either to sink into silence, or endure a continued course of wearisome dissonances.'[90] Furthermore, because no new tunes could be introduced without some expense, 'a church that is thus hampered remains condemned to the original machine which forms [...] so many barrels of legalized error'.[91] In addition to the restricted repertoire, there were also difficulties in setting a suitable tempo, which was often painfully slow. Moreover, inherent mechanical problems included the distracting noise caused by turning the handle, damaged bridges distorting the tunes and the unpredictability of wooden barrels warped in damp churches. In 1842 the editor of the High-Church *Church of England Magazine* recalled being obliged to listen to a damaged barrel organ and highlights what must have been a significant problem for many churches across the country: 'it was the gift of some grandees of the congregation, and its removal, poor groaning creature, would have been an insult.'[92]

In an attempt to maintain sales, in 1839 the organ-builder Gray advertised an 'improved barrel organ', with an operational system that mounted barrels on a rotating frame (Figure 6.8). This had the advantage of reducing wear and tear to the barrels and bridges, and therefore the number of missing or incorrect notes, but its main advantage was that it was no longer necessary to reload a different barrel when choosing a new tune. Gray wrote: 'in many churches it is the custom to commence with the Morning Hymn, and when

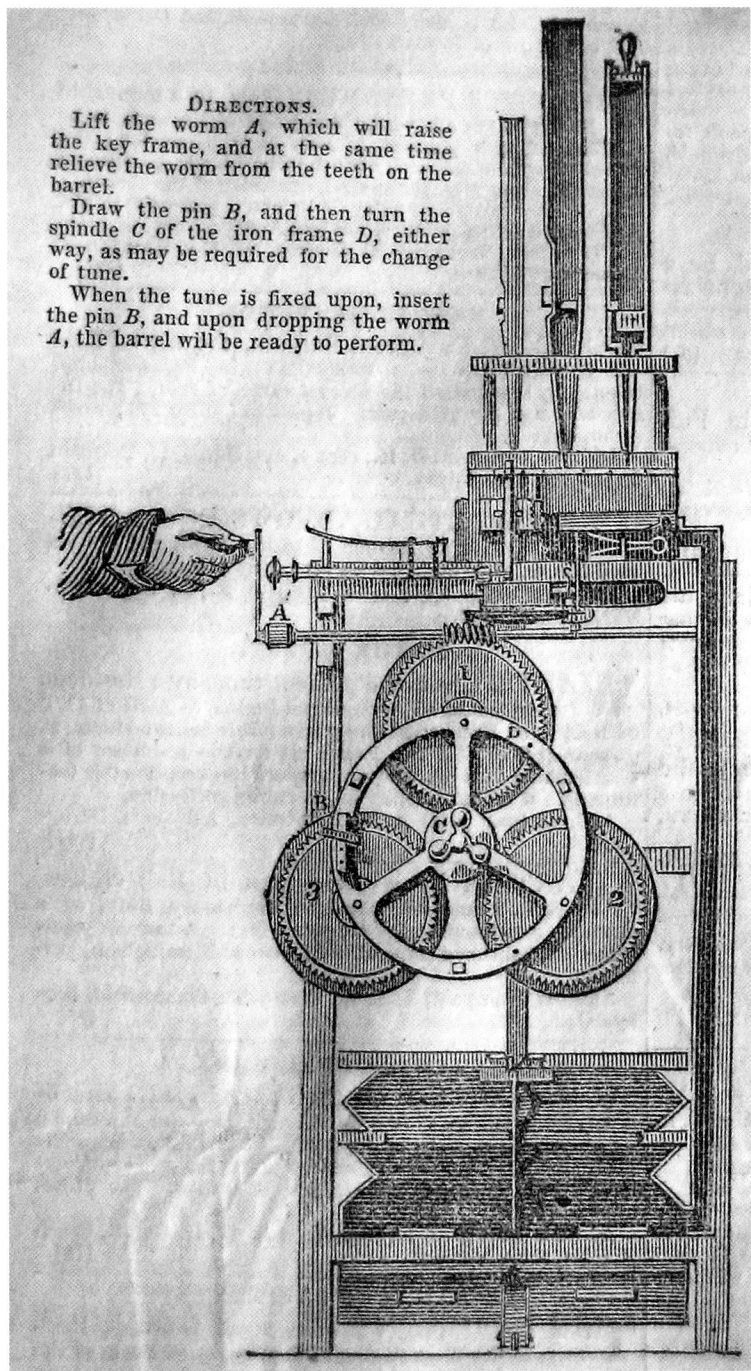

Figure 6.8. Gray's improved church barrel organ (1839). *Ecclesiastical Gazette* (13 August 1839), p. 37.

this is the case, the barrels must be frequently changed, or none but the limited collection of tunes on one barrel will ever be heard during the service.'[93]

Many Hertfordshire churches acquired these instruments, and in 1840 Rev. Watson, vicar of Norton, purchased 'an improved barrel organ no.1' for £63.[94] Other clergy, including Thomas Randolph of Much Hadham in 1844, part-exchanged their existing barrel organ for an 'improved' model.[95] Other organ-builders soon adopted Gray's invention. When Abel Smith (d. 1859) founded the new National School at Bengeo in 1850 the churchwarden Joseph Woodwards gave the parish church a Bates & Son organ. On the invoice it was described as 'A No.5 Trio Church Barrel Organ in solid Oak Case gilt front – three barrels in iron revolving frame ten tunes on each to order'.[96]

Second-hand organs

As a result of changing tastes, by the mid-1800s chamber organs and domestic barrel organs were no longer as fashionable as they had once been, and were often unwanted on the death of their owner. Thus in 1843, following the death of George Alfred Muskett, former MP for St Albans, his '4-barrelled organ' was offered for sale.[97] Other disposals were occasioned by house removals. On leaving the district it was the practice to sell the house contents rather than going to the expense of moving them, which led to further instruments becoming available second-hand. In 1837 a sale of 'Household furniture' in Hoddesden included 'a 4-barrel organ [...] the property of the Misses Sams who are removing'.[98] Similarly, in 1847 a sale of household furniture at Brook House, Cheshunt 'by direction of Charles Chapple, the proprietor, removing' included 'a capital eight-barrelled organ by Gerock'.[99] Because of funding difficulties during this period, many churches could not even afford a new barrel organ, let alone a finger organ and organist, and cheap second-hand instruments such as these became highly sought-after.

The quest for better or more suitable instruments resulted in removals not only from domestic to ecclesiastical surroundings but also from one church to another, and the market for second-hand barrel organs was brisk. Although this might suggest a triumph of hope over experience, it is more likely to have been the result of a desire for a change of repertoire, the search for a more powerful instrument, lack of funds and the willingness of certain churches to part with their old instruments for a pittance, or nothing at all, as the use of finger organs or reed organs became increasingly desirable. In May 1853 the Bovingdon churchwardens purchased a second-hand organ from Stanmore (Middx.).[100] Presumably this was the instrument referred to in *The Musical World* the previous summer:

Last Sunday week we visited the church of St John the Evangelist, Great Stanmore […] when we state that the concluding voluntary was not a chorus of Handel's, or a fugue of Sebastian Bach's, but two verses of the Psalm tune Abingdon, ground on a barrel organ by the village schoolmaster, we cannot imagine that it is what it ought to be in the nineteenth century, nor is it at all in character with the style of the building, which throughout is decorated Gothic.[101]

Stanmore church had just been rebuilt at large expense, and yet the old organ had been brought from the old church, 'where it had remained silent for some years', and now accompanied a few charity children. This was evidently a temporary measure, before it was sold to Bovingdon.

Such was the demand for cheap instruments that some churches advertised for them in terms such as the following: 'A BARREL ORGAN is WANTED, for a small country church. To be of moderate compass, and to contain two or three barrels of the usual psalm tunes.'[102] It is clear from many such examples that the size and appearance of organs were just as important, if not more so, than their precise repertoire. As in this example, there was often a preference for smaller instruments because of space limitations.

Finding little demand from domestic purchasers, vendors attempted to tap into the market for church barrel organs, as seen in numerous advertisements. When George Fry moved from Hertford in 1845 he offered for sale 'a fine-toned large barrel organ, calculated for a Church or Chapel, will play 24 sacred tunes'.[103] Likewise, in 1862 a *Herts Guardian* reader offered: 'A BARREL ORGAN, playing 40 Psalm and Hymn Tunes, with 5 stops; suitable for Church or Chapel. It is 8 feet high, with ornamental front, and in good condition: cost 70 guineas, and will be sold cheap.'[104]

When a new Robson organ was installed at Aspenden in 1856 the old Bryceson barrel organ was taken in part-exchange, but although it had cost £75 in 1821 it was now valued at only £12.[105] It was not unusual for organs to be part-exchanged in this manner. In 1858 J.W. Walker supplied a new finger organ to Broxbourne, taking the old barrel organ in part-exchange. He ruefully observed to Mrs Bosanquet, one of the main subscribers, 'I fear the old organ will stay by me – I was very liberal in my allowance for it.'[106]

So many vendors wanted to take advantage of the demand for cheap second-hand barrel organs that there was soon a glut of instruments. With few church resources to buy them, it was now by no means unusual for households simply to give their local church a domestic barrel organ of which they had tired, as with the instrument given to Cheshunt parish church, and later to Lowewood Museum, Hoddesdon.[107] Although there are no sacred tunes pinned on this particular organ, some domestic barrel organs were pinned with psalm tunes on one or more barrels to accompany family prayers, and it would not have been incongruous to give such an instrument to the church. This accounts for anecdotal stories of dance tunes being played by barrel organs during divine service.

A second-hand chamber organ was equally unsuited to a church with no organist, and therefore many were adapted to be played by barrels. In December 1835 John Smith, rector of Baldock, purchased one from Gray, who added 'a barrel movement complete with draw stops at the back with 3 barrels £31 10s'.[108] On a more ambitious scale, Joseph Stephen Pratt, a canon of Peterborough Cathedral, took up the chaplaincy of Stanstead St Margaret on his retirement. His wife Frances Cecilia was both the church's patron and a member of the Cowper family, daughter of William Cowper MP and granddaughter of Rev. Martin Madan. It was only fitting that Pratt should repair and beautify the church, and in 1837 he arranged for his own William Allen chamber organ to be transported from Peterborough, supplied with four barrels, fitted with a movement to play them and installed in the west gallery (see Figure 6.2).[109] Many of the tunes chosen were typical of those used on other barrel organs of the era, but Pratt's taste was more catholic, perhaps reflecting his experience of music-making in Peterborough and his desire to retain worshippers. To this end he chose several tunes associated with singers and church bands, including 'Portsmouth New' and Joseph Key's 'Psalm 92'.[110]

In many churches the solution to funding difficulties was the installation of a barrel organ, whether new, second-hand or adapted from a chamber organ. Many of these instruments came from country houses, indicating the continuing influence of the elite, although now their priority was often the cheapness of the instrument rather than the superiority of the music it might support. This was seen most clearly at North Mymms. During the late 1700s the local elite had funded high-quality music-making by a metropolitan organist in their parish church, but during the 1830s Mrs Gaussen funded repairs to the church barrel organ used to support singing by the National School children.[111]

Barrel organ repertoire

Most church barrel organs played metrical psalm tunes and were thus sometimes called 'psalmodic' organs, but longer pieces such as anthems or voluntaries could also be played by pinning the barrel spirally, which enabled the performance of a much longer piece of music. In May 1844 Rev. Randolph, rector of Much Hadham, purchased 'An improved barrel-organ with 3 barrels one partly spiral for anthem £78 15s'.[112]

Based on tune-lists given in Langwill and Boston's *Church and Chamber Barrel-organs*, other tune-lists and recordings of surviving instruments, more than 300 different psalm tunes are known to have been played by English church barrel organs.[113] The frequency with which certain tunes occur cannot have been because the choice was limited, but because some were more popular or considered more suitable than others. During the 1790s psalm tune selections by three influential musicians may have affected the choice of tunes. William Mason had his own arrangements set on church barrel organs, and in 1791 Edward Miller offered for sale barrel organs adapted to 'Dr Miller's late Publication of Psalm Tunes'.[114] Miller's tune 'Rockingham' is found on several surviving church barrel organs and is still sung in many churches to the words 'When I survey the Wondrous Cross', a hymn by Watts.[115] Possibly the most influential of the three was the organist John Randall's *Collection of Psalm & Hymn Tunes* (1794).[116] This was compiled especially for an instrument that played sixty tunes installed by Rev. Charles Simeon in Holy Trinity, Cambridge. It included the tune 'Cambridge', composed by Randall for the new organ. Later known as 'Cambridge New', it was frequently pinned on later church barrel organs, including the instrument at St Mary's, Stanstead St Margaret.[117]

Many tune-lists reflected the personal interest of the donor or incumbent. In the case of Hornchurch (Essex), the advowson was held by New College, Oxford, its vicars were fellows of the college and the forty tunes pinned on the barrels of its Bevington organ included 'Hornchurch', 'Essex', 'New College' and 'Oxford'.[118] A barrel organ was installed at Great Amwell in 1825 during the incumbency of William Thomas Say.[119] The organ was pinned with two tunes, 'Stanstead' and 'Aveley', which suggest that the organ was given by the pluralist vicar himself, since Stanstead lies less than a mile from Great Amwell, and Aveley a short distance from his other living in Rainham (Essex). Confusingly, many tunes were known by more than one name. Like 'Cambridge', it is possible that 'Stanstead' and 'Aveley' may have been composed especially, but it is possible they were also known by other names and were repurposed in the hope that the vicar was unfamiliar with them, a device sometimes also used by itinerant singing teachers. However, 'Stanstead' and 'Aveley' may have been names given to tunes Rev. Say particularly associated with his two churches.

The 'Old 100th' was found on almost every church barrel organ, and the frequent occurrence of 'Hanover' is unsurprising given that England had Hanoverian monarchs throughout the period in which church barrel organs were used. Bishop Ken's 'Evening Hymn' was invariably sung to a version of Tallis's Canon and played at afternoon services. The tune used for his 'Morning Hymn' was usually that written by François Hippolyte Barthélémon for the Swedenborg Society. Only one tune was specifically sung at Easter, 'Easter Hymn' (Christ our Lord is risen today), found on half of all barrel organs nationally. A number of different tunes were used at Christmas; most common was 'Portugal New' (O come all ye faithful), a hymn tune first used in the Portuguese Embassy chapel, London, in around 1782.

Two renowned Methodist hymn tunes were often found on barrel organs: 'Mount Ephraim' by Benjamin Milgrove and the advent hymn 'Helmsley'. The frequent inclusion of these two tunes clearly indicates the influence of Methodism on Anglican music-making and the church's attempt to retain worshippers. The Methodists' successful use of parody hymn tunes also led to many 'art' tunes being pinned on church barrel organs, including 'Surrey' by Henry Carey, an operatic composer. Moreover, the presence of 'Bradley Church' from Walker's *Companion*, Thomas Clark of Canterbury's 'Cranbrook' and Zerubbabel Wyvill's 'Eaton' on some church barrel organs provides evidence that Baptist tunes were also considered suitable for use in the established church.[120]

Three tunes commonly pinned on church barrel organs provide further evidence that these instruments were used to support children's voices. 'University' was first published in Hellendaal's *Collection*, which targeted Sunday school patrons as subscribers. It is likely that 'Abingdon', by Musgrave Heighington, organist and children's singing teacher at Yarmouth (Norfolk),[121] and 'Nayland', by the High Churchman William Jones, incumbent of Nayland (Suffolk), were also written for Sunday school children.

Nevertheless, the florid arrangements of simple psalm tunes used on most barrel organs sounded more like 'art' than 'common' tunes, and were therefore considered unacceptable by some. In 1846 'A Choir-Master' wrote to the *Parish Choir* 'On the objectionable character of many psalm tunes in common use' and classified them according to just how objectionable he found them.[122] Many classified as 'light and inferior' and, worse still, 'lax and secular' were commonly pinned on barrel organs, and tunes known to have been played in Hertfordshire are classified according to his opinion in Table 6.2.

The *Parish Choir*'s editors agreed that 'good taste and piety' would never tolerate the use of any 'light and inferior' or 'lax and secular' tunes, including 'Cambridge New' and 'Helmsley', which was later described as 'probably the greatest musical achievement of Methodism'.[123] Apart from the common tunes named by Tate and Brady, authors of the New Version, only around a fifth fell into the category 'solid and ecclesiastical'. Although objections to the repertoire pinned on church barrel organs contributed to a mid-century decline in their use, other factors were involved, as explained in the following section.

Table 6.2
Tunes known to have been played by Hertfordshire church barrel organs, as classified in *The Parish Choir* (1846).

Tune	A common tune named by Tate & Brady?	Parish Choir classification	Where used
Abingdon	No	3	GA, SM, W
Abridge	No	1	GA, SM
Angel's Hymn	No	1	GA
Bedford	No	1	GA, SM, W
Cambridge New	No	2	GA, SM, W
Devizes	No	2	GA, SM, W
Easter Hymn	No	2	GA
Falcon Street	No	3	GA, SM
Gainsboro'	No	2	GA
Hanover (Old 104th)	Yes	1	GA, SM
Helmsley	No	3	GA, SM
Hursley	No	3	SA
Job	No	2	GA
London New	No	1	GA
Manchester New	No	2	A, GA
Mount Ephraim	No	2	GA
New York (Sheffield)	No	3	W
Old 100th	Yes	1	A, GA, W
Portsmouth New	No	3	SM
Portugal New	No	2	GA, SA, W
Sabbath New	No	3	GA, W
Shirland	No	2	GA, SM, W
St Anne	Yes	1	GA
St Mary	Yes	1	SA
St Peter	No	2	SA
Truro	No	2	GA
University	No	3	GA, SM
Warwick	No	1	GA
Winchester	No	1	A, SA

1 = solid and ecclesiastical, 2 = light and inferior, 3 = lax and secular; A = Aldenham, GA = Great Amwell, SA = St Michael's, St Albans, SM = Stanstead St Margaret, W = Watford.
Sources: BL, Add MS 47775 A; HALS, DP/4/29/2 Music played by the barrel organ in the church (1856); *Watford Observer* (28 May 1870), p. 4; St Michael's, St Albans, Correspondence with Mr F.F. Hill (1974); Stanstead St Margaret tunes identified by the author from recordings made by M. Glover.

Demise of the church barrel organ

In 1851 the Great Exhibition provided organ-builders with the opportunity to showcase their products, and Bryceson won a 'Prize Medal' for a church barrel organ 'of superior construction in a gothic case'.[124] The editors of the *Ecclesiologist* were unimpressed:

> We cannot refrain [...] from expressing a hope, that the encouragement given to the manufacture of barrel organs playing metrical psalm tunes and chants will not be such as to tempt future exhibitors to spend time and trouble in these most detestable substitutes for living players; [...] we think that this make-shift can never be excused or tolerated in divine service.[125]

There were also practical objections. New hymnals introduced during the mid-nineteenth century contained a much larger number of tunes than it would have been possible to pin on a barrel organ. The only realistic means of playing them was to replace the instrument with a keyboard and organist, perhaps by converting it to a finger organ, but many churches attempted to avoid this expense by persevering with their existing instrument. The most economical way to do so was to sing only hymns that fitted the existing tunes pinned on the barrels. Alternatively, barrels could be repinned, as was necessary to accompany chanting, a subject discussed in the next chapter.[126] In December 1848 Rev. Morrice, incumbent of Hoddesdon, paid the organ-builders six guineas for 'Resetting barrel with 15 tunes'.[127] Another option for the church was to buy a new barrel. In March 1833 the organ-builder J.C. Bishop provided St Michael's, St Albans, with a new barrel for six guineas, charging a further 10s 6d for resetting the tunes on the existing barrel.[128] But keeping the existing organ was not always practical and by the 1860s may have been seen as throwing good money after bad. Where churches were willing to extend their repertoire and invest in the existing technology by either repinning or purchasing new barrels, despite new developments in instrument-making, it was generally because of financial constraints.

In many churches barrel organs continued to be used during the 1850s and 1860s, and in Hertfordshire at least fourteen of the fifty-seven newly installed organs had some sort of barrel mechanism.[129] In 1850 a finger organ and dumb organist were installed in the west gallery at St Pauls Walden. The Ecclesiologist Henry Dryden may have reluctantly approved, as in 1854 he wrote somewhat despairingly:

> I may just remark that you may as well try to make a silk purse out of a sow's ear as to get good singing with a grinding organ; and, therefore, don't throw away your spare cash on a grinder, if you wish it for *accompaniment*. If, in default of

vocal music, you wish to have voluntaries, a grinder with the spiral-axled barrels may do your turn; but I would advise you never to get a grinder only – get a finger organ with grinding machinery, called 'dumb organist' added.[130]

Nevertheless, a dramatic fall in the acquisition of church barrel organs followed their association by the public with street musicians. In 1831 Latrobe had complained 'What town or village in the country resounds not with the most absurd tunes ground out of these musical boxes, which […] are borne by strolling minstrels from place to place!'[131] When freedom of travel was reinstated after the Napoleonic Wars there was an influx of street musicians, most notably 'organ grinders' from the Duchy of Parma. This resulted in the twin nuisances of incessant noise and blocked thoroughfares in many English towns. Some householders had real grounds for complaint when, rather than being rewarded for their music, certain street musicians demanded hush money before they would move on to a neighbouring street.[132] The problems caused by organ-grinders were seen by some to be a middle-class problem, as servants and the poor positively encouraged them, and wealthy householders could avoid the nuisance by moving to quieter parts of their houses.[133] Street organs caused problems nationally, but especially in London, where a crusade against the 'organ nuisance' had started in the 1850s in *The Times* and continued in *Punch* and elsewhere. The campaign led to the reading of the 'Suppression of Barrel Organs' bill in parliament in 1858. Although this bill was rejected amid claims of anti-Italian racism, the parliamentary proceedings were reported in great detail in *The Times* and many local newspapers, including the *Hertford Mercury and Reformer*.[134] The problem continued until Michael Thomas Bass MP, heir to the Burton-on-Trent brewery, introduced another bill in 1864 for the 'Better Regulation of Street Music within the Metropolitan Police District'.[135] This time the legislation was passed, and it became known as Bass's Act.[136] The Act gave all householders in the district the right to ask any street musician or singer to leave the neighbourhood of their house if they were causing annoyance.[137] *Punch* celebrated appropriately (Figure 6.9).

This was perhaps the final stage in the fall of barrel organs from the elevated position they once held. As a consequence barrel organs were no longer considered appropriate for use in divine service, and quickly forgotten as an embarrassing episode in church music-making. Apart from contemporary newspaper reports and organ-builders' accounts, often the only evidence for their use comes from parish records itemising small payments for their maintenance or operation, or from memoirs. Many were part-exchanged or converted into finger organs, as at Hexton.[138] Some were

Figure 6.9. John Tenniel, 'Clearing the Streets', celebrating the passing of Bass's Act which facilitated the removal of organ-grinders from the capital. *Punch, or the London Charivari*, XLVII (6 August 1864), p. 55.

broken up for parts, and at Westmill lead from the unwanted organ pipes is said to have been melted down by boys for use as catapult pellets.[139]

Other church barrel organs were sold or given away when they fell out of fashion, often to antiquarian clergymen, most prominent among whom was Canon Boston. In 1959 he recalled the circumstances of the visit to Warwickshire that piqued his interest and led to the formation of his own collection in Norfolk:

> It is now some twenty years since, in the house of Rev. Launcelot Mitchell at Curdworth, I was first introduced to the barrel-organ. That delightful, if somewhat eccentric, priest had collected no less than seventeen barrel-organs in his house (there was even one in the bathroom) and they varied in size from tiny instruments little bigger than musical boxes to one splendid organ, which [...] entirely filled the greenhouse [...].[140]

Today, the use of barrel organs in church has been almost completely forgotten, despite the fact that for several generations these instruments featured so prominently in the drive to encourage congregational singing. Because of funding difficulties, in many churches barrel organs continued to be used long after they had fallen out of favour, especially during the period of church rate disputes discussed in the following chapter.

Endnotes

1. J.S. Curwen, 'The Organ in Divine Service', *Congregationalist*, 8 (1879), p. 116.
2. Woodhouse, *Face the Music*; Pacey, *Lincolnshire*; MacDermott, *Sussex*; Weston, *Instrumentation*; Davidson, *Choirs*.
3. See Appendix 3.
4. Drage, 'Reappraisal', p. 175; M. Smith, *Religion in Industrial Society: Oldham and Saddleworth, 1740–1865* (Oxford, 1994), pp. 54–5 and 93.
5. HALS, DP/3/29/17.
6. MacDermott, *Minstrels*, p. 7; K. Baddley, 'Trouble in the Gallery', in C. Turner (ed.), *Georgian Psalmody 1, The Gallery Tradition* (Corby Glen, 1997), pp. 17–25; R. Lee, *Rural Society and the Anglican Clergy, 1815–1914. Encountering and Managing the Poor*, Studies in Modern British Religious History, 11 (Woodbridge, 2006), pp. 50–1; D.A. Spaeth, *The Church in an Age of Danger: Parsons and Parishioners, 1660–1740* (Cambridge, 2000), pp. 237–9.
7. *The Times* (3 December 1841), p. 8.
8. *Chelmsford Chronicle* (5 September 1783), p. 1.
9. A.W.J.G. Ord-Hume, *Barrel Organ: the Story of the Mechanical Organ and its Repair* (London, 1978), pp. 25–6.
10. S. Mayes, *An Organ for the Sultan* (London, 1956).
11. D. Dalrymple (ed.), *The opinions of Sarah Duchess-Dowager of Marlborough (1660–1744). Published from original Mss.* (1788), p. 63.
12. K.W. Schweizer, 'Stuart, John, third Earl of Bute (1713–1792)', *ODNB*.
13. Ord-Hume, *Barrel Organ*, p. 88; W. Malloch, 'The Earl of Bute's Machine Organ: A Touchstone of Taste', *Early Music*, 11/2 (April 1983), pp. 172–83.
14. *St James's Chronicle* (3 January 1784); J.E. May, 'Young, Edward (bap. 1683, d.1765)', *ODNB*.
15. HALS, DE/R/F220 Bills & receipts (1773–4).
16. See Table 2.1.
17. HALS, DE/R/F220.
18. G. Vertue, 'Pinchback's Musical Clock: Jottings of George Vertue, extracted from his Manuscript Notes', *Notes & Queries*, 2nd series, XII (1861), p. 81.
19. *London Evening Post* (22 April 1731), p. 2.
20. J. Boeringer, *Organa Britannica. Organs in Great Britain 1660–1860*, 3 vols (London, 1983–9), 2, p. 30.
21. Arnold, *Compleat Psalmodist*, 5th edn (1761), p. iii; Kilbey, 'Early Use', p. 58.
22. *Ibid.*
23. *Ibid.*
24. *Chelmsford Chronicle* (5 September 1783), p. 1.
25. *Christian Remembrancer* (January 1824) p. 26.
26. *Ibid.*
27. H. Soames, 'Letter VI: Psalmody', in *Parochial Letters from a Beneficed Clergyman to his Curate* (London, 1829), pp. 76–7.
28. Bobbingworth is also known as Bovinger.
29. PP 1835 (62), Abstract of Answers and Returns on State of Education in England and Wales (3 vols), I, p. 271.
30. Ord-Hume, *Barrel Organ*, pp. 101–2.
31. R. Cowgill, 'The London Apollonicon Recitals, 1817–32: A Case-Study in Bach, Mozart and Haydn Reception', *Journal of the Royal Musical Association*, 123/2 (1998), pp. 190–228, p. 192.
32. Ord-Hume, *Barrel Organ*, p. 102.
33. *Ibid.*, p. 127.
34. *Gentleman's Magazine* (April 1797), p. 336.

35 P. Cunningham (ed.), *The Letters of Horace Walpole, Earl of Orford*, 9 vols (London, 1857–9), 9, p. 335; P. Langford, 'Walpole, Horatio, 4th Earl of Orford (1717–1797)', *ODNB*.
36 Bell, *Little Gaddesden*, p. 144.
37 *Christian Observer* (February 1834), p. 95.
38 *British Magazine* (1 December 1835), pp. 679–81.
39 *Ecclesiastical Gazette* (10 July 1849), p. 17.
40 *Ibid.* (13 August 1839), p. 37.
41 Thistlethwaite, *Victorian Organ*, pp. 66–7.
42 *Universal British Directory*, 3, p. 376.
43 HALS, DP/53/8/2 Vestry minutes (1805).
44 *London Gazette* (5 February 1805), p. 175.
45 HALS, DP/53/8/2.
46 Kilbey, 'Early Use', pp. 67–9.
47 National Society, *Fifth Annual Report* (London, 1816), pp. 39–118.
48 LPL, FP Porteus 25/16 (1790).
49 LPL, FP Randolph 9/651–8 (1810).
50 John Longman, organ-builder, formerly of Longman & Broderip.
51 HALS, DE/Hd/F3.
52 HALS, DP/24/5/2–14 Churchwardens' vouchers & accounts (1802–60).
53 HALS, DP/44/5/1 Churchwardens' accounts (1784–1870); DP/44/29/1 Miscellaneous papers (n.d.); R. Hole, 'Randolph, John (1749–1813)', *ODNB*.
54 CRL, BOA, Gray & Davison accounts, vol. 2 (1838–45), p. 166.
55 National Society, *Fifth Annual Report*, pp. 39–118.
56 HALS, DP/61/1/2 Parish notes (1792–1843).
57 T.D.S. Bayley, *Pebmarsh Church, Essex* (Oxford, 1946), p. 48.
58 Cussans, *History*, II, p. 10; M. Kilbey, 'Hexton, Hertfordshire: a Tale of Two Organs', *Organists' Review* (June 2017), pp. 40–1.
59 CRL, BOA, John Gray accounts, vol. 1 (1821–38), p. 35.
60 Mrs Ashley Cooper, *St Faith's Hexton* (n.d.), pp. 15–20.
61 PP 1819 (224) I, p. 355.
62 CRL, BOA, Gray & Davison accounts, vol. 8A (1865–83), p. 351, see also vol. 2 (1838–45), p. 159.
63 *Ibid.*, vol. 2, p. 154.
64 Kilbey, 'Music-making in the English Parish Church', p. 191.
65 *HMR* (10 August 1861), p. 3.
66 Cussans, *History*, III, p. 61; 'Parishes: East Barnet', *VCH Herts*, 2, pp. 337–42; G.E. Cokayne (ed.), *The Complete Baronetage*, reprint (Gloucester, 1983), I, p. 112.
67 HALS, DP/16/5/1–2; LPL, ICBS1091 (1829); F.C. Cass, *East Barnet* (2 pts, 1885–92), I, p. 182.
68 HALS, DP/15/8/3 Vestry minutes (1824–63).
69 LPL, FP Randolph 9/309–18 (1810); England & Wales, Prerogative Court of Canterbury Wills, PROB 11/1791B/258.
70 Mrs Gore, 'Hush!', *Bentley's Miscellany*, XIV (July 1843), pp. 65–73.
71 W. Hughes, 'Gore, Catherine Grace Frances (1798–1861)', *ODNB*.
72 Thistlethwaite, *Victorian Organ*, p. 66.
73 HALS, DP/22/12/4 Vestry minutes (1842).
74 Burg, *Religion*, pp. 44 and 56.
75 *Ibid.*, pp. 141–2.
76 J.J. Page, 'Great Wymondley Church', *Transactions of the East Herts Archaeological Society*, 2/I (1906), p. 18.
77 *HMR* (27 August 1842), p. 2.
78 *HMR* (21 March 1840), p. 2; *Hertfordshire Express and General Advertiser* (17 December 1864), p. 2.
79 D.J. Howlett, 'Malet, Sir Charles Warre, first baronet (1753–1815)', *ODNB*; *HMR* (29 August 1840), p. 3.

80 HMR, *ibid.*
81 *HG* (30 July 1864), p. 4.
82 *Ibid.*
83 BARS, P125/1/5 Register of baptisms (1849).
84 Cussans, 'Hundred of Hertford: Broxbourne', *History*, II, p. 205.
85 UK Register of Duties Paid for Apprentices' Indentures (1710–1811), Class IR 1; Piece 30; HALS, DP/24/5/2–14; DP/4/5/1–8 Churchwardens' accounts, bills & vouchers (1822–61).
86 HALS, DP/126/8/2.
87 P. Harkness, *All Saints … and Sinners* (1999), p. 41.
88 See Table 6.1.
89 See also Chapter 4, p. 110.
90 Latrobe, *Music of the Church*, p. 355.
91 *Ibid.*
92 *Church of England Magazine* (9 April 1842), pp. 245–6.
93 *Ecclesiastical Gazette* (13 August 1839), p. 37.
94 CRL, BOA, Gray & Davison accounts, vol. 3 (1839–41), p. 138.
95 *Ibid.*, vol. 2, p. 166.
96 HALS, DP/17/6/13 Vestry resolution, Bates & Son invoice (1850).
97 *HMR* (22 July 1843), p. 1.
98 *HMR* (17 October 1837), p. 1.
99 *HMR* (22 May 1847), p. 1.
100 CRL, BOA, Gray & Davison accounts, vol. 5 (1849–57), p. 155.
101 *Musical World* (June 1852), p. 373.
102 *The Times* (29 October 1838), p. 1.
103 *HMR* (11 October 1845), p. 1.
104 *HG* (7 January 1862), p. 1.
105 HALS, DP/8/8/3 Lists of subscribers to a new organ (1856).
106 HALS, DP/24/6/4.
107 On display in October 2012.
108 CRL, BOA, John Gray accounts (1821–38), p. 129.
109 Cussans, *History*, II, p. 137; CRL, BOA, John Gray accounts vol. 1 (1821–38), p. 141.
110 Identified by the author from a recording of the instrument made by Marcel Glover.
111 CRL, BOA, John Gray accounts, vol. 1 (1821–38), p. 89.
112 CRL, BOA, Gray & Davison accounts, vol. 2 (1838–45), p. 166.
113 Langwill and Boston, *barrel-organs*; recordings of church barrel organs made by Marcel Glover.
114 *Sheffield Register, Yorkshire, Derbyshire, & Nottinghamshire Universal Advertiser* (9 December 1791), 2. Advertisements were also placed in the *Derby Mercury*, *Northampton Mercury* and *Stamford Mercury*.
115 For example, on barrel organs at Sutton (Beds) and Fobbing (Essex).
116 J. Randall, *A collection of psalm & hymn tunes some of which are new & others by permission of the authors [...] for the use of congregations in general* (Cambridge, 1794); Kilbey, 'Early Use', pp. 68–9.
117 Kilbey, 'Early Use', pp. 68–9.
118 H. Bevington, *A Selection of Psalm & Hymn Tunes as set on the NEW ORGAN, lately Erected in Horn Church Essex by H. Bevington* (London, c.1830).
119 HALS, DP/4/5/1–8.
120 For example at Hampton Gay (Oxon) and Wardley (Rutland).
121 T. Fawcett, *Music in Eighteenth-Century Norwich and Norfolk* (Norwich, 1979), p. 33.
122 *Parish Choir* (May 1846), pp. 31–2.
123 Bradley, *Abide With Me*, p. 10.
124 *London Journal of Arts, Sciences, and Manufactures, and Repertory of Patent Inventions* (London, 1851), p. 196.
125 *Ecclesiologist* (June 1851), p. 189.

126 See Chapter 7, p. 193.
127 CRL, BOA, Gray & Davison accounts, vol. 4 (1842–8), p. 258.
128 St Albans, St Michael's, Churchwardens' papers 4 (1831–40).
129 See Appendix 3.
130 *Ecclesiologist* (April 1854), p. 100.
131 Latrobe, *Music of the Church*, p. 355.
132 J.M. Picker, *Victorian Soundscapes* (Oxford, 2003), pp. 41–64.
133 L. Sponza, *Italian Immigrants in Nineteenth Century Britain: Realities and Images* (Leicester, 1988), p. 170.
134 *The Times* (30 April 1858), p. 8; *HMR* (1 May 1858), p. 2.
135 *HMR* (7 May 1864), p. 4.
136 27 & 28 Vict. c. 55.
137 *HG* (August 1864), p. 2.
138 Kilbey, 'Hexton', p. 41.
139 Ewing, *Westmill*, p. 96.
140 Boston, 'The Barrel-Organ', p. 99.

Chapter 7
Disputes and Tractarianism

During the nineteenth century church rate disputes had a disruptive effect on church music-making in many Hertfordshire towns. Changing employment patterns had led many to seek work in towns, where dissenting meetings flourished. As the number of dissenters grew, so too did their objections to funding the upkeep of organs and payments to organists in the churches of their new parishes, which they did not attend.

The same disruptive result was seen in certain Hertfordshire churches after the introduction of new styles of worship by clergymen influenced by Tractarianism. But in these churches the objections came from members of the congregation themselves.

Church rates

During the early nineteenth century the existing system of collecting rates to fund local concerns, outlined in Chapter 1, became progressively more difficult to manage owing to the increasingly mobile population and the growing number of poor. A reform of this arrangement was one aspect of the growing demand for both the restructuring of local government and parliamentary reform. Predictably, sweeping changes to the *status quo* were strongly opposed by traditionalists, and in October 1831 bishops in the House of Lords failed to support the Reform Bill that would have changed the electoral system and widened the franchise for male voters. Frustration at this failed opportunity inflamed antipathy towards the Tory-dominated established church in general, and bishops in particular. One manifestation of this was the burning of effigies of bishops on 5 November 1831, and in Hertfordshire a guy dressed as a bishop instead of Guy Fawkes was carried through the streets of Ware before being burnt 'amid the execrations of the people assembled to witness it'.[1]

In 1832 the Reform Bill was finally passed and within a few years a series of further parliamentary acts brought to an end the parish's responsibility for secular affairs. One of these was the Poor Law Amendment Act of

1834. Under this new system parishes were grouped together in 'unions', greatly reducing the cost of supporting the poor. Although this lessened the burden on the poor rate, the collection of the church rate to fund the church fabric and divine service continued, and many demanded a reform of this system, too.

In those churches where a church band had received payments from the church rate a natural progression, if an organ was later installed, might have been for the organ and organist to be funded similarly. But purchases of instruments out of the church rate were infrequent in Hertfordshire, indicating that most were privately funded. Any suggestion that payments relating to an organ should come from the church rate is therefore likely to have been seen as an imposition. Although vestry resolutions authorising payments to organists out of the church rate do survive for some Hertfordshire parishes, in most instances there are none, either because the records do not survive or, more frequently, because none were made.

As early as 1817 a correspondent to the *Bury and Norwich Post* questioned the legality of the vestry's decision to pay the organist of St Mary's, Bury St Edmunds (Suffolk), a salary of thirty guineas out of the church rate. They pointed out that, until recently, the organist had been paid by voluntary subscription, and added:

> charging an Organist's salary to the Church Rate, may, I fear, be deemed an *Innovation*; and you know, Mr Editor, that good and loyal subjects are very apt to be alarmed at *Innovations*. Besides, doubts may arise in the minds of some, as to the legality of the Churchwardens' charging such salaries in their accounts; and some of those who, unhappily not having the taste to admire the beautiful simplicity of the Church Service, or from some other cause, secede therefrom, may object to paying the Rates, on account of such charge.[2]

Funding a church organist would probably have been considered even more of an imposition to householders newly settled in towns such as Bury and rapidly growing towns in Hertfordshire because, even if their former rural parishes had an organ, it would almost certainly have been a barrel organ, and the 'organist' would have been paid only a nominal sum to operate it.

The influence of dissent

As Hertfordshire towns grew, so did opposition to making payments to organists from the church rate. Many dissenters became prominent, were actively involved in the vestry and, perhaps understandably, were reluctant to contribute towards expenses associated with a church that offered them no spiritual or financial support and that they had no intention of attending. In Hertfordshire the earliest known questions regarding the legality of paying the organist out of the church rate were raised in towns in the south and west of the county, those which had seen the greatest population growth. In April 1827 George Miller was appointed organist of St Andrew's, Totteridge, for the sum of 'six shillings per day for every Sunday and such other days as he might be required to attend'.[3] Although he started at this daily rate, by 1831 it had dropped to four shillings, and he was already owed £16 10 s, eighteen months' pay, presumably because the church rate had not been paid by certain parishioners. Totteridge had a large and well-attended Independent Chapel whose members appear to have been active in the vestry. In October 1833 the vestry questioned the legality of paying the organist at all. No conclusive decision was made, and the discussion was postponed until the Easter vestry, when the minutes recorded:

> Resolved that a special vestry be called for the purpose of auditing the churchwardens bills before they are paid – and that the question of the legality of paying the organist's salary out of the church rates be then discussed, and if it be proved – that the same may be legally charged upon the rate that it be allowed for this year, but if on the contrary, it is not legal, that such charges be then struck out of the churchwardens accounts.[4]

Fortunately for Miller, on this occasion the vestry agreed to pay the outstanding sum, but unfortunately no further payments were sanctioned.

In December 1828 Emma Smith of Tring Park married James Edward Austen-Leigh, curate of the parish church.[5] Tring was a growing town with a very strong Baptist presence and singers with a history of disputing with the rector.[6] Emma's sisters appear to have taken an interest in reforming the church's music-making, and in September 1832 the vestry discussed a proposal 'on the part of the Miss Smiths of Tring to present the church with an organ'.[7] In 1830 the ecclesiastical lawyer John Haggard had reported a ruling that parishioners could not be forced to pay for the installation or upkeep of an organ, even if the bishop had granted a faculty.[8] Unaware of this ruling, the Tring vestry accepted the barrel organ, authorising 'such alterations in the Gallery as may be requisite for the proper reception of the organ', but at the following vestry it was made clear that the parishioners themselves would be called upon to pay for these alterations.[9] After being compelled to pay almost £22 for installing the 'free' organ, in 1833 the vestry retaliated by ordering that the £1 annual salary of the barrel-organist would no longer be paid out of the church rate.

Initially, disputes such as these were relatively isolated, but broadening readership following the 1836 reduction in newspaper tax[10] and widespread dissemination of reports of such incidents presented a new problem for many town churches. An escalation in disputes followed.

Hitchin had not only Independent and Baptist chapels but also a significant Methodist and Quaker presence. When the Easter 1837 vestry was held at St Mary's, the *Hertford Mercury and Reformer* reported 'From the large attendance of Churchmen and Dissenters it was evident that an opposition to the rate was expected.'[11] Sure enough, William Hainworth, sometime preacher at Tilehouse Street Baptist Chapel,[12] proposed that the two years' salary due to the organist Edwin Theodore Nicholls, formerly organist of the Abbey Church, St Albans, should not be paid out of the church rate. The chairman appealed to Frederick Delmé Radcliffe, whose father had presented the organ to the church. He replied that it appeared 'unreasonable thus to compel Dissenters to pay for what he considered a luxury of the church'.[13] The Hitchin vestry agreed to pay Nicholls his overdue salary, but that in future the organist should be paid by private subscription.

Subscribing towards the organist's salary seemed to offer a practical alternative in some parishes, but this still did not offer the organist job security. In 1840 Frederick Walker replaced Nicholls as Hitchin organist at an annual salary of £40 to be raised by subscription. This continued until March 1848, when the number of subscribers had fallen so substantially that they were obliged to offer a reduced salary of £30, which Walker considered 'illiberal':

> with a large family like mine – the loss of ten pounds a year would be a serious inconvenience, but at times like the present when my teaching is so greatly reduced and the wants of my family so much greater than before – the reduction of one fourth of my yearly stipend is a hardship I severely feel and may indeed ultimately prove of the most disastrous consequences. I therefore still hope that some means will be adopted so that I may not become a sufferer from the loss of subscribers to the organ and that faith may still be kept with me.[14]

Walker stated that, if forced to accept the terms, he would play only on Sundays, Christmas Day and Good Friday, 'all other requirements to be specially paid for'. He attempted to make ends meet by advertising in February 1850:

> MR F.C. WALKER, Organist of St Mary's Church, HITCHIN, late of London, Professor of Harmony and Composition, and Teacher of the Organ, Pianoforte, and Singing, attends his Pupils at HATFIELD, WELWYN, and their Vicinities, on

MONDAYS; STEVENAGE and its Vicinity, on WEDNESDAYS; and BALDOCK and its Vicinity, on FRIDAYS. TERMS: *Five Lessons for One Guinea*. Church Choirs instructed and properly regulated.[15]

In October 1851 Walker's plea for extra payments came to nothing and he was dismissed by the churchwardens 'in consequence of their inability to collect the sum requisite to pay your salary'.[16]

By 1841 objections to paying organists from the church rate had clearly become a widespread national issue, with a legal periodical advising:

Q.: Can parishioners assembled in vestry legally make a *church-rate* to pay the salary of an organist?
A.: The parishioners cannot make a church-rate for the specific purpose of paying an organist's salary; but the majority of those present in vestry may legally agree that the organist's salary shall be paid out of the church-rate. The ecclesiastical courts have repeatedly recognized this power.[17]

With Independents, Wesleyan Methodists and large numbers of Baptists in Watford, the celebrated Thomas Parker finger organ at St Mary's was part-exchanged in 1842 for a J. Walker barrel-and-finger organ.[18] This is suggestive both of indifference on the part of the vicar, the Hon. & Rev. William Robert Capel, and severe funding difficulties, so much so that the organ-builder's invoice was not paid in full until some three years later, when 'directed by the Archdeacon'.[19] Yet extraordinarily, and for reasons unknown, in 1845 the Watford vestry appointed Thomas Warne organist 'at the salary of £50 per annum and that it be paid out of the church rate'.[20] This was an unusually high salary and when a church rate was proposed in 1849 'for the purpose of paying the salary of the organist and for such other expences as are by law chargeable to the church rate' there was widespread rebellion. The entire parish was polled, but with 187 votes for and 142 against, the organist kept his job, albeit at a significantly reduced salary of £30.[21] Unable to manage his affairs on this reduced salary, Warne was reported by the *Hertford Mercury and Reformer* to have been declared insolvent in 1851.[22]

Cheshunt also had a significant proportion of Nonconformists in the parish, and the Easter 1849 vestry at St Mary's was so large that it adjourned to the Green Dragon inn 'in consequence of the insufficiency of the vestry room'.[23] When it was proposed that an annual payment of £30 should be paid to the organist out of the church rate, an amendment was put forward that it should instead be paid by private subscription. The amendment was thrown out, again after a poll of the entire parish. Similar objections were raised annually, until finally in April 1857 the vestry resolved to discontinue the salaries of the parish clerk, organist, organ-blower, beadle and pew opener 'upon the principle that those persons only who require their services should contribute to their support'. With no-one willing to pay the organist, the organ became surplus to requirements and temporarily removed by the organ-builders Bishop & Starr, but later re-instated.[24]

In Berkhamsted 'a considerable sum' had been raised in 1849 towards the purchase of a new finger organ to replace the barrel organ in St Peter's, and it was proposed that an organist should be appointed at an annual salary of £25, to be paid out of the church rate.[25] With many Baptists, Independents, Wesleyans and Quakers in the parish this was strongly opposed, some ratepayers asserting that it was illegal and others 'that those who had been dissatisfied with the old organ should subscribe for the salary of the organist required for the new instrument'. After 'a warm discussion', the churchwardens sought legal advice, again from John Haggard. They asked whether it was justifiable 'under the authority of a resolution of vestry, or otherwise' to pay the organist and organ-related expenses out of the church rate and, if so, whether it should be specified in advance that this would be the purpose of the vestry meeting. Haggard's opinion was:

> That a majority of ratepayers in the parish of Gt Berkhampstead may legally vote a salary to an organist, & a sufficient sum for tuning the organ, & for necessary repairs as occasion may require. If the vestry be convened mainly for the above objects, they certainly should be specified in the notice.[26]

He went on to explain that 'Generally, such expences form a part of the annual items submitted to the rate-payers to be included in a rate, applied for annually by the churchwardens as expences incident to the performance of Divine Service, to the churchwardens' office', but added, 'In this case, the item being new, it is advisable to specify it.' Haggard drew their attention to the 1830 ruling that parishioners could not be forced to pay for the installation or upkeep of an organ, even if the bishop had granted a faculty, and reiterated that a faculty to erect an organ 'would not saddle the expenses of performance upon the church rate'.[27] He also advised that a faculty would not be refused 'merely on the ground of those expences not being specially provided for'.[28] So, in other words, when giving permission for the installation of an organ, the bishop did not take into account the parish's ability or willingness to pay for the upkeep of the organ or for the organist.

An additional comment provides a partial explanation as to why so few faculties for Hertfordshire church organs survive from this period.

Haggard's wording clearly implies that few churches went to the trouble and expense of applying for one, but he cautioned that parishioners might feel justified in opposing organ-related expenses without such a faculty: 'Strictly, I apprehend, a faculty is required for the erection of an organ, and if opposition to payments in respect of it be anticipated, it may be worth consideration whether the instrument itself should be erected without legal authority.'[29] In this instance the Berkhamsted vestry did decide to appoint an organist. Having chosen Thomas Crabb, he appears to have been paid regularly and without any further opposition, but this outcome was atypical in Hertfordshire, perhaps because the legal implications had been so thoroughly examined from the outset.

The Hertfordshire town with the largest and most active body of dissenters was St Albans, with Baptists, Independents, Wesleyan and Primitive Methodists. The St Albans Corporation held the advowson of the Abbey Church until the 1835 Reform of Municipal Corporations Bill. From this date onwards all corporation members had to be elected by ratepayers, so that, in addition to having vestry voting rights in their parish church, Nonconformists and non-church-goers could now also be elected to the corporation. Problems with funding the Abbey Church organist quickly became apparent, and in August 1838 it was necessary to hold a collection after morning and evening service 'in lieu of an appointed salary' for the organist Thomas Brooks.[30] Although regular payments resumed, with Brooks paid an annual salary of £40 between 1840 and 1844, it became the norm for the numerous Baptists in the parish to refuse to pay the Abbey Church rate, largely because they objected to this being used to fund the organist. The goods of several Baptists who attended Dagnall Street Chapel, including two tables and some cheese belonging to their minister William Upton, were seized for non-payment of the rate in 1848.[31] In addition to coverage in the local press, the Baptist printer Richard Gibbs responded by printing and circulating handbills that highlighted the absurdity of the items seized and, more importantly, the fact that their expected resale value was in all cases far higher than the amount owed. The matter was reported widely in newspapers, including the *Hampshire Telegraph*, which reprinted Gibbs' handbill:

CAUTION!!!

Whereas the houses of the undermentioned inhabitants of the Abbey Parish, have been recently entered, and the following articles forcibly taken from them, viz –

From Mr Richard Gibbs's (Church-rate 10s 6d)
23 gilt-edged bibles!!! And 6 do. Prayer books.
Value £2 0s 6d

From Mr T Bonds (Rate 10s)
Four pair of men's high shoes Value £1 14s

From Mr H Whitbread's (Rate 10s)
An Easy Chair, 2 Windsor chairs, a table and a music stand
Value £2 10s

From Mr T Harris's (Rate 9s)
3 dozen fine Brazilian hats Value £2 14s

From Miss Wood's (Rate 6s)
2 tables, a fender, hearth-rug, 4 chairs, 8 knives and 6 forks,
a tea-tray, and a washing-tub (much needed by the offender)
Value £3

From Mr Jesse Hulks's (Rate 5s 6d)
3 pair of Boots
Value £1 7s

And whereas, this was done by persons well known as the agents of an aged and notorious offender named CHURCH (OF ENGLAND)!

This is to caution all persons of respectability from holding any communication with the said offender, and to invite the assistance of the virtuous part of the community in bringing her to justice.[32]

In 1849 the defaulters purchased a second-hand organ for their Dagnall Street chapel by means of a private subscription and the proceeds of the tea meeting. The Liberal *Hertford Mercury and Reformer* pointedly remarked that by these means 'the whole of the expenses created by the purchase of the instrument had been covered'.[33] Unlike at the Abbey Church, there had been no reliance on contributions from the parish to fund their music-making.

The *Herts Guardian* reported that in April 1853 several St Albans dissenters, mostly Baptists, had been summonsed for non-payment of the church rate. Specifically, 'Mr Hucks [Hulks] objected to the sums for organist's salary and clock chimes coming out of the rate; the bench made an order for payment.'[34] One of the dissenters was John Lewis, a member of both Dagnall Street Baptist Chapel and St Albans Corporation, who is reported as saying that, had he been mayor, he would not have signed the summons. Indicating support for the established church, William Pollard, the paper's editor, commented, 'If Mr Lewis ever does become Mayor and refuses to sign summonses for rates when applied to, he will find himself in a very unenviable predicament.'[35]

No church rate
In the early decades of the nineteenth century voting against setting the church rate had been merely a means of registering a protest, because the churchwardens had the final decision. But in August 1853 the House of Lords finally settled the sixteen-year-long church rate dispute at Braintree in Essex. The *Hertford Mercury and Reformer* reported that churchwardens would now no longer be permitted to impose a church rate, so, unless the majority of the vestry agreed, no rate could be made.[36] Dissenters and non-church-goers were now able to block both the payment of specific items from the church rate and the setting of the rate itself, and from this date onwards disputes are said to have multiplied fivefold, partly because many parishes had been awaiting the verdict.[37] Members of numerous town vestries now began to vote against setting a church rate that would have made provision for payments to the organist. Many church organists were already in a very difficult position financially, and the 1853 ruling made a bad situation worse.

In April 1854 more than ninety parishioners attended the Abbey Church vestry in St Albans, where the motion was put forward 'that no rate be made'.[38] Following an inconclusive vote the entire parish was polled, as in Cheshunt and Watford. A total of 179 votes was cast for the rate, but 189 against, so no funding was allocated to pay 11s to the singing boys and £30 to the organist John Brooks, who had taken over from his brother Thomas. Following this meeting John Brooks resigned to become organist of St Mary's, Watford, believing that this 'would eventually be much to the benefit of himself and his family'.[39] He assured the vestry that he was not leaving because he anticipated losing his salary, believing that 'those parishioners who attend the church service would gladly continue to do what they had recently done, subscribe sufficient to pay an organist, in addition to the other expenses, rather than have the musical portion of the service abridged'.[40] The vestry agreed 'to leave the appointment of an organist to those parishioners who subscribe to carry on the church service, the refusal of a church-rate having put an end to the fund out of which the organist was formerly paid'.[41] But unfortunately things went from bad to worse for Brooks in Watford owing to the influence of Tractarianism, as explained below.

Archdeacon Grant summarised the *status quo* during his 1859 visitation held at All Saints, Hertford. He advised churchwardens to be careful not to admit into their accounts 'any item which cannot legally be charged upon that fund', warning that this would invalidate the church rate if contested.[42] Items he considered to be 'lawful where assented to by a majority of the vestry, though not compulsory' included 'fuel, lights, mattings, clerk's, organist's and pew-opener's salaries, improvements in the sittings, and so forth'.

Although attempts were made in 1834 and 1837 to pass legislation to abolish church rates, this was not finally achieved until the Compulsory Church Rates Abolition Act of 1868.[43] In the Abbey Church no attempt was made to collect church rates after Easter 1866. Instead, voluntary contributions and offertory collections were made to defray expenses associated with church services. At the end of the first full year the churchwardens printed a detailed list of contributions and expenses, which showed a substantial deficit, with outgoings of £123 but receipts of only £69.[44] The music department accounted for over £61 of the outgoings, including the organist's salary of £31. That such a large proportion of the total should be spent on music-making in this town church gives an indication as to why there should have been so much discontent among those parishioners who, although unwilling or unable to attend, had formerly been expected to contribute towards it.

Today, the Church of England continues to make use of voluntary contributions and collections to help defray expenses. Unfortunately in the majority of parish churches there is little or no dedicated funding available to pay an organist, let alone for the upkeep of an organ.

Tractarian influence

In certain Hertfordshire parishes church rate disputes were fuelled by opposition to clergy who had come under the influence of the Tractarian or Oxford Movement. In 1833 Rev. John Keble, Fellow of Oriel College, Oxford, preached a highly influential sermon on 'National Apostasy' at the University Church. This addressed the threats posed to the established church by the recent passing of various parliamentary acts. His arguments were subsequently developed in 'Tracts for the Times' by members of his circle, most notably Edward Pusey and John Henry Newman. This new 'Tractarian' or 'Oxford Movement' developed into a fundamental shift towards Catholicism within the established church, only lacking recognition of the pope's authority. Although the Evangelical movement continued to flourish throughout the 1800s, by the end of the century Oxford-influenced Anglo-Catholics had become the dominant group in the Church of England, taking the initiative from the old High Churchmen.

Closely related to the growing Oxford Movement, 1839 saw the founding of the Oxford Society for Promoting the Study of Gothic Architecture. The Cambridge Society for the Study of Church Architecture, almost immediately renamed the Cambridge Camden Society (CCS), was also founded in this year, and was renamed again in 1845 as the Ecclesiological Society. In addition to publishing the *Ecclesiologist*, the CCS produced a series of pamphlets entitled *A Few Words to [...]*, with the aim of reaching every parish in the country, as had the High-Church *Ecclesiastical Gazette*. These university societies actively encouraged the scholarly study of mediaeval art and architecture in order to promote both the restoration of old churches and the building of new, to provide what they considered to be more suitable liturgical settings.[45] Their focus on the Eucharist required the provision of suitably reverential church buildings, worship and music-making, and radically altered the way in which the church operated.

During the early nineteenth century many Hertfordshire parishes found themselves with a resident incumbent for the first time in living memory. This was a result of a reduction in absenteeism and pluralism, a consequence of political and theological radicals successfully fighting for improvements to conditions for poor clergy, and a reduction in the influence of patrons and wealth of bishops.[46] By the mid-1800s many newly ordained clergymen were attracted by the dynamic approach of the Oxford Movement, but the changes they introduced in their parish churches reinforced the church–chapel dichotomy and fuelled long-running church rate disputes, with serious consequences for church music-making.

Some musicians were in the habit of playing in both church and chapel, and likewise some Nonconformists attended their parish church in the morning and their own chapel in the afternoon or evening as a supplement. Many newly resident Tractarian incumbents disapproved of this. In his Survey, the Baptist minister William Upton described Richard Gee, appointed vicar of Abbots Langley in 1844 at the age of 27, as 'Puseyite', adding 'A flag on the Church announces and calls to church on Saints days – All quite Anglo

Catholic.'[47] Gee and his curate were 'indefatigable in denouncing Dissent, urging and bribing people to attend the Church'.[48] Similarly, when a young St Albans boy was taken to the Dagnall Street Methodist chapel by his parents in 1843 it was considered 'a grave offence' by the National School committee, who ordered him to be birched.[49]

Tractarians continued to see singing children as a means of reforming parochial psalmody, as had the elite associated with charity and Sunday schools and early supporters of National Schools. But Tractarians initially wished to do away with *any* sort of instrumental support for children's and adult's singing, and disapproved of the use of instruments and organs alike. Frances Ann Head of Awlescombe in Devon argued against 'the whimsical flourishes of the wind and stringed instruments […] which now fill the galleries of our country churches'.[50] Head was a member of the Devon gentry who took it upon herself to reform the music-making in her parish church. She sought the advice of the Tractarian Arthur Henry Dyke Acland, younger son of Sir Thomas Dyke Acland, a major landowner in nearby Killerton. A.H.D. Acland took the name Troyte in 1852 under the terms of an inheritance, and it is by this name that he is known as a composer of hymn tunes and Anglican chants.[51] Referring to the 'vile instruments' in her parish church, Head argued that 'the music best calculated for these instruments is *not* that of the Psalmody, the harmony of which has *no proper instrumental accompaniment* at all, and the place of these bands therefore is *not* in the *church*'.[52]

Letters to the Tractarian *Educational Magazine* enlarged upon this theme. In May 1840 'E.T.' offered 'a few remarks on the best method of improving Parochial or Village Psalmody': 'Many of your readers may be doomed to listen with aching ears, and tastes and feelings sorely wounded, to the miserable attempts at sacred music in their parish Church, and would be rejoiced if so pleasing and important a part of the service could be better conducted.'[53] The influence of church rate disputes can again be seen in E.T.'s argument that singers were tolerated 'because they are volunteers and cost the parish nothing except a trifling gratuity at Christmas', yet were permitted to 'introduce their own instruments' and 'to reign supreme in the singing gallery'. Continuing the trend witnessed throughout this period, the proposed solution was to use children:

> In any place where there is a daily boys' or girls' school, the elements of this choir may be found. […] once well begun, and singing established as a regular part of school tuition, the Clergyman and his people will be secure of a succession of tolerable vocalists. Though the children pass off from the school, some remain in the village; and these, whether in the gallery or in the body of the Church, are useful both by their better singing and better taste.[54]

In early 1841 Acland took up the theme in earnest in a short series of articles for the magazine, in which he praised Head's teaching method.[55] The following month this was detailed in a letter from Miss Head herself, at Acland's request. At first she familiarised children to sing at the pianoforte, before moving on to using only a pitch-pipe to give the first note. Using the familiar argument that the results would be self-perpetuating she wrote:

> Should this plan [...] be at all extensively adopted, the trouble – such as it is – will in the next generation totally cease. The children of those who now, as children themselves, sing by note the first and second parts, would learn almost unconsciously of their *parents*. [...] every child, boy or girl, in every parish, who may have either voice or ear, may learn; and our Village Churches may henceforward be filled, not only with good Choirs, but with *the voices of the whole congregations*.[56]

It is clear that this approach was adopted in other churches, perhaps making a virtue out of necessity, as funding was at such a low ebb. During the 1850s the rector of Westmill's wife Mrs Ewing, and afterwards her daughter, led the choir of men, women and children equipped only with a pitch-pipe.[57]

In 1845 the amateur musician Robert Druitt attracted support from both clergymen and laity after the publication of his *Popular Tract on Church Music*.[58] His supporters collaborated to form the Tractarian 'Society for Promoting Church Music', and in 1846 the first issue of their journal *The Parish Choir* was published under Druitt's editorship. The very first issue indicated that in both rural and town parishes the singing was left to the children. In rural parishes there was either no organ or no resident organist, and an untrained choir of 'a few children of the parish school', considered a hindrance to any attempt at singing made by members of the congregation.[59] In towns, school children taught by the organist were 'the psalm-singers for the congregation', which was also considered inappropriate, in this instance because the children sang instead of the congregation. The *Parish Choir* argued:

> something may be done, and ought to be done, to improve the style of music and singing in our churches [...] Therefore, as a first step, we say, let all children be taught to sing, not only in the national and charity schools, but also in the private schools to which people in good circumstances send their children.[60]

This goes further than other contemporary suggestions that only poor children should lead the singing in church, and is reminiscent of Riley's 1762 advice that the children of polite families should also play their part.[61]

Like the *Educational Magazine*, the *Parish Choir* campaigned against gallery singers and church bands, pleading for a more decorous approach to worship. Each issue included supplements of church music, ideally to be sung unaccompanied, with the aim of reaching every parish to promote congregational psalmody among 'all members of the Church, high and low, rich and poor'.[62] The Tractarians' promotion of this 'special style' of music emphasised their ideal that there should be a clear distinction between the church and the secular world.[63] This is one reason why clergy with Tractarian leanings pressed for the introduction of congregational chanting instead of singing metrical psalms.

Anglican chants
Rather than being an innovation of the Oxford Movement, the introduction of the chanting of psalms was a gradual and complex process.[64] Gregorian chant (plainchant) had been promoted by certain Evangelical clergymen, but Tractarians were most prominent in attempts to induce the congregation to sing it.[65] However, congregations found the unpredictable rhythms of Gregorian chant very difficult to master, and those with no organ or choir to lead them would have found it even more of a challenge.[66] The more tuneful Anglican chants used in cathedrals were widely adopted instead, particularly after the *Parish Choir* began to distribute a complete set of them, starting in its second issue, but these too required much practice.[67] Prompted by a letter suggesting that the roles of schoolmaster and organist could be combined to save money, the editor wrote, 'it is very desirable that the schoolmaster should be able to accompany the chant on a small organ, so that that horrible makeshift, the grinding organ, need not be thought of'.[68] In churches with an existing barrel organ capable of accompanying chanting it was necessary to re-pin at least one of the barrels with chants, and in 1831 Mrs Gaussen, patron of North Mymms, paid the organ-builder Gray for repairs that included 'resetting both barrels' and 'resetting 2 tunes and altering chaunt'.[69] Similarly, an instrument offered for sale in the *Hertford Mercury and Reformer* in 1849 drew attention to the fact that its barrels were 'newly marked'.[70] But chanting did not lend itself to performance by a barrel organ operated and blown by one handle, because of the impossibility of extending the length of the chanting note without loss of wind pressure. Organ-builders took note of the difficulties involved. If the organ had separate handles to crank the barrel and blow the bellows, it would be possible to sustain the chanting note, and in 1839 Flight & Sons advertised 'Psalmodic Organs for Churches and Chapels, which, by the improvements effected in them, are made to execute Psalms, Responses, and Chants, in a manner quite equal to the performance on a Finger-organ.'[71]

Among Tractarians there were heated discussions as to whether churches should have organs at all. In 1843 the CCS declared that the use of organs could not be justified owing to the vocal nature of 'church musick' before the invention of the organ. It gave a stark example:

> compare a church where metrical psalms have been wont to be lustily sung with no accompaniment except (perhaps) a bass; and the same church, when some illjudged liberality has given a barrel-organ. [...] we think nothing can be much more revolting than to hear the feeble singing of a congregation to a jingling, shaking, barrel-organ, which plays about three tunes like 'Cambridge New'.[72]

After enumerating further objections, including the cost, but especially the wanton manner in which organs and galleries blocked arches and western windows, the CCS baldly asserted, 'We do therefore earnestly deplore and deprecate the introduction of organs into old churches not yet provided with them, or new churches to be built.'[73]

In addition to finding no precedent for the use of instruments, Ecclesiologists argued against the involvement of women in church music-making for the same reason. Although women organists would have been hidden behind the curtain normally hung around the organ console, their very presence may have caused unease to the prominent Ecclesiologist John Mason Neale, who argued in 1843 that 'where women-singers are allowed [...] the notice which they attract from their station in front of the gallery might well enough befit a theatre, but is highly indecorous in the House of God'.[74]

The CCS acknowledged Cambridge University's failure to educate potential clergymen in the niceties of church music, as the university was then a place with 'A few miserable and effete singers running about from choir to choir, and performing, to a crashing and bellowing of organs, the most meagre and washy musick'.[75] This appears to have fuelled the CCS's prejudice against organ music, and they added 'Most earnestly do we hope that no more organs – we can scarcely condescend to say, or *barrel-organs* – may be put up in our beautiful old churches.'[76]

The Tractarian insistence on unaccompanied singing and the Ecclesiological drive to remove galleries were significant factors in the demise of both church bands and barrel organs. Yet this stance quickly began to soften, so that in 1842 the CCS advised churchwardens that they could 'do much for the more solemn and reverent performance of Divine Service, by encouraging the organist to teach the children to sing', repeating an argument used time and again during the eighteenth and nineteenth centuries.[77]

By 1850 little progress appears to have been made in 'regulating' singers and church bands. The *Parish Choir* asked of the clergyman: 'Supposing utmost care has failed to win the confidence of his choir. If the flute, fife, clarionet, and bassoon are huffed, and combine with the vocalists to revenge his interference by withdrawing their assistance, how shall he act?'[78] Once again, the obvious solution presented itself:

> The way is open – let him turn to his Sunday-school. There are rich materials for forming a choir. There he will have fewer tempers to contend with. There he will discover a mine of vocal beauty; for no finer voices exist whether for leading or swelling a chorus, than those of children.[79]

Perhaps suggesting that disposing of singers was something akin to shooing wasps – 'the petty vexation for the time would be unpleasant' – the article assured any doubters that 'a more favourable event could hardly happen to a country clergyman than to be deserted by his singers and thrown upon the resources of his Sunday-school'.

Objections to Tractarianism

Strong objections were made in several Hertfordshire parishes whose clergy had come under the influence of the Oxford Movement, and again this caught the attention of the local press. Opposition was probably felt particularly keenly in Ware owing to the location of St Edmund's College, a large Roman Catholic teaching establishment, in the parish of Standon, close by. Henry Coddington, vicar of St Mary's, Ware, was regarded with increasing suspicion by his parishioners, who considered him to be 'imbued with Tractarianism'.[80] In June 1843 vestry members did not mince their words when they wrote to Charles Blomfield, Bishop of London:

> My Lord, we the undersigned inhabitants and ratepayers of the parish of Ware respectfully beg leave to represent to your lordship that the alterations lately made in the celebration of Divine Worship in this parish are utterly inconsistent with our views and feelings, nay more, we may say so entirely repugnant to them, that we are fully convinced if they are persisted in it will ultimately endanger the true interests of the church.[81]

The dispute escalated. By September the churchwardens had entered into correspondence with William Howley, Archbishop of Canterbury. A discussion was held as to whether the organ should continue to be used, and the *Hertford Mercury and Reformer* reported that 'It now only played two psalms in which the congregation engaged, and was employed during the rest of the service merely for the accommodation of the minister, while he was marching about the church.'[82]

As anticipated, when the Ware Easter vestry was held 'a considerable number of the principal rate-payers were present' – always a sign of potential trouble.[83] Several items were struck out, and the vestry agreed that notice should be given to the organist T.W. Luppino 'that after Easter next his services will be dispensed with, as his salary [£35] will not be allowed out of the church rate'. By May 1844, 230 of the congregation had broken away to form a separate meeting in the Town Hall led by a Wesleyan Connexion minister, with 'prayers, lessons, and singing psalms [...] in strict accordance with the usage of the established church'.[84]

Until this point the organ's major role would have been to support singing, preferably by the congregation, rather than to provide liturgical embellishment, but this incident provides an interesting example of how a change in the use of the organ was instrumental in repelling rather than attracting worshippers. As a locally renowned music teacher and impresario of musical and theatrical entertainments, Luppino may have selected an ambitious repertoire to accompany the minister's 'marching about'. He next became organist of Cheshunt parish church, where he continued until 1850.[85] Although briefly reinstated at Ware, Luppino retired in his early 60s in 1852, when the vestry felt 'the duty of organist has now perhaps become too laborious for his advanced years'.[86]

By 1858 the Ware churchwardens were unable to collect a church rate at all. According to Joseph Blakesley, who had replaced Coddington as vicar in 1845:

> feeling that persons who did a public service had a right to be paid for their services, and having no funds at command for the purpose of paying those who performed services in connection with the church, the churchwardens gave notice to those persons to discontinue their services. Accordingly the organ did not play, for there were no means of paying the organist and the organ blower; the bells no longer chimed because there was no money to pay the ringers, the clock had stopped, because there was no funds to pay the person who wound it up.[87]

Ware was not the only town to see strong opposition to Tractarianism. In October 1855 the *Hertford Mercury and Reformer* reported:

> In two Hertfordshire towns, connected by a few miles of railway, we have the same contest going on between youthful Romanizing vicars and curates and their Protestant parishioners. In each case the Bishop sides with the parishioners, and remonstrates with and entreats the clergy. He can do nothing more.[88]

This referred to disputes in Hemel Hempstead and Watford, then connected by the London and North Western Railway. The newspaper carried a report of a 'numerously attended' meeting held in Hemel Hempstead Town Hall 'to consider what steps should be taken to resist the innovations recently introduced into the Church service' by the vicar William Henry Mountain.[89] A proposal was made to oppose the making of any church rate in the parish, and to adopt 'every other legal and constitutional means whatsoever for the purpose'. This was seconded by Thomas Rolph, the local bank manager, who said: 'He was determined to do everything in his power to resist the introduction of Popery amongst them, and by the term Popery he meant not only the old corrupt tree of Rome, but also every offshoot of that tree, of which Puseyism was one.'[90] The resolution was carried unanimously. The organist at the time was none other than Edwin Theodore Nicholls. Having lost his position as organist of St Mary's, Hitchin, because of a dispute initiated by dissent, he now lost his appointment at St Mary's, Hemel Hempstead, because of a dispute initiated by the introduction of Tractarian ritualism.

Meanwhile, in Watford the smouldering flames of discontent, initially provoked by matters of principle and financial considerations, had also been fanned by the introduction of ritualism. Following the death of the notorious and elderly Hon. & Rev. Capel in December 1854, Richard Lee James, a young and enthusiastic Tractarian, was appointed vicar and immediately set about introducing 'changes of a Puseyite character' to the service.[91] It had been the custom to sing a psalm at the end of Morning Prayer, but instead James introduced both the ringing of a bell for five minutes to announce the Communion service and the Prayer for the Church Militant. According to the *Herts Guardian*, 'As soon as the bell began to ring, the Hon. Mrs. Villiers rose from her seat in a pew near the pulpit and left the church – an example which was immediately followed by the whole of the congregation.'[92] At this time, Arthur Capel, 6th Earl of Essex, was patron of Watford parish church, and Mrs Villiers was a prominent member of his family.

The new vicar left the parish for a while, under a cloud of bad feeling. Yet on his return he explained his determination to continue with the changes, and preached a sermon that 'excited renewed apprehension', fuelled by the rumour that he was planning to 'clothe twelve of the National School boys in surplices, practise them as choristers, and place them in the chancel of the Church'.[93] Because the patron was also lay rector of the church, locating the choir in the chancel without his express permission to do so would have been seen as a provocative action. In November 1856 the vestry agreed not to set a church rate 'to mark their sense of the unhappy feeling of discord which has recently been introduced amongst them, by the extreme and altered mode of conducting the Church Services, which have proved detrimental to the moral well being of the parishioners'.[94]

The organist John Brooks found himself in circumstances similar to those of Nicholls. Having left his post at the Abbey Church a few months previously because of a dissent-led church rate dispute, Brooks now lost his salary in Watford 'by the discontinuance of the church rate' provoked by the introduction of ritualism.[95] Rev. James responded by introducing voluntary contributions and church collections, but collected only £50 in 1856 and £33 in 1857, making good the shortfall as best he could.[96] With his poor financial situation exacerbated by a tenant's rent arrears and outstanding payments for pupils' music lessons, Brooks was arrested in Watford High Street on Whit Monday 1859 for non-payment of a trifling debt associated with a loss-making concert he had given in St Albans.[97] When Brooks explained to the Sheriff's officer that he was on his way to play at St Mary's, and would lose his job if detained, the officer agreed to sit with him while he played for the service. Brooks then spent five days in Hertford gaol and was declared insolvent. Subsequently Rev. James appealed to his parishioners for help in clearing the considerable arrears due, including £20 to John Brooks. But a strong point of principle was at play here, and there was little response. According to the *Herts Guardian*, 'if it were not that the payment of these arrears would appear to countenance the service as carried on by Mr. James, there would be no doubt about raising the money immediately'.[98] In September 1862 the Watford vestry resolved to dispose of the organ altogether, but with poetic justice were thwarted by a complete lack of funds to pay for its removal.[99]

In 1863 the new organist of St Mary's, Watford, was the National School master Charles Lawrence. Calling attention to his Hullah training, the significance of which is explained in the next chapter, Lawrence innocently advertised:

> Mr C. Lawrence (*Organist of the Parish Church, Watford*) BEGS respectfully to inform the inhabitants of Watford and its vicinity, that he is prepared to instruct pupils on the Organ, Pianoforte, or Harmonium, upon the following terms: In Watford 10s. 6d. per Quarter; Elsewhere 1 Guinea per Quarter; Mr L. (formerly a pupil of Hullah) will also teach *Vocal Music* upon the same terms.[100]

Lawrence appears to have been blissfully unaware of the financial arguments that beset his immediate predecessors. Almost inevitably, objections were raised when it became apparent that some of his pupils had no connection with the parish church and were, by having lessons on the church organ, seen to be taking advantage of an asset to which they had not contributed. The correspondent 'Fair Play' wrote to the editor of the *Watford Observer* in 1864:

> SIR, Some time since an effort was made to provide a better organ for our noble old church, or to improve the present instrument. That effort, however, failed as most such things do in 'money-getting Watford'. Under these circumstances it is obvious that *some* care should be taken of the old organ; but, from what I hear, the contrary is the case, inasmuch as among the persons who have access to the organ, and are regularly receiving lessons and 'grinding' upon it, will be found the *organist of a baptist chapel*, and a member of the choir of a popular church in this neighbourhood (both chapel and church being bitterly opposed to our parish church and its services). Surely these aspirants for musical fame ought to practice upon the organs in their own places of worship, instead of availing themselves of a privilege which they have not the courtesy to reciprocate.[101]

By the time of the 1871 census Lawrence and his wife had found new teaching posts in Wales.[102]

Disputes driven by both dissent and objections to Tractarianism contributed to severe difficulties in paying organists during the mid-nineteenth century. Once more the church became dependent on voluntary donations and the willingness of parishioners to fund music-making. When no money was forthcoming, unless the church became entirely reliant upon voluntary organists or a barrel organ, there was no organ-playing to support congregational singing. Yet this was not the case in every parish, because during the mid-1800s a renewed interest in singing began to lead to an increase in fundraising for church music, as discussed in the next chapter. Nevertheless, the Tractarian drive to remove galleries, and preferably the church bands and barrel organs that had been located in them, had a lasting influence on church buildings, as is discussed further in Chapter 9.

Endnotes

1. *Bucks Gazette* (12 November 1831), p. 4.
2. *Bury and Norwich Post* (26 February 1817), p. 2.
3. HALS, DP/46B/12/5 Vestry minutes (1827–34).
4. *Ibid.*
5. D. Le Faye, *A Chronology of Jane Austen and Her Family: 1700–2000* (Cambridge, 2006), p. 638.
6. See Chapter 4, p. 93.
7. HALS, DP/111/8/20.
8. J. Haggard, *Reports of Cases Argued and Determined in the Ecclesiastical Courts at Doctors' Commons and in the High Court of Delegates*, 4 vols (London, 1829–33), III, pp. 4–10.
9. HALS, DP/111/8/20.
10. See Chapter 3, p. 81–2.
11. *HMR* (9 May 1837), pp. 2–3.
12. HALS, DE/Gr/46 Gerish Collection.
13. *HMR* (9 May 1837), pp. 2–3.
14. HALS, DP/53/7/4 Minutes of meetings of subscribers to the organist's salary (1837–56).
15. *HMR* (23 February 1850), p. 1.
16. HALS, DP/53/7/4.
17. *The Justice of the Peace and County, Borough, Poor Law Union and Parish Law Recorder* (24 April 1841), p. 245.
18. HALS, DP/117/5/1 Churchwardens' accounts (1841–4); *Watford Observer* (28 May 1870), p. 4.
19. HALS, DP/117/5/1.
20. HALS, DP/117/8/1–3.
21. *Ibid.*
22. *HMR* (13 September 1851), p. 1.
23. HALS, DP/29/8/48–57.
24. *Ibid.*
25. HALS, DP/19/6/1 Papers relating to the organ (1849); *HMR* (28 April 1849), p. 3.
26. HALS, DP/19/6/1; *HMR* (28 April 1849), p. 3.
27. HALS, DP/19/6/1; *HMR* (28 April 1849), p. 3.
28. HALS, DP/19/6/1; *HMR* (28 April 1849), p. 3.
29. HALS, DP/19/6/1; *HMR* (28 April 1849), p. 3.
30. *County Press* (18 August 1838), n.p.
31. *HMR* (13 May 1848), p. 3; *Hampshire Telegraph* (20 May 1848), p. 8; *Leeds Times* (27 May 1848), p. 6.
32. *Hampshire Telegraph* (20 May 1848), p. 8.
33. *HMR* (13 January 1849), p. 3.
34. *HG* (14 May 1853), p. 8.
35. *Ibid.*; John Lewis *was* elected mayor of St Albans in 1856.
36. *HMR* (20 August 1853), pp. 5–6.
37. Owen Chadwick, *The Victorian Church*, 2 vols, 3rd edn (London, 1971), 1, p. 158.
38. HALS, DP/90/8/1–3 Vestry minutes (1799–61).
39. *HMR* (5 May 1855), p. 3.
40. *Ibid.*
41. *Ibid.*
42. *HG* (9 July 1859), p. 5.
43. PP 1831–32 (199).
44. Cathedral & Abbey Church of St Alban Muniment Room, Voluntary Contributions Towards the Church Service from Easter 1866 to Easter 1867.
45. N. Yates, *Buildings, Faith and Worship* (Oxford, 1991), p. 150.

46 *Ibid.*, p. 127.
47 Burg, *Religion*, pp. 46–7.
48 *Ibid.*
49 Greaves, *Methodism*, p. 49.
50 F.A. Head, *Choral Psalmody, or a collection of tunes to be sung in parts without instruments [...]* (London, 1840), p. 8.
51 J.E. Acland, *A Layman's Life in the days of the Tractarian Movement* (Oxford, 1904), p. 71.
52 Head, *Choral Psalmody*, p. 8.
53 *Educational Magazine* (May 1840), pp. 309–14.
54 *Ibid.*
55 *Ibid.* (January 1841), pp. 39–50.
56 *Ibid.* (February 1841), pp. 88–92.
57 Ewing, *Westmill*, p. 95.
58 B. Rainbow, *The Choral Revival in the Anglican Church (1839–1872)* (Oxford, 1970), pp. 96–8.
59 *Parish Choir* (February 1846), p. 7.
60 *Ibid.*, p. 1.
61 See Chapter 2, pp. 51–2.
62 *Parish Choir* (February 1846), p. 2; Rainbow, *Choral Revival*, p. 98.
63 Temperley, *Parish Church*, pp. 248–9.
64 *Ibid.*, pp. 259–61.
65 *Ibid.*
66 *Ibid.*
67 Rainbow, *Choral Revival*, p. 102.
68 *Parish Choir* (November 1846), p. 79; (July 1847), pp. 154–5.
69 CRL, BOA, John Gray accounts, vol. 1 (1821–38), p. 89; see Chapter 6, p. 168.
70 *HMR* (17 March 1849), p. 1.
71 *Ecclesiastical Gazette* (12 November 1839), p. 95.
72 *Ecclesiologist* (September 1843), pp. 1–5. See Chapter 6, p. 169.
73 *Ibid.*
74 J.M. Neale, *Church Enlargement and Church Arrangement* (Cambridge, 1843), p. 15.
75 *Ecclesiologist* (September 1843), pp. 1–5.
76 *Ibid.*
77 Cambridge Camden Society, *A Few Words to Churchwardens on Churches and Church Ornaments. No. II Suited to Town and Manufacturing Parishes* (Cambridge, 1841), p. 12.
78 *Parish Choir* (June 1850), pp. 31–2.
79 *Ibid.*
80 *HMR* (16 September 1843), p. 3.
81 HALS, DP/116/8/10 Vestry minutes (1843–52).
82 *HMR* (16 September 1843), p. 3.
83 *HMR* (9 December 1843), p. 2.
84 *HMR* (11 May 1844), pp. 2–3.
85 HALS, DP/29/8/48–57.
86 HALS, DP/116/8/10.
87 *HMR* (30 October 1858), pp. 2–3.
88 *HMR* (13 October 1855), p. 3.
89 *Ibid.*
90 *Ibid.*
91 *HG* (12 June 1855), p. 2.
92 *Ibid.*
93 *HM* (13 October 1855), p. 3.
94 HALS, DP/117/8/1–3.
95 *HMR* (25 April 1857), p. 3.
96 *HG* (12 June 1858), p. 5.

97 *HMR* (3 July 1858), p. 3; *HMR* (9 July 1859), p. 5.
98 *HG* (12 June 1858), p. 5.
99 HALS, DP/117/8/1–3.
100 *Watford Observer* (22 August 1863), p. 1.
101 *Ibid.* (25 June 1864), p. 1.
102 1871 Wales Census RG10/5336/f.52/p.6.

Chapter 8
Singing classes and choirs

During the mid-nineteenth century a national reform of secular music education led to a popular demand for singing classes for children and adults alike. As a result, many church choral associations and choirs began to be established, in some cases supported by the local elite. The enthusiasm for forming church choirs was usually allied with the demand for new hymn books, and often for a new organ, as discussed in Chapters 3 and 5.

Reform of music education

The first national attempts to reform music education were made during the 1830s, when two school textbooks were published to teach children how to read music. John Turner's *A Manual of Instruction in Vocal Music, Chiefly with a View To Psalmody* was published in 1833 under the auspices of the National Society. Rather than aiming to teach children by ear, this book set out a method for teaching the rudiments of music theory before starting singing lessons. Turner's *Manual* was adopted in many churches, and his method received a warm endorsement in 1839 when 'Ecclesiasticus' wrote to *The Church Magazine* advocating its use to form a small choir of National School boys, who would be more tractable than 'village musicians'. He argued that in many churches there was no psalmody at all and in others it was still

> left to the direction of the village choir; who, not having much knowledge of music, and being moreover greatly disposed to magnify what they have, in about the inverse ratio of their acquirements, either sing to the praise and glory of themselves rather than of God, or inflict torment upon tender ears by the most merciless disregard of time and tune.[1]

In 1835 Sarah Anna Glover, a Sunday school teacher and daughter of a Norwich clergyman, published her *Scheme for Rendering Psalmody Congregational*. Observing that many congregations were unable or unwilling to sing, she advocated teaching poor children to sing in order to lead them, like Gibson and Porteus before her.[2] Teaching the rudiments of music was not easy, and various aids were employed. Glover invented an innovative system termed the 'Norwich Sol-Fa Ladder' to teach her sol-fa method. Yet it was only after the congregationalist minister John Curwen adapted her system as the 'tonic sol-fa', and used it in his 1843 *Singing for Schools and Congregations*, that this method was widely adopted.[3]

Glover was by no means the only person to suggest ingenious devices to teach singing. In 1838 William Cecil, rector of Longstanton St Michael (Cambs.), found that in rural parishes 'The singing is confined almost exclusively to the gallery of performers', and proposed 'A syllabus of directions for training untaught children in the knowledge and practice of psalmody'.[4] Cecil's 'Specification of the mechanical apparatus for teaching psalmody, to large assemblies of children' described in detail how an iron frame was to be filled with a 'mattress' of old carpet or similar, covered with white fabric, across which black tapes were stretched to form staves. Individual notes and musical symbols were made of black-painted tin, with the advice 'from the above description they may be made by any common tinman'. A single tune was then displayed on the apparatus in large characters:

> While the master plays or sings the melody, one child stands before the chart, and points with a wand to the notes as they are played. The other children sing the tune, following the notes so pointed, by the eye, and the tune by the ear. Several children in succession, sometimes two or three together, act this part of Fugleman to the rest, till every child in the room can do it with ease.[5]

The High-Church *Christian Guardian* commented:

> This is very ingenious and so clearly defined that we doubt not it will be found generally useful. We could wish that it should be adopted in every grade of school; indeed teachers and governesses would not find the drudgery of first lessons in music half so intolerable, were they to have recourse to this amusing invention [...].[6]

A.H.D. Acland suggested another Tractarian method of teaching singing that did away with the need for any instrumental support. Like Cecil, he had a practical scientific mind, and in 1841 proposed representing the music stave with wires and balls already used for teaching arithmetic. He suggested they should be 'arranged in two rows of five wires with balls on; and between each, a wire of another colour being used for the ledger C line'.[7] It is unclear how he proposed to represent the length of each note.

Of far greater significance was the opening of the National Society's first teacher-training establishment at Battersea in 1840. The education secretary Sir James Kay appointed the composer John Hullah to teach music as an integral part of the masters' and mistresses' training, following successful reports of children's singing in church. Hullah went on to take charge of music in all National Society teacher-training colleges, including St Mark's College, Chelsea, where all trainees were taught to sing psalms, chants and anthems in the college's 'parochial choir'.[8] The Society sought prospective candidates with considerable proficiency in reading, writing, arithmetic, history, geography, scriptural history, church catechism and preferably Latin and Greek, advising:

> Superior musical abilities are not often found, and still less often cultivated, in this country, in conjunction with the other and higher requisites mentioned above. Much attention will, however, be bestowed upon this department of education in the College, in the hope of diffusing through the country a better style of psalmody, along with the practice of congregational singing.[9]

Indicating that those who already had some grounding in music would be looked upon favourably, the prospectus added that 'a turn for music' in applicants otherwise well qualified 'will be an additional recommendation'.

The Council on Education drew up significant new instructions for school inspectors, clearly indicating that, although choirs of school children continued to be seen as a means of improving congregational psalmody, they were now required to be able to sing from notation rather than relying on a barrel organ:

> *Attainments.* [...] *In Singing*: Having by ear an acquaintance with psalmody and labour songs; acquainted with the elements of the notation of music; able to sing common psalm tunes and labour songs from notes at sight; able to sing chants, anthems and more difficult sacred music, from notes.[10]

Singing classes

Under government sanction, in 1841 Hullah started massed singing classes for adults at Exeter Hall, London, using the same teaching method employed in the National Society's teacher-training colleges. One year later he was presented with a commemorative music stand by grateful members of his first 'Workman's Singing Class'. In front of a packed Exeter Hall audience, Mr T.H. Headland, a member of the class, thanked Hullah for providing the working man with a cheap and innocent means of relaxation after work 'in his own home, and with his own family': in other words, an alternative to spending his wages on drink or perhaps worse. It is apparent from what he said next that, despite numerous and widespread efforts to teach children to sing, by the 1840s there were still few signs this had resulted in congregational singing becoming general:

> An improvement of congregational singing has long been deemed necessary; its inefficiency has probably arisen from the want of a more general acquaintance with the science of music; in consequence of which, this important portion of public worship has commonly been entrusted to the children of elementary schools, from whose little voices, childish apathy, and unconscious irreverence, cannot be obtained those solemn effects of piety which ought to be produced by the multitude of voices engaged in devout sympathy and holy earnestness in singing the praises of Almighty God.[11]

Those successfully completing Hullah's courses were awarded certificates of competence to teach music from *Hullah's Manual*, his translation of Guillaume Wilhem's method, which was used in Parisian schools and public singing classes.[12] This presented an additional income stream to impoverished church organists with no guaranteed salaries, at this time largely a result of the church rate disputes discussed in the previous chapter. In May 1842 the Hitchin organist Frederick Walker delivered a lecture on 'Hullah's, or rather Wilhem's' system of teaching singing.[13] He had already established classes in Hitchin, Weston and Ashwell, and planned to extend to other Hertfordshire parishes. The following November Thomas Brooks, organist of the Abbey Church, St Albans, announced that he too had 'qualified himself under Mr Hullah as an instructor of Wilhem's Method of teaching singing' and intended to give lessons at the Town Hall.[14] Brooks had the full support of the local clergy, numbering among his patrons the incumbents of the Abbey Church, St Peter's, St Michael's, St Stephen's, Redbourn and Abbots Langley. This suggests that attempts to use children's voices alone to lead congregational singing were beginning to peter out. The Ware organist T.W. Luppino was not far behind, advertising his own singing classes in April 1843, although he appears to have had his own ideas about how it should be taught. He explained that his plan 'was not exactly that of Hullah, or of Mainzer, but an adaptation of both'.[15] Here Luppino referred to Joseph Mainzer, who had recently set up London singing classes to rival Hullah's, with an accompanying textbook entitled *Singing for the Million* (1841). The mid-century enthusiasm for singing that developed out of the popularity of Hullah and Mainzer's classes is discussed further below.

In January 1843 Thomas Brooks lectured at Shenley with a view to setting up singing classes there, and 'dwelt with considerable earnestness on the necessity of persons acquiring a knowledge of vocal music to enable them to join in congregational singing'.[16] A few months later his work received a resounding endorsement from Hullah himself when he agreed to conduct the St Albans class in the Town Hall, which was 'nearly filled by the fashionables of the town and neighbourhood', with many others unable to gain admission.[17] Hullah explained to the assembled company that his primary motive had been 'to increase and improve congregational singing, and to substitute a creditable style of singing in places of worship for the imperfect strains that were sent forth from most of the churches in England'.[18]

According to the *Herts Guardian*, the popularity of efforts made by the government in the early 1840s to establish singing classes 'in every part of the kingdom' had confounded the suggestion that 'the English are an unmusical people'.[19] Yet classes were very short-lived, owing to over-ambitious expectations, leaving towns and villages in the same position as before.[20] Some recipients of this tuition had joined their local church choir, but with little commitment. 'A Churchman who likes Music' was so disappointed by the music-making at All Saints, Hertford, on Christmas Day 1850 that he complained to the *Hertford Mercury and Reformer*:

> I have no doubt that most of the parishioners who attend All Saints' Church, are obliged to the gentlemen amateurs who assist so regularly in the singing portion of the service [...] but in common with many others, I have to express my surprise and regret that on Christmas Day, one of the highest festivals of our Church, not *one singer* attended, and consequently the *Te Deum* was performed *in all its parts* by the boys and the organ only, as well as the chaunts and other musical parts of the service.[21]

Nevertheless, certain Hertfordshire landowners persisted in efforts to encourage congregational singing in their parish church, as explained below.

George William Martin

In 1850 the *Parish Choir* reported the recent formation of the Cheadle Association for Promoting Church Music in Staffordshire, established to encourage good congregational singing.[22] Others were urged to follow this example, and the Hertfordshire clergyman Lowther Barrington was among the first to do so. In 1850 Abel Smith (d. 1859) installed Lowther Barrington as rector of Watton-at-Stone. Shortly afterwards, Barrington was introduced to George William Martin of St Paul's Cathedral, music teacher, composer, organist and resident music master of the National Society's Battersea teacher-training college.[23] Having already taught in several villages, Martin now aimed 'to prove that music, as a most powerful agent in cultivating the intellect and improving the moral condition of our working population, can be successfully cultivated in our towns and villages [...]'.[24]

Barrington suggested that Martin should test his theory at Watton-at-Stone, and undertook to pay his expenses. The weekly class soon comprised sixty men, women and boys, 'all from the humbler classes', and, reporting its success, the *Herts Guardian* concluded that singing should be made an essential element of instruction for the poor:

> it is very common to meet with mere children belonging to this class who have made extraordinary progress in sight singing; moreover amongst the members are men accustomed to field work, who possess score copies of some of the Oratorios, and are able by merely looking at the scores to form a correct idea of the beauties and difficulties of those parts which they have never heard.[25]

William Pollard commented: 'a singing class on Mr Hullah's system is about to be established in Hertford. The incredulous in such matters should pay a visit to Watton some Monday evening and see and hear for themselves what Mr Martin has effected by his system among village rustics.'[26]

In 1855 Martin began a second singing class at Newgate Street, in the parish of Hatfield, 'for the purpose of affording a rational recreation to the inhabitants of the hamlet, and also of furthering congregational singing in the Church'.[27] This time it was funded by the landowner Thomas Mills MP, who had already built the Newgate Street schools and chapel-of-ease, to which he had given not one but two barrel organs.[28] The *Hertford Mercury and Reformer* commented:

> If such singing may be heard amongst a population which cannot number more than 100, what might we not hear in some of our larger villages? All that is wanted is a little of that support and encouragement on the part of our gentry which Mr Mills appears to have given in this case.[29]

In 1858 Martin lectured at Cheshunt 'with a view to form classes for the improvement of Church Psalmody' at the request of the vicar James Grantham Faithfull, who 'thought considerable improvement was needed in the singing at the church'.[30] This is hardly surprising, given that the organ had been removed as a result of church rate disputes the previous year, and it was probably an attempt to attract worshippers back.

Martin went on to establish singing classes in many other Hertfordshire parishes. In October 1863 the *Choir and Musical Record* reprinted a letter from 'A Working Man' to the *Hertfordshire Express* outlining their merits.[31] Describing himself as 'deeply interested in the improvement of Church

Psalmody', he explained that the vicar of his Hitchin church had invited the congregation 'to attend once a month at the National Schools and practice with the choir the psalms, hymns, and chants appointed to be sung in the church'. Many of the congregation readily accepted the invitation, and the clergy were also present, 'not as spectators merely, but as genuine working members'. The correspondent argued that the objective of congregational singing should be:

> to avoid on the one hand the *high* style (if I may be permitted so to call it), such as anthems with solos in them, the canticles set to services of such a character as would place the choir in a false position, as not being leaders of the congregation in singing the praises of God: and, on the other, the *low* style, such as falling back to the "good old times" of the gallery with its company of wind and stringed instruments, to wit, the melancholy trombone, the irate clarionet, and the scraping fiddle. These, Sir, are the two extremes. The latter there is happily little fear of our falling back to: but the ambition to aspire to the former is by no means uncommon.[32]

It is perhaps uncharitable to suggest that the vicar may have penned the letter himself.

Tonic sol-fa

Although Hullah's method continued to be taught until the early 1860s, by this time schoolteachers had become increasingly disillusioned by its inflexibility, and most preferred to use John Curwen's tonic sol-fa method. Such was its success that the Tonic Sol-fa Association for the Promotion of Vocal Music in Schools, Homes, and Congregations was established in 1853. The *Herts Guardian* reported that by teaching both sacred and secular music to people from all walks of life the association was 'patiently hoping for its reward', in that gradual improvement of psalmody, which is its chief aim'.[33] In September 1857 a massed choir of some 3,000 tonic-sol-fa-educated school children assembled at Crystal Palace, a gathering akin to the Anniversary Meetings at St Paul's.[34] Although both children and adults used the system very widely, it found its greatest success in the late nineteenth century, which lies outside the scope of this book. The Tonic Sol-fa Association was just one symptom of the mid-century singing craze described by Rainbow as 'one of the most remarkable social phenomena of early Victorian England'.[35]

Church choral associations and choirs

A plethora of locally organised singing associations, societies, unions and festivals sprang up, many concerned with parish music-making. In 1856 the first diocesan choral festival was held in Lichfield Cathedral, and by 1864 seventeen other English and Welsh cathedrals held them.[36] In Hertfordshire,

Table 8.1
Vice-presidents of the Herts Church Choral Association (1861).

Vice-president	Occupation	Notes
Hon. & Rev. Godolphin Hastings	Rector of Hertingfordbury	Son of the Earl of Huntingdon
Hon. & Rev. Lewis William Denman	Rector of Willian	Son of Baron Denman
Hon. & Rev. Lowther Barrington	Rector of Watton-at-Stone	2nd cousin of the Duke of Bedford
Hon. & Rev. William Whitworth Chetwynd-Talbot	Rector of Hatfield	Brother of the Earl of Shrewsbury
Rev. Sir Brooke Boothby	Rector of Welwyn	Baronet
Rev. Canon Blomfield	Rector of Stevenage	Brother of the Bishop of London
Christopher William Giles Puller	Barrister, MP for Hertfordshire	Brother of the rector of Standon
Thomas Mills, Newgate Street	Barrister, landowner, MP	
William Wilshere, Welwyn	Banker, landowner, MP	
William Robert Baker, Bayfordbury	Landowner	
Lionel Ames, Ayot St Lawrence	Landowner	

Source: HMR (30 November 1861), p. 2.

George Becher Blomfield, rector of Stevenage and brother of the Bishop of London, took the lead in October 1861 when he chaired a meeting in his parish 'to consider the propriety of forming a Church Choral Association for the encouragement of music and promotion of congregational singing in the county of Hertford'.[37] The meeting proposed 'that the association should offer to those parishes joining it, instruction in music and singing [...] with the understanding that there shall be no interference with the existing choirs, or the order of Divine Service in any church without the consent of the clergyman'.[38] With Francis Thomas de Grey Cowper, 7th Earl Cowper, as its president, vice-presidents included Canon Blomfield, together with many Honourable and Reverend Hertfordshire incumbents and a number of major landowners (see Table 8.1).

The Herts Church Choral Association engaged a singing master to teach a weekly evening class in the committee members' parishes for a one-off fee of a guinea per parish, plus a small weekly charge for each lesson, depending on the number of attendees. The first members were choirs 'chiefly composed of members of the congregation' from these and a handful of other parishes.[39] In 1862 the association's first annual festival was held at Hitchin, and came to the attention of the *Musical Standard*, which reported that 'upwards of 750 have been and are under the training given by the three choir masters constantly employed' and praised the encouragement of an 'improvement in the standard of knowledge and good taste on the part of the present and rising generation of churchmen'.[40] As with the opening of a new organ or consecration of a restored church, the event attracted a very large congregation, in this instance nearly 2,000 persons. Additional transport was required, and 'the Great Northern Railway Company kindly provided a special train to convey the [singing] classes to their respective homes'.[41]

There was no cathedral in Hertfordshire in which to hold a large choral festival until 1877, when the Abbey Church became the cathedral of the new St Albans diocese. Nevertheless, large choral festivals were held in this building before its elevation to cathedral status. In July 1862 a Grand Musical Festival with a choir of some 150 local volunteers was held in the Abbey Church on the anniversary of the opening of the new organ 'with a view to the improvement of church music', raising funds for 'the maintenance of an efficient choir' and 'the ultimate completion of the organ according to the original specifications of the builders'.[42] The appearance of the town signified the day's importance:

> The Union Jack floated from the top of the massive tower of the Abbey, and the 'College Youths'[43] rang out a merry peal from the bells of old St Alban's. About two o'clock the principal shops in the town were closed, and the streets began to throng with carriages, and well-dressed people on foot hastened in the direction of the Abbey.[44]

On this occasion, a special train brought a large number of visitors from Watford, so that the church was filled with an estimated crowd of at least 3,000, of whom approximately three-quarters were ladies. The *Hertford Mercury and Reformer* attributed the popularity of this event to 'the spread of a practical knowledge of music amongst the masses', which had led 'not only to the holding of monster Handel Festivals in the Crystal Palace, but also to humbler musical celebrations in almost every town in the kingdom'.[45] Singing festivals had the power to attract back disenchanted church-goers and challenge the rival singing attractions found in places with a strong dissenting presence, and were not restricted to market towns such as St Albans and Hitchin. In May 1863 Association choirs trained by George William Martin from Westmill, Standon, Hormead, Little Munden and Braughing, numbering some 170 voices, came together for a festival at the newly restored church in the little village of Westmill.[46] The choice of music clearly reflected the Tractarian influence of the association: the choir chanted the Magnificat, Nunc Dimittis and psalms, and sang Keble's hymn 'Sun of my soul' after the sermon. Perhaps making a virtue out of necessity, the singing throughout was 'unaccompanied by any instrument'. Although this might have reflected the Tractarians' early stance that no organs should be used, it may have had as much to do with the impossibility of using the church's barrel organ to support this repertoire. Indeed, only one of the participating parishes is known to have had a finger organ at this date.

In 1864 Bishop Blomfield praised the association's efforts in replacing the use of children's voices alone, saying:

> the diffusion of a musical knowledge in general, thereby fitting the congregation to take their share in those exercises of praise which are too often either left to the feeble efforts of a few children, or are given in a style which compels the people to be mute listeners, instead of being the principal performers, while the praises of God are sung.[47]

But he closed with an earnest appeal on behalf of the association, which was 'in danger of being crippled in its usefulness through want of adequate [financial] support from the county at large'.

Notwithstanding reports of huge congregations and special trains, a journal kept by Samuel Pryer Field, vicar of Sawbridgeworth and secretary of the Herts Church Choral Association, provides a candid insider's assessment of the association's progress. In 1861 he recorded the initial struggle of finding the minimum number of thirty parishioners stipulated per singing class and persuading eight lapsed choir members to join, 'knowing the independent disposition of many of my parishioners, and how delusive enthusiasm, exhibited hastily at the first, often proves to be – especially in Sawbridgeworth'.[48] Perhaps with this in mind, in 1863 and 1865 festivals were held at Newgate Street 'for the encouragement of the juvenile members' of the association.[49] Some 100 children from local schools took the treble parts, this time supported by a smattering of adult association members who sang alto, tenor and bass. In 1865 the preacher urged the children, 'as the leaders of the church psalmody[,] to be patterns of devotion to the rest of the congregation'. The *Hertford Mercury and Reformer* commented:

> In most of our rural parishes there is not the material to form an efficient choir; and even when through some unusual exertion on the part of the clergyman, the squire, or some ardent musician in the parish, a choir is formed, too often does the attendance of the adults become irregular when the novelty has passed away; and were it not for the children of the school, whose presence can be depended upon, there would frequently be no choir of any kind, to lead the praises of the congregation.[50]

This indicates that during the 1860s congregational singing continued to be heavily dependent on children's singing. After the service Mr Mills regaled the children with 'a plentiful supply of tea and buns' before they mounted their waggons home, again suggesting a continuation of the tradition of rewarding singers with food and drink.

Although the aim of these societies was to promote congregational singing, in some instances their members went on to form or supplement the church choir itself. In 1864 a choir was formed at St Andrew's, Hertford, under the direction of John Marchant, secretary to the Literary and Scientific Institution and a member of the Local Educational Board, suggesting a strong didactic motive. The object was 'to improve and encourage congregational singing in St Andrew's church, Hertford; and also to familiarise its members with the practice of singing in sacred and secular harmony'.[51] A list of choir members given in the *Herts Guardian* demonstrates a wide age range, the youngest being 13 and the eldest 63 (see Table 8.2). Correlation with their given occupations in census returns also indicates both that they were all middle class and that half the ladies had been born outside Hertfordshire, which may perhaps have led to some resentment of outside interference among locally born parishioners.

Again, there were difficulties in retaining adult choir-members. 'A Country Bumpkin' visited St Andrew's in February 1865 expecting to hear 'the voices of trained ladies and gentlemen', but

> The rendering was irreverent, common-place, and slovenly, to a degree that I never heard out of Hertford, which is so much behind the age, that the villages and hamlets around completely eclipse her, although they have some right to look to her for a lead in such matters.[52]

1871 census returns reveal the transitory nature of St Andrew's choir. Two of the young ladies had married and moved away, and four choir members had died by 1871, including Marchant himself.[53] Martin's Watton-at-Stone choir had also quickly dwindled, and the *Hertford Mercury and Reformer* observed that

> The great thing to contend against in societies of this kind is the secession of individuals through marriage and change of residence, or other causes which often frustrate the attempt to improve the taste for music in general, and to animate the too-often dull Psalmody of our village churches.[54]

In 1845 all Hertfordshire parishes had been transferred to the Diocese of Rochester, and in 1862 Rev. Field, secretary of the Herts Church Choral

Table 8.2
Members of St Andrew's, Hertford, church choir (1864).

	Age in 1864	Occupation in 1861	Place of birth	Notes
Female	17	Lodging house keeper's daughter	Hertford	
	17	Widow's daughter	Hertford	1871 living in Hants.
	18	Daughter of Stephen Austin, proprietor & editor of the *Hertford Mercury and Reformer*	Hertford	
	18	Pupil teacher	Hertford	1871 living in Kent
	19	Tax collector's niece	London	
	19	Rector's daughter	Derbys.	
	20	Solicitor's daughter (Marchant's sister-in-law)	Hertford	
	25	Victualler's daughter	Essendon	
	37	Brewer's wife	London	
	40	Coal merchant's wife	London	
	56	Rector's wife	London	1871 living in Gloucs.
	63	Town councillor's wife (Marchant's mother)	Yorks.	d. 1866
Male	13	Rector's son	Isle of Wight	1871 serving in the Navy
	24	Hairdresser	Hertford	
	25	Compositor, market gardener's son	Baldock	
	28	Mason	Ware	d. 1868
	33	Solicitor (John Marchant)	Ware	d. 1868
	41	Ostler	Bengeo	d. 1868
	45	Classics master, Christ's Hospital	Essex	

Sources: *HG* (28 June 1864), p. 4; 1861 Census RG9/655/f.138/p.5, RG9/805/f.5/p.5, RG9/823/f.98/p.10, RG9/823/f.101/p.16, RG9/824/f.5/p.3, RG9/824/f.10/pp.13-14, RG9/824/f.15/p.24, RG9/824/f.21/p.35, RG9/824/f.24/p.42, RG9/824/f.25/p.44, RG9/824/f.26/p.45, RG9/824/f.42/p.24, RG9/824/f.49/p.38, RG9/824/f.62/p.11; 1871 Census RG10/875/f.9/p.10, RG10/1126/f.74/p.16, RG10/1372/f.50/p.49, RG10/1372/f.103/p.8, RG10/1372/f.116/p.33, RG10/1372/f.134/p.13, RG10/1372/f.139/p.24, RG10/1372/f.150/p.46, RG10/1372/f.151/p.50, RG10/1372/f.152/p.51, RG10/1373/f.9/p.13, RG10/1373/f.28/p.1, RG10/2680/f.46/p.8 ; England & Wales, National Probate Calendar (Index of Wills and Administrations), 1858–1966.

Association, set up a new group for clergymen and their existing church choirs 'with a view to increase congregational singing and to promote the love and practice of good church music'.[55] With a more ambitious diocesan rather than county emphasis, it was named the Church Choral Union in the Diocese of Rochester. A significant point of difference from the Association was 'That the choirs enrolled consist only of men and boys', as in the cathedral tradition.[56] Choirs from Harlow (Essex), High Wych, Sawbridgeworth and Hatfield immediately enrolled in the Union, again with G.W. Martin as its choirmaster, and the Union endured for at least two years.[57] The exclusion of women from the Union's choirs suggests an adherence to Ecclesiological principles and a desire to emulate cathedral service. At Wheathampstead a grand procession of clergy and choristers was assembled by Rev. Davys for the reopening of the restored church in April 1866, singing Gregorian chant as they entered the church. The choir comprised men and boys only, and the use of Gregorian chant provides a further indication of Tractarianism. But an additional motive for choirs to include only boy choristers may have been to encourage them to continue to attend church – girls were considered less likely to need such encouragement. Joseph Wigram, Bishop of Rochester, in his 1864 visitation, asked what measures were taken to retain young people in the Sunday school after leaving the daily school, to which Field replied 'The church choir keeps a few together.'[58]

By 1866 yet another initiative had come into being, this time 'The St Alban's Church Choral Association for promoting and improving Congregational Psalmody throughout West Hertfordshire', the name carefully chosen to reflect Bishop Claughton's express wish to encourage congregational singing, rather than singing by choirs alone.[59] The Association's second choral festival was another huge event held in the Abbey Church and attended by between 500 and 600 choristers from local villages and a congregation of at least 2,000, necessitating the loan of 600 seats from Rochester Cathedral in Kent.[60] And yet, the choirs' singing offered the assembled congregation an opportunity to admire, rather than participate to any great extent. With the exclusion of women and girls from at least some of its church choirs, it would appear that the greatest contribution many made to church music-making was to show off the male choristers to good effect. The *Herts Advertiser* commented: 'The sun shone in at the great west window upon a vast congregation, and the variety and beauty of the ladies costumes were pleasantly contrasted with the white robes of the choristers, and of the clergy and church dignitaries beyond.'[61]

Excluding women reignited the old complaint that the gentry and middle classes disassociated themselves from church music-making. Referring to Hitchin church choir, in 1864 'A Lover of Music' wrote to the *Hertfordshire Express*:

SIR, I cannot allow the week to pass without having a say about our Church Choir singing, which on Sunday morning [...] was most execrable. Could not something be done to induce members of a choral class to join and improve the church choir – is it from a little over nicety on the part of ladies? Surely no stigma can attach thereto. I think with a little management this might be effected. We should then have a church choir second to none in this county or the next.[62]

Following the establishment of a choir, the need to accommodate both choir and organ led to changes in the church layout, often resulting in structural alterations, and these consequences are examined in the next chapter. Although the choirs themselves often proved to be short-lived, the associated changes in the fabric can still be seen in many churches today.

Endnotes

1. *Church Magazine* (November 1839), pp. 343–4.
2. S.A. Glover, *Scheme for Rendering Psalmody Congregational; comprising a Key to the Sol-fa Notation of Music and Directions for Instructing a School* (Norwich, 1835), pp. 5–7.
3. J. Curwen, *Singing for Schools and Congregations* (London, 1843). J.S. Curwen was his son.
4. W. Cecil, *The Church Choir. A Collection of Psalm and Hymn Tunes* (1838), Preface, cited by G.U. Yule, 'In Memory of the Rev. William Cecil', *Proceedings of the Cambridge Philosophical Society*, 27 (Cambridge, 1931), pp. 9–11.
5. *Ibid*.
6. *Christian Guardian* (December 1839), p. 488.
7. *Educational Magazine* (February 1841), p. 97.
8. Burgess, *Enterprise*, p. 117.
9. National Society, *30th Annual Report* (London, 1841), p. 96.
10. *Christian Guardian* (May 1840), p. 194.
11. *Illustrated London News* (1 November 1842), p. 437.
12. P.A. Scholes, 'The Hullah Movement', in *The Mirror of Music 1844–1944*, 2 vols (London, 1947), 1, p. 11; B. Rainbow, 'Hullah, John' in *Grove Music Online*, accessed at <http://www.oxfordmusiconline.com>.
13. *HMR* (7 May 1842), p. 3.
14. *HMR* (5 November 1842), p. 2.
15. *HMR* (15 April 1843), p. 2.
16. *HMR* (14 January 1843), p. 2.
17. *HMR* (5 August 1843), p. 2.
18. *Ibid*.
19. *HG* (11 February 1854), p. 8.
20. *Ibid*.
21. *HMR* (4 January 1851), p. 2.
22. *Parish Choir* (November 1850).
23. National Society, *Monthly Paper* (September 1848), p. 43.
24. *HG* (14 March 1854), p. 3.
25. *Ibid*.
26. *HG* (14 October 1854), p. 2.
27. *HMR* (8 August 1857), p. 3.
28. CRL, BOA, Gray & Davison accounts, vol. 4 (1842–8), p. 156; vol. 5 (1849–57), p. 145.
29. *HMR* (8 August 1857), p. 3.
30. *HMR* (16 October 1858), p. 3.
31. *Choir and Musical Record* (31 October 1863), p. 190.
32. *Ibid*.
33. *HG* (30 July 1853), p. 6.
34. B. Rainbow, *Bernarr Rainbow on Music: Memoirs and Selected Writings* (Woodbridge, 2010), pp. 111–12.
35. B. Rainbow, 'The Rise of Popular Music Education in 19th-century England', *Victorian Studies*, 30 (Autumn 1986), p. 35.
36. Adelmann, *Contribution*, pp. 205–7.
37. *HMR* (5 October 1861), p. 3.
38. *Ibid*.
39. *HG* (22 July 1862), p. 3.
40. *Musical Standard* (15 August 1862), pp. 16–17.
41. *Ibid*.
42. *HMR* (12 July 1862), p. 3.
43. The prestigious London change-ringing society.
44. *HMR* (12 July 1862), p. 3.

45 *Ibid.*
46 *HG* (19 May 1863), p. 3.
47 *HMR* (6 August 1864), p. 3.
48 HALS, DP/98/29/5 Rev. S.P. Field, Memoranda (1864).
49 *HMR* (21 February 1863), p. 2; *HG* (29 April 1865), pp. 3 and 8.
50 *HMR* (29 April 1865), p. 3.
51 *HG* (28 June 1864), p. 4.
52 *HG* (11 March 1865), p. 5.
53 1871 Census RG10/1373/f.18/p.31; *HMR* (18 July 1868), p. 2.
54 *HMR* (21 January 1865), p. 3.
55 HALS, DP/98/29/5.
56 *Ibid.*
57 *HMR* (4 June 1864), p. 3.
58 HALS, DP/98/29/5.
59 *Herts Advertiser* (3 March 1866), p. 2.
60 *Herts Advertiser* (3 August 1867), p. 2.
61 *Ibid.*
62 *Hertfordshire Express and General Advertiser* (26 November 1864), p. 3.

Chapter 9
Church buildings

Changing fashions in landscaping and architecture affected music-making in certain Hertfordshire parish churches and, conversely, changes in music-making led to alterations in the fabric of many others. Galleries in some churches were built to house organs or seat singers, but most were built to seat charity children, the poor and artisan classes, for whom no adequate accommodation was provided elsewhere in the building. Some town parishes found it necessary to install multiple galleries because so many children were obliged to attend divine service, where they were expected to take their part in leading congregational singing.

The removal of galleries during the nineteenth century contributed to the need for many churches to extend or rebuild to provide enough seating, and there was much discussion concerning the location of the choir and organ.

Landscaping
During the eighteenth century it was by no means unusual for landowners to demolish entire villages in the name of landscaping, and by dominating local politics they were able to pass many enclosure acts and divert highways. A 'golden age of landscape gardening' in Hertfordshire started in 1753, and by the time of Dury and Andrews' 1766 map there were forty-five parks enclosed by palings, with a further thirty-four unenclosed gardens and pleasure grounds larger than 100 acres.[1] Humphry Repton was consulted by seventeen landowners in Hertfordshire, where his most extensive work was at Panshanger, begun in 1799, when the 5th Earl Cowper acceded to the title.[2] This swept away work previously undertaken by 'Capability' Brown for the 2nd Earl and covered an extensive tract of land including most of the parishes of Hertingfordbury and St Andrew's, Hertford.[3]

In many rural Hertfordshire parishes the manor house, usually owned by the patron, was situated very near to the church, but, following landscaping, some churches became isolated from the local village. Although the resentment felt by parishioners towards emparkment is

Figure 9.1. Above: St Lawrence's, Ayot St Lawrence from the east; below: interior, looking towards the patron's gallery at the east end. The organ can be seen on the north side (2013).

well documented, until now no consideration appears to have been given to the effect these developments had on church music-making. Physically separating the church building from the majority of parishioners would have given landowners an even greater opportunity to gain control over the style of worship.

On occasion, the landowner rebuilt the parish church in a location considered more aesthetically pleasing. During the mid-eighteenth century William Mason designed the gardens for Simon Harcourt, 1st Earl Harcourt, as part of his major landscaping at Nuneham Courtenay (Oxon.).[4] The works included demolishing the old parish church and building a new one in Greek Revival style, which was fitted up *c*.1777.[5] In the old parish church the music had been provided by singers, but the new church housed a barrel organ set with Mason's 'music for the responses to the commandments, and for some of his psalms and his Sunday hymns, which are sung here'.[6]

Perhaps influenced by the fashionable new church at Nuneham Courtenay, in 1779 Lionel Lyde invested money made through the tobacco trade in demolishing the parish church of Ayot St Lawrence and building a new one.[7] As at Nuneham Courtenay, the church was relocated and rebuilt in Greek Revival style (Figure 9.1). It was designed with the communion table placed at the west end so that a grand entrance portico could be built at the east, facing Lyde's Ayot House. A church patron such as Lyde clearly felt he had *carte blanche* to do as he pleased and, although he assigned the church to the rector and churchwarden, he stipulated that worshippers should enter and leave it via a designated path through the park so as not to interrupt his view.[8] Shortly after the consecration Lyde installed a chamber organ with an added barrel mechanism, 'one of the things over which Sir Lionel had not economized'.[9] This is the earliest known example of a barrel-and-finger organ being used in a Hertfordshire church, and one of the earliest in the country.

Ayot St Lawrence church was designed with a prestigiously located gallery over the grand entrance, but there is no evidence to suggest the organ was ever placed there. In this very small parish with no charity school, the gallery was built for the private use of the patron. At both Nuneham Courtenay and Ayot St Lawrence the primary function of the barrel organ was not to encourage children to sing but probably to support congregational psalmody, perhaps to play a voluntary by Handel and, above all, to be fashionable. In 1782 the organist Jonas Blewitt was resident in Ayot St Lawrence.[10] It would be unrealistic to expect that Blewitt would have been able to earn a supplementary income in such a small parish, and nor perhaps would he have wished to be isolated from metropolitan music-making, and the Ayot organ may have been fitted with barrels for use in his absence.

Church layout and accommodation

At the end of the eighteenth century the typical layout of a parish church was an auditorium or 'preaching-box' with good acoustics, and preferably good sight-lines to the pulpit, so that the preacher could be heard and seen. Therefore in many churches the pulpit and reading desk were to be found mid-way down the nave against the wall, as at Stanstead Abbots (Figure 9.2). A major disadvantage was that some of the congregation were obliged to sit with their backs to the communion table, an arrangement considered disrespectful by High Churchmen.[11] As illustrated in Figure 1.3, many churches had galleries, and the most highly prized location for elite private galleries was near the pulpit. Yet those seated beneath a low gallery would have been unable to see a pulpit located mid-way down the nave, and nor could they clearly hear what was being said. To make matters worse, where an organ had been placed at the front of a gallery it blocked the view of those seated behind it. These problems were common, owing to the widespread building of several other types of gallery during this period.

Figure 9.2. Interior of St James's, Stanstead Abbots, with pulpit situated mid-way down the nave (2014).

Figure 9.3. Daniel Hollingsworth, *Plans and elevations of gallery*, St Michael's, St Albans (1846). The barrel organ shown in this figure was added some years after the gallery was originally built. Reproduced by permission of the Vicar and Churchwardens, St Michael's Church, St Albans.

Singing galleries
During the late eighteenth century, although singers could theoretically sing in the nave or an aisle, a 'singing gallery' was often built if no space was available to accommodate them as a group elsewhere. Singing galleries were usually built at the less prestigious west end of the church.

James, 3rd Viscount Grimston, was patron of St Michael's, St Albans, which was situated on his Gorhambury estate, and in 1777 he began rebuilding the house and making alterations to the church. As part of these works he ordered the removal of Gorhambury chapel's gallery to the church, where it was fashionably supported on Corinthian columns (Figure 9.3).[12] Grimston installed his brother Harbottle as vicar, and in 1785 recorded in his personal accounts: 'Musical instruments given to St Michael's church, 8 guineas'.[13] In London, Grimston had paid in excess of £36 to rent a pew in the Grosvenor Chapel in the years 1774–86, subscribed £63 to the opera and purchased tickets for masquerades and concerts at the Pantheon in St James.[14] The timing of these alterations and purchases suggest that the patron and his Honourable and Reverend brother had high expectations of the quality of music-making at St Michael's, perhaps hoping to emulate on a small scale the Grosvenor Chapel music-making with which they were familiar.[15]

Other singing galleries were built by subscription. Bishop Porteus was patron of Sawbridgeworth when in the autumn of 1787 seventy-eight men and eleven women subscribed to a new gallery.[16] This parish had no shortage of wealthy parishioners, and subscribers included William Plumer MP (New Place), Jeremiah Milles, former Dean of Exeter (Pishiobury), and Conyers Jocelyn, Earl of Roden, who owned Hyde Hall, just over the border in Essex.[17] None subscribed substantial sums, suggesting that, rather than being intended for their own use, it may have been built as a singing gallery to further Porteus's desire to promote music-making. With the Earl of Hardwicke among the subscribers, it may also have been intended to seat the children of the charity school, again supported by local landowners.[18]

Certain galleries built by subscription in Hertfordshire suggest the influence of the local 'middling sort' on parish music-making. At Braughing a gallery was built in 1784 'for the use of the Psalm-singers and the music accompanying them', and in Northchurch forty-one men subscribed to 'a Gallery for singers' in November 1775.[19] Correlation with militia ballot lists reveals that most were of middling rank, and almost half were farmers or their sons.[20]

In other parishes the singing gallery was funded from the church rate in the late 1700s. In June 1779 the St Andrew's, Hertford, vestry agreed to set a church rate of fourpence in the pound 'in order to erect a Gallery for the Singers and for other purposes relating to their said Office'.[21] Likewise, in

March 1794 the Baldock vestry agreed 'that a Gallery shall be erected at the West end of the middle aisle for the accommodation of the Singers & other Inhabitants of this parish', indicating that it was not exclusively for the use of the singers.[22]

Organ galleries

During the late eighteenth and early nineteenth century, if a church had an organ it was usually located in the centre of a west gallery. In some cases this was because it was installed in a pre-existing singing gallery, but in others it was because there was no room in the body of the church. Perhaps the most important consideration was that it could be prominently seen and heard by most of the congregation. While the appearance of donated church organs drew attention to the generosity and wealth of the donors, often 'commemorated on a plaque',[23] the prominent display of charity children in organ galleries fulfilled a similar role. In 1787 William Vincent had urged that children should be taught to sing properly so that 'they would become not merely ornamental to the Church as an exhibition of benevolence, but an useful and essential part of the congregation'.[24] As with the 'display of virtue rendered visible' at St Paul's Cathedral, the visual impact of charity children prominently displayed in provincial church galleries, and their elevated position, 'illustrated the fruit of the charity of parishioners'.[25] The display of organ and charity children together reinforced the impact of each on its own. When the Watford organ was installed in 1766 the vestry resolved that 'the Charity Children both Boys and Girls […] will be advantageously placed for Singing with the Organ if they are removed from their present seats […] into the said Gallery, and that such removal of the Charity Children will also be an ornament to the Church'.[26] Rather than suggesting that the children were decorative, the term 'ornament' indicates they were a living embodiment of a plaque or charity board, displaying the benevolence of the parish towards its poor. This proposal was considered so desirable that the Watford vestry sanctioned the alterations to be paid out of the church rate.

Canon Davidson asked whether such children were taught psalmody, 'imitating the London charity-children who were taught to lead the metrical psalms, and sat by the organs in the City churches?'[27] Evidence of the frequency with which this gallery arrangement was replicated from the late eighteenth to the mid-nineteenth centuries, even when the church had only a barrel organ, suggests that this metropolitan fashion had both a significant and enduring influence. When the Broxbourne barrel organ was installed following the establishment of the Sunday school in 1804 the carpenter was paid 'To 2 Days ¼ Cutting out the Peughs in Gallery for the Orgin & helping

Figure 9.4. Benches provided for the poor at St Mary's, Albury (1866). W.B. Gerish, 'Albury Church', *Transactions of the East Herts Archaeological Society*, 2/III (1904), p. 229, reproduced by permission of the East Herts Archaeological Society.

to fix ditto 9s'.[28] In 1820 the Abbey Church installed its first organ since the restoration of the monarchy and built a gallery to seat the National School children who were now to be taught singing by the organist.[29] In 1838 Flaunden parish church was demolished and rebuilt nearer the village, largely at the expense of the incumbent, Samuel King. He commissioned his nephew George Gilbert Scott to build the church, and his plans show children's seats to either side of the west gallery, which eventually housed a barrel organ.[30] This was Scott's first church, and one of the last to be designed with a gallery purpose-built to house children.

Lack of seating

Although pews and galleries provided certain members of the congregation with seating, in many instances there was little or no accommodation for the poor. This situation was aggravated by the requirement to seat so many charity children, itself a consequence of the desire to improve congregational psalmody.

At Bishops Stortford and other town churches benches were placed all the way down the central aisle, and similar seating problems were seen in many village churches.[31] At Albury a south gallery had been erected by the Brograve family, and underneath were 'several miserable little pens, where the labourers sat, and where, being quite out of sight, they used to play pitch and toss for beer, crack nuts, and go to sleep'.[32] At Albury, and in many other churches, the poor sat on benches or forms wherever they could be squeezed in (Figure 9.4). In churches with no side aisles and a fully pewed nave there was no room at all in the nave for benches, let alone for an organ.

Lack of seating was a problem that increased during the early nineteenth century in rapidly growing Hertfordshire towns. With no room in the parish church, some poor parishioners turned to dissenting meetings, where accommodation was not usually such an issue. In Bishop Randolph's 1810 visitation, Edward Hodgson, vicar of Rickmansworth and nephew of Bishop Porteus, stated that 'The parish church though very considerable is quite inadequate to the accommodation of so populous a parish [...] this circumstance must contribute to the increase of Dissenters.'[33] He successfully campaigned to rebuild the church, and in 1826 the church was completely reconstructed to seat 2,000 people, with pews and galleries supported by iron pillars ranged on three sides. The west gallery housed the barrel organ and choir, and the men and boys sat in the south gallery.[34]

A similar problem was found at All Saints, Hertford. In April 1824 the curate Thomas Lloyd stated that 'The parishioners are extremely anxious to afford accommodation to the Inhabitants, and particularly to the lower classes, who are literally driven to the meeting houses for want of room.'[35] The situation was no better in 1855, when the vestry found 'A great want of accommodation [...] for mechanics and artisans, a class of persons who [...] are deterred from attending divine worship', which they attributed to having to sit in free seating with the poor rather than pews with the gentry.[36]

Incorporated Church Building Society

In an attempt to stem the perceived exodus of poor parishioners from the church, in 1817 a group of High Churchmen resolved to form a society for 'promoting public worship by obtaining additional church-room for the middle and lower classes'. The following January the Church Building Society was formed (incorporated in 1828, when it became the Incorporated Church Building Society, or ICBS). Its chief aim was to provide increased church accommodation through the provision of grants to reorder or extend existing churches, or to build new ones. When applying for funding, the applicant, usually the incumbent, was asked to declare the size of the parish's population and provide figures showing the difference between the number of inhabitants and the present church accommodation. Preference was given to parishes that had already raised a large proportion of the amount required, and to those planning to provide the greatest number of free sittings. When the recently appointed Rev. Vaughan applied for ICBS funding to rebuild Harpenden parish church in 1861 he said that, owing to lack of accommodation, 'many have been driven, almost against their will, into the ranks of dissent, and a very large number (especially of the working men) are, it is to be feared, worshippers neither in church nor chapel'.[37] Those seeking funds to repair dilapidated churches had to demonstrate that the state of the building was not the result of negligence on the part of the parishioners, that they were able to raise at least part of the funds from rates or subscription and that repairs would increase accommodation for the poor.

In 1818 the government passed an Act for Promoting the Building of Additional Churches in Populous Parishes, with a budget of £1,000,000 to be administered by newly created Commissioners for Building New Churches. Previously, although a dissenting chapel could be opened merely by taking out a licence, a church could usually be built or repaired only following an individual act of parliament.[38] Although the passing of this Act facilitated the work of the ICBS, many alterations made during the nineteenth century continued to be privately financed, not least because the promoters knew their designs would not meet with ICBS approval. Designs considered unsuitable included the provision of additional seating not intended for the use of the poor, or rebuilding in what was considered to be a more fashionable style without providing any additional seating at all.

Children's galleries

The situation in fashionable Bath Abbey, where the entire nave was filled with charity children, may have been exceptional (see Figure 2.4). Nevertheless, it highlights the increased seating difficulties encountered following the establishment of a charity school associated with the church, because pupils

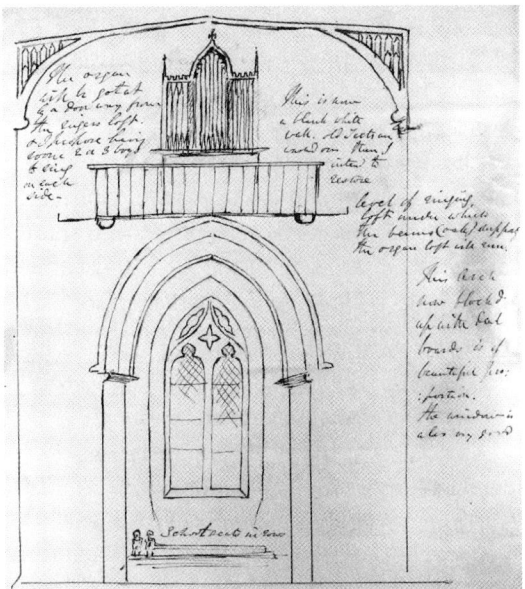

Figure 9.5. W.W. Malet, *Proposed relocation of organ at St Lawrence's, Ardeley* (1844). LPL, ICBS 3466 reproduced with permission from Lambeth Palace Library.

were obliged to attend church on Sundays. Apart from using benches, the cheapest, quickest and least intrusive way to seat charity children was to place them in an existing or new gallery. Numerous applications were submitted to the ICBS following the establishment of a National School, with plans showing the extra accommodation needed for children. By 1815 Broxbourne's schools had become affiliated with the National Society, and a payment to George Cheffins for 'Carpenters' Work in the Church for National School children' confirms that more accommodation was needed to seat all the children.[39] Datchworth National School was founded by local landowners in 1820, and in 1824 the church applied for ICBS funding towards a new children's gallery with 'additional seats below where there were none before for the poor'.[40]

All ICBS applications had to be accompanied by a plan, elevations, sections and a detailed estimate. Needless to say, many parishes were unable to find the funds to pay an architect to draw up the plans, and so the clergyman drew them himself. This was the case at Ardeley, where W.W. Malet had been appointed vicar in 1839. Clearly a Tractarian, he was described as 'Decidedly Puseyite' and 'an ultra Ritualist [wearing] all the vestments of a Roman Catholic priest'.[41] With more room required for the National School children, in 1844 Malet applied for funding to convert the ringing chamber into a seating area for the children, with the organ behind them (Figure 9.5). Although his application was successful he was offered only £14, and it seems unlikely that the alterations were made.

It was usual to seat school boys and girls separately in church, just as they were taught separately, and at Markyate they were seated at opposite ends of the gallery, boys on the left, girls on the right, either side of the barrel organ (Figure 9.6).[42] Children were not treated any differently from adults in this respect, since traditionally men and women were seated separately in many churches, including Cheshunt, Anstey and the Abbey Church, St Albans, among others.[43] There was no consensus as to how seating should be arranged. In some churches men sat on one side of the nave and women on the other, as at Sawbridgeworth until 1879, while in others men sat in the nave, women in the gallery, or *vice versa*.[44] Elsewhere polite men and women sat together in allocated seating, but the servants and labouring classes were segregated.[45] At Redbourn, during the 1850s,

> The Vicar's family, together with a few parishioners who lived in the larger houses, were allowed to sit in the Chancel; the central aisle was occupied by the farmers and trades people; the south side by labouring men; the north by women. [...] An old inhabitant, still living, distinctly remembers his Grandfather playing a clarinet in the men's gallery over the Rood Screen – the women's gallery was at the west end [...].[46]

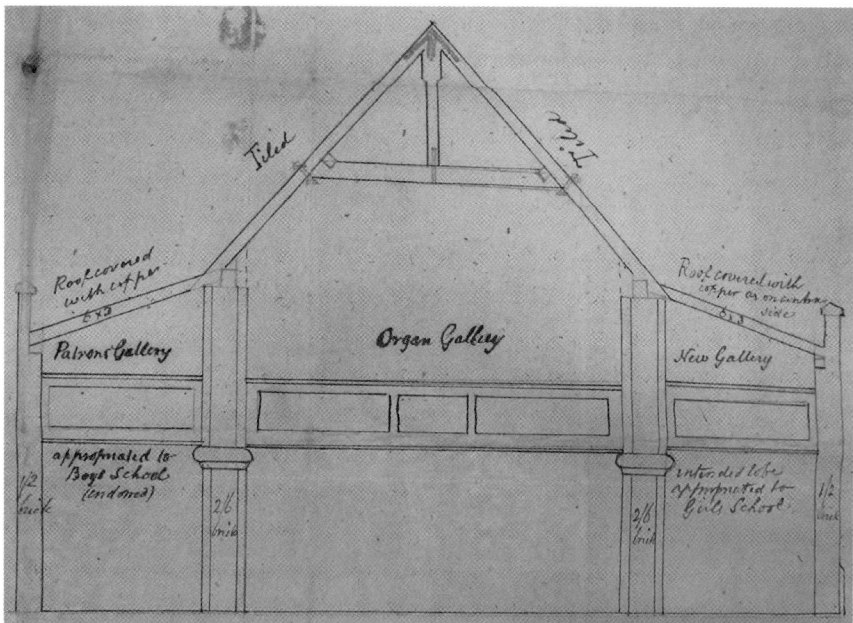

Figure 9.6. Elevation of gallery, St John's, Markyate (1843) showing seating for boys on the left, girls on the right. LPL, ICBS 2868, f. 28 reproduced with permission from Lambeth Palace Library.

Poor children rarely sat with their families owing to the obligation for charity school children to attend church as a group. In 1856 'G.W.O.' commented on problems associated with children's attendance at church. He reminisced about his own more privileged childhood, when he had sat with his family in the family pew, but had seen 'the National-school children in the gallery – boys on one side of the organ, and girls on the other; the workhouse-children arranged on forms under the gallery'.[47] 'G.W.O.' argued that children should sit with their families rather than in segregated seating, and that this would draw the congregation back from dissenting places of worship. But in many churches this would have led to a further requirement for increased accommodation. When accommodation problems were discussed in Harpenden, Frederic Spackman, the local doctor, argued that instead of segregating charity children he was 'very desirous that the seats in the South Transept should be devoted to family sittings'.[48]

Shared galleries
In 1825 the Little Hadham vestry agreed to raise a voluntary subscription to build a gallery for school children and psalm singers.[49] Similarly, in 1841 Rev. Tucker, vicar of Sandon, made a successful application for funding towards a gallery because there was 'no accommodation for the children, or for the singers'.[50] Singers often occupied a few seats at the front or side of a gallery, the rest being used by children or ordinary members of the congregation.[51] Again, the vicar himself supplied a number of drawings and plans to support his ICBS application, on this occasion for a gallery 'to accommodate 80 persons including the schoolchildren – the two front seats for the singers' (Figure 9.7). As at Markyate, boys are shown seated on the left and girls on the right. In some cases children and singers shared a gallery owing to space restrictions, but in other churches this arrangement was adopted so that children could sing with adults or with the support of instrumentalists.

Galleries in other churches accommodated an organ, children, singers, the labouring poor, servants, tradesmen or various combinations of these groups. A large west gallery built in 1819 at Berkhamsted accommodated twenty-four 'poorer inhabitants', together with an organ flanked by 'thirty children educated in the Charity School'.[52] In June 1834 Samuel Johnes Knight, rector of Welwyn, applied for ICBS funding to erect a large new gallery to seat singers, children and the poor. In a covering letter a committee member wrote: 'Mr Knight is very anxious this project should be effected during his ministry and he hopes now especially that there is a Division among them, that increased room may be the means of bringing back several Dissenters to the Right Fold.'[53] Although the wording of this application hints at a formulaic argument to increase the likelihood of being granted funding, the

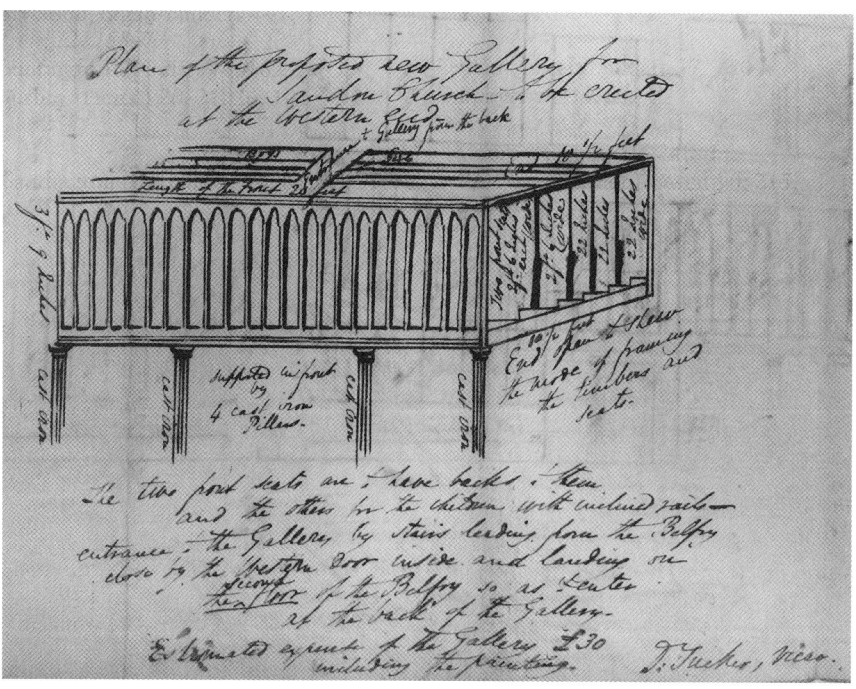

Figure 9.7. Above: Dennis Tucker, *Western end of All Saints, Sandon, showing the proposed new gallery*; below: *Plan of gallery* (1841). LPL, ICBS 2944, ff. 9–10 reproduced with permission from Lambeth Palace Library.

involvement of both the rector and his wife in the welfare and moral well-being of the Welwyn parishioners suggests that they had their best interests at heart. The village infant school at Woolmer Green was entirely supported by Mrs Johnes Knight, and she and her husband were liberal contributors towards several other schools, in addition to the town band and 'Singing Classes, on Hullah's system'.[54]

Yet by 1835 the gallery arrangement at Welwyn had clearly become troublesome, and Rev. Johnes Knight had second thoughts. He decided instead to seat the poor in the gallery, the children in the chancel, 'which enables the clergyman to judge of their behaviour in church', and the singers in the body of the church 'under the immediate observance of the clergyman'.[55] He advised the ICBS that 'In consequence of this alteration the Psalmody has become general throughout the body of the church.'

Extended and double galleries

In some churches space was at such a premium that existing west galleries were enlarged. At St Michael's, St Albans, children were seated on either side of the barrel organ, but in 1846 the gallery was extended to accommodate new seating at the front (see Figure 9.3). Furthermore, many parish churches in towns found it necessary to build a second west gallery above the first, resulting in a double gallery. Organs presented to both Hitchin and Hoddesdon during the early 1800s were installed in an upper west gallery, partly because this is where the singers already sat, but also because there was no room elsewhere.[56] Finding it necessary to seat more than 130 charity children, in 1822 St Etheldreda's, Hatfield, had two galleries at the west end, with 'eight raised seats or forms for the accommodation of the children' in the enlarged part of the upper gallery.[57]

East Barnet provides a striking example of the unforeseen consequences of the need to accommodate large numbers of National School children. In 1829 the rector and churchwardens made an application for ICBS funding towards a new gallery to replace the two existing west galleries. Submitted plans of the existing galleries carefully depicted sightlines to the pulpit on the south side of the nave, shown top left in the plans (Figure 9.8). Other than those seated at the front of the galleries, few could see the minister, 'Owing to the proximity of the Pulpit and intervention of the organ'. Situated at the front of the lower west gallery, the organ was so tall that it blocked the view for many in both the lower gallery, with 'bare headway under the upper gallery', and the upper gallery, 'so close to the ceiling of the church that at the back there was scarcely any room to stand up'.[58] The adopted remedy was to move the pulpit further away and build a large replacement west gallery with the organ next to the west wall and the children of the National School seated on either side.

Figure 9.8. Richard Kelsey, *Reordering of galleries at St Mary's, East Barnet* (1829). LPL, ICBS 1091, f.10 reproduced with permission from Lambeth Palace Library. Above: existing upper gallery: 'for children of the National School […] It had no light except the reflected rays from the nave, and was only ventilated by a small hole in the ceiling and a grating in the back partition'; middle: existing lower gallery; below: proposed replacement gallery.

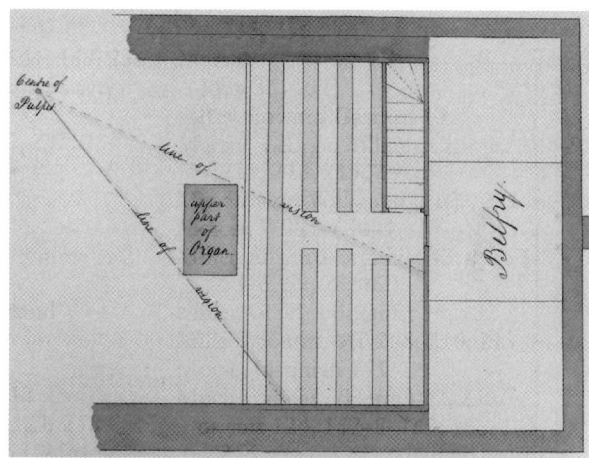

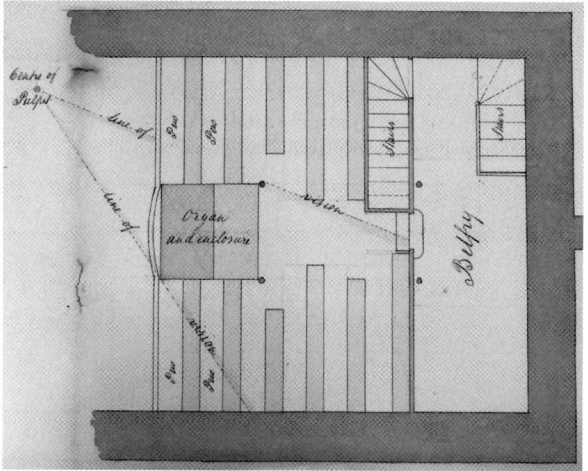

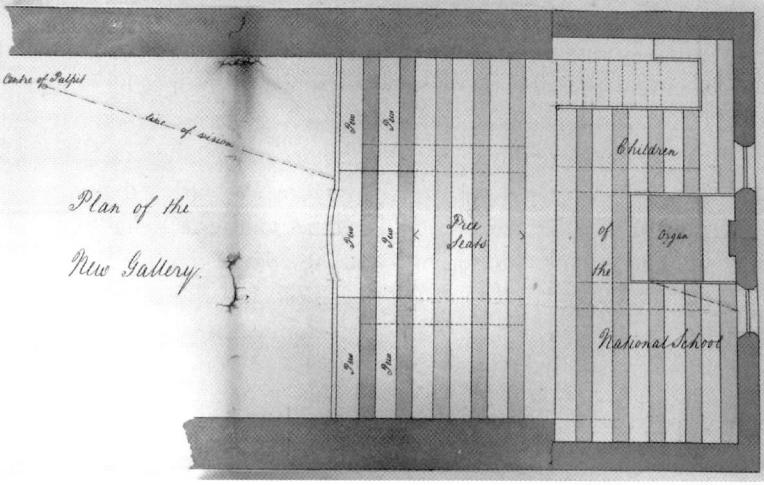

Gallery removal

Owing to the unforeseen consequences of trying to seat so many adults and children, some galleries were already being removed by the 1820s. In March 1828 the curate of Bushey preached a sermon urging that his church should be rebuilt, arguing that the seats beneath the singers' and children's galleries were dark, poorly ventilated and badly placed to hear the preacher.[59] (See Figure 1.3). Nevertheless, although the singers' gallery was eventually removed in 1842, the church was not restored until 1871.

An ICBS application made in September 1834 suggested that the sounding board at the back of the Ware organ should be removed from the gallery, presumably because it was blocking the view of the pulpit for those seated behind it.[60] Describing a situation similar to that at Bushey, the applicant stated that the west gallery, where the organ and children were located, was too deep and low, making the seats beneath 'dark, unpleasant and nearly useless'. Because of the obligation for charity school children to attend church, they often found themselves crammed into seating such as this. In January 1832 Daniel Goodson Adey, incumbent of Markyate, made a fresh application to the ICBS. Annotating his plan of the seats in the gallery, which housed both children and barrel organ, he noted 'a grown up person can hardly sit in them. It is now proposed to widen them to a proper size, and to make the stairs (at present little better than a ladder) to them more convenient'.[61] A similarly cramped gallery at St Pauls Walden seated seventy children.[62]

Correspondents to the *Ecclesiologist* began to draw attention to the cramped and uncomfortable seating endured by many children. In July 1842 'Gamma' wrote to the editor:

> I think it a token of no little want of feeling, that in many churches, though pewed up to the very teeth, the children of the Sunday School are made to sit erect on backless forms; the only distinction between them and the rest of the congregation being that they are not able to remonstrate.[63]

The *Ecclesiologist* also published 'Suggestions and Instructions' drawn up by the ICBS, two of which had a significant effect on music-making. Fervently campaigning for the removal of all 'Pues or Pens', such as those in Bushey parish church, they stated: 'Much accommodation is gained by the adoption, instead of pews, of open seats with backs.'[64] Unlike the pews that they replaced, the new seating was not enclosed by high sides and a door and all faced the same direction, so that nobody had their back to the preacher or communion table. This 'free' seating was available for use by any member of the congregation, rather than being allocated to a particular person or property.

The ICBS also suggested that seats intended exclusively for children should be slightly lower in height than those intended for adults, and spaced more closely together. Although a width of twenty inches was allowed for each adult seated in the pew, fourteen inches was allowed for a child.[65] This resulted in the introduction of a new style of ICBS application form during the mid-1840s.[66] In addition to pre-existing questions regarding the present and proposed number of appropriated and free seats, the form now asked applicants to estimate how many were for adults and how many for children. Although the ICBS continued to ask whether or not the church had galleries, it discouraged the building of new ones and announced that 'The Society will not sanction any plan involving the erection of a gallery, unless in cases where it is distinctly shown that no room is unnecessarily sacrificed, by inconvenient arrangements, on the floor.'[67] When a barrel-and-finger organ was presented to Braughing (c.1850) it was erected on a 'platform' in the south-west corner of the church, with four tiers of benches in front to seat the choir and schoolgirls.[68] The plan, however, showed an organ 'gallery', suggesting that the word 'platform' may been chosen to circumvent opposition.

The CCS finally drew attention to the use of two or even three tiers of church galleries:

> Another evil, which is now becoming more common, and reaching even to country parishes, is the use of double or even triple galleries, one above the other. The upper tier is often given to the charity-children or national schools: or sometimes these are put behind the organ. Neither of these places is a good one for the children, and the first quite spoils a church besides.[69]

Despite the practical considerations highlighted above, Ecclesiological disapproval of galleries had been based on the fact that they blocked arches and on the lack of pre-Reformation precedent for their use. Perhaps it is cynical to suggest that Ecclesiologists should suddenly show concern for the well-being of those obliged to sit in them. According to one correspondent, at St Andrew's, Headington (Oxon.):

> From a large pen in the same church springs a small rough ladder, by which children ascend to the cill of the east window of the south Aisle. Here a bench is placed for their accommodation; and a crazy erection of laths in front serves the double purpose of supporting their books, and shielding the occupants of the inferior pen from the casual infliction of a falling child.[70]

The High-Church *Oxford and Cambridge Review* did not concur with the Ecclesiologists' argument that galleries should be dismantled, but they did object to their occupation by organs and children – a desirable reform during a previous period. They stated: 'Many country churches there are, we grieve to say, in which the old choir has been swept away to make place for that miscreated machine the grinding organ, and the *twang twang* of charity children.'[71]

In 1862 the ICBS finally began to publish its own journal, *The Church Builder*, 'to set forth in a popular form the progress of Church Extension in connexion with Church Building', with accounts of model church 'restorations' and advertisements from suppliers of church fitments to encourage others to follow suit.[72] The editors commented 'we hope to find it on the drawing-room table of the rich, as well as the cottage shelf of the poor'. This resulted in more numerous, but not necessarily sizeable, financial contributions to church 'improvements' from all levels of society. In 1863 the *Church Builder* announced that rules regarding children's seating were to be further modified: the distance from back to front was increased to 'at least twenty-six inches', and for the first time there was a requirement for their seats to have backs.[73]

In 1864 'J.C.' reported in the *Church Builder* that the future prime minister William Gladstone had himself drawn attention to the defective and 'in many respects highly mischievous' arrangements under which schoolchildren attended church, inspiring 'a rooted and very intelligible disinclination to attendance at church'.[74] In 1848 Dickens had described the experience of 'Rob the Grinder', a 'clothed' charity school boy. His:

> reverence for the inspired writings, under the admirable system of the Grinders' School, had been developed [...] by the parading of him at six years old in leather breeches, three times a Sunday, very high up, in a very hot church, with a great organ buzzing against his drowsy head, like an exceedingly busy bee.[75]

This illustrates the continuing importance attached to the display of charity children in countless parish churches. But Gladstone now highlighted the discomfort, sometimes amounting to real suffering, of being confined to cramped seating, and the difficulties faced by the preacher in attempting to address both adults and children. Yet his main concerns were the stuffy conditions in and below their galleries, 'commonly the worst in the church', and the length of time spent there.

'J.C.' expected children to occupy 'one-fifth to one-fourth' of the seats in the church, depending on circumstances.[76] Although this might seem excessive, during this extended period of high population growth children formed a considerable proportion of the parish. Furthermore, in some churches the fraction was even greater, and in Wigginton parish church children comprised the greater part of the congregation.[77]

In 1866 All Saints, Hertford, was restored, but the *Herts Guardian* considered the work incomplete until something could be done to address the poor ventilation caused by the 'excessive space occupied by galleries'.[78] The scaremongering article referred its readership to a recent case in Wisbech (Cambs.) in which a woman seated in a gallery was asphyxiated 'by the foul atmosphere which arose from the body of the church, and was pent up between the galleries and the roof'. Since warm air rises, those seated in galleries were in the stuffiest part of the church. Although they may have frozen in winter, during the summer the heat was probably as unbearable as it had been for 'Rob the Grinder'.

Although the ICBS no longer provided grants for galleries or cramped children's seating, in many churches they remained. Nevertheless, in 1864 'J.C.' was pleased to report that:

> From the gradual extinction of galleries; the unbecoming sight of the singing children forming the front row, and singing for the congregation, has happily almost passed away, and the position and duties of the choir are now as well defined as any other portion of the service.[79]

This provides a further example of how one generation's reforming efforts were considered to be abhorrent by the next. Few examples of children's seats survive today, because the narrow spacing between their rows made it impossible for all but the smallest of adults to fit into them, and the removal of such seats enabled church accommodation to be more flexible.

Restoration

Although the 'preaching-box' church layout had suited Evangelicals, it was not suited to Tractarian ideals, which placed the Eucharist at the heart of worship. Architectural rearrangements were therefore needed to recreate pre-Reformation places of worship and give prominence to the communion table by building a larger chancel to house it. This was itself to be separated from the nave by having a higher floor level, a chancel arch and preferably a screen to preserve a sense of mystery.

Between 1840 and 1875 nearly 80 per cent of all old English parish churches were restored, rebuilt or enlarged, with the majority of restoration work undertaken between 1856 and 1874.[80] From its foundation in 1839, the CCS actively promoted the restoration of churches to provide idealised pre-Reformation liturgical settings for worship, preferably in 'pointed gothic' style. Tractarians built in this style for a number of reasons. The church had been central to society during the era of Gothic architecture in a way strikingly different from the recent, increasingly secular, time, which was characterised by a preference for the neo-classical style. The choice of neo-Gothic architecture also referred to a more idyllic pre-industrial age.[81] But most important of all was the anti-Protestant influence of the architect Augustus Welby Pugin, who referred to Gothic architecture as 'Christian architecture' to the exclusion of all other styles.[82]

Those Hertfordshire parishes with no shortage of gentry, wealthy incomers or ladies susceptible to the fundraising efforts of young clergymen saw a surge in church rebuilding and restoration. In some cases restoration involved 'improving' upon the original, and at St Mary's, Standon, the old font, which was 'almost Norman in character', was restored to look even more Norman in 1864.[83] In other cases 'restoration' involved very substantial rebuilding work. The 1860s saw a surge in Hertfordshire church restorations, and the *Hertford Mercury and Reformer* commented that the diocese of Rochester had 'certainly not been backward' in efforts to provide for the spiritual wants of the population: 'Very frequently, of late, has it been our pleasing duty to chronicle in these columns, the erection of new churches, or the restoration and enlargement of old churches.'[84] At All Saints, Hertford, accommodation was greatly increased following the installation of seats made of the 'best description of pine, stained in imitation of oak', an artifice of which Pugin would definitely not have approved.[85] Holy Cross, Sarratt, was said to be 'miserably ruinous' prior to restoration by George Gilbert Scott, 'blocked up with unsightly galleries' and high-backed pews that were replaced with open seats to provide seating for an additional seventy-five parishioners.[86]

As the century progressed, restoration work was thought incomplete without the removal of all galleries and the installation of an organ, and organ-builders became essential members of the architectural and ecclesiastical supply industry. When Holy Trinity, Bengeo, was built in 1855 to replace the old parish church of St Leonard's, the work was considered unfinished until a finger organ was finally acquired in 1860 'so that the arrangements of this beautiful edifice for sacred worship are now nearly all complete'.[87] If funds did not stretch to the immediate provision of an organ, then space was allocated for one. At Sawbridgeworth both west galleries were removed during 1859 restoration work and space allowed for an organ: 'A very elegant arch between the chancel and south aisle, for many years blocked up by a colossal monument of late date, has been thrown open, and repaired space has thus been gained for an organ, and its position is well adapted for leading a choir in the chancel.'[88]

How much more of an impression could be made by the opening of a newly built or rebuilt church complete with an organ from the start. When

St Nicholas', Harpenden, was restored in 1862 a new organ was installed in time for the reopening by Joseph Wigram, Bishop of Rochester, in November.[89] At Tring the organ was rebuilt, enlarged and placed near the east end of the north aisle, so that when the church was reopened by the bishop on New Year's Day 1863 'the whole congregation took their part well both in the chanting and singing'.[90]

Under the supervision of Rev. Davys, St Helen's, Wheathampstead, said to be in 'a state of grievous decay', was transformed in 1866 by a restoration costing in excess of £3,000. Its newly gleaming exterior was said to be 'almost startling'.[91] Moreover, the description of the finger organ installed in place of the old west gallery barrel organ suggests that its suitably reverential appearance was just as important as its speaking tone, or perhaps even more so. On the anniversary of the church's reopening the *Herts Guardian* reported:

> the organ was suspended on the north side the chancel, in accordance with the paper recently read by the Rev. gentleman at St Albans Archaeological Society, on the 'Choral arrangement of Churches'. The pipes of the organ are very beautifully ornamented: there is variety of colors, but they blend in perfection, and the combined effect of windows, organ, and ceiling is rich beyond description.[92]

In Davys's paper he had explained to the society why he felt provision for music-making should now be an integral part of any church rebuilding or restoration work:

> there has grown up a desire that the living church should prosper as well as the material building, so that we seldom see a church restored without seeing decency and order restored in its services; and since good music is so generally esteemed as a needful part of an orderly worship, it is not surprising that church choirs, and how to organize, train, and arrange them, should have become a very popular subject for enquiry and discussion. This is, indeed, a comparatively new subject, for the time is not long since the best arrangement possible for many a so-called choir was to remove it as far as possible from the inside of a building […].[93]

Davys was the son of George Davys, Bishop of Peterborough, who, as explained in Chapter 2, had been so strongly in favour of teaching children to sing in order to lead the congregation. The bishop's son stated that, 'till very lately', in most churches choirs were located in a gallery at the west end, but that, as this 'singing loft' was now generally condemned, they should now be placed 'in accordance with the true principles of choral arrangement', modestly echoing Pugin's *True Principles*. He stated:

I will suppose that you have a choir composed, as the model choirs of the Church of England are composed, of men and boys, that you have got them clothed in the surplice, which has ever been recognised in the Church of England as the appropriate dress for those, whether lay, or clerical, who minister in her services, and that, having done all this, you are about to lead your choir into church, and want to know where to place them.[94]

The CCS initially advised that the chancel should be reserved for the clergy.[95] Yet Ecclesiologists soon agreed, reluctantly, that choristers should be seated there because, like the clergy, they were taking part in the performance of divine service. Davys argued that the proper place for the singers was 'undoubtedly' the 'constructive choir' or chancel.[96] However, any use of the chancel for music-making was still subject to the approval of the rector. Davys drew attention to churches with no such approval, stating that in such cases the choir should be situated west of the chancel arch: 'This plan has been adopted by Mr Scott with excellent effect in the choral arrangements of St Michael's church, near St Albans.'[97] In this case it was because there was little room in the chancel, which houses a large monument to the philosopher Francis Bacon, 1st Viscount St Alban. Scott's work at St Michael's was a far cry from his first church at Flaunden, built with a gallery to seat singing children and a barrel organ, and clearly illustrates how the approach to reforming music-making had dramatically altered during the course of one generation. George Davys had promoted the use of children's voices to lead congregational singing, whereas his son promoted a choir of men and boys.

Two-thirds of rebuilding or restoration work during the mid to late nineteenth century was started within five years of the appointment of a new, often Tractarian, incumbent.[98] Davys instigated building work within five years of his arrival at Wheathampstead, as had Rev. King at Flaunden and Rev. Vaughan at Harpenden. A grand impression could be made if an existing choir could be found to fill the new choirstalls in newly restored or rebuilt churches. In 1856 the new organ at Aspenden was opened by Richard Limpus, organist of St Michael's, Cornhill, supported by 'several members of his own choir'.[99] In 1853 the remotely situated St Mary's, Thundridge, had been demolished and a new parish church built nearer the village by the brewer and local landowner Robert Hanbury.[100] He managed to secure the offices of G.W. Martin as organist on the brand-new £200 Bishop organ for the grand opening, together with a choir of girls from the village school he had also funded, supplemented by the renowned Watton-at-Stone choir to fill the new choirstalls.[101] As a token of his appreciation he presented the choir with the music cupboard which still stands in the church at Watton, long after the choir had been disbanded (Figure 9.9).

Figure 9.9. Music cupboard presented to the Watton-at-Stone choir by Robert Hanbury (1853).

Relocation of the organ

Because the campaign to remove galleries had been so successful, numerous churches now had to find a new location for their organ. Many proposals and counter-proposals were made. By 1843 the CCS stated 'Few things give more trouble to church-arrangers or church-builders than the position of the organ.'[102] Initially they found fault with all suggestions, and argued that the organ should not be placed in an organ chamber built off the chancel, as such an arrangement 'offends all rules concerning Aisles, Chapels, Transepts, or Sacristies'.[103] Furthermore, the rector still had the right to object to an organ being placed in the chancel.

Where children had been seated in a gallery next to an organ a new location also had to be found for them, and a clear example of Ecclesiological influence in this regard comes from Widford. The CCS had originally objected to the use of organs, but reluctantly conceded that if a church already had one it should be placed 'at the west end, either of the Nave or either Aisle, *and on the ground*'.[104] Plans drawn up in 1868 show Widford children seated next to the organ in a west gallery before restoration, but in children's seating next to the organ on the ground at the west end after restoration (Figure 9.10).

The positioning of church organs continued to be a contentious issue. At Leeds parish church the High Churchman John Jebb had placed the choir in the chancel with the organ to one side of it, and in 1843 argued this was the only proper place for them.[105] In Hertfordshire the 1851 ICBS application from Aston was the first to show Jebb's arrangement, with an organ located in a newly built organ chamber off the chancel, and therefore near the choir.[106] This arrangement allowed organs to be located adjacent to chancels not originally designed to hold them, and often had the added

CHURCH BUILDINGS

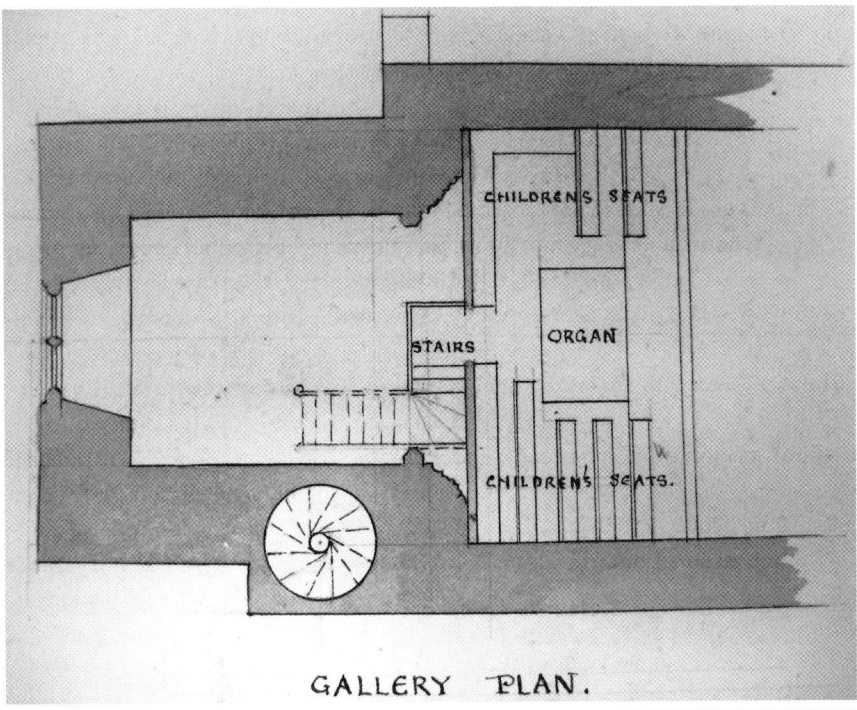

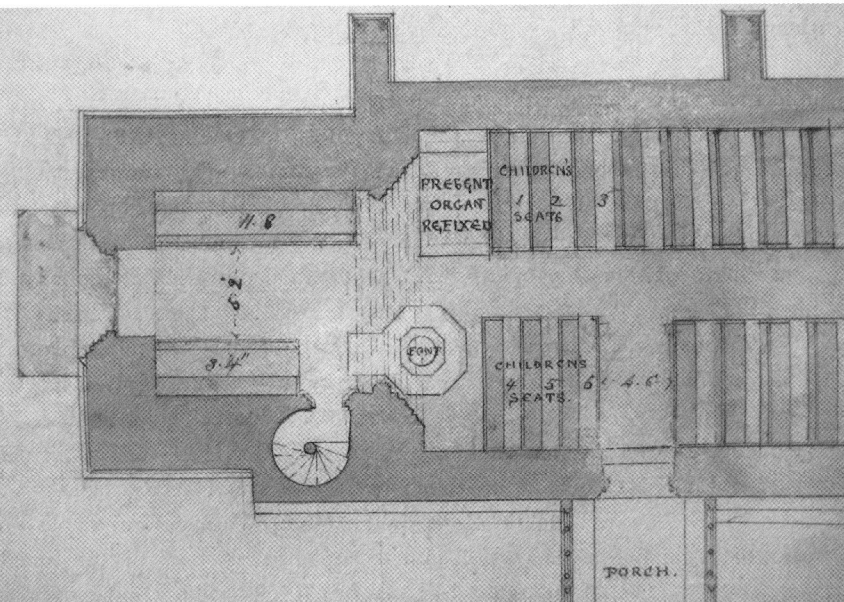

Figure 9.10. G.E. Pritchett, *Detailed plans of St Luke's, Widford* (1868). Above: children's seats on either side of the organ in the west gallery before reordering; below: children's seats and organ at the back of the nave after removal of the gallery. HALS, DP/123/6/1 reproduced with permission from Hertfordshire Archives & Local Studies.

Figure 9.11 Gray organ relocated next to the chancel of St Faith's, Hexton (2017). This instrument was originally a barrel organ located in the church's west gallery.

benefit of allowing the organist to be discreetly hidden behind a curtain or other screen. In Hexton and many other churches, following the removal of the west gallery the barrel organ was converted to a finger organ and relocated to a situation adjacent to the chancel (Figure 9.11).

Although this became usual in the later nineteenth century, it was by no means the only arrangement. William Spark, deputy organist of Leeds parish church, disagreed with Jebb and in 1852 gave a paper to the Yorkshire Architectural Society entitled 'Choirs and Organs: Their Proper Position in Churches', which received widespread coverage when reprinted in full in the *Musical Times*.[107] Spark contended that there was no historical precedent for 'any uniform rule for our guidance in the locating of organs and choirs'.[108] Consequently the answer to the question of where to locate the organ, especially following the removal of one or more galleries, was not obvious. The new Bishop, Starr & Richardson organ purchased by subscription at St Andrew's, Hertford, in 1861 was placed in the west gallery, but the *Hertford Mercury and Reformer* objected that 'the organ appears to us to be placed too far back and too high up in the gallery of the church, which is not well adapted for the conveyance of sound'.[109] In 1859 the Hemel Hempstead vestry agreed that as part of restoration work the 'organ and west gallery remain in the same position for the present'.[110] But the following year they discussed removing both on the grounds that 'the interior of the church would be much improved thereby' and 'the organ be placed in the north transept'. However, the vicar protested against placing the organ in the transept, 'because it would sacrifice many seats, and also be illegal unless the consent of the Bishop was first obtained'. The following vestry rescinded the resolution and decided that the organ should be 'placed in the chamber on the north side of the chancel end of the church'.

In 1862 the *Church Builder* carried advertisements for harmoniums and organs, often now described as 'chancel organs', yet when the organ-builder Bevington advertised his 'chancel organs' in 1863 the question of where to locate an organ was by no means settled, as he stated that they were 'Suitable for the Chancel or Gallery of Church or Chapel'.[111] In 1864 the Ardeley choir and harmonium were located in the chancel, which was, according to the *Herts Guardian*, 'the proper place for choirs': 'Indeed the recent decision in the case of "Griffin v. Dighton" proves that the chancels of [...] churches are intended for the use of the parishioners generally *i.e.* for their choirs, and for those who attend at Holy Communion and at Weddings.'[112]

'Griffin v Dighton' was an action brought in 1863 by the lay rector of a church in Monmouthshire against her vicar and churchwardens. Because only the lay rector held the key to the external door into the chancel, and she withheld permission to use it, the churchwardens had changed the lock after being denied access. The judge found in favour of the defendents, ruling that the lay rector had no superior right to control the use of the chancel over that of the vicar.[113] This significant ruling eased the way for both choirs and organs to be located in the chancel. From this date onwards it became aspirational for churches to have their congregational singing led by a choir of men and boys facing each other across the chancel, and in the early twenty-first century this collegiate-style seating can still be found in most Hertfordshire parish churches.

Many eighteenth- and nineteenth-century alterations to the church layout and fabric were made to accommodate those participating in music-making. Choirs of children seated next to organs in galleries were replaced by choirs of men and boys in the chancel, in many cases with an organ located nearby. From the 1810s onwards the ICBS gave grants towards many of these alterations on the assumption that a large percentage of the population would attend church, and churches were built accordingly. Although so many church seats are empty today, this is partly because so many seats were provided for charity school children in attempts to improve congregational singing that persisted throughout the period from the 1760s to the 1860s.

Endnotes

1. Prince, *Parks*, pp. 93 and 107.
2. *Ibid.*, pp. 118–22.
3. *Ibid.*, pp. 96–7 and 122.
4. J. Smith, 'Mason, William (1725–1797)', *ODNB*; see Chapter 6, p. 169.
5. Kilbey, 'Early Use', pp. 63–5.
6. G. Hannah (ed.), *The Deserted Village. The Diary of an Oxfordshire Rector JAMES NEWTON of Nuneham Courtenay 1736–86* (Stroud, 1992), pp. xvi and 59; Anon., *Description of Nuneham-Courtenay, in the County of Oxford* (1797), pp. 10–11.
7. *Gentleman's Magazine* (25 July 1791), p. 682; see also T. Friedman, *The Eighteenth-Century Church in Britain* (London, 2011), pp. 551–5.
8. Prince, *Parks*, pp. 149–50.
9. Oman, *Ayot Rectory*, p. 144; Langwill and Boston, *Barrel-organs*, p. 79; N. Pevsner and B. Cherry, *Hertfordshire*, Buildings of England, 2nd edn (London, 1977), p. 80; organ still present, mechanism removed 1964.
10. Hertfordshire Family History Society, *Militia Ballot Lists: Ayot St Lawrence* (Hertford, 1999), p. 1.
11. N. Yates, *Liturgical Space. Christian Worship and Church Buildings in Western Europe 1500–2000*, Liturgy, Worship and Society Series (Aldershot, 2008), pp. 79–81.
12. E.W. Brayley, *The Beauties of England and Wales*, 18 vols (London, 1801–15), 7, part 1, pp. 93–4.
13. Grimston, *Manuscripts*, pp. 216–18.
14. *Ibid.*
15. See Table 2.1.
16. HALS, DP/98/5/1 List of subscribers (1787).
17. LPL, FP Porteus 30/10 (1790); see Appendix 1.
18. LPL, FP Randolph 12/11 (1810).
19. HALS, DP/23/3/1; DP/74/8/1–3 Vestry book; list of subscriptions for gallery for singers (1775).
20. Hertfordshire Family History Society, *Militia Ballot Lists: Northchurch* (Hertford, 1999).
21. HALS, DP/49/8/2–5.
22. HALS, DP/12/8/1 Vestry book (1794).
23. Temperley, *Parish Church*, p. 101.
24. Vincent, *Considerations*, p. 24.
25. M.G. Jones, *The Charity School Movement: A Study of Eighteenth Century Puritanism in Action* (Cambridge, 1938), p. 61; Jacob, 'Congregation', p. 301.
26. HALS, DP/117/8/1–3.
27. Davidson, *Choirs*, p. 68.
28. HALS, DP/24/5/2–14.
29. LPL, ICBS General committee minute book, no.1 (1820), p. 168; HALS, DP/90/7.
30. Cussans, *History*, III, p. 176; LPL, ICBS 2154 (1837); *National Pipe Organ Register* N14073.
31. HALS DP/21/6/15 Papers relating to St Michael's church (n.d.).
32. Gerish, 'Albury Church', pp. 229–37.
33. LPL, FP Randolph 11/99 (1810).
34. HALS, DE/X840/7/13 St Mary the Virgin, Rickmansworth (n.d.).
35. LPL, ICBS 557 (1824).
36. HALS, DP/48/8/4 Vestry minutes (1855).
37. LPL, ICBS 5754 (1862).
38. M.H. Port, *600 New Churches. The Church Building Commission 1818–1856*, 2nd edn (Reading, 2006), p. 24.
39. National Society, *Third Annual Report* (London, 1815); HALS, DP/24/5/2–14.

40 HALS, DP/33/1/24 Notes on the erection of parish school (1820); LPL, ICBS 574 (1824).
41 Burg, *Religion*, p. 6; A. Deacon and P. Walne (eds), '*A professional Hertfordshire tramp*': *John Edwin Cussans*, Hertfordshire Record Society, vol. III (Ware, 1987), pp. 104–5.
42 LPL, ICBS 2868 (1843), f. 28
43 HALS, DP/29/8/48–57; DP/90/8/1–3; F.R. Williams, *Anstey: A Hertfordshire Parish* (Cambridge, 1929), pp. 58–9.
44 Anon., *Great St Mary's Through the Ages* (Margate, n.d.), p. 29.
45 J.E. Vaux, *Church Folklore. A record of some post-Reformation usages in the Church of England*, 2nd edn(London, 1902), pp. 30–7.
46 H. Miller, *Redbourn Parish Magazine* (August 1910), cited by A. Featherstone, *Redbourn's History* (Redbourn, 2001), pp. 208–9.
47 National Society, *Monthly Paper* (October 1856), pp. 275–7.
48 LPL, ICBS 5754 (1861).
49 HALS, DP/43/5/1 Churchwardens' accounts (1825).
50 LPL, ICBS 2944 (1841).
51 G.W.O. Addleshaw and F. Etchells, *The Architectural Setting of Anglican Worship* (London, 1948), pp. 93 and 98.
52 HALS, AHH19/2 Faculty for a gallery, Berkhamsted (1819).
53 LPL, ICBS 1669 (1834).
54 *HMR* (6 July 1844), p. 3.
55 LPL, ICBS 1669 (1835).
56 *HMR* (27 February 1858), p. 3; HALS, DP/24A/6/10 Specification for re-seating and other works to Hoddesdon church (1864).
57 National Society, *Ninth Annual Report* (London, 1820) pp. 24–157; HALS, 64394 Faculty book (1822).
58 LPL, ICBS 1091 (1829).
59 HALS, DP/26/29/5 'Bushey Reports' (1828).
60 LPL, ICBS 1784 (1834).
61 LPL, ICBS 1133 (1832).
62 S.F. Clarkson, 'St Pauls Walden', *Transactions 1888*, St Albans Architectural and Archaeological Society (1889), p. 27; Burg, *Religion*, p. 149.
63 *Ecclesiologist* (July 1842), p. 170.
64 *Ibid*., p. 156.
65 *Ibid*.
66 See, for example, LPL, ICBS 3425 (1846).
67 *Ecclesiologist* (July 1842), p. 156.
68 P.G. Ward, *A History of Braughing Church and its Benefactors* (1888), pp. 17 and 24.
69 Cambridge Camden Society, *A Few Words to Churchwardens*, II, p. 7.
70 *Ecclesiologist* (February 1843), p. 107.
71 *Oxford and Cambridge Review* (May 1846), p. 344.
72 *Church Builder*, I (1862), p. 2.
73 *Ibid*., VIII (1863), p. 165.
74 *Ibid*., IX (1864), pp. 24–7.
75 C. Dickens, *Dombey and Son* (London, 1848), p. 386.
76 *Church Builder*, IX (1864), pp. 24–7.
77 HALS, DP/124/29/1.
78 *HG* (25 August 1866) p. 4.
79 *Church Builder*, IX (1864), pp. 24–7.
80 C. Miele, '"Their interest and habit": Professionalism and the Restoration of Medieval Churches, 1837–1877', in C. Brooks and A. Saint (eds), *The Victorian Church: Architecture and Society* (Manchester, 1995), p. 156.
81 F. Knight, *The Nineteenth-Century Church and English Society* (Cambridge, 1995), p. 61.
82 A.W. Pugin, *The True Principles of Pointed or Christian Architecture* (London, 1841).
83 *Hertfordshire Almanac* (24 December 1864), pp. 102–3.

84 *HMR* (15 November 1862), p. 3.
85 *Hertfordshire Almanac* (4 July 1866), p. 94; (12 December 1867), p. 103.
86 *Church Builder*, XXVI (1867), p. 72.
87 *HG* (3 July 1855), p. 3; (24 March 1860), p. 5.
88 *HG* (22 November 1859), p. 3.
89 *HMR* (15 November 1862), p. 3.
90 *HG* (10 January 1863), p. 5.
91 *HMR* (28 April 1866), p. 3.
92 *HG* (11 May 1867), p. 5.
93 Davys, 'Choral Arrangements', pp. 262–4.
94 *Ibid.*
95 Cambridge Camden Society, *A Few Words to Church Builders* (Cambridge, 1841), pp. 10 and 23.
96 Davys, 'Choral Arrangements', pp. 268–9.
97 *Ibid.*
98 Miele, 'Interest and habit', pp. 169–70.
99 *HMR* (24 May 1856), p. 3.
100 Cussans, *History*, I, p. 160.
101 *HMR* (12 November 1853), p. 3.
102 *Ecclesiologist* (September 1843), pp. 1–4.
103 *Ibid.*
104 *Ibid.*
105 Temperley, *Parish Church*, p. 257.
106 LPL, ICBS 4358 (1851).
107 *Musical Times* (October 1853), pp. 259–62; (November 1853), pp. 275–8.
108 *Ibid.*, p. 278.
109 *HMR* (11 May 1861), p. 2.
110 HALS, DP/47/8/4 Vestry minutes (1858–61).
111 *Church Builder*, III (1862), p. 7; *Choir and Musical Record* (25 July 1863).
112 *HG* (5 April 1864), p. 3.
113 *London Daily News* (26 May 1863), p. 6.

Conclusion

This book has demonstrated that constant attempts were made to improve parochial congregational singing in Hertfordshire throughout the whole period between 1760 and 1870. In theory the entire congregation was expected to join in singing psalmody, but in practice few sang. Little improvement can be detected, with scarce evidence for congregational singing.

The use of charity children's voices to promote congregational psalmody was repeatedly attempted following continuing episcopal guidance and encouragement, and children were taught to sing by elite patrons, organists, singers, parish clerks and schoolteachers. Although a variety of different teaching methods were adopted, the most widespread and enduring support for their singing came from church barrel organs. Attempts to use children's voices to improve psalmody met with disappointment time after time, often because of the adults' reluctance or inability to sing with them.

During the late eighteenth and early nineteenth centuries charity and Sunday schools and their choirs were enthusiastically promoted by the elite, aware of episcopal and lay concerns regarding the state of congregational psalmody through their shared cultural experience and exclusive access to reading matter. Many advantages were anticipated, including encouraging children to continue to attend church as singing adults, attracting their parents to church, retaining worshippers in the face of Nonconformity and saving the expense of paying adult musicians.

The metropolitan fashion of placing choirs of charity children in a gallery where their singing was supported by an organ was of significant and enduring influence, resulting in the adoption of this practice in rural parishes, even if the instrument was a barrel organ. The founding of the National Society in 1811 was of particular significance for both the development of music-making and for church architecture because, following the incorporation of an existing or new charity school into the Society, it was usually a continuing requirement for children to attend church, and an organ of some sort was often introduced to support their singing. But elite members of the congregation did not sing with school children because they did not wish to be associated with the objects of their charity.

The significant influence of the elite on church music-making also found expression in parish churches with no organ, and perhaps even no charity school. The introduction of wind instruments to church bands during the Napoleonic Wars was in some cases influenced by their use in military bands and, as was the case with organs, initially allied to their use in polite music-making favoured by the gentry.

Music-making in local dissenting and Methodist meetings was seen as a rival attraction. Its influence was seen not only in the church's original desire to retain worshippers by improving church music-making but also in the inclusion of works by Nonconformists in both collections of psalms and hymns and tunes pinned on church barrel organs. But some children, on reaching adulthood, preferred to sing the hymn tunes learnt as school children instead of the psalm tunes used in church. As these hymn tunes were often used in Nonconformist places of worship they served as an attraction towards the chapel and away from the parish church.

During the early 1800s central discussions on the improvement of church music-making shifted from the elite to the clergy, part of a discernible trend from the lay-dominated eighteenth and early nineteenth centuries to the more clerically dominated late nineteenth century. The *Ecclesiastical Gazette*, sent to every church, encouraged the clergy to purchase barrel organs, but with waning financial support for the church mid-century the clergy often paid for them themselves. Long-running church rate disputes resulted in difficulties paying organists in certain Hertfordshire towns and ensured that barrel organs remained in use long after the beginnings of Tractarian influence, which was initially opposed to the use of any instruments in church. Dissenters and non-church-goers were not the only parishioners who revolted against church rates, as in some parishes it was members of the congregation themselves who raised objections following the introduction of Tractarian-led ritualism. Most church organists would have already supplemented their income through teaching, concert-giving, organ tuning, music editing or other employment. But the inability to collect church rates, and then their abolition in 1868, meant that in the absence of bequests or funding from private individuals church organists had to become more reliant on this supplementary revenue or face insolvency.

The need to accommodate poor children, whether or not they sang, meant that in many churches, particularly those in towns, most seating was appropriated to the elite or to school children despite the building of galleries. The charity children's own families were therefore unable to sing in their parish church because there was insufficient available space to accommodate them. Those adults able to find seats found it difficult or impossible to sing in the same range as children, whose voices were described as shrieking, chirping, screaming, strained, squalling, shouting, croaky, noisy and generally 'most unsatisfactory'. Others associated the church with their own unpleasant childhood experience of compulsory attendance, and so may not have attended any place of worship.

By the mid-nineteenth century local newspapers and national publications engaged a wider, democratic readership and encouraged the support of all in ambitious schemes that included the extension or rebuilding of parish churches. As additional accommodation was made available for the poor some of the artisan class with no appropriated seats were unwilling to share unappropriated sittings with them, refused to attend church and consequently did not sing there.

Time and again reform introduced in one period was regarded as inappropriate during the next. The fashionable barrel organs introduced to improve congregational singing in the late 1700s became the grinding organs abominated in the 1860s. During the 1760s a gallery had been considered a desirable location for organs and choirs of children and an acceptable location for singers and church bands. But by 1870 the building of galleries in parish churches had been forbidden, and any remaining galleries were considered objectionable. An adult singing craze, often transitory, had led to collegiate-style choir seating being placed in the chancel, often with an organ close by. This became the typical church layout, still found in perhaps the majority of English parish churches in the early twenty-first century.

Although this book is concerned with music-making in the English parish church, it also casts light on some more general features of the Church of England itself. On the one hand, it has provided an example of the effectiveness of bishops in promoting their agendas, which in this case was the improvement of congregational psalmody. Their success in making their guidance known, and the extent to which it influenced both their clergy and certain elite parishioners, has been underappreciated. Channels of communication, including the SPCK, National Society and ICBS, proved to be an increasingly effective network for the dissemination of both clerical guidance and information in terms of encouraging singing by charity and Sunday school children and providing guidelines for suitable church architecture in which to do so. But, on the other hand, this book has also highlighted the Church of England's shortcomings with regard to its ability to learn from experience, seen for example in persistent efforts to use children's voices to lead congregational singing and the constant underfunding of organists. Its repeated attempts to improve music-making reflect a broader picture in which there was change, but no change.

Encouraging the congregation to sing and retaining worshippers remain very relevant issues today. Although 'worshiptainment', based on a style of music more traditionally associated with the entertainment industry, attracts many worshippers to some churches, it drives away others. Perhaps unsurprisingly in the Church of England, there is no single answer that would satisfy all church-goers.

Appendix 1

Map of Hertfordshire *c.*1800 showing major routes, towns and selected country houses

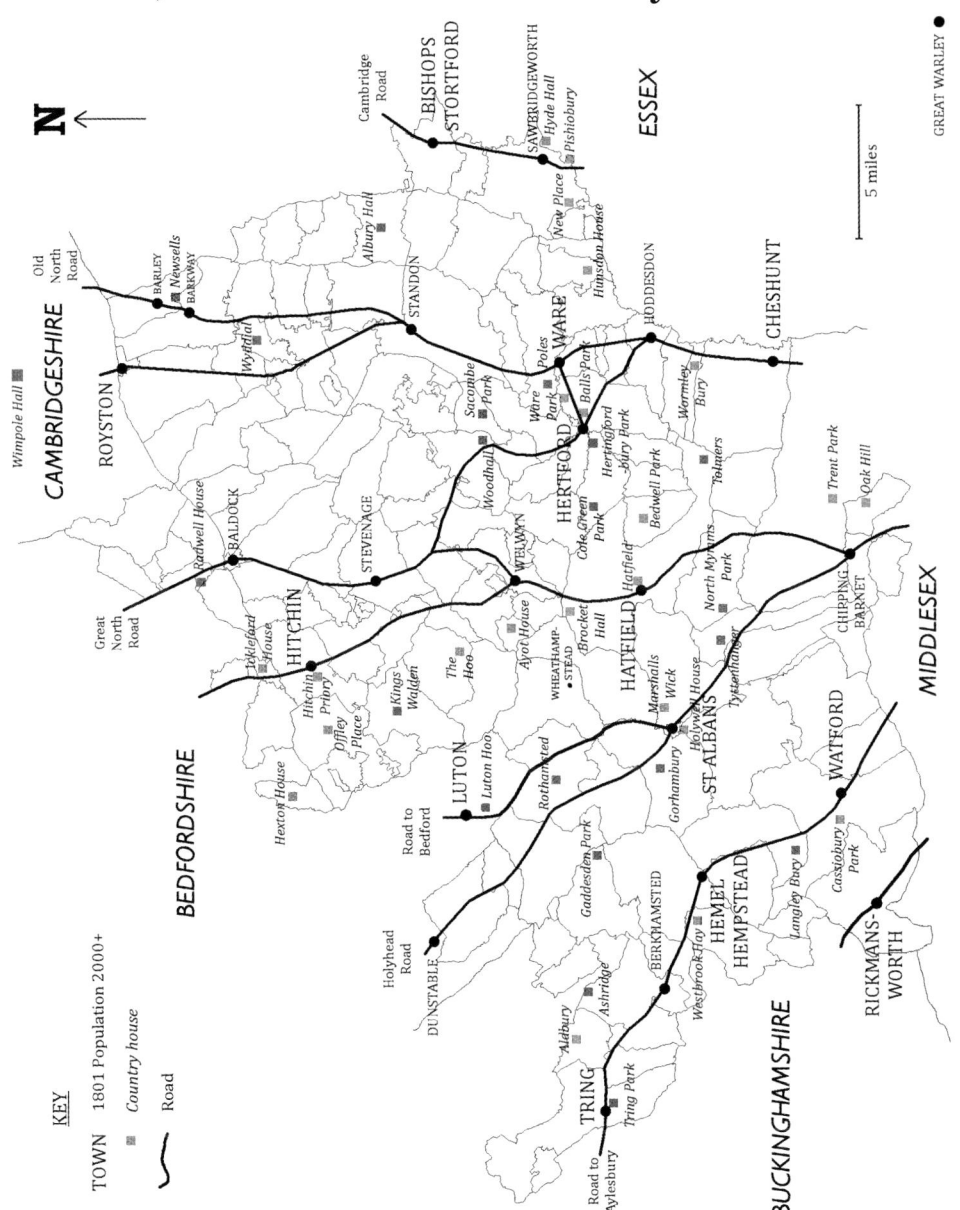

Note: see Figure 5.1 for North Mymms area.

Appendix 2
Map of Hertfordshire parishes included in this book

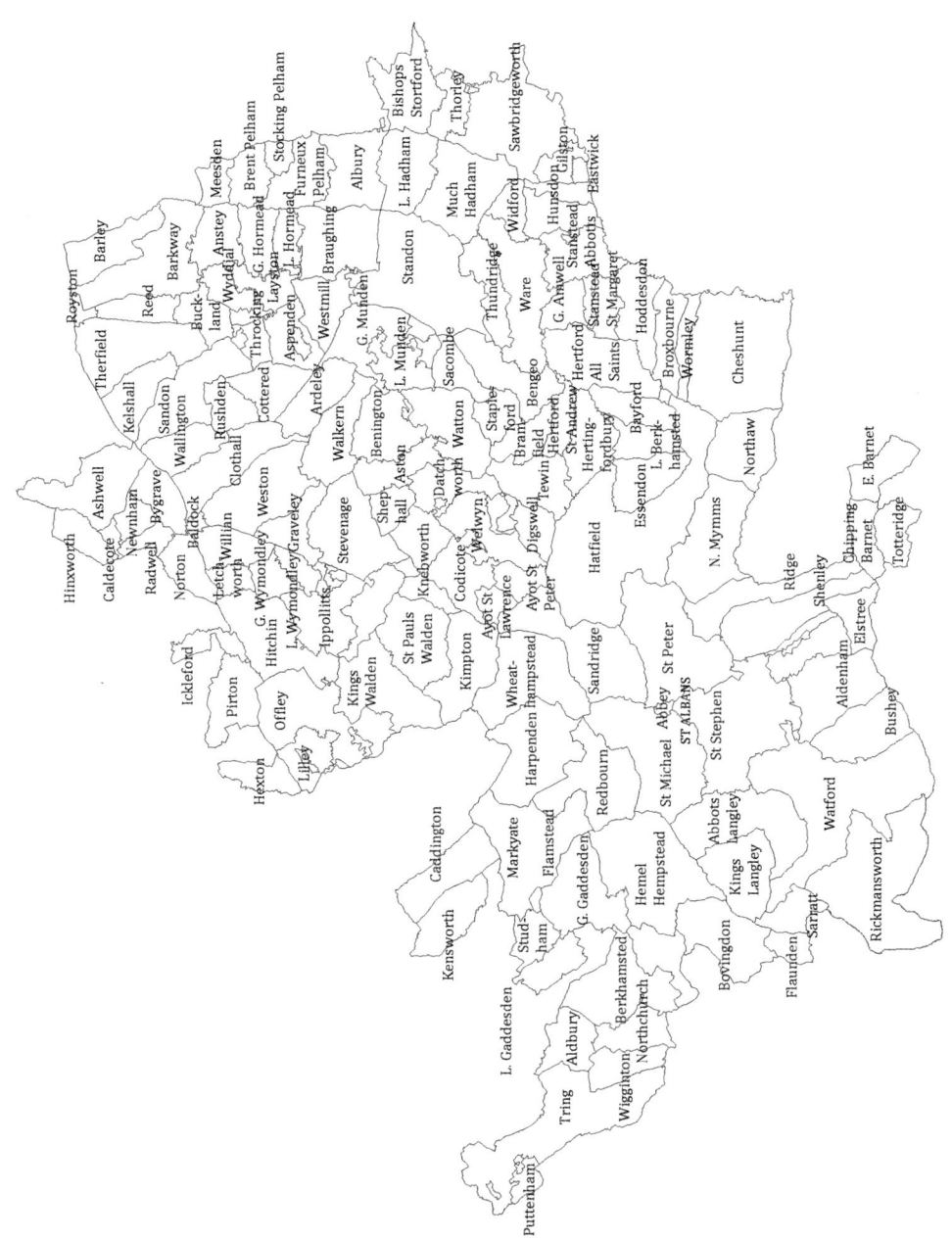

Appendix 3
Evidence for organs installed in Hertfordshire parish churches 1760–1869

Parish church	Organ(s) and date of first known use
Abbots Langley*	c.1840 BO; 1850 O (Gray & Davison)
Aldbury*	1866 O (Gray & Davison)
Aldenham*	c.1820 BO (Gray); 1853 B/F (Gray & Davison); 1866 O (Gray & Davison)
Ardeley	1840 BO
Ashwell	1868 O (J.W. Walker)
Aspenden	1821 BO (H. Bryceson); 1856 O (T.J.F. Robson)
Ayot St Lawrence	c.1780 B/F
Baldock*	1835 Organ with added barrel mechanism
Barkway*	1844 [B]O
Bayford*	c.1860 O (Henry Willis)
Bengeo	1850 Improved BO (Bates & Son); 1860 O
Benington*	1867 O (Bryceson)
Berkhamsted*	1819 BO; c.1849 O (H. Bryceson)
Bovingdon*	1853 [B]O
Bramfield	1842 [B]O
Braughing*	1810 BO; c.1850 B/F (Bishop & Sons)
Broxbourne	1804 BO; 1831[B]O (H.C. Lincoln); 1858 O (J.W. Walker)
Cheshunt	1791 O (Longman & Broderip)
Chipping Barnet	1824 BO (Flight & Robson); 1850 O (H. Bevington)
Cottered	1832 BO (B. Flight & Sons)
East Barnet	1824 BO (Flight & Robson); 1862 O
Elstree*	1826 BO (George Parsons); 1854 O (Gray & Davison)
Essendon*	1851 BO (?Pilcher)
Flaunden	c.1838 BO
Great Amwell*	1825 BO (?William Allen); 1866 O
Great Gaddesden*	1850 O & dumb organist; 1863 O (Samuel Parsons)
Great Hormead	1855 [B]O
Great Wymondley	c.1844 BO
Harpenden*	1862 O (T.J.F. Robson)
Hatfield*	1851 O (James Eagles)
Hemel Hempstead	c.1820 O (H.C. Lincoln); 1861 O (Gray & Davison)
All Saints, Hertford	1840 O (Gray & Son)
St Andrew's, Hertford*	1822 O (?Bishop); c.1850 O; 1861 O (Bishop, Starr & Richardson); 1867 O (G.M. Holdich)
Hertingfordbury	1842 [B]O

Parish church	Organ(s) and date of first known use
Hexton	1826 BO (John Gray)
Hitchin*	1805 BO (Charles Green)
Hoddesdon	1805 BO (?R.W. Keith); 1865 O (Henry Willis)
Hunsdon	1827 BO (?Walker); 1865 O (John Fincham)
Ickleford	1849 BO (T.C. Bates & Son); c.1860 O (Henry Willis)
Kimpton	c.1819 BO
Kings Langley*	1843 BO (Gray & Davison); 1856 O (Gray & Davison)
Kings Walden	1869 O (Walker)
Little Berkhamsted	1857 O
Little Gaddesden*	c.1849 BO
Little Hadham*	1868 O (Gray & Davison)
Markyate	1830 BO; 1840 BO (Gray & Son); 1844 BO (Gray & Davison)
Much Hadham*	1827 BO; 1844 Improved BO (Gray & Davison); c.1856 O; 1859 O (Gray & Davison)
Newnham	c.1860 O (A.T. Miller)
North Mymms	c.1784 O; 1820 B/F (?Gray)
Northchurch*	1836 BO
Norton	1840 Improved BO (Gray & Son)
Offley*	1861 [B]O
Pirton*	1854 [B]O
Radwell	1837 BO (H. Bryceson)
Redbourn*	1848 BO
Rickmansworth*	1826 BO (H. Bryceson)
Ridge	1851 [B]O (Bevington)
Royston*	c.1820 BO
Sacombe	c.1840 BO (Bevington & Sons)
Abbey Church, St Albans*	1820 O (Father Smith); 1861 O (Hill & Son)
St Michael's, St Albans*	1833 BO (?J.C. Bishop); 1867 O (Bevington)
St Stephen's, St Albans*	1849 O (John Godman jnr.)
St Ippolyts	1844 BO; 1866 O (William Carling)
St Pauls Walden*	1850 O & dumb organist
Sarratt*	1866 O
Sawbridgeworth*	1860 O (Gray & Davison)
Shenley	1839 O
Standon*	1859 O (G.M. Holdich)
Stanstead Abbots*	c.1832 BO (?Flight); 1867 O (Bevington)
Stanstead St Margaret	1837 Barrel mechanism (John Gray) added to chamber organ (William Allen)
Stevenage*	1836 B/F (John Gray)
Stocking Pelham	c.1848 BO (T.C. Bates & Son)
Studham	1842 Improved BO (Gray & Davison)
Therfield	1862 O (?Walker)
Thorley	1850 [B]O
Thundridge	1849 [B]O; 1853 O (Bishop & Sons)
Totteridge	1823 O
Tring*	1832 BO; 1863 O (Hill & Son)
Walkern	1842 BO
Ware	1812 O (?J.C. Bishop)
Watford	1766 O (Thomas Parker); 1842 B/F (J. Walker)
Watton-at-Stone	1839 [B]O (J.C. Bishop)

Parish church	Organ(s) and date of first known use
Welwyn*	1854 BO (Gray & Davison)
Westmill	1829 BO (H. Bryceson)
Weston	1842 B/F (?Hill)
Wheathampstead*	1829 BO (?Allen); 1866 O (J.W. Walker)
Widford	1868 BO
Willian	c.1831 BO; 1864 O (J.W. Walker)
Wormley	1844 BO; 1860 (Henry Willis)

Notes: BO = barrel organ; [B]O = organ, probably barrel organ; B/F = barrel-and-finger organ; O = finger organ; * also evidence of singers/church bands (see Appendix 4).

Sources: BL, Add MS 47775A; CRL, BOA, John Gray accounts, vol. 1, Gray & Davison accounts, vols 2–8A, Hill & Son estimate book, vol. 1; HALS DE/Hd/F3, DE/R/F220, DP/3/29/17, DP/4/5/1–8, DP/7/6/1, DP/8/1/3, DP/13/5/2–3, DP/15/5/2, DP/15/12/5, DP/17/6/13, DP/18/5/3, DP/19/6/1–11, DP/22/12/4, DP/23/5/1, DP/24/5/2–14, DP/24/6/4, DP/24A/5/1–3, DP/24A/6/10, DP/24A/8/10, DP/36/5/1, DP/37/5/4, DP/44/5/1, DP/46B/8/12, DP/47/8/4, DP/48/6/2, DP/49/8/2–5, DP/50/8/3, DP/53/8/2, DP/53/29/9, DP/55/5/1, DP/57/5/2, DP/58/5/1, DP/59/5/2, DP/61/1/2, DP/69/5/1, DP/74/5/24, DP/76/5/1, DP/80/4/1–2, DP/85/5/1, DP/86/5/2, DP/90/3/1, DP/94/29/4, DP/98/29/5, DP/105/3/3, DP/108/5/1, DP/110/8/2, DP/111/8/20, DP/114/8/1, DP/117/5/1, DP/117/8/1–3, DP/118/8/13, DP/120/1/4, DP/122/5/1, DP/122/29/9, DP/123/6/1, DP/125/1/3, DP/125/5/1, DP/126/8, RDC/7/69/35; LPL, ICBS 291, ICBS 1133, ICBS 3423, ICBS 4042; St Michael's, St Albans, Churchwardens' papers (1831–40), Correspondence with Mr F.F. Hill (1974), Vestry order book 21 (1819–34); J. Baron, *Scudamore Organs* (1862); Cass, *East Barnet*; Cussans, *History*, I–II; *Hertfordshire Almanac* (1864–66); *HG* (1856–67); *HM* (1837–66); *Kelly's Post Office Directory of Hertfordshire* (1851); *Pigot's & Co.'s Commercial Directory* (1839); Lewis, *Topographical Dictionary of England* (1831); G. Aylott, 'Norton Manor and Church', *Transactions of the East Herts Archaeological Society*, 2/III (1904), pp. 273–8; Bell, *Little Gaddesden*; Featherstone, *Redbourn's History*; Forbes, *Artist*; A.E. Gibbs, *The parish registers of Aldenham, Hertfordshire, 1559–1659* (St Albans, 1902); Harkness, *All Saints*; Langwill and Boston, *Barrel-organs*; J.E. Morris, 'Hunsdon Church', *Transactions of the East Herts Archaeological Society*, 2/I (1902), pp. 46–56; Ord-Hume, *Barrel Organ*; Pevsner and Cherry, *Hertfordshire*; H.T. Pollard, 'Cottered Church', *Transactions of the East Herts Archaeological Society*, 3/II (1907), pp. 160–5; H.T. Pollard, 'Stocking Pelham Church', *Transactions of the East Herts Archaeological Society*, 2/I (1906), pp. 75–8; J. Pollington, *Kimpton Parish Church* (1978); Senar, *Little Gaddesden*; E.E. Squires, 'St Faith's Church, Hexton', *Transactions of the East Herts Archaeological Society*, 4/I (1909), pp. 43–6; Ward, *Braughing*; R.S. Wilkinson, *The Church and Parish of Abbots Langley* (Abbots Langley, 1959); British Institute of Organ Studies, *National Pipe Organ Register*, accessed at <http://www.npor.org.uk>

Appendix 4
Evidence of singers and church bands in Hertfordshire parish churches 1760–1850

	Singers	Singing gallery/pew	Music books	Bassoon	Clarinet/clarionet	Oboe/hautboy	Flute	Cello/bass viol	Violin/fiddle	Unspecified instruments
Abbots Langley	•	•						•		
Albury					•			•		
Aldbury	•	•	•	•	•					
Aldenham					•	•		•	•	
Baldock	•	•	•		•			•	•	
Barkway	•	•	•	•	•		•	•		
Barley	•	•								
Bayford	•									
Benington	•									
Berkhamsted	•	•			•			•		
Bovingdon	•	•								
Braughing	•	•								•
Brent Pelham										•
Bushey	•	•			•			•		
Caddington	•	•	•	•	•	•				
Elstree	•	•	•							•
Essendon	•	•	•							
Furneux Pelham								•		•
Great Amwell			•							
Great Gaddesden										•
Harpenden			•	•	•	•				
Hatfield									•	•
St Andrew's, Hertford	•	•								
Hitchin	•	•	•							
Kensworth				•	•					
Kings Langley	•		•	•		•		•		

258

APPENDIX 4

	Singers	Singing gallery/pew	Music books	Bassoon	Clarinet/clarionet	Oboe/hautboy	Flute	Cello/bass viol	Violin/fiddle	Unspecified instruments
Lilley	•	•			•			•	•	
Little Gaddesden	•	•								
Little Hadham	•	•								
Much Hadham	•									
Northchurch	•	•	•							
Offley	•	•			•					
Pirton			•							
Redbourn	•	•			•					
Rickmansworth	•		•							
Royston			•		•			•	•	
Rushden	•									
Abbey Church, St Albans	•	•	•		•					
St Michael's, St Albans	•	•	•							•
St Stephen's, St Albans	•	•	•	•				•		
St Pauls Walden	•	•		•	•	•		•	•	•
Sandon	•	•								
Sarratt								•		
Sawbridgeworth	•	•								
Standon		•	•					•	•	
Stanstead Abbots				•						
Stevenage	•									
Tring	•	•			•					
Wallington	•	•			•					
Welwyn	•	•		•						
Wheathampstead	•			•						
Total	37	28	20	11	16	4	4	14	6	7

Sources: BARS, P34/5/1–3, P35/5/1–2; BL, Add MS 47775A; HALS ASA17/17/1/2, DE/X228/Z5–6, DP/1/29/2, DP/2/5/2, DP/3/5/1, DP/12/5/3, DP/12/8/1, DP/13/5/2–3, DP/13/8/21–30, DP/18/29/7–12, DP/19/5/1–2, DP/23/3/1, DP/26/5/1–2, DP/36/5/1, DP/37A/5/1, DP/39/5/2, DP/43/5/1, DP/44/5/1, DP/49/8/2–5, DP/64/5/1–2, DP/67/5/2, DP/74/5/24, DP/74/8/1–3, DP/76/5/1, DP/78/3/3, DP/78/5/1, DP/80/4/1–2, DP/85/25/1, DP/90/5/1, DP/90/7, DP/94/5/1, DP/98/5/1, DP/105/5/1, DP/111/8/20, DP/115/5/1, DP/122/5/1, DP/122A/5/1–2; LPL, ICBS 1570, ICBS 1669, ICBS 2944, ICBS 3321; St Michael's, St Albans, Churchwardens' papers 2; Anderson, 'Old Church Bands'; Bell, *Little Gaddesden*; Brayley, *Beauties*; W. d'A Crofton, 'Standon Church', *Transactions of the East Herts Archaeological Society*, I (1901), pp. 273–88; *English Church History Exhibition*; Feakes, 'Lilley'; Featherstone, *Redbourn's History*; Grimston, *Manuscripts*; Hall, 'Essendon Church'; Hellendaal, *Psalms*; *Herts Advertiser* (1866); Kingston, *Fragments*; Luppino, *Psalms and Hymns*; Trollope, *What I Remember*; Wilkinson, *Abbots Langley*; Luton Museum, BL/53/45, 4-keyed bassoon from St Pauls Walden; St Albans Museum, 88.3187, 8-keyed bassoon from Welwyn; The Higgins Art Gallery and Museum (Bedford), 7692 & 7693, clarinets from Wallington.

Bibliography

Manuscript and archival sources
Bedfordshire Archives and Record Service (BARS)
Ecclesiastical Parish Records
P34/5/1–3 Churchwardens' accounts (1805–60)
P35/5/1 Churchwardens' accounts (1779–1838)
P35/5/2 Vouchers (1787–1840)
P118/5/4 Churchwardens' accounts (1778–1813)
P125/1/5 Register of baptisms (1849)

Russell (Dukes of Bedford) archive
R4/608/35/20–1 Harland and Salmon correspondence (1816)

British Library (BL)
Add MS 47775 A–B, K.H. MacDermott, 'The Old Church Gallery Minstrels' collections (1934–52)

Cadbury Research Library, University of Birmingham (CRL)
British Organ Archive (BOA)
John Gray accounts, vol. 1 (1821–38)
Gray & Davison accounts, vol. 2 (1838–45)
Gray & Davison accounts, vol. 3 (1839–41)
Gray & Davison accounts, vol. 4 (1842–8)
Gray & Davison accounts, vol. 5 (1849–57)
Gray & Davison accounts, vol. 8A (1865–83)

Camden Local Studies and Archives Centre
Ecclesiastical Parish Records
P/GB/M/1/1 Vestry minutes (1788)

BIBLIOGRAPHY

Cathedral and Abbey Church of St Alban, Muniment Room
Shelf F Kent Book
Voluntary Contributions Towards the Church Service from Easter 1866 to Easter 1867

Hertfordshire Archives and Local Studies (HALS)
Diaries of John Carrington, senior and junior, farmers
DE/X3/12 Diaries of John Carrington, senior, vol. XII (April–December 1809)

Ecclesiastical Parish Records
DP/1/29/2 ms history of the parish of Albury (1939)
DP/2/5/2 Churchwardens' accounts (1764–1813)
DP/2/29/9 Churchwardens' bills (1772–4)
DP/3/5/1–2 Churchwardens' accounts (1760–1870)
DP/3/5/3 Receipted bills (1822)
DP/3/25/12 Establishment of Elstree National School (1814)
DP/3/29/17 Correspondence (1902–25)
DP/4/5/1–8 Churchwardens' accounts, bills & vouchers (1822–61)
DP/4/29/2 Music played by the barrel organ in the church (1856)
DP/7/6/1 Invoice for church organ (1868)
DP/8/1/3 Register of baptisms, includes list of subscribers to new organ (1821)
DP/8/8/3 Lists of subscribers to a new organ (1856)
DP/12/5/2 Churchwardens' bills & vouchers (1821)
DP/12/5/3 Churchwardens' accounts (1826–68)
DP/12/8/1 Vestry book (1794)
DP/12/29/5 Miscellaneous papers (1814–34)
DP/13/5/2–3 Churchwardens' accounts (1817–44)
DP/13/8/21–30 Bills & vouchers (1803–33)
DP/13/25/6 Rough sketch plan of the old pews in Barkway Church (*c*.1863)
DP/13/25/14 National School minute book (1839–54)
DP/15/5/2 Churchwardens' accounts (1762–1840)
DP/15/8/3 Vestry minutes (1824–63)
DP/15/12/5 Churchwardens' accounts (1840–50)
DP/17/6/13 Vestry resolution, Bates & Son invoice (1850)
DP/18/5/3 Churchwardens' accounts (1867)
DP/18/29/7–12 Account books of the Rev. John Haggard (1770–1805)
DP/19/5/1–2 Churchwardens' accounts & vestry minutes (1810–45)
DP/19/5/4 Churchwardens' bills (1812–14)
DP/19/6/1 Papers relating to the organ (1849)
DP/21/5/5 Churchwardens' accounts (1827–9)
DP/21/5/10–11 Churchwardens' bills & vouchers (1760–1841)

DP/21/6/15 Papers relating to St Michael's church (n.d.)
DP/22/12/4 Vestry minutes (1842)
DP/23/3/1 Vicar's notes & memoranda (1680–1912)
DP/23/5/1 Churchwardens' accounts (1810)
DP/24/5/2–14 Churchwardens' vouchers & accounts (1802–60)
DP/24/6/4 Papers relating to repairs & restoration of church (1858–9)
DP/24A/5/1–3 Churchwardens' accounts (1823–51)
DP/24A/6/10 Specification for re-seating and other works to Hoddesdon church (1864)
DP/24A/8/10 Vestry minutes (1805–09)
DP/26/5/1–2 Churchwardens' accounts (1785–1831)
DP/26/29/5 'Bushey Reports' (1828)
DP/29/8/48–54 Churchwardens' accounts & vestry minutes (1750–1857)
DP/33/1/24 Notes on the erection of parish school (1820)
DP/36/5/1 Churchwardens' accounts (1791–1826)
DP/37/5/4 Churchwardens' accounts (1835–73)
DP/37A/5/1 Churchwardens' accounts (1812)
DP/39/5/2 Churchwardens' accounts (1817–62)
DP/43/5/1 Churchwardens' accounts (1825)
DP/44/5/1 Churchwardens' accounts (1784–1870)
DP/44/29/1 Miscellaneous papers (n.d.)
DP/46B/8/12 Churchwardens' accounts (1821–3)
DP/46B/12/5 Vestry minutes (1827–34)
DP/47/8/4 Vestry minutes (1858–61)
DP/48/6/2 Papers relating to new organ (1839–40)
DP/48/8/4 Vestry minutes (1855)
DP/49/8/2–5 Vestry minutes (1779–1867)
DP/50/8/3 Vestry minutes (1842)
DP/53/7/4 Minutes of meetings of subscribers to the organist's salary (1837–56)
DP/53/8/2 Vestry minutes (1805)
DP/53/29/9 Miscellaneous items (1805)
DP/55/5/1 Churchwardens' accounts (1855–59)
DP/57/5/2 Churchwardens' accounts (1827–79)
DP/58/5/1 Churchwardens' accounts (1849–59)
DP/59/5/2 Churchwardens' accounts (1844-66)
DP/61/1/2 Parish notes (1792–1843)
DP/64/5/1–2 Churchwardens' accounts (1793–1853)
DP/64/25/9–10 Sunday School minutes & accounts (1786–1801)
DP/67/5/2 Churchwardens' accounts (1824–61)
DP/69/5/1 Accounts (1762–1860)
DP/74/5/24 Churchwardens' accounts (1836)

DP/74/8/1–3 Vestry book & minutes (1775–1847)
DP/76/5/1 Churchwardens' accounts (1810–70)
DP/78/3/3 Vicars' account book (1725–47)
DP/78/5/1 Churchwardens' accounts (1842–52)
DP/80/4/1–2 Churchwardens' accounts (1791–1861)
DP/85/5/1 Churchwardens' accounts (1828–55)
DP/85/25/1 Charity School accounts (1761)
DP/86/5/2 Churchwardens' accounts (1851)
DP/90/3/1 Rector's correspondence (1820)
DP/90/5/1 Churchwardens' accounts (1811–49)
DP/90/7 Bills & vouchers (1814–48)
DP/90/8/1–3 Vestry minutes (1799–61)
DP/93/1/28 Register of burials (1815)
DP/93/5/3–5 Churchwardens' accounts (1760–1870)
DP/93/29/8 Extracts from the records of the church of St Peters (*c*.1890)
DP/94/5/1 Churchwardens' accounts (1805–24)
DP/94/8/1 Vestry minutes (1841)
DP/94/29/4 Frederick Henshaw, ms history of St Stephens (1935)
DP/96/29/1 Accounts of various parish clubs (1831–72)
DP/98/5/1 List of subscribers (1787)
DP/98/29/5 Rev. S.P. Field, Memoranda (1864)
DP/105/3/3 Letter presenting organ (1836)
DP/105/5/1 Churchwardens' accounts (1829)
DP/108/5/1 Churchwardens' bills & receipts (1850)
DP/110/8/2 Vestry minutes (1849)
DP/111/8/20 Vestry minutes (1824–33)
DP/114/8/1 Vestry minutes (1842)
DP/115/5/1 Plans of church pews (n.d.)
DP/116/5/1–2 Churchwardens' accounts (1794–1868)
DP/116/8/10 Vestry minutes (1843–52)
DP/117/5/1 Churchwardens' accounts (1841–4)
DP/117/8/1–3 Vestry minutes (1766–1862)
DP/118/8/13 Vestry minutes (1839)
DP/119/8/5 Vestry minutes (1812)
DP/120/1/4 Register of baptisms (1829)
DP/120/8/1 Vestry minutes (1829)
DP/122/5/1 Churchwardens' accounts (1818–29)
DP/122/29/9 Canon Owen Davys, Typescript of history and guide to church (1908)
DP/122A/5/1–2 Churchwardens' accounts (1800–18)
DP/123/6/1 G.E. Pritchett, Plans (1868)

DP/124/29/1 George Gaisford, Some notes concerning Wigginton (1901)
DP/125/1/3 Register of baptisms (1864)
DP/125/5/1 Churchwardens' accounts (1857–64)
DP/126/5/1 Churchwardens' accounts (1861)
DP/126/8/2 Vestry minutes (1852–61)

Estate Collections
DE/R/F220 Family, business papers & correspondence of the Radcliffe family of Hitchin Priory: bills & receipts (1773–4)

Hatfield Rural District Council
RDC/7/69/35 List of subscribers (1851)

Hertford Museum, family and personal papers
DE/Hd/F3 Journal of William Jones (1802–5)
DE/Hx/F9 Draft of letter sent by Charles Bridgeman (1800)

Papers of Flora Humm, Hockerill Training College
DE/X840/7/1 Sir James Craufurd, 'Aldbury Church, Hertfordshire' (1961)
DE/X840/7/13 St Mary the Virgin, Rickmansworth (n.d.)

Quarter Sessions, Liberty of St Albans
LSGB/2 Gaol Book (1798)

Records of the Archdeaconry of Huntingdon, Hitchin Division
AHH10/1 Churchwarden's presentment (1772)
AHH19/2 Faculty for a gallery, Berkhamsted (1819)

Records of the Archdeaconry of St Albans
ASA17/14/1 Churchwardens' presentment (1803)
ASA17/17/1/2 Churchwardens' presentment (1820)

Records of Parish Councils and Parish Meetings
CP44/8/2 Vestry minutes (1843–87)

Standon, miscellaneous
DE/X228/Z5–6 ms volumes of metrical psalm tunes and church anthems, titled on spine 'James Whitaker 1829'

The William Blyth Gerish Collection
DE/Gr/46 Gerish Collection

Miscellaneous
64394 Faculty book (1822)
Acc 13/Box 3/1–5 Hitchin Volunteer infantry (1800–04)

Lambeth Palace Library (LPL)
FP: Fulham Papers: papers of the Bishops of London
Visitation returns
FP Porteus 24/65 (1790)
FP Porteus 25/16 (1790)
FP Porteus 27/40 (1790)
FP Porteus 29/4 (1790)
FP Porteus 29/34 (1790)
FP Porteus 30/8 (1790)
FP Porteus 30/10 (1790)
FP Randolph 9/17–26 (1810)
FP Randolph 9/107–14 (1810)
FP Randolph 9/301–8 (1810)
FP Randolph 9/309–18 (1810)
FP Randolph 9/651–8 (1810)
FP Randolph 9/784–91 (1810)
FP Randolph 10/66 (1810)
FP Randolph 10/100 (1810)
FP Randolph 11/99 (1810)
FP Randolph 12/11 (1810)
FP Randolph 12/30 (1810)
FP Randolph 12/49 (1810)
FP Randolph 12/94 (1810)

ICBS: Incorporated Church Building Society
ICBS 291 (1821)
ICBS 557 (1824)
ICBS 574 (1824)
ICBS 1091 (1829)
ICBS 1133 (1832)
ICBS 1570 (1833)
ICBS 1669 (1834–5)
ICBS 1784 (1834)
ICBS 2154 (1837)
ICBS 2868 (1843)
ICBS 2944 (1841)
ICBS 3321 (1843)

ICBS 3423 (1844)
ICBS 3425 (1846)
ICBS 4042 (1848)
ICBS 4358 (1851)
ICBS 5754 (1861)
General committee minute book, no.1 (1820)

Lincolnshire Archives
DIOC/FAC/1/26 Faculty (1678)

Little Gaddesden, St Peter & St Paul
Churchwardens' bills & vouchers (1824)

St Albans, St Michael's
Churchwardens' papers (1831–40)
Vestry order book 21 (1819–34)

UK manuscript census returns, UK register of duties paid for apprentices' indentures, wills and probate records <http://www.ancestry.co.uk>
1841 England Census
HO107/438/f.7/p.8
HO107/438/f.23/p.15
HO107/438/f.34/p.24
HO107/439/f.11/p.16
HO107/440/f.5/p.5
HO107/440/f.17/p.4
HO107/441/f.11/p.16
HO107/443/f.16/p.1
HO107/443/f.30/p.26
HO107/444/f.26/p.3
HO107/447/f.4/p.1

1851 England Census
HO107/444/f.26/p.3
HO107/447/f.6/p.5
HO107/1500/f.509/p.14
HO107/1701/f.274/p.10
HO107/1705/f.89/p.26
HO107/1705/f.205/p.12
HO107/1705/f.558/p.21
HO107/1706/f.647/p.13

HO107/1707/f.13/p.18
HO107/1709/f.135/p.4
HO107/1710/f.283/p.25
HO107/1711/f.285/p.12
HO107/1712/f.5/p.3
HO107/1712/f.75/p.16
HO107/1714/f.260/p.11
HO107/1715/f.453/p.18
HO107/1723/f.109/p.4
HO107/1723/f.110/p.5
HO107/1723/f.122/p.31

1861 England Census
RG9/655/f.138/p.5
RG9/805/f.5/p.5
RG9/812/f.34/p.25
RG9/812/f.43/p.3
RG9/820/f.28/p.5
RG9/821/f.24/p.14
RG9/823/f.98/p.10
RG9/823/f.101/p.16
RG9/824/f.5/p.3
RG9/824/f.10/pp.13–14
RG9/824/f.15/p.24
RG9/824/f.21/p.35
RG9/824/f.24/p.42
RG9/824/f.25/p.44
RG9/824/f.26/p.45
RG9/824/f.42/p.24
RG9/824/f.49/p.38
RG9/824/f.62/p.11

1871 England Census
RG10/875/f.9/p.10
RG10/1126/f.74/p.16
RG10/1349/fol.29/p.16
RG10/1372/f.50/p.49
RG10/1372/f.103/p.8
RG10/1372/f.116/p.33
RG10/1372/f.134/p.13
RG10/1372/f.139/p.24

RG10/1372/f.150/p.46
RG10/1372/f.151/p.50
RG10/1372/f.152/p.51
RG10/1373/f.9/p.13
RG10/1373/f.18/p.31
RG10/1373/f.28/p.1
RG10/2680/f.46/p.8

1871 Wales Census
RG10/5336/f.52/p.6

1911 England Census
RG14/7731/9

England & Wales, National Probate Calendar (Index of Wills and Administrations), 1858–1966
England & Wales, Prerogative Court of Canterbury Wills, PROB 11/1791B/258
UK Register of Duties Paid for Apprentices' Indentures (1710–1811), Class IR 1; Piece 30

Directories, newspapers and periodicals
Bentley's Miscellany (1843)
British Magazine (1832–6)
Bucks Gazette (1831)
Bury and Norwich Post (1817)
Chelmsford Chronicle (1783–1928)
Choir and Musical Record (1863)
Christian Guardian (1839)
Christian Observer (1806–34)
Christian Remembrancer (1821–4)
Church Builder (1862–4)
Church Magazine (1839)
Church of England Magazine (1842)
Church of England Quarterly Review (1857)
Church Times (1895–1905)
Connoisseur (1756)
Cornishman (1924)
County Press (1838)
Court Magazine and Monthly Critic (1845)
Ecclesiastical Gazette (1839–47)
Ecclesiologist (1842–54)

Eclectic Review (1838)
Educational Magazine (1838–41)
Gazetteer and London Daily Advertiser (1763)
General Evening Post (1761)
Gentleman's Magazine (1766–1800)
Hampshire Telegraph (1848)
Hertford Mercury and Reformer (1834–87)
Hertfordshire Almanac (1864)
Hertfordshire Express and General Advertiser (1864–5)
Herts Advertiser (1867)
Herts Guardian, Agricultural Journal, and General Advertiser (1853–67)
Illustrated London News (1842)
Ipswich Journal (1778)
Journal of the House of Lords (1643)
Justice of the Peace & County, Borough, Poor Law Union and Parish Law Recorder (1841)
Kelly's Post Office Directory of Hertfordshire (1851)
Lady's Companion (1854)
Leeds Times (1848)
London Courier & Evening Gazette (1827)
London Daily News (1863)
London Evening Post (1731)
London Gazette (1798–1829)
London Journal of Arts, Sciences, & Manufactures, and Repertory of Patent Inventions (1851)
London Literary Gazette (1819–29)
London Magazine, Or, Gentleman's Monthly Intelligencer (1751–79)
Monthly Review (1796)
Morning Post (1776–1837)
Musical Standard (1862–7)
Musical Times (1852–1905)
Musical World (1850–7)
New Evangelical Magazine (1823)
New Lady's Magazine, or, Polite & entertaining companion for the fair sex (1787)
New Monthly Magazine (1814–15)
Northampton Mercury (1797–1804)
Oxford and Cambridge Review (1846)
Oxford Parochial Magazine (1860–1)
Parish Choir (1846–7)
Pigot's & Co.'s Commercial Directory (1839)
Public Advertiser (1766)

Punch, or the London Charivari (1864)
Radio Times (1935)
St James's Chronicle (1761–84)
Sheffield Register, Yorkshire, Derbyshire, & Nottinghamshire Universal Advertiser (1791)
Stamford Mercury (1778–1821)
The Times (1786–1858)
Universal British Directory (5 vols, London, 1790–8)
Watford Observer (1863–70)
Windsor and Eton Express (1824)
World and Fashionable Advertiser (1790–2)
Yorkshire Post and Leeds Intelligencer (1905)

UK parliamentary papers
Command Papers
PP 1835 [67] Royal Commission to inquire into Ecclesiastical Revenues and Patronage of England and Wales Report
PP 1852–53 [1631] Census of Great Britain, 1851. Population tables. I. Numbers of the inhabitants, in the years 1801, 1811, 1821, 1831, 1841 and 1851, vol. I
PP 1868–69 [4202] [4202-I] Royal Commission on Employment of Children, Young Persons and Women in Agriculture, Second Report, Appendix
PP 1874 [C.1097] Return for each County in England and Wales of Name and Address of every Owner of Acre and upwards [...]

House of Commons Papers
PP 1819 (224) Select Committee on Education of Poor (1818). Digest of Parochial Returns (3 vols)
PP 1831–32 (199) Royal Commission to inquire into practice and jurisdiction of Ecclesiastical Courts in England and Wales: Reports, Appendix
PP 1833 (60) 25, PP 1834 (225) 27 and PP 1835 (216) 29 Reports of the commissioners appointed in pursuance of an act of Parliament, made and passed in the 1st and 2nd years of His Present Majesty, c. 34, intituled, 'an act for appointing commissioners to continue the inquiries concerning charities in England and Wales for two years, and from thence to the end of the then next session of Parliament'
PP 1835 (62) Abstract of Answers and Returns on State of Education in England and Wales (3 vols)
PP 1835 (216) Commissions of Inquiry into Charities in England and Wales: Twenty-ninth Report

Primary sources (printed)

Acland, J.E., *A Layman's Life in the days of the Tractarian Movement* (Oxford, 1904)

Anon., *An Account of Charity Schools in Great Britain and Ireland [...]* (London, 1713)

Anon., *Methods used for erecting Charity Schools, with the Rules and Orders by which they are governed* (London, 1715)

Anon., *A list of the governors and guardians, of the Hospital for the Maintenance and Education of Exposed and Deserted Young Children* (London, 1740–99)

Anon., *An Account of the Hospital for the Maintenance and Education of Exposed and Deserted Young Children* (London, 1749)

Anon., *List of the Patrons of the Anniversary of the Charity-Schools* (London, 1790)

Anon., *Concerts of Antient Music* (London, 1791)

Anon., *Description of Nuneham-Courtenay, in the County of Oxford* (1797)

Anon., *A narrative of the preparations made at Hatfield* (London, 1818)

Anon., *English Church History Exhibition: at the Town Hall, St Albans, from 27th June to 15th July 1905* (St Albans, 1905)

Arnold, J., *The Compleat Psalmodist*, 3rd–7th edns (1753–79)

Arnold, J., *Church Music Reformed* (London, 1765)

Arnold, S., *The Psalms of David [...] The words selected by the Revd. Sir Adam Gordon Bart.* (London, 1791)

Bacon, R., *Ode on the Royal Review of the Hertfordshire Volunteers in Hatfield Park June 13th 1800* (London, 1800)

Baron, J., *Scudamore organs, or, Practical hints respecting organs for village churches and small chancels, on improved principles* (London, 1858 and 1862)

Bedford, A., *The Excellency of Divine Music* (London, 1733)

Benbow, W., 'Account of the Honourable and Rev. William Capel', in *The Crimes of the Clergy, or, the Pillars of Priestcraft Shaken*, no. 2 (London, 1823), pp. 28–30

Bevington, H., *A Selection of Psalm & Hymn Tunes as set on the NEW ORGAN, lately Erected in Horn Church Essex by H. Bevington* (London, c.1830)

Bickersteth, E., *Christian Psalmody: A Collection of Above 700 Psalms, Hymns, and Spiritual Songs; Selected and Arranged for Public, Social, Family and Private Worship* (London and Hertford, 1833)

Blewitt, J., *A Complete Treatise on the Organ* (London, 1795)

Boase, F., *Modern English Biography*, VI (London, 1965)

Brayley, E.W., *The Beauties of England and Wales*, 18 vols (London, 1801–15), 7, part 1

Bridgeman, C., *Marches composed for the Use of the Hertfordshire Volunteers* (London, 1800)

Bridgeman, C., *A Collection of Psalms and Hymns for the use of the Congregation of All Saints, Hertford* (Hertford, 1821)

Cambridge Camden Society, *A Few Words to Church Builders* (Cambridge, 1841)

Cambridge Camden Society, *A Few Words to Churchwardens on Churches and Church Ornaments. No. II Suited to Town and Manufacturing Parishes* (Cambridge, 1841)

Clark, T., *The Union Tune Book, a selection of Psalm and Hymn tunes, suitable for use in Congregations and Sunday Schools. Arranged by Thomas Clark of Canterbury*, 2nd edn (London, 1842)

Cooke, M., *Twelve Psalm Tunes (in Four Parts) Composed for the Use of the Church at North Mims [...]* (London, ?1790)

Crompton, J., *The psalm singer's assistant, or, a key to psalmody [...]* (London, 1778)

Cunningham, P. (ed.), *The Letters of Horace Walpole, Earl of Orford*, 9 vols (London, 1857–9), 9

Curwen, J., *Singing for Schools and Congregations* (London, 1843)

Curwen, J.S., 'The Organ in Divine Service', *Congregationalist*, 8 (1879), pp. 115–25

Curwen, J.S., *Studies in Church Music* (London, 1880)

Curwen, J.S., 'The Old Village Musicians', *Strand Magazine*, 33 (11 September 1897), pp. 137–9

Cussans, J.E., *History of Hertfordshire*, 3 vols (London, 1870–81)

Dalrymple, D. (ed.), *The opinions of Sarah Duchess-Dowager of Marlborough (1660–1744). Published from original Mss.* (1788)

Davys, G., *Village Conversations on the Liturgy of the Church of England* (London, 1820)

Davys, O.W., 'The Choral Arrangements of Churches', *Reports and Papers of the Architectural and Archaeological Societies of the Counties of Lincoln and Northampton*, 10 (1870), pp. 261–70

Dickens, C., *Dombey and Son* (London, 1848)

Dickens, C., *All the Year Round* (26 March 1864)

Doane, J., *A musical directory for the year 1794* (London, 1794)

Fawcett, J., *A New Set of Sacred Music* (London, c.1811)

Ford, D.E., *Observations on psalmody, by a composer* (London, 1827)

Fowler, T., *An Enlarged Selection of Psalms and Hymns, for the use of the parish church of St Peter, St Alban's: and adapted to the congregations of the Established Church in general* (St Albans, 1817)

Fowler, T., *A Selection of Psalms and Hymns, adapted for the use of the Abbey Church, St Albans* (St Albans, 1820)

Gibson, E., *Directions given by Edmund Lord Bishop of London to the Masters and Mistresses of the Charity-schools* (London, 1724)

Gibson, E., *Directions given to the Clergy of the Diocese of London, in the year 1724* (London, 1727)

Glover, S.A., *Scheme for Rendering Psalmody Congregational; comprising a Key to the Sol-fa Notation of Music and Directions for Instructing a School* (Norwich, 1835)

Gordon, A., *Sermons on several subjects and occasions*, 2 vols (London, 1790), 1

Goulding, Phipps and d'Almaine, *Catalogue of instrumental and vocal music* (London, 1800)

Gresham, J., *Psalmody Improved [...]* (London, 1797)

Greville, C.C.F., *The Greville Memoirs*, 3 vols (London, 1885), II

Grimston, J.W. (3rd Earl of Verulam), *Report on the Manuscripts of the Earl of Verulam, preserved at Gorhambury*, Historic Manuscripts Commission, no. 64 (London, 1906)

Haggard, J., *Reports of Cases Argued and Determined in the Ecclesiastical Courts at Doctors' Commons and in the High Court of Delegates*, 4 vols (London, 1829–33), III

Hall, W.J. (ed.), *Psalms and Hymns adapted to the Service of the Church of England, approved by Bishop Blomfield* (London, 1836). Also known as 'The Mitre Hymn Book'

Hardy, T., *Under the Greenwood Tree or the Mellstock Quire. A Rural Painting of the Dutch School* (London, 1872; 1896 edn)

Head, F.A., *Choral Psalmody, or a collection of tunes to be sung in parts without instruments [...]* (London, 1840)

Hellendaal, P., *A Collection of Psalms for the use of Parish Churches* (Cambridge, 1794)

Hurt, J.S., *Bringing Literacy to Rural England. The Hertfordshire Example* (Chichester, 1972).

Hymns ancient and modern for use in the services of the Church (London, 1861)

Ivery, J., *The Hertfordshire Melody; or, Psalm-Singers Recreation* (Hertford, 1772; London, 1773)

Jackson, T., *The Life of the Rev. Charles Wesley*, 2 vols (London, 1841), 2

Jacob, B., *National psalmody, a collection of tunes, set to a course of psalms selected from the New Version by J.T. Barrett* (London, 1818)

Kemp, J., *The New System of Musical Education* (London, 1819)

Kingston, A., *Fragments of Two Centuries, Glimpses of Country Life when George III was King* (Royston, 1893)

Lamborn, C., *The Dunstaplelogia* (Dunstable, 1859)

Latrobe, J.A., *The Music of the Church Considered in its Various Branches* (London, 1831)

Leach, T., *The Hertfordshire Yeomanry Cavalry, A new song composed by Mr Leach organist of Cheshunt, Herts* (London, 1796)

Luppino, T.W., *Psalms and Hymns for Ware Church* (Hertford, 1821)

Mann, H., *Census of Great Britain, 1851. Education in Great Britain, the official report of H. Mann* (London, 1854)

Mann, H., *Census of Great Britain, 1851: Religious Worship, England and Wales – Report and Tables* (London, 1854)

Mason, W., 'On Parochial Psalmody' (1795), in *Essays on English Church Music*, 4 vols (London, 1811), III

Mercer, W., *The Church Psalter and Hymn Book* (London, 1855; 2nd edn., 1857)

Miller, E., *The Psalms of David for the use of Parish Churches the words selected from the version of Tate & Brady by the Revd. George Hay Drummond* (London, 1790)

Miller, E., *Thoughts on the Present Performance of Psalmody in the Established Church of England* (London, 1791)

Morrell, T.B. and How, W.W., *Psalms and Hymns* (London, 1858)

National Society, *Annual Reports* (1812–47)

National Society, *Monthly Papers* (1848–56)

Neale, J.M., *Church Enlargement and Church Arrangement* (Cambridge, 1843)

Nichols, J., *Literary Anecdotes of the Eighteenth Century*, 9 vols (London, 1815), IX

Novello, V., *The Psalmist: a Collection of Psalm and Hymn Tunes, suited to all the varieties of Metrical Psalmody; consisting principally of Tunes already in general use for Congregational Worship [...]* (London, 1838)

Otway, T., *The Orphan, or, the Unhappy Marriage* (London, 1680)

P[ayne], B., *The Parish-Clerk's Guide* (London, 1709 edn)

Pearce, C.W., *Notes on English Organs of the Period 1800–1810* (London, 1912)

Peck, J., *The Union Tune Book, being a collection of psalm and hymn tunes, adapted for use in Sunday schools and congregations. Arranged by John Peck. To which is prefixed a short introduction to singing* (London, 1837)

Porteus, B., *A charge delivered to the clergy of the diocese of London at the primary visitation of that diocese in 1790* (London, 1790)

Porteus, B., 'Sermon XII', in *Sermons on Several Subjects*, vol. II (London, 1794)

Porteus, B., *A charge delivered to the clergy of the diocese of London, in the year 1803* (London, 1804)

Pugin, A.W., *The True Principles of Pointed or Christian Architecture* (London, 1841)

Randall, J., *A collection of psalm & hymn tunes some of which are new & others by permission of the authors [...] for the use of congregations in general* (Cambridge, 1794)

Randolph, J. (ed.), *The Clergyman's Instructor* (Oxford, 1807)

Randolph, J., *A charge delivered to the clergy of the diocese of Bangor* (Bangor, 1808)

Riley, William, *Parochial music corrected. Containing remarks on the performance of psalmody in country churches, and on the ridiculous and profane Manner of Singing practised by the Methodists* (London, 1762)

Rippon, J., *A Selection of Hymns from the Best Authors, Intended to be An Appendix to Dr. Watts's Psalms and Hymns* (London, 1787)

Royal Commission on Historical Monuments (England), *An Inventory of the Historical Monuments in London, 2: West London* (London, 1925)

Shaw, J., *Parish Law* (London, 1733)

Shaw, S., *History of Verulam and St Albans* (St Albans, 1815)
Soames, H., 'Letter VI: Psalmody', in *Parochial Letters from a Beneficed Clergyman to his Curate* (London, 1829)
Stephenson, J., *Church Harmony Sacred to Devotion. Being a choice Set of New Anthems & Psalm Tunes on various Subjects*, 3rd edn (London, 1760)
Sternhold, T., Hopkins, J. et al., *The Whole Book of Psalms* (London, 1562)
Sturges, C., *Mr West's Annual Charity Sermon* (Reading, 1795)
Sunday School Society, *Plan of a Society established in London, AD 1785, for the support and encouragement of Sunday-Schools in the different counties of England* (London, 1788 and 1793)
Tate, N. and Brady, N., *A New Version of the Psalms of David, fitted to the Tunes used in Churches* (London, 1696)
Tattersall, W.D., *A version of the Psalms [...]* (London, 1797)
Trimmer, S., *The Oeconomy of Charity, or, An address to ladies concerning Sunday-schools* (London, 1787)
Trimmer, S., *Family Magazine*, vol. 1 (June 1788)
Trimmer, S., *The Oeconomy of Charity, or, An address to ladies concerning Sunday-schools*, 2 vols (London, 1801), 1
Trollope, A., *The Small House at Allington*, 2 vols, 2nd edn (London, 1864), 1
Trollope, T.A., *What I Remember*, 3 vols (London, 1887), 1
Urwick, W., *Nonconformity in Herts. Being Lectures upon the Nonconforming Worthies of St. Albans, and Memorials of Puritanism and Nonconformity in all the Parishes of the County of Hertford* (London, 1884)
Urwick, W., *Bible Truths & Church Errors* (London, 1888)
Vaux, J.E., *Church Folklore. A record of some post-Reformation usages in the Church of England*, 2nd edn (London, 1902)
Vertue, G., 'Pinchback's Musical Clock: Jottings of George Vertue, extracted from his Manuscript Notes', *Notes & Queries*, 2nd series, XII (1861)
Vincent, W., *Considerations on parochial music* (London, 1787)
Walker, T., *Walker's Companion to Dr Rippon's tune book* (London, 1811)
Watts, I., *Divine Songs Attempted in Easy Language, for the Use of Children* (London, 1715)
Watts, I., *The Psalms of David Imitated in the Language of the New Testament* (London, 1719)
Wesley, J., *Select Hymns: with Tunes annext: Designed chiefly for the use of the People called Methodists*, 4th edn (Bristol, 1773)
Wesley, J., 'Thoughts on the Power of Music', *The Works of the Rev. John Wesley*, 16 vols (London, 1812), XV
Wesley, J., *The Journal of the Rev. John Wesley in Four Volumes*, 4 vols (London, 1827), 4
Whitaker, J., *The Seraph, a Collection of Sacred Music [...]* (London, 1818)

White, W.J., of St Albans, *The Sacred Herald [...]* (London, *c*.1820)
Wilkins, M., *An Introduction to Psalmody. Containing some easy instructions for young beginers [...]* (London, 1750)
Wilkins, M., *A Second Book of Psalmody* (London, 1750)
Wilks, S.C., *Correlative Claims and Duties; or, an Essay on The Necessity of a Church Establishment in a Christian Country [...]* (London, 1821)

Secondary sources

Addleshaw, G.W.O. and Etchells, F., *The Architectural Setting of Anglican Worship* (London, 1948)
Adelmann, D., *The Contribution of Cambridge Ecclesiologists to the Revival of Anglican Choral Worship 1839–62*, Music in Nineteenth-Century Britain (Aldershot, 1997)
Anderson, G., 'The Old Church Bands', *The Antiquary*, 10 (July 1914), pp. 267–9
Andrew, D.T., *Philanthropy and Police. London Charity in the Eighteenth Century* (Princeton, 1989)
Andrews, C.B. (ed.), *The Torrington Diaries*, 4 vols (London, 1934–8), 3
Andrews, C.B. (ed.), *The Torrington Diaries: A Selection from the Tours of the Hon John Byng* (London, 1954)
Anon., *Great St Mary's Through the Ages* (Margate, n.d.)
Ashley Cooper, Mrs, *St Faith's Hexton* (n.d.)
Aylott, G., 'Norton Manor and Church', *Transactions of the East Herts Archaeological Society*, 2/III (1904), pp. 273–8
Ayres, J. (ed.), *Paupers and Pigkillers: The Diary of William Holland, a Somerset Parson 1799–1818* (Gloucester, 1984)
Baddley, K., 'Trouble in the Gallery', in C. Turner (ed.), *Georgian Psalmody 1, The Gallery Tradition* (Corby Glen, 1997), pp. 17–25
Barger, J., *Elizabeth Stirling and the Musical Life of Female Organists in Nineteenth-Century England*, Music in Nineteenth-Century Britain (Aldershot, 2007)
Bayley, T.D.S., *Pebmarsh Church, Essex* (Oxford, 1946)
Bell, V., *Little Gaddesden. The Story of an English Parish* (London, 1949)
Boeringer, J., *Organa Britannica. Organs in Great Britain 1660–1860*, 3 vols (London, 1983–9), 2
Boston, N., 'Music of the Eighteenth Century Village Church', *Archaeological Journal*, 99 (1942), pp. 53–66
Boston, N., 'Barrel Full of Tunes', *Church Times* (9 July 1954), p. 531
Boston, N., 'The Barrel-Organ', *Transactions of the Ancient Monuments Society*, New Series, 7 (1959), pp. 99–124
Boston, N. and Langwill, L.G., *Church and chamber barrel-organs: their origin, makers, music and location: a chapter in English church music* (Edinburgh, 1970). See Langwill and Boston for 2nd edn

Bradley, I., *Abide with Me. The World of Victorian Hymns* (London, 1997)

Bradley, I., 'Nonconformist Hymnody', in R. Pope (ed.), *T & T Clark Companion to Nonconformity* (London, 2013), pp. 235–46

Bradley, I., 'The Theology of the Victorian Hymn Tune', in M. Clarke (ed.), *Music and Theology in Nineteenth-Century Britain*, Music in Nineteenth-Century Britain (Abingdon, 2016), p. 13

Breihan, J. and Caplan, C., 'Jane Austen and the Militia', *Journal of the Jane Austen Society of North America*, 14 (1992), pp. 16–26

Brewer, J., *The Pleasures of the Imagination. English Culture in the Eighteenth Century* (London, 2013)

Burg, J., *Religion in Hertfordshire 1847 to 1851*, Hertfordshire Record Society, vol. XI (Hertford, 1995)

Burg, J., 'Religious Worship in 1851', in Short, *Historical Atlas*, pp. 140–1

Burgess, H.J., *Enterprise in Education. The Story of the work of the Established Church in the education of the people prior to 1870* (London, 1958)

Carrington, J. and Johnson, W.B. (ed.), '*Memorandoms for …*', *The Diary between 1798 and 1810 of John Carrington* (Chichester, 1973)

Cass, F.C., *East Barnet*, 2 pts (1885–92), I

Chadwick, O., *The Victorian Church*, 2 vols, 3rd edn (London, 1971), 1

Clarkson, S.F., 'St Pauls Walden', *Transactions 1888*, St Albans Architectural and Archaeological Society (1889), pp. 19–33

Cokayne, G.E. (ed.), *The Complete Baronetage*, reprint (Gloucester, 1983), I

Corke, S.G., *John Wesley and the Methodists in Hertford* (n.d.)

Cowgill, R., 'The London Apollonicon Recitals, 1817–32: A Case-Study in Bach, Mozart and Haydn Reception', *Journal of the Royal Musical Association*, 123/2 (1998), pp. 190–228

Cowgill, R. and Holman, P. (eds), *Music in the British Provinces 1690–1914* (Aldershot, 2007)

Crofton, W. d'A, 'Standon Church', *Transactions of the East Herts Archaeological Society*, I (1901), pp. 273–88

Cutts, I. (ed.), *Twelve psalm tunes composed for the use of the church at North Mymms* (Peterborough, 2016)

Davidson, H., *Choirs, Bands and Organs. A History of Church Music in Northamptonshire and Rutland* (Oxford, 2003)

Dawe, D., *Organists of the City of London 1666–1850. A Record of one Thousand Organists with an Annotated Index* (Purley, 1983)

Deacon, A., 'John Bunyan in Hertfordshire', *Hertfordshire's Past*, 22 (Spring 1987), pp. 5–8

Deacon, A. and Walne, P. (eds), '*A professional Hertfordshire tramp*': *John Edwin Cussans*, Hertfordshire Record Society, vol. III (Ware, 1987), pp. 104–5

Dibble, J. and Zon, B. (eds), *Nineteenth-Century British Music Studies*, Music in

Nineteenth-Century Britain (Aldershot, 2002)

Ditchfield, P.H., *The Parish Clerk* (London, 1907)

Dolman, B., '"Everything Curious": Samuel Hieronymus Grimm and Sir Richard Kaye', *Electronic British Library Journal* (2003), pp. 4–6, accessed at <http://www.bl.uk/eblj/2003articles/article2.html>

Drage, S., 'A Reappraisal of Provincial Church Music', in Wyn Jones, *Music*, pp. 172–90

Drage, S., 'John Fawcett of Bolton: the Changing Face of Psalmody', in Dibble and Zon, *Nineteenth-Century British Music Studies*, pp. 59–69

Evans, J., *The Endless Web* (London, 1954)

Ewing, G., *Westmill. The Story of a Hertfordshire Parish* (Tunbridge Wells, 1928)

Fawcett, T., *Music in Eighteenth-Century Norwich and Norfolk* (Norwich, 1979)

Feakes, M., 'St Peter's Church, Lilley', *Transactions of the East Herts Archaeological Society*, 4/II (1910), pp. 188–9

Featherstone, A., *Redbourn's History* (Redbourn, 2001)

Flood, S., 'Probate Divisions', in Short, *Historical Atlas*, pp. 14–15

Forbes, D., *The Artist and the Organist* (Ware, 2005)

Friedman, T., *The Eighteenth-Century Church in Britain* (London, 2011)

Galpin, F.W., 'The Village Band. An Interesting Survival', *Musical News*, 5 (8 July 1893), pp. 31–2; (15 July 1893), pp. 56–8

Galpin, F.W., 'Notes on the Old Church Bands and Village Choirs of the Past Century', *Proceedings of the Dorset Natural History and Antiquarian Field Club*, 26 (1905), pp. xl and 172–81

Galpin, F.W., *Old English Instruments of Music: their History and Character* (London, 1910)

Gammon, V., '"Babylonian Performances": the Rise and Suppression of Popular Church Music, 1660–1870', in E. Yeo and S. Yeo (eds), *Popular Culture and Class Conflict 1590–1914: Explorations in the History of Labour and Leisure* (Brighton, 1981), pp. 63–88

Gant, A., *O Sing unto the Lord: A History of English Church Music* (London, 2015)

Garrod, H., 'Chew's House', *Dunstable & District Local History Newsletter*, 23 (February 2005), pp. 154–7

Gee, A., *The British Volunteer Movement, 1794–1814* (Oxford, 2003)

Gerish, W.B., 'Albury Church', *Transactions of the East Herts Archaeological Society*, 2/III (1904), pp. 229–37

Gibbs, A.E., *The parish registers of Aldenham, Hertfordshire, 1559–1659* (St Albans, 1902)

Goose, N., 'Population, 1801–1901', in Short, *Historical Atlas*, pp. 56–7

Goose, N., 'Straw-Plaiting and Hat-Making', in Short, *Historical Atlas*, pp. 90–1

Greaves, J.G., *Wesleyan Methodism in the City of the Proto-Martyr and the St Albans Circuit* (St Albans, 1907)

Grey, E., *Cottage Life in a Hertfordshire Village* (Harpenden, 1977)

Gróf, L., *Children of straw: the story of straw plait, a vanished craft and industry* (Buckingham, 2002)

Hall, H.R.W., 'Essendon Church', *Transactions of the East Herts Archaeological Society*, 3/III (1907), pp. 233–57

Hamlyn, F.C., 'In Quires and Places where they Sing ... The Gallery Musicians of Bedfordshire', *The Bedfordshire Magazine*, III/19 (Winter 1951/2), pp. 99–103

Hannah, G. (ed.), *The Deserted Village. The Diary of an Oxfordshire Rector JAMES NEWTON of Nuneham Courtenay 1736–86* (Stroud, 1992)

Harkness, P., *All Saints ... and Sinners* (1999)

Harwood, K., 'Some Hertfordshire Nabobs', in A. Rowe (ed.), *Hertfordshire Garden History: A Miscellany* (Hatfield, 2007), pp. 49–77

Hatfield W.E.A., *Hatfield and Its People: Part 7: Churches* (Hatfield, 2014)

Herbert, T. and Barlow, H., *Music and the British Military in the Long Eighteenth Century* (Oxford, 2013)

Hertfordshire Family History Society, *Militia Ballot Lists* (Hertford, 1999)

Hillsman, W., 'Women in Victorian Church Music: Their Social, Liturgical and Performing Roles in Anglicanism', in W.J. Sheils and D. Wood (eds), *Studies in Church History, 27: Women in the Church* (Oxford, 1990), pp. 443–52

Hilton, B., *A mad, bad, and dangerous people? England 1783–1846* (Oxford, 2008)

The History of Parliament, accessed at <http://www.historyofparliamentonline.org/>

Holman, P., 'Eighteenth-Century English Music: Past, Present, Future', in Wyn Jones, *Music*, pp. 1–13

Hunn, J., 'County, Hundred and Ecclesiastical Boundary Changes', in Short, *Historical Atlas*, pp. 12–13

Hurford, P., *The Organs of St Albans Abbey* (St Albans, 1969)

Jacob, W.M., *Lay People and Religion in the Early Eighteenth Century* (Cambridge, 1996)

Jacob, W.M., '"... This congregation here present ...": Seating in Parish Churches during the Long Eighteenth Century', in K. Cooper and J. Gregory (eds), *Studies in Church History, 42: Elite and Popular Religion* (Woodbridge, 2006), pp. 294–304

Jennings, S., 'The Silk Industry', in Short, *Historical Atlas*, pp. 96–7

Jones, M.G., *The Charity School Movement: A Study of Eighteenth Century Puritanism in Action* (Cambridge, 1938)

Keene, D., Burns, R.A. and Saint, A. (eds), *St Paul's: the Cathedral Church of London, 604–2004* (London, 2004)

Kilbey, M., 'Hexton, Hertfordshire: a Tale of Two Organs', *Organists' Review* (June 2017), pp. 40–1

Kilbey, M., 'A "St Cecilia Organ" for Wormley', *Organists' Review* (September 2018), pp. 54–5

Kilbey, M., 'The Early Use of Barrel Organs in the English Parish Church', *Journal of the British Institute of Organ Studies*, 43 (2019), pp. 58–71

King, N., *The Grimstons of Gorhambury* (Chichester, 1983)

Knight, F., *The Nineteenth-Century Church and English Society* (Cambridge, 1995)

Langwill, L.G. and Boston, N., *Church and chamber barrel-organs: their origin, makers, music and location: a chapter in English church music*, 2nd edn (Edinburgh, 1970)

Lasocki, D., 'New Light on Eighteenth-Century English Woodwind Makers from Newspaper Advertisements', *Galpin Society Journal*, LXIII (May 2010), pp. 73–142

Le Faye, D., *A Chronology of Jane Austen and Her Family: 1700–2000* (Cambridge, 2006)

Le Hardy, W., *Notes & Extracts from The Sessions Records*, Hertfordshire County Records, vol. IV (Hertford, 1923)

Lee, R., *Rural Society and the Anglican Clergy, 1815–1914. Encountering and Managing the Poor*, Studies in Modern British Religious History, 11 (Woodbridge, 2006)

Leppert, R., *Music and Image. Domesticity, Ideology and Socio-cultural Formation in Eighteenth-century England* (Cambridge, 1988)

Lomas, M.J., 'Militia and Volunteer Wind Bands in Southern England in the Late Eighteenth and Early Nineteenth Centuries', *Journal of the Society of Army Historical Research*, 67 (1989), pp. 154–66

Lomas, M.J., 'The Wiltshire Militia Band, 1769–c.1831', *Wiltshire Archaeological and Natural History Magazine*, 85 (1992), pp. 91–100

Longstaffe-Gowan, T., *The London Square* (London, 2012)

McCart, T.K., *The Matter and Manner of Praise. The Controversial Evolution of Hymnody in the Church of England 1760–1820*, Drew Studies in Liturgy Series, 5 (Lanham, 1998)

McCormack, M., '"Turning Out for Twenty-Days Amusement": The Militia in Georgian Satirical Prints', in E. Charters, E.Rosenhaft and H. Smith (eds), *Civilians and War in Europe, 1618–1815* (Liverpool, 2014), pp. 157–81

MacDermott, K.H., *Sussex Church Music in the Past* (Chichester, 1922)

MacDermott, K.H., *The Old Church Gallery Minstrels: an Account of the Church Bands and Singers in England from about 1660 to 1860* (London, 1948)

McGuinness, R. and Johnstone, H.D., 'Concert Life in England I', in H.D. Johnstone and R. Fiske (eds), *The Eighteenth Century: Music in Britain*, The Blackwell History of Music in Britain, vol. 4 (Oxford, 1990), pp. 31–95

McKendrick, N., Brewer, J. and Plumb, J.H., *The Birth of a Consumer Society. The Commercialization of Eighteenth-century England* (London, 1982)

Macnair, A., Rowe, A. and Williamson, T., *Dury and Andrews' Map of Hertfordshire: Society and Landscape in the Eighteenth Century* (Oxford, 2016)

McVeigh, S., 'Introduction', in S. Wollenberg and S. McVeigh (eds), *Concert Life in Eighteenth-Century Britain* (Aldershot, 2004), pp. 1–18

Malloch, W., 'The Earl of Bute's Machine Organ: A Touchstone of Taste', *Early Music*, 11/2 (April 1983), pp. 172–83

Manley, K.R., 'John Rippon and Baptist Hymnody', in Rivers and Wykes, *Dissenting Praise*, pp. 95–123

Mayes, S., *An Organ for the Sultan* (London, 1956)

Miele, C., '"Their interest and habit": Professionalism and the Restoration of Medieval Churches, 1837–1877', in C. Brooks and A. Saint (eds), *The Victorian Church: Architecture and Society* (Manchester, 1995), pp. 151–72

Morgan, W.C., 'St Peter's Church, St Albans', *Transactions 1897 & 1898*, St Albans Architectural and Archaeological Society, New Series, 1 part II (St Albans, 1899), pp. 135–73

Morris, J.E., 'Hunsdon Church', *Transactions of the East Herts Archaeological Society*, 2/I (1902), pp. 46–56

Munby, L.M., *The Common People are not Nothing. Conflict in Religion and Politics in Hertfordshire 1575–1780* (Hatfield, 1995)

Nash, H., *Reminiscences of Berkhamsted* (Berkhamsted, 1890)

Obelkevich, J., *Religion and Rural Society: South Lindsey 1825–1875* (Oxford, 1976)

Olleson, P., *Samuel Wesley: the Man and his Music* (Woodbridge, 2003)

Oman, C., *Ayot Rectory. A Family Memoir* (London, 1965)

Ord-Hume, A.W.J.G., *Barrel Organ: the Story of the Mechanical Organ and its Repair* (London, 1978)

Pacey, R., *Lincolnshire Church Organs [...]* (Burgh-le-Marsh, 2002)

Page, F.M., *Christ's Hospital Hertford* (London, 1953)

Page, J.J., 'Great Wymondley Church', *Transactions of the East Herts Archaeological Society*, 2/I (1906), p. 18

Parry, J.D., *History and description of Woburn and its abbey* (London, 1831)

Pevsner, N. and Cherry, B., *Hertfordshire*, Buildings of England, 2nd edn (London, 1977)

Picker, J.M., *Victorian Soundscapes* (Oxford, 2003)

Pollard, H.T., 'Stocking Pelham Church', *Transactions of the East Herts Archaeological Society*, 2/I (1906), pp. 75–8

Pollard, H.T., 'Cottered Church', *Transactions of the East Herts Archaeological Society*, 3/II (1907), pp. 160–5

Pollington, J., *Kimpton Parish Church* (1978)

Port, M.H., *600 New Churches. The Church Building Commission 1818–1856*, 2nd edn (Reading, 2006)

Prescott, H.M., *Notes on Caddington Church* (Luton, 1937)

Prince, H., *Parks in Hertfordshire since 1500* (Hatfield, 2008)
Rainbow, B., *The Choral Revival in the Anglican Church (1839–1872)* (Oxford, 1970)
Rainbow, B., 'Singing for Their Supper', *Musical Times* (April 1984), pp. 227–9
Rainbow, B., 'The Rise of Popular Music Education in 19th-century England', *Victorian Studies*, 30 (Autumn 1986), pp. 25–49
Rainbow, B., *Bernarr Rainbow on Music: Memoirs and Selected Writings* (Woodbridge, 2010)
Rainbow, B., 'Hullah, John', in *Grove Music Online*, accessed at <http://www.oxfordmusiconline.com>
Rivers, I. and Wykes, D. L. (eds), *Dissenting Praise* (Oxford, 2011)
Robins, B. (ed.), *The John Marsh Journals. The Life and Times of a Gentleman Composer (1752–1828)*, Sociology of Music, no. 9, 2 vols (New York, 1998–2013)
Rodgers, B., *Cloak of Charity. Studies in Eighteenth-Century Philanthropy* (London, 1949)
Rohr, D., *The Careers of British Musicians 1750–1810* (Cambridge, 2001)
Royal Society of Musicians of Great Britain, *RSM Membership 1738–1749*, accessed at <http://www.royalsocietyofmusicians.co.uk/>
Ruston, A., 'Protestant Nonconformity', in Short, *Historical Atlas*, pp. 134–6
Ruston, A.R., 'Sermon Tasting in St Albans 1835', *Hertfordshire's Past*, 22 (Spring 1987), pp. 12–17
Sainsbury, J.D., *The Hertfordshire Yeomanry – An Illustrated History 1794–1920* (Welwyn, 1994)
Scholes, P.A., 'The Hullah Movement', in *The Mirror of Music 1844–1944*, 2 vols (London, 1947), 1
Senar, H., *Little Gaddesden and Ashridge* (Chichester, 1983)
Sharpe, J.F.B., 'Christ's Hospital at Ware and Hertford', *Transactions of the East Herts Archaeological Society*, 3/III (1908), pp. 304–5
Shaw, P., 'Local History', *The Greenwood Quire*, accessed at <http://www.greenwoodquire.co.uk/GreenwoodWestGalleryQuire/Local_History.html> (accessed 19 September 2014)
Sheldrick, G., *Three Centuries of Music at All Saints Church Hertford* (Hertford, 1987)
Sheldrick, G. (ed.), *The Accounts of Thomas Green, Music teacher and tuner of musical instruments 1742–1790*, Hertfordshire Record Society, vol. VIII (Hertford, 1992)
Sheppard, F.H.W. (ed.), *Survey of London*, accessed at <http://www.british-history.ac.uk/search/series/survey-london>
Short, D., *An Historical Atlas of Hertfordshire* (Hatfield, 2011)
Shuker, D., 'More than "Distinguished Ornaments"? Women Organists in Late-Georgian England', *Organists' Review*, XCVI (February 2010), pp. 7–11

Shuker, D., 'The Pitfalls of Received Wisdom: Women Organists in Anglian Churches and Chapels in Great Britain from 1750 to 1850', *Organ Yearbook*, XXXIX (2010), pp. 101–12

Slater, T. and Goose, N., *A County of Small Towns: The Development of Hertfordshire's Urban Landscape to 1800* (Hatfield, 2008)

Smith, J.T., '"The Parson's Fag": the Schoolteacher as the Servant of the Church in the second half of the Nineteenth Century', *Journal of Educational Administration and History*, 34/1 (2002), pp. 1–22

Smith, M., *Religion in Industrial Society: Oldham and Saddleworth, 1740–1865* (Oxford, 1994)

Southey, R., *Music-making in North-east England during the Eighteenth Century* (Aldershot, 2006)

Spaeth, D.A., *The Church in an Age of Danger: Parsons and Parishioners, 1660–1740* (Cambridge, 2000)

Spink, I., 'Haydn at St Paul's: 1791 or 1792?', *Early Music*, 33/2 (May 2005), pp. 273–80

Sponza, L., *Italian Immigrants in Nineteenth Century Britain: Realities and Images* (Leicester, 1988)

Squires, E.E., 'St Faith's Church, Hexton', *Transactions of the East Herts Archaeological Society*, 4/I (1909), pp. 43–6

Stanyon, M., 'Papermaking', in Short, *Historical Atlas*, pp. 80–1

Stevens, R.J.S. and Argent, M. (eds), *Recollections of R.J.S. Stevens, an Organist in Georgian London* (London, 1992)

Stone, L. and Stone, J.C.F., 'Country Houses and their Owners in Hertfordshire, 1540–1879', in W.O. Aydelotte, A.G. Bogue and R.W. Fogel (eds), *The Dimensions of Quantitative Research in History* (London, 1972), pp. 56–123

Stone, L. and Stone, J.C.F., *An Open Elite? England 1540–1880* (Oxford, 1984)

Straker, G.C., *A History of the Organs at the Cathedral of St Alban* (London, 1929)

Temperley, N., *The Music of the English Parish Church*, Cambridge Studies in Church Music, 2 vols (Cambridge, 1979), 1

Temperley, N., 'Music in Church', in H.D. Johnstone and R. Fiske (eds), *The Eighteenth Century: Music in Britain*, The Blackwell History of Music in Britain, vol. 4 (Oxford, 1990), pp. 357–95

Temperley, N., 'The Hymn Books of the Foundling and Magdalen Hospital Chapels', in D. Hunter (ed.), *Music Publishing and Collecting: Essays in Honor of Donald W. Krummel* (Urbana, 1994), pp. 3–37

Temperley, N., 'John Wesley, Music, and the People Called Methodists', in Temperley and Banfield, *Music and the Wesleys*, pp. 3–25

Temperley, N., 'The Music of Dissent', in Rivers and Wykes, *Dissenting Praise*, pp. 197–228

Temperley, N., 'The Modern English Hymn', *Grove Music Online*, accessed at <http://www.oxfordmusiconline.com>

Temperley, N. *et al.*, 'Psalms, metrical', *Grove Music Online*, accessed at <http://www.oxfordmusiconline.com>

Temperley, N. and Banfield, S., *Music and the Wesleys* (Urbana, 2010)

Thistlethwaite, N., *The Making of the Victorian Organ* (Cambridge, 1990)

Thompson, D.M., 'The Religious Census of 1851', in R. Lawton (ed.), *The Census and Social Structure* (London, 1978), pp. 241–88

Thompson, F.M.L., 'Town and City', in F.M.L. Thompson (ed.), *The Cambridge Social History of Britain*, vol. 1 (Cambridge, 1990), pp. 1–86

Tiller, K., *English Local History: An Introduction*, 2nd edn (Stroud, 2002)

Turner, C., 'The Decline of the Gallery Tradition', in C. Turner (ed.), *Georgian Psalmody 1* (Corby Glen, 1997), pp. 71–9

Turner, C., 'Miserable Machines: The Role of the Barrel Organ within Georgian Psalmody', in C. Turner (ed.), *Georgian Psalmody 2. The Interaction Between Urban and Rural Practice* (Corby Glen, 1999), pp. 65–72

Turner, C., 'Psalmody Singing and the Role of the Barrel Organ in the Anglican Church of the Nineteenth Century', in Dibble and Zon, *Nineteenth-Century British Music Studies*, pp. 32–45

Turner, D., *With Cheerful Zeal: A History of Dagnall Street Baptist Church St Albans* (St Albans, 1999)

Virgin, P., *The Church in an Age of Negligence: Ecclesiastical Structure and Problems of Church Reform 1700–1840* (Cambridge, 1989)

Wallace, E., *Children of the Labouring Poor: The working lives of children in nineteenth-century Hertfordshire* (Hatfield, 2010)

Wallace, E., 'Schools 1833–1902', in Short, *Historical Atlas*, pp. 148–9

Ward, P.G., *A History of Braughing Church and its Benefactors* (1888)

Ward, W.R., *Religion and Society in England 1790–1850* (London, 1972)

Watson, J.R., 'The Hymns of Isaac Watts and the Tradition of Dissent', in Rivers and Wykes, *Dissenting Praise*

Watts, M.R., *The Dissenters, vol. II. The Expansion of Evangelical Nonconformity* (Oxford, 1995)

Western, J.R., *The English Militia in the Eighteenth Century. The Story of a Political Issue 1660–1802* (London, 1965)

Whitehead, L. and Myers, A., 'The Köhler Family of Brasswind Instrument Makers', *Historic Brass Society Journal*, 16 (2004), pp. 90–1

Wilkinson, R.S., *The Church and Parish of Abbots Langley* (Abbots Langley, 1959)

Williams, F.R., *Anstey: A Hertfordshire Parish* (Cambridge, 1929)

Williams, P. (ed.), *The Leffler Manuscript*, facsimile edition (Reigate, 2010)

Woodhouse, H., *Face the Music: Church and Chapel Bands in Cornwall* (St Austell, 1997)

Wrigley, E.A. and Schofield, R.S., *The Population History of England 1541–1871: A Reconstruction, Cambridge Studies in Population, Economy and Society in Past Time* (Cambridge, 1981)

Wyn Jones, D. (ed.), *Music in Eighteenth-Century Britain* (Aldershot, 2000)
Yates, N., *Buildings, Faith and Worship* (Oxford, 1991)
Yates, N., *Liturgical Space. Christian Worship and Church Buildings in Western Europe 1500–2000*, Liturgy, Worship and Society Series (Aldershot, 2008)
Yule, G.U., 'In Memory of the Rev. William Cecil', *Proceedings of the Cambridge Philosophical Society*, 27 (Cambridge, 1931), pp. 1–14

Unpublished theses
Kilbey, M.J., 'Music-making in the English Parish Church from the 1760s to 1860s, with Particular Reference to Hertfordshire', DPhil thesis (Oxford Univ., 2017)
Weston, S.J., 'The Instrumentation and Music of the Church Choir-Band in Eastern England, with Particular Reference to Northamptonshire, during the Late Eighteenth and Early Nineteenth Centuries', PhD thesis (Leicester Univ., 1995)
Williams, P., 'English Organ Music and the English Organ under the First Four Georges', PhD thesis (Cambridge Univ., 1962)

Index

Page numbers in *italic* refer to Figures, Tables and Appendices

1851 Census of Accommodation and Attendance at Worship 22–5
1851 Census of Education 58, 60

Abbots Langley (Herts.) 11, 190–1, *255*, *258*
  singing teachers 57, 73, 93
Acland (later Troyte), Arthur Henry Dyke 191–2, 204
Albury (Herts.) 16–7, 135, 226, 227, *258*
Aldbury (Herts.) 5, 72, 121, *255*, *258*
  singers, singing 85, 91, 99
Aldenham (Herts.) 91, 162, *163*, *171*, *255*
  band 93, 98, 106, 145, *258*
Allen, organ-builders 168, *255–7*
Anniversary Meetings *see* St Paul's Cathedral
Anstey (Herts.) 230
Apollonicon 154, 155, 158, 159
Apsley (Herts.) 28–9
Ardeley (Herts.) 15, 161–2, 229, *229*, 245, *255*
Arnold, John, organist 52, 103, 105–6, 117, 148, 152
Ashwell (Herts.) 206, *255*
Aspenden (Herts.) 57, 85, 124, 167, 241, *255*
Aston (Herts.) 57, 242
Ayot St Lawrence (Herts.) 36, 106, *210*, 221
  organ, organists 116, 128, 135, *220*, *255*

Baldock (Herts.) 26, 49, 57, 103, 168, *255*
  singers, band 70, 72–3, 85, 225, *258*
Barkway (Herts.) 25, 58, 137, *255*
  band 98, 101, 106, *258*
Barley (Herts.) 23–4, 25, *44*, *258*
Barrington, Hon. & Rev. Lowther 207–8, *210*
Bass viol *see* Cello
Bassoon 98, 105, 107–10, *108*, 118, 129, 195, *258–9*
  reeds 99, 106
  trumpet top 107, *108*, 109
Bass's Act 173, *174*
Bates, organ-builders *145*, *146*, 149, 155, 166, *256–7*
Bayford (Herts.) 18, 122, *255*, *258*
Beauclerk, Hon. & Rev. Frederick de Vere 15
Bengeo (Herts.) 83, 123, 135, 166, 239, *255*
Benington (Herts.) *255*, *258*
Berkhamsted (Herts.) 13, 26, 28, 91, 231, 258
  organ, organists 61, *132*, *163*, 185–6, *255*
Bevington, organ-builders 169, 245, *255–6*
Bickersteth, Rev. Edward 78
Bird, William, organist 73, 74
Bishop, organ-builders 172, 185, 241, 244, *255–6*
Bishops Stortford (Herts.) 16, 17, 26, 72, 79, 227
  charity children *44*, 53,

organ, organists 53, *116*, 118, 120, 128, 131, *132*
singers 91, 120
Volunteers *116*, 128
Blewitt, Jonas, organist *116*, 128, 221
Blomfield
  Charles, Bishop 17, 79, *195*, 212
  Rev. George Becher 210
Boston, Canon Noel 5, 94, 175
Bovingdon (Herts.) 16, 18, 166–7, *255*, *258*
Bow Brickhill (Beds.) 94
Bramfield (Herts.) 161, *255*
Brand, Thomas, MP, Lord Dacre 36, 158
Braughing (Herts.) 44, 45, 211, 224, 236, *255*, *258*
Brent Pelham (Herts.) 100, *258*
Bridgeman
  Anna Maria, organist *116*
  Charles, organist 78, *116*, 129, 131
  Henry, organist *54*
Brooks
  John, organist 188–9, 198
  Thomas, organist 186, 188, 206
Broxbourne (Herts.) 25–6, 35
  organ, organists *132*, 135, 156–7, 162, *163*, 167, 225, *255*
Bryceson, organ-builders *147*, 148, 167, 172, *255–7*
Buntingford (Herts.) 44, 162
Bushey (Herts.) 20, 21, 26, 101, 235, *258*

Caddington (Herts.) 51, 74, 85, 93, 99, 121, *258*
Caldecote (Herts.) 121
Capel family; Earl of Essex 17, *36*, 117, 197
  Hon. & Rev. William Robert 17, 184, 197
Carrington, John 48, 104, 107
Cecil; Gascoyne-Cecil family; Marquess of Salisbury 12, *36*, 43, 105, 107, 129
Cecil, Rev. William 204
Cello, bass viol 49, 92–3, 95, 98, 100–1, 104, 107, 109–10, 118, *258–9*
Cheshunt (Herts.) 25, 26, 44, 55, 208, 230
  disputes 184–5

organ, organists *54*, *116*, 128, *132*, 167, 196, *255*
Volunteers *116*, 128
Chipping Barnet (Herts.) 26, *54*, 85, 137, 159
  organ, organists *116*, 151, 159, *163*, *255*
Cholmondeley, Hon. & Rev. Robert 17, 69
Church Choral Union in the Diocese of Rochester 215
Clarinet 21, *54*, 92, 94–5, 98–109, 129, 151, *195*, 209, 230, *258–9*
Clark, Thomas, of Canterbury 80, 170
Claughton, Thomas Legh, Bishop 125–6, 215
Clothall (Herts.) 121, *122*
Codicote (Herts.) 161
Cooke, Matthew, organist *116*, 118–9
Cottered (Herts.) *255*
Cowper family 14, 210, 219
  Frances Cecilia 168
  George, 3rd Earl Cowper 13, *14*
  William, MP 13, 168
  William, poet 13, 16
Curwen
  John Spencer 3, 143, 217n3
  John 204, 209

Dallam, organ-builders 37, 150
Datchworth (Herts.) 229
Davys
  George, Bishop 59, 240–1
  Rev. (later Canon) Owen 90, 215, 240–1
Dickens, Charles 138, 237
Dumb organist 148, *149*, 172–3, *256*
Dunstable (Beds.) 74, 99
  charity children 39

East Barnet (Herts.) *54*, 137, 159, *163*, 233–4, *255*
Elstree (Herts.) 58, 91, 93, 95, *255*, *258*
Essendon (Herts.) *54*, 57, *163*, *255*, *258*
  singers, singing 35, 85, 91

Fawcett, John 72, 74, 107
Field, Rev. Samuel Pryer 212, 213
Flamstead (Herts.) 23
Flaunden (Herts.) 18, 226, 241, *255*

INDEX

Flight; Flight & Robson; Robson, organ-builders 86, 154, 155, 159, 167, 193, *255–6*
Flute 14, 15, 49, 92, 98, 100, 103, 107, 118, 154, 195, *258–9*
Ford, Rev. David Everard 52, 55, 92
Foundling Hospital (London) 34–5, *36*
Fowler, Thomas, organist *54*, 74, 77, 120
Frogmore (Herts.) 28, 73
Furneux Pelham (Herts.) 56, 95, 100, *258*

Galpin, Canon Francis W. 4, 5
Gee, Rev. Richard 57, 158, 190–1
George III 41, 43, 126–7, 129, *130*, 151
Gibbs, Richard 81, 83, 186–7
Gibson, Edmund, Bishop 16, 37–9, 47–51
Glover, Sarah Ann 203–4
Godman family 93, 121, *256*
Gordon, Rev. Sir Adam 49
Gore, Mrs 159–61, *160*
Gray; Gray & Davison, organ-builders 155, 158, 164–6, *165*, 168, 193, *244, 255–6*
Great Amwell (Herts.) 16, 133, *163*, 169, *171, 255, 258*
Great Gaddesden (Herts.) 99, *163, 255, 258*
Great Hormead (Herts.) 25, *163*, 211, *255*
Great Warley (Essex) 52, 103, 105, 129
Great Wymondley (Herts.) 161, *255*
Green, Thomas, organist 45, *116*
Gresham family 74, 85, 99, 129
Grimston
  Charlotte, Countess 127
  James, 3rd Viscount 13, *36*, 43, 105, 224

Haggard, John 182, 185–6
Hall, Rev. William John 79
Hanbury, Robert 241–2
Handel, George Frederick 115, 127–8, 150–1, 167, 211, 221
Hardy, Thomas 4–5, 97, 99
Harmonium *see* Reed organ
Harpenden (Herts.) 13, 27, 74, 228, 240, *255, 258*
  charity children 61, 231

Harpsichord 15, 45, 51–2, 115, *116*, 118, 127
Hatfield (Herts.) 12–3, 24, 98, 183, 215, *258*
  charity children *44*, 137, 233
  House, Park *36*, 105, 106, 107, 129, *130*
  organ, organists 137, *255*
Head, Frances Ann 191–2
Hellendaal, Peter 73, 156, 170
Hemel Hempstead (Herts.) 18, 23, 27, 28, *44*, 73, 85
  disputes 196–7
  organ, organists 138, 196–7, 244–5, *255*
Hertford (Herts.)
  All Saints 48, 81, 82, 98, 189, 207
    accommodation 21, 227, 238, 239
    organ, organists 36, 78, *116*, 120, 129, 131, *132*, 161, *255*
    charity children 36, 39, *54*
  St Andrew's *54*, 79, 81–2, 219, 224
    absent rector 17, 69–70
    choir 125, 213, *214*
    organ, organists *116*, 124–6, *132*, *244, 255, 258*
  Volunteers *116*, 128, 129
Hertfordshire Union 24, 72
Hertingfordbury (Herts.) 17, *44*, *210*, 219, *255*
Herts Church Choral Association 210–3, 215
Hexton (Herts.) 158, *244*, *256*
Higdon, John 54, 71, 95, 98, 120
High Wych (Herts.) 215
Hinxworth (Herts.) 25, *44*, 49
Hitchin (Herts.) 77, 81, 85, 209, 210, 215, *258*
  disputes 183–4
  organ, organists *132*, 155–6, 197, 206, 233, *256*
  Priory 36, 151, 156
  schools 26, 121
  singers 54, 73
  Volunteers 103–4, 129
Hoddesdon (Herts.) 156, 162, *163*, 166, 167, 172, 233, *256*
Hullah, John 198, 205–9, 233
Hunsdon (Herts.) *163*, *256*
Huntingdon, Countess of 25, 73
Hymns Ancient and Modern 82–3, 85

289

Ickleford (Herts.) *44*, 122, 161, *163*, *256*
Incorporated Church Building Society (ICBS) 228–38, 242, 245
  plans, elevations *229*, *230*, *232*, *234*
Ivery, John 47, 85

Jacob, Benjamin, organist 77
Jones, Rev. William, of Broxbourne and Hoddesdon 35, 156–7
Jones, Rev. William, of Nayland (Suffolk) 170

Keble, Rev. John 189–90, 212
Kensworth (Herts.) 23, 85, 121, *258*
Kimpton (Herts.) 15, *36*, 158, *256*
Kings Langley (Herts.) *44*, *54*, 71, 121, *256*
  singers, band 91, 93–4, 98, *258*
Kings Walden (Herts.) 13, *256*

Latrobe, John Antes 110, 164, 173
Lawrence, Charles, organist 198–9
Leach, Thomas, organist *54*, *55*, *116*, 128
Levesque, John Baptiste, organist *116*
Lilley (Herts.) 51, 121, *259*
Little Berkhamsted (Herts.) 68, *256*
Little Gaddesden (Herts.) *54*, *55*, 95, 121, 155, *256*, *259*
Little Hadham (Herts.) 12, 231, *256*, *259*
Little Hormead (Herts.) 25, 47
Little Munden (Herts.) 135, 211
Little Wymondley (Herts.) 13
Lock Hospital (London) 13, 34
Luppino, Thomas William, organist 76, 78, *116*, 121, 127–8, 196, 206
Luton (Beds.) 5, 93, 150–1
Lyde, Lionel *36*, 106, 128, 221

MacDermott, Canon Kenneth Holland 3, 5, 97–8
Madan, Rev. Martin 13, 168
Magdalen Chapel (London) 34–5
Malet, Rev. William Wyndham 161–2, *229*
Mann, Horace 22, 26, 58, 60
Marchant, John 82, 125–6, 213, *214*
Markyate (Herts.) 18, 23, 230–1, *230*, 235, *256*

Marsh
  John 15, 104
  Rev. Edward Garrard 15
Martin, George William, organist 207–9, 211, 213, 215, 241
Mason, Rev. William 92, 169, 221
Mercer, William 80–4
Miller, Edward, organist 43, 45, 52–3, 55–6, 69, 73, 169
Miller, George, organist 54, 182
Mills, Thomas, MP 208, *210*, 213
Morse, Justinian 151
Much Hadham (Herts.) 12, *259*
  organs 124, 157–8, *163*, 166, 168, *256*

Napoleonic Wars 27, 50, 101, 128, 173, 250
Newgate Street (Herts.) 208, *210*, 212
Newnham (Herts.) 16, *256*
Nicholls, Edwin Theodore, organist *54*, 183, 197–8
North Creake (Norfolk) 46, 71
North Mymms (Herts.) *36*, *116*, 118–9, *119*, *132*, 138, *256*
  barrel organ *163*, 168, 193
Northaw (Herts.) 47
Northchurch (Herts.) *132*, *163*, 224, *256*, *259*
Norton (Herts.) 166, *256*
Novello, Vincent 61, 77, 80
Nuneham Courtenay (Oxon.) 221

Oboe 85, 92, 98–100, 105–7, 109, *258–9*
Offley (Herts.) 100–1, *163*, *256*, *259*
Osborne, Francis, 5th Duke of Leeds *36*, 118–9
Otway, Thomas 107

Perry
  Charles, organist *116*
  Robert, organist *54*, *116*, 131
Piano 13, *14*, 15, 127, 137, 183, 192, 198
Pirton (Herts.) *44*, 85, 99, *256*, *259*
Pitch-pipe 5, 99, 192
Pollard, William 81–2, 84, 126, 188, 208
Popely, William, organist *116*, 118

Porteus, Beilby, Bishop 39, 47–50, 73–4, 156, 224, 227
Pretyman
  George, Bishop 13, 49, 157–8
  Rev. George Thomas 13, 158
Puddephatt family 99

Radcliffe family 36, 151, 156, 183
Radwell (Herts.) 135–6, *256*
Randall, John, organist 169
Randolph
  John, Bishop 13, 49, 157, 227
  Rev. Thomas 13, 124, 157–8, 166, 168
Redbourn (Herts.) 13, 15, 28, 206, 230, 256, *259*
Reed organ 120–2, *122*
  Harmonium 15, 120–1, 133, 135–6, 198, 245
  Seraphine 15, 120–1
Rickmansworth (Herts.) 23, 26, 28, *54*, 227, *256*
  singers 49, 84, 93, 95, *259*
Ridge (Herts.) *256*
Riley, William 24, 51–2
Rippon, John 71–3, 74
Robson *see* Flight & Robson
Royston (Herts.) 26, 61, 99, 103, *256*
  singers, band 73, 101, 104, *259*
  Volunteers 129
Rushden (Herts.) 15, 92, *259*
Russell family; Duke of Bedford 99, 109–110, 118
Ryley, Emily, organist *134*, 135

Sacombe (Herts.) *256*
St Albans (Herts.) 5, 19, 23, 26, 28, 36, 81, 115, 166
  Abbey Church 19, 46, 55, 72, 83, 98, 230, *259*
    disputes 183, 186–9, 198
    organ, organists *54*, 75, 77, 123–4, *132*, 206, 226, *256*
    choral festivals 211, 215
  charity schools 43, *44*, 46, *54*, 95, 226
  Church Choral Association 215
  Dagnall Street 24, 70, 71, 186, 188, 191
  Holywell House 36, 45–6, 150
  St Michael's 13, 15, 72, 83, *171*, 224, 233, 241, *259*
    organ, organists 136, 158, *163*, 172, *223*, *256*
  St Peter's 21, 53, 55, 83, 85
    organ, organists *37*, *54*, 74, 77, *116*, 120, 131, *132*
  St Stephen's 21, 77, 91, 93, 98, 121, *256*, *259*
  Town Hall 4, 206–7
St Ippolyts (Herts.) 161, *163*, *256*
St Paul's Cathedral (London) 16, 39–43, *40*, 46–7, 81–2, 85, 207, 225
  Anniversary Meetings 39–43, *40*, 46–7
St Pauls Walden (Herts.) 172, 235, *256*
Sandon (Herts.) 15, 79, 121, 231, *232*, *259*
Sandridge (Herts.) 16, 83
Sarratt (Herts.) 15, *134*, 135, 239, *256*, *259*
Sawbridgeworth (Herts.) 15, 212, 215, 230, *256*, *259*
  galleries 224, 239
Scott, George Gilbert 227, 239, 241
Scudamore organ 122, *123*
Seraphine *see* Reed organ
Shenley (Herts.) 206–7, *256*
Shephall (Herts.) 27
Sherman
  Anna Sophia, organist 53, 74, 116, 131
  George Ferdinand 85, 116, 131
Shield, Rev. Thomas 104, 129
Simeon, Rev. Charles 25, 156, 169
Singers, singing 90–7, *258–9*
  children and adults 94–96
  disputes 92–3, 145
  feasts 91, 213
  galleries 17, 69, 93, 191, 224–5, *258–9*
  pews 91, 100
  teachers 38, 73, 74, 84, 169–70
    children's singing teachers 53–6
  visiting 93–4
Smith, Abel MP (d.1859) 11–2, 161, 166, 207
Smith, Felix, organist *116*, 120, 129, 131
Society for Promoting Christian Knowledge (SPCK) 10, 33, 38, 83, 155, 251
Sol-fa; Tonic Sol-fa 204, 209
Spencer, Georgiana, Countess 36, 45–6, 71
Standon (Herts.) 25, 28, 85, 94, 211, 239, *256*, *259*

St Edmund's College 195
Stanstead Abbots (Herts.) 25, *222*, *256*, *259*
Stanstead St Margaret (Herts.) 143, *144*, 148, 168, 169, *171*, *256*
Stevenage (Herts.) 24, 184, 210, *256*, *259*
Stocking Pelham (Herts.) 47, *146*, *256*
Stuart, John, 3rd Earl of Bute 150–1
Studham (Herts.) *256*

Tewin (Herts.) *44*, 107
Theatre *116*, 127–8, 194, 196
Therfield (Herts.) *256*
Thorley (Herts.) *256*
Thundridge (Herts.) *44*, 241, *256*
Tonic Sol-fa *see* Sol-fa
Totteridge (Herts.) 18, *54*, 77, *132*, *256*
  disputes 182
Trimmer, Sarah 41, 46–7, 50, 55, 94
Tring (Herts.) 28, 57, 83, 106, *259*
  disputes 93, 182
  organs, organists *132*, *163*, 240, 182, *256*
Trollope
  Anthony 95
  Thomas Adolphus 92
Turner, John 203

Union Tune Book 79–80
Upton, Rev. William 15, 24, 186, 190–1

Villiers family; Earl of Clarendon 45, 197
Vincent, William, Dean of Westminster 39–40, 43, 47–8, 56, 69, 225
Violin, fiddle 49, 92, 98, 99, 105–6, *116*, 118, 154, 209, *258–9*

Walker, Frederick, organist 183–4, 206
Walker, Thomas 72, 170
Walker, organ-builders 167, 184, *255–7*
Walkern (Herts.) *256*
Wallington (Herts.) 27, *259*
Walpole family; Earl of Orford 104, 154
Ware (Herts.) 25, 26, 76, 103, 195
  charity children 36, 39, *44*, *54*
  disputes 180, 196
  organ, organists 78, *116*, 120, *132*, 206, 235, *256*
  Volunteers 104

Wareside (Herts.) 121
Warne, Thomas, organist 184
Watford (Herts.) 17, 24, 26, 28, *36*, 56, 211
  charity children *44*, 45, *54*, 55, 62–3, 225
  disputes 184, 188–9, 197–9
  organ, organists *54*, 73–4, *116*, 117, 120, *132*, *171*, *256*
Watton-at-Stone (Herts.) 78, 210, *256*
  choir 207–8, 213, 241, *242*
Watts, Isaac 71, 72, 73, 74, 169
Welwyn (Herts.) 24, 151, *210*, *257*
  singers, band 107, 231, 233, *259*
Wesley
  Rev. John 24–5, 69–70, 72, 73, 92
  Rev. Samuel 39
  Samuel, organist 74
Westmill (Herts.) 61, 85, 192, 211, *257*
  organ, organists 57, *147*, 148, *163*, 175
Weston (Herts.) 161, 206, *257*
Wheathampstead (Herts.) 13, 28, 158, 215, *257*, *259*
  restoration 240–1
Wheatam 159–61, *160*
Whitaker, James 85, 94
Whitaker, John 77–8, 133
White, W.J., of St Albans 72–3, 93
Widford (Herts.) 242, *243*, *257*
Wigginton (Herts.) 28, 59, 237
Wigram, Joseph, Bishop 125, 215, 240
Wilkins, Matthew 53, *55*
Willian (Herts.) *163*, 164, *210*, *257*
Willis, Henry, organ-builder 122, *123*, *255–6*
Wilshere
  William (d. 1824) 103–4, 129
  William, MP (d. 1867) 210
Woburn (Beds.) 100, 109–10
Wood, Sarah, organist *54*, 131
Wormley (Herts.) 122, *123*, 162, 164, *257*

Yorke, Philip, 3rd Earl of Hardwicke *36*, 45, 57, 73, 103, 224